On the Self-Regulation of Behavior

On the Self-Regulation of Behavior presents a thorough overview of a model of human functioning based on the idea that behavior is goal-directed and regulated by feedback control processes. It describes feedback processes and their application to behavior, considers goals and the idea that goals are organized hierarchically, examines affect as deriving from a different kind of feedback process, and analyzes how success expectancies influence whether people keep trying to attain goals or disengage. Later sections consider a series of emerging themes, including dynamic systems as a model for shifting among goals, catastrophe theory as a model for persistence, and the question of whether behavior is controlled or instead "emerges." Three chapters consider the implications of these various ideas for understanding maladaptive behavior, and the closing chapter asks whether goals are a necessity of life. Throughout, theory is presented in the context of diverse issues that link the theory to other literatures.

Charles S. Carver is a professor of psychology at the University of Miami. Michael F. Scheier is a professor of psychology at Carnegie Mellon University. They have conducted research on personality processes and motivation in a variety of laboratory and applied settings, most recently focusing on the role of personality variables in responding to health crises such as coronary disease and cancer. Their research has been supported by the National Science Foundation; the National Institute of Alcohol Abuse and Alcoholism; the National Cancer Institute; the National Heart, Lung, and Blood Institute; and the American Cancer Society.

On the Self-Regulation of Behavior

Charles S. Carver
Michael F. Scheier

CAMBRIDGE
UNIVERSITY PRESS

PUBLISHED BY THE PRESS SYNDICATE OF THE UNIVERSITY OF CAMBRIDGE
The Pitt Building, Trumpington Street, Cambridge, United Kingdom

CAMBRIDGE UNIVERSITY PRESS
The Edinburgh Building, Cambridge CB2 2RU, UK   http://www.cup.cam.ac.uk
40 West 20th Street, New York, NY 10011-4211, USA   http://www.cup.org
10 Stamford Road, Oakleigh, Melbourne 3166, Australia

First published 1998

Printed in the United States of America

Typeset in Times Roman 11/13 pt, in LATEX 2_ε [TB]

*A catalog record for this book is available from
the British Library.*

Library of Congress Cataloging-in-Publication Data
Carver, Charles S.
On the self-regulation of behavior / Charles S. Carver, Michael F.
Scheier.
p.   cm.
ISBN 0-521-57204-5
1. Control (Psychology).   2. Goal (Psychology).   3. Feedback
(Psychology).   I. Scheier, Michael.   II. Title.
BF611.C35   1998
153.8 – dc21   98-15204
                                                                          CIP

ISBN 0 521 57204 5 hardback

For one of the world's great writers of
psychological science fiction: Jeffrey A. Carver
csc

For Howard F. Matthews, father-in-law extraordinaire
mfs

Contents

Contents

Preface

In 1981 we published a book in which we argued that feedback processes are important in the self-regulation of human behavior, that these processes underlie not just the body's internal maintenance activities, but even behavior that's consciously controlled. That book was a research monograph, reporting many experiments in detail. It was hard to read for plot.

Since 1981 we've realized that the line of thought we described there can be extended in several additional ways. This book revisits the themes of 1981 and adds several extrapolations from the earlier model – some our own, some developed by others. We discuss the latter in a way that's maximally compatible with our own ideas, to try to tell a coherent story. In doing this, we've tried not to do serious violence to ideas whose origins lie with people other than ourselves.

This book is in some respects a continuation of the earlier one. It's an easier read, partly because it's thinner on data. What dominates the stage in this book are ideas and speculations. This is very much a point-of-view book, and speculation plays a larger role here than in the earlier one. We've stretched to make connections across literatures, even where the links are tenuous. We hope these connections will cause you to consider some possibilities you might not otherwise have thought about.

To Whom This Book Is Written

We wrote this book to overview a set of ideas that we find interesting and useful about how behavior occurs in the behaving person. In the main, it's intended for graduate students and professionals in personality–social phychology (and related areas such as clinical, counseling, health, developmental, and organizational psychology). This doesn't mean it won't be of interest to others, or that it's too technical for nonpsychologists to follow. We've actually assumed very little technical knowledge on the reader's part.

Because we want to present as coherent a picture as we can, we've included some things we've said before. Early sections are partly (not entirely) redundant with our earlier book. Some points made in later sections have been aired in articles published in the past few years. But there are also a good many extrapolations and speculations, particularly in later sections, that we *haven't* entertained elsewhere.

We've tried to present here the bones of a cybernetic view on human self-regulation, somewhat unencumbered by the details of the literature that tends to support the viewpoint. On the other hand, we've tried to bring into the discussion a range of issues and questions that have been raised in our own minds (and in the minds of people who disagree with us about the usefulness of these ideas) during the years in which we've worked on these topics. Not all the issues are resolved, which leaves a residual tension in some parts of the discussion that we hope will prompt further work. In any case, we hope that the picture sketched across these pages will be of interest to others who are interested, as we are, in the structure of the self-regulation of behavior.

Acknowledgments

We'd both like to acknowledge the help of the following people, who contributed in important ways to the book's development:

- Deborah Stipek, for careful and thoughtful reading of many of the early chapters.
- Melanie Harris, who provided valuable assistance in tracking down several sources of information for later chapters, and for her thoughtful comments on several chapters.
- John Cacioppo, Alan Cobo-Lewis, Adele Hayes, Janine Shelby, Jennifer Strauss, Robin Vallacher, Barbara Wolfsdorf, Rex Wright, and Bob Wyer for their comments on material contained in various chapters.
- Craig Mason and particularly Alan Cobo-Lewis for helping create Figures 18.2 and 18.3.
- Annette Stanton, for her very helpful reading of the complete manuscript.

We also have some individual acknowledgments.

From Coral Gables:

About half of the first draft of this book was written while I was a Visiting Scholar at the University of California, Los Angeles. I appreciate the services (and hospitality and consultation) provided to me by people there. I am particularly grateful to Janine Shelby and Shelley Taylor, who collaborated in making it possible for me to spend a sabbatical in Los Angeles (and to experience the Northridge earthquake).

I'd also like to express my personal thanks to the following:

- Linda Cahan, my secretary, who dealt with a torrent of faxes during my year away, and the usual chaos since my return.
- Dorothy Crawley and especially Diane Thurston, for helping patch the raveled sleeve.

- Janine Shelby, who I once believed was Emily, but who eventually realized she was not. I hope you will recognize some of the ways you've shaped the book's content. This (book) is my hand.
- My co-author, Michael Scheier, who exhibited a salutory tendency to keep me at least somewhat tethered to reality when I tended to drift.
- Last but not least, Calvin, my shag terrier, who's made the past two years of my life much more interesting than they would otherwise have been.

From Pittsburgh:

There are four sets of people I would like to thank:

- At the top of the list, Karen, Meredith, and Jeremy, the rest of the members of the Matthews/Scheier family. The longer I live, the more important they become.
- Jim Staszewski and Rich Schulz, for being rascals and for allowing me to be a rascal with them from time to time.
- Mike Bridges and Ginger Placone, for facilitating my professional life so that I could find time to work on the book.
- And finally, Chuck Carver, who has once again exposed me to a set of ideas that has changed my view of the world in a fundamental way.

Charles S. Carver
http://www.psy.miami.edu/Faculty/CCarver/
Michael F. Scheier

1

Introduction and Plan

Throughout our careers we've been interested in the structure of behavioral self-regulation. Sometimes when relatives or acquaintances ask us what we do for a living, we use that phrase. Often enough, what we get in return is a blank look. In truth, it's a pretty abstract phrase. It's hard to know what it means unless you already know what it means. The term *self-regulation* in itself says more than we intend. After all, control of such qualities as body temperature, blood pressure, and blood chemistry all represent self-regulation. But these aren't what we're interested in.

Even adding the qualifier *behavioral* to self-regulation doesn't entirely solve the problem. This leaves a door open to a large body of work on the regulation of physical action – motor control. There are links between the processes of motor control and the processes we focus on (to carry out any kind of behavior, you somehow have to translate the intent to act into actual movement). Yet the topics are different enough to draw a line between them. For the most part, movement control is outside our focus.

Behavioral self-regulation in this book concerns mostly behavior at the level of interest to personality–social (and health, organizational, clinical, and counseling) psychologists. The question we're interested in is how behavior – at that level of abstraction – happens. This restricts the topic a little. In another sense, though, we're using the word *behavior* broadly. We're interested both in action and in emotion. Both of these aspects of the human experience are important to behavioral self-regulation, and we've tried to bring them together in a way that's internally consistent.

WHAT MAKES BEHAVIOR HAPPEN?

What are the processes that underlie behavior? There are many ways to answer this question – indeed, many paths to take in *approaching* it. The concept of motivation owes its existence to the effort to understand how and why behavior happens. From the vantage point of this concept, people act in various ways because they're "motivated" to do so. This is a start, but it leaves a lot unsaid. To say that motives underlie behavior says nothing about the processes referenced by (or following from) the term *motive*. It implies only that some such processes exist, somewhere, in some form.

What's the nature of these processes? Wildly diverse answers have been proposed over the decades. Human behavior is sometimes seen as reflecting internal energy systems competing for ascendence (Freud, 1949/1940; Hull, 1943). Another view holds that behavior emerges directly from a set of needs (Murray, 1938). Another is that behavior reflects patterns coded into human genes over eons of evolution (e.g., Buss, 1991, 1994; Wilson, 1975). Behavior has been seen as reflecting patterns of childhood relationships carried in symbolic form into adulthood (e.g., Bowlby, 1988; Fairbairn, 1954), and as reflecting deeply rooted traits (e.g., Costa & McCrae, 1992; Digman, 1990; Eysenck, 1967). It's also been argued that the concept of motive is irrelevant and misleading – that human behavior is the product of a history of external events coming together to form a pattern of reinforcement contingencies (Skinner, 1938).

In this book we argue that human behavior is a continual process of moving toward, and away from, various kinds of mental goal representations, and that this movement occurs by a process of feedback control. This view treats behavior as the consequence of an internal guidance system inherent in the way living beings are organized. The guidance system regulates a quality of experience that's important to it. For that reason, we refer to the guidance process as a system of *self-regulation*.[1] In the chapters to come, we describe aspects of this view, which has long been central in our thinking about human behavior (Carver, 1979; Carver & Scheier, 1981a). The overall goal of the book is to create a sense of how such a model of behavior can be fit to various aspects of the human experience.

Some Limitations and Some Grandiosity

Before we begin, we should note a couple of further limitations. One is that the model is incomplete. Many motivational theorists would

---

[1] Block (1996) has argued that it's preferable to call this *autoregulation*. In his view, that label does a better job of evading the implication that the *self* is always involved in the regulatory process, an implication that often isn't intended. For example, most people wouldn't want to argue that processes such as blood pressure control are managed by the self. Although Block's point is well taken, the term self-regulation has by now become so well entrenched in the literature that we continue to use it here.

not see what we describe here as a complete picture of motivation or even self-regulation (cf. Kuhl, 1984, 1994a; see Ford, 1987, for an even broader perspective). We won't examine every issue that might be raised. Doing that would require a longer book, and more answers than we have. Our aim isn't to paint a complete picture but rather to create a sense of the importance of certain kinds of ideas in thinking about human functioning.

Second, we don't necessarily mean to argue that the conceptualization presented here should be adopted *in place of* other ways of thinking. The view we're presenting is separate from – but a ready collaborator with – many other ideas. It's a view of the structure of behavior that can accommodate diverse ways of thinking about which goals matter and why. For this reason, we believe it can be seen as complementing and supplementing a wide variety of other ideas about what goes on when humans live out the moments, hours, and days in their lives (cf. Carver, 1996b; Carver & Scheier, 1996a).

We'll even go a little further. We think that the ideas presented in this book have important and useful things to say to everyone who's interested in the behavior of human beings (at the level of abstraction indicated earlier). These ideas paint a useful picture of what goes on when behavior is rolling smoothly forward, and they also have implications about some of the ways in which self-regulation goes awry.

Observations and Origins

The starting point for some aspects of what we say in this book is an observation that also underlies the writings of the behaviorists: The consequences of behavior are important to the behaving organism. Our view on this observation differs in important ways from that of behaviorists, however. The consequences of behavior have both a short-term effect and a longer-term effect. The longer-term effect is learning. The shorter-term effect is captured in the phrase *feedback process*.

Learning, we believe, isn't about the stamping in of action tendencies through reinforcement, but rather about the linking together of information (cf. Bolles, 1972; Rescorla, 1987; Timberlake, 1993; Tolman, 1932). Sometimes the information that's linked is that particular actions were effective in moving toward a particular goal. Thus, the person learns that the action is potentially good to take when that goal is in place in similar circumstances. In a similar situation later on, the person may well repeat the action. Although this phenomenon is important, we will for the most part disregard this longer-term effect of the consequences of action.

Our focus instead is on the shorter-term effect. The consequence of an act informs you about whether or not the act moved you toward a desired end (or away from an undesired end). In the short term, that information is useful in determining whether to continue the action, change the action, or perhaps discontinue the activity altogether. The information conveyed by the act's consequence thus constitutes feedback. This idea lies at the heart of the book.[2]

THE BOOK'S PLAN

The plan we follow in this book is to start simple and add layers of complexity. We begin by talking about the basic elements of our viewpoint on self-regulatory phenomena, in which feedback processes are centrally important. In doing so (in Chapter 2), we use a variety of illustrations, but we generally avoid examples from human behavior. Instead, our treatment in Chapter 2 is abstract, intended to make clear the meanings of key concepts before going on to address behavior.

Goal-Directed Action

The application of these ideas to human behavior begins in earnest in Chapters 3 and 4. There we address a variety of topics within personality and social psychology, indicating how the elements of the feedback loop are embodied in the flow of several kinds of experience. Both negative (goal-seeking) loops and positive (goal-evading) loops are important in human action, and these chapters represent an initial mapping of these concepts to behavior.

In many people's minds the feedback-loop concept has esoteric origins. But it's actually been with psychology for centuries, hidden inside another, perhaps simpler, certainly more familiar concept: the goal (cf. Tolman, 1932). A goal (or something very much like a goal) is inherently embedded in the feedback process. Though not constituting the *whole* of the feedback loop, a goal is *essential* to the feedback loop.

[2] A number of others in psychology have found these concepts to be useful, though the angles they've taken have been somewhat different from the one taken here (e.g., Ford, 1987; Hyland, 1987; Karoly, 1993; Levine & Fitzgerald 1992a, 1992b). Further, although these applications aren't our focus here, we note in passing that feedback models have been found useful in a number of other fields involving human behavior, including sociology, organizational behavior, politics, and economics (e.g., Denning, 1992; Levine, 1992; Maruyama, 1986).

The goal concept is a broad one, useful for many purposes. There's great diversity among human goals, and that diversity has important implications for our story. In Chapter 5 we describe several goal constructs introduced to psychology over the past decade or so and consider aspects of their diversity. One important aspect of this diversity among goals is their breadth or abstractness. One way of thinking about this difference is to think of goals as ordered in a hierarchy, such that very abstract goals subsume many goals that are more concrete. This idea represents one kind of complexity to be layered onto the more basic idea that behavior reflects feedback processes.

The idea that such a goal hierarchy is embedded in behavior has many implications, and it also raises a number of questions. After discussing the goal construct and its diversity in Chapter 5, we take up some of these implications and questions in Chapter 6. In doing so, we begin a pattern that recurs twice more in the book: a chapter of theoretical principles, followed by a chapter on issues that are raised by a close consideration of the principles.

There's yet one more distinction that we need to address among the goals that underlie human behavior, a distinction that's particularly important in thinking about social behavior. The distinction is between goals that are personal (taking into account only your own preferences and desires) and goals that in some fashion or other involve other people. The latter goals, whether they're communal or self-presentational, entail the consideration of one's relationships to others, and how others view oneself. Chapter 7 addresses how these classes of goals influence action – how the influences are the same and how they're different.

Emotion

Thus far in the story, discussion focuses on goals, actions, and how actions are managed. No model of human action can go too far, though, without considering emotional experience. Chapters 8 and 9 deal with these experiences. We argue there that the principles of feedback control apply to the understanding of feelings as well as to the understanding of action. Chapter 8 is our conceptual account of the nature and origins of affect, along with results of some research bearing on that view. This account of affect also adds a layer of complexity to the model constructed in early chapters, but it's a layer that's very different from the one added by the notion of hierarchicality.

This conceptual analysis of affect is followed by another "issues" chapter. The model of affect we've proposed has a number of implications that go well beyond its basic themes, and the nature of the model raises many questions. Further, important points of contact (both similarities and contrasts) exist between this model and other ideas that are currently prominent in psychology. Chapter 9 takes up a series of these implications, questions, and comparisons among theories. Our goal there is, in part, to show how this model threads together in a coherent fashion a substantial number of points made elsewhere.

Confidence and Doubt, Persisting and Giving Up

Another issue that any analysis of human behavior must address is that people sometimes confront difficulties in trying to reach their goals. Although affect is one response to these difficulties, there are behavioral responses as well. Sometimes people remain fully engaged in the struggle to move ahead. Sometimes they slow down, stop, and give up. Sometimes the behavioral responses seem directly parallel to affective experiences, but sometimes they don't. How are these aspects of behavior to be understood?

Chapter 10 presents theory and data bearing on this set of issues. We argue that the same mechanism that produces affect produces a sense of confidence versus doubt, but that this sense can be superseded in some circumstances by information consolidated in memory that's taken as relevant to the present situation. Thus, whether confidence or doubt prevails is a matter that extends beyond the stimuli of the present moment.

We also argue in that context that confidence (past some threshold) keeps people in the chase toward attainment of their goals, whereas doubt (again, past a threshold) tends to promote abandonment of those goals. Our postulating a threshold or watershed past which persistence gives way to giving up is the first sounding of a broader theme about discontinuity in behavior. This theme emerges in full force later on.

Questions that surround persistence and abandonment of efforts are among the most fundamental to the psychology of human behavior. There are many theories of the processes by which these outcomes are created. Although these theories have a good deal in common, there are also differences among them. These differences are explored in another issues chapter, Chapter 11. Along with discussion of theoretical distinctions, we also point to a number of literatures where issues of confidence versus doubt appear to play a very important (though often unrecognized) role.

Problems in Behavior

Any approach to understanding normal behavior has implications for understanding problems in behavior. The view on behavior sketched out in the first part of the book is no exception in that regard. Because we think some of these implications are important, we briefly interrupt the layering on of further complexities to describe some of them.

These implications for understanding problems range from the simple and straightforward to the more complex and convoluted. There are enough points to be made here to fill two chapters. Again, we start simple in Chapter 12 and work our way toward matters of greater complexity in Chapter 13. Among the complexities that seem most important is the set of issues surrounding giving up. Sometimes people give up *trying* but can't seem to give up *wanting*. Sometimes people remain *committed* to trying but can't seem to make themselves *really* try. How to conceptualize these problems is a question that we don't think has been well answered. These chapters contain our contributions to the evolving discussion.

Newer Themes: Dynamic Systems and Catastrophes

The conceptual girders of the book up to this point are the principles of feedback processes. Cross-members and framing are provided by extensions and connections to the more typical constructs of personality–social psychology. The extended discussion of problems in Chapters 12 and 13 brings us to something of a point of closure on the principles addressed in the preceding chapters. At this point, we turn to a set of topics that in some ways differ considerably from what came before.

Recent years have seen increasing discussion of the themes of dynamic systems theory, and how these themes may relate to the phenomena of psychology. Some of the initial steps taken in these discussions were halting, others were more bold. Today it seems apparent that these ideas raise interesting questions and suggest methodologies that weren't obvious before. More and more, these ideas are beginning to be seen as important elements in the tool kit of the psychological theorist.

We are far from the first to consider the relevance of these ideas for understanding behavior, even at the personality–social psychological level of abstraction. In the past few years, however, we've come to find them useful as a conceptual heuristic. In Chapter 14 we lay out some of the basics of dynamic systems thinking and consider how these ideas may integrate with themes presented earlier in the book.

Although some have asserted that these ideas represent a totally new angle on behavior, destined to replace other concepts, we're inclined to disagree. Rather, we see them as complements and supplements to the concepts contained in earlier parts of the book. As do all useful conceptual tools, the ideas of dynamic systems suggest hypotheses that aren't obvious from other angles. But we think these tools add to, rather than replace, the tools already in the kit.

A body of thought related to dynamic systems theory, though distinct in its origins, is catastrophe theory. As is true of dynamic systems theory, catastrophe theory provides a different perspective on understanding experience. Catastrophe theory concerns the topology of surfaces, focusing on surfaces with folds. Thus it bears on the existence of discontinuities in whatever can be mapped onto the surface. Some people believe that aspects of behavior can be portrayed in this way, and this topic provides the basis for Chapter 15.

The ideas of dynamic systems and catastrophe theories create a framework for raising issues in ways that might not have been apparent without those ideas. This is true for issues about behavior that flows smoothly, and also for problems in behavior. Enough implications and issues about problems and their treatment have been identified to fill another chapter. Chapter 16 examines problems from the perspective of these newer conceptual tools.

Control versus Emergence of Behavior

One more side trip in our journey occurs in the penultimate chapter. The model developed throughout the book assumes a kind of top-down regulation of behavior. We've assumed that people take up goals, form intentions, and try to realize those goals and intentions in their actions. However, several literatures question the accuracy of this portrayal. In Chapter 17 we explore the emergence of self-organization in coordinations, the concepts of connectionism, and some work in robotics. Each of these literatures suggests the plausibility of bottom-up control of behavior. A better answer, however, may be that both views are right.

There are reasons to believe that influence on behavior flows both ways, that there are two modes of thinking that have different characteristics. These ideas are also discussed there.

Goal Engagement and Life

In Chapter 18 we consider another broad theme: that goal involvement is critical to life. Without goals, behavior loses form. People's lives fall apart. In discussing that theme, we describe the results of studies – some old, some very new – that seem to imply that life requires engagement. When engagement remains, when people can accept even tragedy and move forward, life retains its vibrancy. When people lose that sense of engagement, they lose a great deal psychologically, and even the physical reality of life is threatened.

This, then, concludes our brief overview of the book's themes. Let us commence.

2

Principles of Feedback Control

This chapter describes a set of basic principles underlying the conceptual analysis presented in the remainder of the book. We describe the principles here abstractly, with examples and illustrations taken mostly from domains other than personality–social psychology. Our goal is to create a clear sense of the nature of particular processes (for a more detailed account see Clark, 1996) without pressing the argument that human behavior embodies them. We move on to that argument in due course.

CYBERNETICS, FEEDBACK, AND CONTROL

Wiener (1948) defined cybernetics as the science of communication and control. *Cybernetics* is one of several terms intertwined with one another – terms such as *control processes, feedback processes*, and *servomechanisms* (or *servos*). These terms have varying origins, they're used preferentially by different people in different lines of work, and they differ in shades of meaning. For our purposes, though, they refer to roughly the same things. Cybernetics is the science of feedback processes; feedback processes involve the control or regulation of certain values within a system (see also Ashby, 1961; Clark, 1996).

Negative Feedback

A negative feedback loop, the basic unit of cybernetic control, is a system of four elements in a particular kind of organization. The elements are an input function, a reference value, a comparator, and an output function (Figure 2.1). An input function is a sensor. It brings information into the loop. In later discussions we'll treat this input function as equivalent to perception. In the abstract, however, it's simply a process by which information of some sort arrives to be used in a particular way.

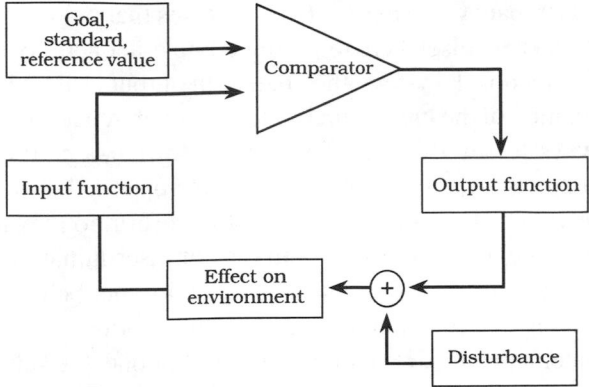

Figure 2.1. Schematic depiction of a feedback loop, the basic unit of cybernetic control. In such a loop a sensed value is compared to a reference value
or standard, and adjustments are made in an output function (if necessary) to
shift the sensed value in the direction of the standard.

The next step in describing a feedback loop is handled most easily
by introducing two elements at the same time: the comparator and the
reference value. The comparator is a structure that makes comparisons.
Comparison can be made in different ways in different physical systems,
and how it takes place is less important than *that* it takes place. The
reference value is a source of information other than the information from
the input function. As the input enters the system, a comparison occurs
between the input and the reference value. This comparison yields one of
two outcomes: The values being compared are discriminably different
from one another or they're not.

What follows this comparison is an output function (Figure 2.1). In
later discussions we'll treat this output function as equivalent to behavior. In the abstract, however, it's more general than that. It's simply
an *effector* of some sort – a process that in some way or other has an
effect on the system's environment (whatever's external to the system
itself). If the comparison fails to find a difference, the output remains
whatever it is now (which may be zero or may be some other value). If
the comparison finds a discrepancy, the output changes.

These functions in the negative feedback loop were described by
Miller, Galanter, and Pribram (1960), in an early statement on feedback
control, as what they termed a TOTE unit. TOTE is an acronym for test-
operate-test-exit. *Test* is comparison. If comparison reveals a discrepancy, an *operate* (output function) occurs, after which *test* recurs to see

whether the discrepancy still exists. *Exit* indicates that, with no discrepancy, control transfers elsewhere to permit some other activity to occur.

In a negative feedback system, the change in output is aimed at countering any deviation of the input function from the reference value. There are several ways to say this, all of which mean the same thing: The change in output is aimed at reducing the discrepancy between input and reference value, at causing the former to conform to the latter. It's an attempt to create input information that's not discriminable from the standard. It isn't behavior for the sake of behavior, but behavior in the service of creating and maintaining a desired perception.

This last statement has several implications. For one, the value the input function senses depends on more than what happens as output. The output function operates on the system's environment, but so do other forces. Disturbances can change present conditions, either adversely (creating a discrepancy from the reference value) or favorably (closing a discrepancy). In the former case, noting a discrepancy prompts a change in output, as always. In the latter case, however, the result of the disturbance is that *there's no need for an output adjustment*, because the system sees no discrepancy.

Feedback systems are often called "purposive" because it isn't just the pieces of the system that have roles to play. Rather, the system as a whole serves a purpose: to keep sensed values in conformity to the standard that's in place as a reference value. They're called *self-regulatory* systems because they regulate specific qualities via an internal organization. They're referred to as *closed loop* systems because there's an endless cycle among functions, with output having an impact on subsequent input. They're also referred to as *control systems* for at least two reasons. First, there's an interdependence of processes in the loop, such that the result of each function partially determines (controls) what happens in the next function. Second, the overall purpose of the loop is to determine (control) the quality of the sensed input.

A brief comment on the word *control*: This is a word with several meanings in the vocabulary of psychology. One meaning that's particularly likely to become confused with the meaning intended through most of this book is control as personal causal responsibility for events. We don't mean that here. Here, control refers to the process of maintaining conformity of a sensed input to a reference value, regardless of the source of the influence that does so. That is, it doesn't matter to the feedback loop whether conformity is created by its own output function or by a disturbance from outside. Sometimes the loop's actions are

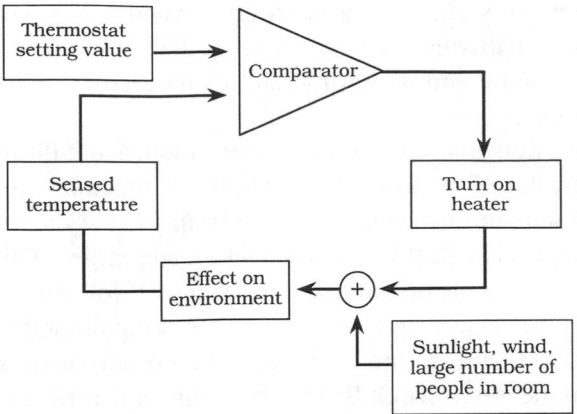

Figure 2.2. The elements of the feedback loop are often illustrated by the functions manifest in a room thermostat and furnace/air conditioner, with sensing of air temperature as the input function, a thermostat setting as the reference value, the turning on and off of the heater as the output function, and a variety of environmental influences as sources of disturbances.

critical, but sometimes a loop creates the desired outcome by *not* acting. Thus, control in this context has more to do with ensuring a result than with having causal primacy.

An Example: The Ubiquitous Thermostat

Let's illustrate some points we've made in abstract terms with a couple of examples from the behavior of physical systems. A commonly used example is the thermostat. The simplest point this example makes is that feedback processes can occur in diverse physical systems. What matters isn't the nature of the physical elements, but the logical relationships among the functions in which the elements engage (see Braitenberg, 1984).

Figure 2.2 shows the schematic displayed earlier in Figure 2.1, re-labeled so the functions are identified with the elements of a thermostat and ancillary devices (e.g., heat pump). The system has an input function, continuously sampling current air temperature. This input information goes to the device that compares the sensed value to the thermostat's setting. As long as the two values aren't discernibly different, nothing else happens. If the comparator detects a difference between values, it sends a message that turns on the heater and air transport system, which begins to dump warm air (or cold, depending on the application) into the room. Eventually enough warm air arrives and mixes with the air in the room that the thermostat can no longer tell the difference between the room temperature and its setting, and its request for activity from the heater ceases.

This example illustrates the elements of the loop, and it illustrates the purposive character of the system as a whole: It functions to keep the room's temperature in reasonably close conformity to the value of its setting. The example also illustrates other points made earlier. This system doesn't act by turning the output function on and off for certain specific periods of time, because it isn't the action of the compressor that's being controlled, but the temperature of the air. If a hot afternoon sun temporarily warms the room on a chilly fall afternoon, or if a crowd of people who are standing in the room radiate excess body heat, the heater doesn't have to heat, and the call to heat doesn't come. The room temperature is controlled by disturbances, rather than by the output function.

This example also illustrates that a not very clearly specified process intervenes between output and input functions, labeled only "effect on environment" in Figures 2.1 and 2.2. The output function has an indirect effect on the input function, rather than a direct one. The output changes reality in some fashion, but the path by which this change influences subsequent input may be quite circuitous. In the case of a heating system, you don't place the heat vent so it points directly at the thermostat, though this would be the fastest way to get the thermostat to register no discrepancy. Rather, you place the vent to dump warm air on the far side of the room, so the entire room is warmed when the thermostat senses no discrepancy.

Although the thermostat is a convenient illustration of feedback processes in a device with which most people are familiar, it's certainly not the only example one could use. Indeed, in some ways it's a poor example. For one thing, it tends to imply that feedback systems can produce only conformity to a steady state, which isn't correct. Feedback systems can conform to constantly changing reference values (see Clark, 1996, chap. 10). Another problem is that the purposive quality of the system isn't too striking in the thermostat. It's seen more easily in systems such as the gyroscopic steering system used on a large ship. This system uses feedback principles to keep the ship on course, despite outside influences (changing winds and currents). Such a steering system is a nice metaphor for human action (see also Klein, 1987). Indeed, we'll argue shortly that people have their own internal gyroscopes that keep them on track toward the goals they've put before themselves.

ADDITIONAL ISSUES IN FEEDBACK CONTROL

Many further issues can be raised about feedback principles. We consider three of them, each stemming in some way from the fact that our portrayal thus far has been somewhat idealized. Each suggests at least one way in which the self-regulation displayed by a feedback system can be less than perfect.

Sloppy versus Tight Control

In discussing the elements of a feedback loop, we said that the input information is compared against a reference value and that what happens next depends on whether the comparator detects a discrepancy between them. A question that's rarely raised, but has clear implications for the functioning of the system, is this: How good is the comparator's ability to detect differences? There must be variability in this capability, such that sometimes a comparator can detect minor deviations but sometimes it can detect only substantial ones.

How well a system can detect errors has a straightforward implication for the system's ability to self-regulate (assuming a constant ability to adjust output). A system with precise error detection (high error sensitivity) can maintain close self-regulation. The slightest deviation from the reference value is noted, and compensatory action is taken immediately. A system with poor error detection is more variable. There is a range within which deviations from the reference value won't be noted, and thus won't be countered. Only when the input deviates far enough that it falls outside that range will the discrepancy be noted and an output called for. The functioning of this system will appear sloppier than that of the other system. This is one of several ways in which self-regulation can be less than optimal, while still embodying the elements of feedback control.

Lag Time

Just as we idealized the function of the comparator, we've also idealized the role of time in the self-regulatory process. That is, the influence of the output function isn't instantaneous. As noted earlier, the output has its impact on the input via some "effect on the environment." The time it takes for the effect of an output to influence the input function (an interval sometimes called *lag time*) must be taken into account in the

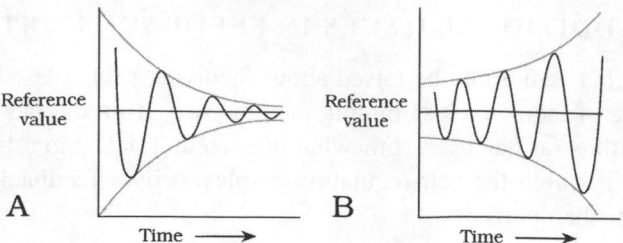

Figure 2.3. Failure to take into account the time required for feedback to register on the system can result in overcompensation, which in turn creates oscillation about the reference value. (A) If the overcompensation is less than the overshoot, the system will converge on the value. (B) If the overcompensation is larger than that, however, the system goes out of control, with deviations becoming more and more extreme.

loop's functioning (Clark, 1996, chap. 9). That is, the system has only one way of knowing whether its output has had the desired effect. Its only source of information on this question is the input function. The desired effect has occurred if the input is no longer discrepant from the reference value. But what if the output of this system takes a long time to exert its influence? What if the influence takes a long time to work its way back through the "effect on the environment" to show up in the input function?

If the system is "well designed," it takes the time lag into account. If the time lag isn't taken into account, the system continues to register a discrepancy long after it has executed the output needed to counter the initially sensed error. Consequently, the output function will continue longer than needed. At some point, the comparator will indicate that the discrepancy no longer exists and stop the output, but by this time a great deal of action has already taken place. Most of the effects of this action haven't yet registered on the input function. When these effects arrive, they'll create a deviation away from the reference value *opposite* to the initial deviation (see Figure 2.3).

This overcompensation (from failure to take into account the system's response time) can potentially lead to repetitive oscillation, as the system overcompensates first one way, then the other. If the overcompensation is smaller than the overshoot, self-regulation is erratic but eventually closes in on the reference value (Figure 2.3A). If it's larger, though, the system spins out of control (Figure 2.3B). It's important, then, to take lag time into account in considering how a feedback system is functioning. Failure to do so is a second way in which self-regulation can be less than optimal, even while embodying the character of feedback control.

Intermittent Feedback

A third way in which we over-idealized our description of feedback systems was to describe the loop in terms of continuous cycling of its component processes. This might imply that all the component processes function all the time. Sometimes this is so, but sometimes it's not. Schmidt (1988) provides a good description of the difference between these kinds of systems.

A continuous servo is one in which the effects of the output are continuously related to the reference value, and output varies continuously in response to variations in input. An example is the automatic steering mechanism in a ship, in which deviations are sensed continuously and changes in output are also made continuously (although even here it's important to note the need to consider lag time in the system's response).

A discontinuous, or intermittent, system is one in which the input and output functions don't track each other perfectly; rather, one function or the other occurs only intermittently. Sometimes the output is altered intermittently, as in the thermostat and furnace. That is, the room temperature changes continuously and these changes are noted continuously, but the heater is either off (when the temperature is within the range where the comparator doesn't notice the deviation) or on (when a deviation is noted).

There are also cases where the intermittency is on the input side. In such cases an output that's elaborate may be put into action, and its effects are checked only occasionally or only at the conclusion of the output. It's sometimes argued that fast body movements (too rapid for continuous feedback) rely on systems functioning this way (Schmidt, 1988, p. 221). It's also easy to see, however, how intermittency can produce erratic self-regulation. If input is checked only rarely, an output that's actually inappropriate won't be noticed as such until it's been largely or wholly carried out. This idea has obvious application to human concerns. If a person carries out an entire plan of action before checking to see whether it's having the desired effect, a great deal of effort may be spent on a plan that's actually counterproductive.

DISTINCTIONS AND FURTHER CONSTRUCTS

Although the negative feedback loop is the focal control structure in most of what follows, other concepts should also be mentioned. In this section we describe several, and indicate how they differ from those introduced thus far.

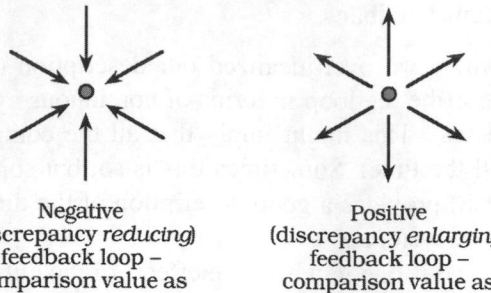

Negative
(discrepancy *reducing*)
feedback loop –
comparison value as
attractor or goal

Positive
(discrepancy *enlarging*)
feedback loop –
comparison value as
repeller or anti-goal

Figure 2.4. Negative feedback loops cause sensed qualities to shift *toward* positively valenced reference points. Positive feedback loops cause sensed qualities to shift *away from* negatively valenced reference points.

Positive Feedback Loops

The systems described thus far are called negative feedback loops, because their function is to negate (remove or diminish) a discrepancy between sensed input and reference value. These systems can be thought of as having reference values that are desired goals. These loops act to create conformity with reference values (see Figure 2.4). No matter the nature or direction of the deviation, the effort is to reduce it.

A positive feedback loop, in contrast, is a discrepancy amplifying system (DeAngelis, Post, & Travis, 1986; Ford, 1987; Maruyama, 1963). These loops create movement *away* from the reference value (Figure 2.4). Think of this as a system with an undesired goal, or an "anti-goal," as its reference value. Discrepancy amplifying loops try to move the currently perceived value away from the reference value. They are believed to be less common in naturally occurring systems than discrepancy reducing systems, because they're unstable. That is, they push away, and awayness goes on without limit. Whereas the conformity caused by a negative loop has a specific goal, the anticonformity caused by a positive loop doesn't. This creates instability, as they go on forever trying to create larger and larger deviations.

Positive feedback processes occur in functional ways in living systems (e.g., McFarland, 1971), but their action is typically constrained in some way by negative loops. Figure 2.5 illustrates symbolically how this can happen. A positive or avoidance loop creates pressure toward deviation from its reference value. Moving away occurs to a point, but the tendency to move away is captured by the influence of a negative loop. This loop then serves as an attractor, working to pull the sensed input into its orbit.

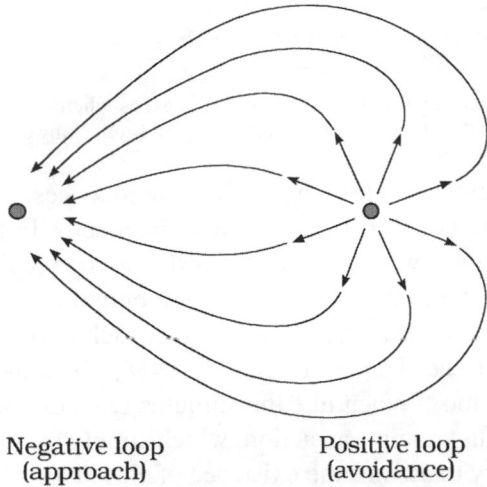

Negative loop   Positive loop
(approach)   (avoidance)

Figure 2.5.   The effects of positive (avoidance) feedback systems are often
bounded or constrained by negative (approach) feedback systems. A value
moves away from an undesired condition in a positive loop, and then comes
under the influence of a negative loop, moving toward the latter's desired
condition.

The use of the word *orbit* in the preceding sentence suggests a
metaphor that may be useful for readers to whom these concepts don't
feel terribly intuitive. The metaphor is feedback processes as gravity
and antigravity. The negative loop exerts a kind of gravitational pull
on the sensed input it's controlling, pulling the input closer to it. The
positive loop has a kind of antigravitational push, moving sensed values
ever farther away. A similar metaphor is feedback as magnetism: negative feedback as similar to magnetic attraction, and positive feedback
as similar to the repulsion that occurs when two poles of the same sign
face each other.

Open Loop Systems

Most of our emphasis in this book will be on the closed loop systems described in the preceding sections, systems in which the effects of actions
have an impact on the future perceptions of the systems, and ultimately
on subsequent outcomes. We should also note, however, the difference
between these systems and what have been termed open loop systems.

In an open loop system (Figure 2.6), the output of the system is
triggered by the recognition of a particular state of affairs, and output

Figure 2.6.   What's called an open loop system exists when some input cue triggers an output that is executed without subsequently checking on its impact.

simply executes. There's no checking on its consequences. There is a presumption that the consequence will be as intended. In an open loop system the output is always preprogrammed, with no provision for modifying it. Such systems are invoked when the output is very rapid, where there appears to be insufficient time for feedback information to be used (for discussion see chap. 7 of Schmidt, 1988). To some extent, the open loop system looks much like the stimulus-response depiction of behavior: A stimulus prompts an action, which simply occurs.

When is it necessary to assume the existence of closed loop systems, and when will an open loop system do? This is an important issue in discussions of movement control, and there remain substantial disagreements as to the answer (for a critique of the idea that open loop systems are used in movement control, see Marken, 1986, p. 275). Schmidt (1988, pp. 145–146) also pointed out that complex systems can be hybrids of closed and open loop subsystems. As an illustration, car engines have elements that follow closed loop principles – regulation of engine temperature through an arrangement of thermostat and control of coolant flow. They also have elements that are open loop – order and timing of the spark plugs.

The issue of combining open and closed loop systems is one that's important in discussions of movement control. In general, at the level of abstraction we're interested in, we'll argue that open loop systems are dysfunctional. In general, human functioning at this level involves closed loops.

Feedforward

Another concept to address here is feedforward. The principle of feedforward is used in somewhat different ways in different contexts, but the uses have some commonalities. Whereas feedback is information about the consequences of an output (reflected in a subsequent input), feedforward is anticipatory. This principle can be conceptualized in two ways.

First, feedforward can be considered as *anticipatory output*. In the cases of most interest to us, feedforward represents a first approximation of output, which occurs before any input is taken into account. Because it would seem to precede the noting of any discrepancy between present state and reference value, the feedforward theoretically comes first. It doesn't take into account the present state, because nothing has come in yet to take into account.

The feedforward signal can be viewed as a "best estimate" of the output that's going to be needed (e.g., Marteniuk, 1992), an output that's "in the ballpark" (Greene, 1972). If the first approximation is good enough, the outcome will occur exactly as desired, with little or no subsequent correction needed. This result – behavior as intended with no need for correction – is often what leads people to invoke the concept of feedforward. (Indeed, this also can cause people to infer open loop control when that's not the case; even if the first approximation is exactly on the mark, it doesn't mean the system isn't checking to be sure.)

This use of the feedforward concept raises questions that are hard to answer. It's convenient in some respects to assume that the feedforward somehow bypasses the comparator (Figure 2.7A), but it's hard to be sure this is right. Maybe the feedforward instead occurs through the ordinary mechanism of the loop, *but is simply the first cycle of output to occur* (Figure 2.7B). That is, given the sudden presence of a reference value but no input yet available, the comparator by default should register a discrepancy. Thus the feedforward may be no different in principle from any other output.

In either case, this application of the feedforward concept raises questions about how the first-approximation output is created. In an electronic system the answer is often quite easy: The reference signal is sent directly on as the output, and the feedback loop acts simply to eliminate subsequent unwanted disturbances from sources outside the system. In a behavioral application of these ideas, all this becomes a little trickier.

A second application of the feedforward concept treats feedforward as creating a change in reference value. This application occurs in discussions of functioning of visual centers in the nervous system. When your eye makes a shift in position, you rarely notice it. If the room shifted the same amount, however, you'd notice it and be disoriented. You can tell whether you've made a movement in a stable environment or whether the environment itself has suddenly shifted, but how?

The usual answer (Evarts, 1973; Gallistel, 1980; Sperry, 1950) is that when the instruction to shift is sent to the muscles that move the eye (an output function within its own loop), a copy of that instruction (termed *efference copy*) is sent to the part of the brain that interprets the visual input. This copy causes the movement to be taken into account in interpreting

A

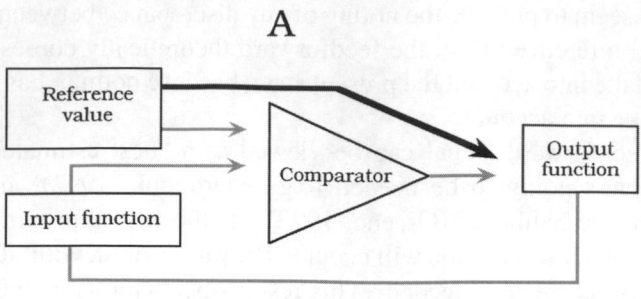

B

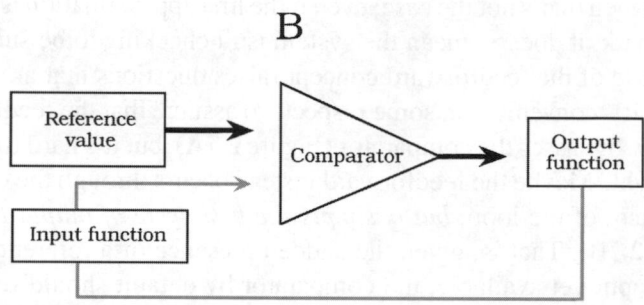

Figure 2.7.   Two construals of feedforward as a first approximation of the output needed to create a desired result (i.e., to be identical to the reference value). Paths that are associated with feedback are gray, to indicate that they've not yet conveyed information when the feedforward occurs. (A) Here the feedforward signal is shown as bypassing the comparator as first-cycle output. (B) Here the feedforward signal is portrayed as occurring within the structure of the loop. This portrayal assumes that the comparison in the absence of input information registers a discrepancy, and the initial output is the feedforward signal. In this latter view, there's some question as to whether the feedforward signal really differs from any other output.

the visual input. The signal that a movement was ordered causes the visual system to adjust its reference value, to compensate for the fact that the movement had been ordered by some other part of the nervous system. The signal to make this adjustment is termed a *feedforward* signal.

INTERRELATIONS AMONG FEEDBACK PROCESSES

Thus far in the chapter we've described the functioning of feedback processes in terms of single cases, one loop at a time, although we've made occasional reference to information coming to the loop from elsewhere in a broader organization. We turn now to a consideration of several ways in which organizations can exist among feedback loops.

Interdependency

One way in which feedback loops can be related constitutes a kind of interdependency between separate feedback systems. In this arrangement, two systems that have their own goals and purposes are both responsive to the outputs of the other system.

An example often used in discussions of feedback processes in ecology concerns population sizes. Imagine a closed ecosystem (perhaps a small island) where there's a population of rabbits and a population of foxes. The rabbits constitute the major food source for the foxes, who are the only predators to threaten the rabbits. The size of each population is influenced by changes in the other population.

Given plentiful vegetation, the rabbits multiply rapidly and populate the island. As the rabbit population grows, the population of foxes also grows, because there's now more food (rabbits) for them. As the population of foxes grows larger, the population of rabbits begins to shrink, because so many of them are being eaten. This reduction in the available food supply has an adverse effect on the population of foxes, which also begins to diminish. With a depletion in the ranks of the predators, the rabbit population begins to reemerge.

In a well-balanced ecosystem, the populations of both species will find levels at which there is mutual stability. However, it's not impossible for the system to be driven outside this stability. For example, if the rabbit population is reduced to zero, the foxes have no food source, and the fox population also dies out. Here's a case where both population sizes are causes and both are also effects. Each changes over time in response to changes in the other, and each helps determine how the other changes.

Another example of interrelated feedback processes embeds one within the other, such that the output of each one acts as a disturbance on the other. Consider (from Schmidt, 1988) the case of two temperature-controlling feedback processes that are active simultaneously in many homes: a refrigerator and a furnace. The refrigerator keeps the temperature inside it at a set level, through a feedback loop with an internal thermostat. The furnace does the same thing, but with respect to the temperature inside the house.

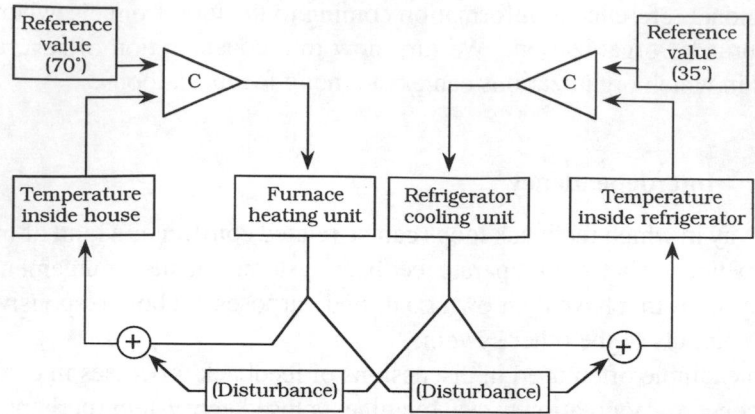

Figure 2.8.   Interdependent feedback loops: One loop controls the temperature inside the refrigerator; the other controls the temperature inside the room.
The output function of each loop acts as a disturbance on the other loop, influencing the perception registered in its input function. (Adapted from Schmidt,
1988, p. 145.)

Each of these systems also has an impact on the other (Figure 2.8). The
output function of the refrigerator cools the air inside the refrigerator by
transferring heat from inside to outside. The input function of the furnace
(indicating the temperature of the room) responds not only to the actions
of the furnace, but also to disturbances. One disturbance is the behavior
of the refrigerator, which periodically dumps some heat from inside it
into the rest of the room. When the refrigerator's compressor is running,
it's not just cooling the refrigerator but heating the room.

In the same way, the furnace is acting as a disturbance on the refrigerator. Why does the refrigerator have to run its compressor periodically
in the first place? Because heat gets into the refrigerator, raising its temperature. Where does the heat come from? From the air surrounding
the refrigerator, the very air that the furnace is trying to keep warm.
Thus the furnace's action makes the refrigerator work harder to keep its
temperature down.

Reference Value and Input Function:
How Do They Differ?

Let's return to the beginning of this chapter's story for a moment, think
again about the elements that make up a feedback loop, and consider a

question. The loop has two sources of information, the input function and the reference value. It should be apparent that both sources are important – indeed, both are necessary for a feedback loop to exist and to function. The two aren't entirely equivalent, however. There's a sense in which the reference value is more important, in that it's more "demanding" than the input function.

We said earlier in this chapter that detecting a discrepancy between input and reference value leads to an attempt to reduce it. In principle, there are two ways by which the discrepancy might be reduced (leaving aside fortuitous environmental disturbances). The path we've focused on involves changing the output function in order to change the input so that it comes into closer conformity with the reference value. Why not change the reference value so that it more closely matches the input?

If these two values didn't differ in their stability, self-regulation would be truly haphazard. Instead of holding fast to some reference standard, the system would be all over the place, shifting the standard and shifting the input erratically, as a function of which moved first. Although there do appear to be cases in which standards change, such changes indicate something more complex than a single feedback loop. In a single loop, the reference value is rigidly in place (compared to the input function), and adjustments try to move input toward the standard.

A shift in standard appears to imply the operation of a second feedback path. The second path shown in Figure 2.9 uses the same information about the relation between input and reference value as the original loop uses. Its action is aimed not at changing the input, but at changing the reference value. We're not going to explore how it actually does so; we're only going to note that this path typically has a more gradual effect than the other path. As a result, this path has a discernible effect on the reference value only if a great deal of attempted output fails to reduce the discrepancy.

Such a secondary process probably is not inevitably in effect, but it is there sometimes. For example, most people sleep roughly eight hours per night (as a standard). If you get too little sleep over a night or two, your body typically compensates by catching up on a later night. Anecdotal evidence (from one of our colleagues) suggests that if you get smaller amounts of sleep over a long enough time, the standard appears to undergo a shift, so your body asks for less sleep than it used to. Because this change in reference value seems to occur through a secondary output

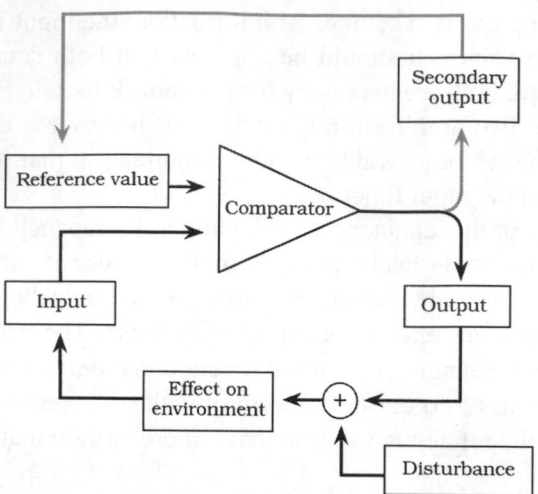

Figure 2.9.   Feedback loops act to create changes in the input function, to shift its value toward the reference value. *Sometimes* another process is also in place (indicated by gray lines), which works to adjust the reference value toward the input. If it's in place, this additional process is typically very gradual, which keeps the reference value comparatively stable.

of the very comparison process that's using the reference value, we'll call this a "self-referential" change in standard, to distinguish it from the idea we're just about to introduce.

Hierarchies

Thus far we've talked about individual feedback loops and loops that are mutually interdependent. Even in the latter cases, the loops implicitly exist at the same level of abstraction. It's also been argued, though, that feedback loops can be organized in a hierarchical fashion, such that there are superordinate systems and subordinate systems (Powers, 1973a, 1973b). In this view, superordinate systems don't act directly on the outside environment. They act on subordinate systems. More specifically, they act by resetting the reference values of the subordinate systems.

Consider the thermostat one last time. As is true of many control structures, it's a flexible device that can operate with respect to a wide range of reference values. It gets its reference value from a superordinate system, the woman on whose wall the thermostat is wired. This woman also has a reference value (be comfortably warm). Rather than operate directly on the environment to produce heat – for example, by building a fire – she operates by providing a new reference value to the subordinate system – resetting the thermostat from 60 degrees to 75 degrees. Given this change in reference value, the thermostat calls on the furnace, and the room temperature rises.

This example illustrates several points. First, the action of the superordinate system involves changing a reference value. Unlike the change discussed in the preceding section, however, this change process isn't self-referential. Rather, it occurs by the action of one system on the other system. A second point is that as the two systems act to create their desired conditions, each is monitoring its own input, which exists at its own level of abstraction. The thermostat assesses air temperature; the woman assesses her comfort level. Third, since the subordinate system is operating in the service of the superordinate system, progress toward discrepancy reduction occurs simultaneously for both systems as the air temperature rises.

A final point is that it's possible for a superordinate system to exist but not to act in a superordinate fashion. The woman in our example has actually been sitting in her living room for a long time, inattentive to the fact that she isn't comfortably warm, because she's been thinking about a problem she's facing at work. Only when someone came into the room and asked her if she was warm enough did she realize she wasn't. At that point she walked across to the thermostat and adjusted it. Until then, the superordinate system wasn't acting in a superordinate way. It was as though it had been temporarily disconnected. The fact that the higher-level system wasn't being used doesn't mean that it and its reference value weren't there. But while the superordinate system wasn't engaged, this two-level hierarchy was operating with the thermostat functionally superordinate.

In principle, it's possible for there to be many levels in a hierarchy of control (Figure 2.10). Among theorists interested in the control of movement of the human body, it isn't unusual for models to be proposed in which several layers of control are assumed (see, e.g., Greene, 1972; Rosenbaum, 1987, 1991b), though how to conceptualize their arrangement is debated among the theorists (Schmidt, 1988). William Powers (1973a, 1973b), whose background is in engineering rather than motor control, argued that the sensorimotor aspects of the nervous system are organized in such a way that as many as nine layers of control may be involved in voluntary movement. Because Powers tried to take higher-order intentions into account, as well as motor control, his model has some interesting implications, which we consider later.

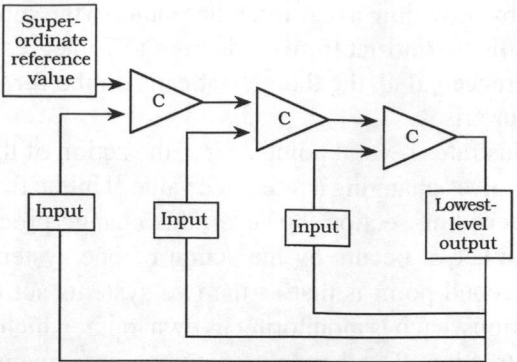

Figure 2.10.   A hypothetical three-level hierarchy of feedback loops. The output function of the superordinate loop consists of the resetting of the reference value of the loop at the next lower level, a pattern that is repeated to the bottom level, where the output function takes another form. All levels are construed as monitoring feedback at the level of abstraction relevant to that level.

CONCLUDING COMMENT

This completes our description of the principles of feedback control. This was the hardest part. In many ways, the rest is all applications. That is, we use virtually all the ideas presented here as descriptive and explanatory principles in examining self-regulation in human behavior. This we do now, beginning with Chapter 3.

3

Discrepancy-Reducing Feedback Processes in Behavior

Our waking lives are filled with behavior. We haul ourselves out of bed each morning and set off for the day. We do much that's mundane and even trivial. Sometimes we do things we think are important at the moment but will later decide didn't matter much after all. Sometimes we do things that seem trivial at the time but will later seem more momentous. Occasionally our actions involve our core sense of self, though this is probably rare for most people. A lot of human behavior, after all, is an extended process of maintenance activity – buying groceries, washing dishes, driving from place to place to get things. Some behavior involves a lot of physical movement, but some of our most important behavior involves moving little more than our mouths and eyes.

FEEDBACK CONTROL IN HUMAN BEHAVIOR

In this chapter we argue that all these behaviors embody the processes of feedback control. We didn't invent this idea. Explicit statements about it go back at least to Miller, Galanter, and Pribram's (1960) book *Plans and the Structure of Behavior* (see also Hunt, 1965; MacKay, 1963, 1966; Powers, 1973a, 1973b), and ideas underlying it go back much further (chap. 3 of Miller et al., 1960, reviews the history of related thought). We're part of a second generation of psychologists who regard it as plausible.[1]

---

[1] We reiterate that *behavior* as discussed here means primarily behavior at the level of personality and social psychology. Keep in mind, though, that theorists examining how the body controls movement find feedback ideas indispensable. This point is relevant for two reasons. First, the nervous system that moves the body is the same one that forms abstract intentions and carries them out. If feedback concepts are useful in the movement part, they're likely to be useful in other parts as well, since it's unlikely that different aspects of the nervous system depend on entirely different principles (cf. Gallistel, 1980). Second, even abstract intentions must be carried out by physical movements. Thus, having built-in conceptual links to theories about how the body carries out actions is a bonus for a theory about self-regulation of behavior at a higher level.

Early Applications of Feedback Principles

The first theorists to argue for the idea that feedback processes are important in macro-level human behavior were Miller, Galanter, and Pribram (1960). Their arguments appeared in a slim, engaging volume that presented a picture of human behavior guided by plans and goals and self-regulated by discrepancy-reducing feedback processes. It's a book of ideas and research possibilities rather than a description of support for the ideas. It articulated a feedback-based vision of behavior, inviting others to consider its usefulness.

Another well-known early user of feedback ideas was Bowlby (1969). He viewed the mind as a hierarchy of evaluating and controlling mechanisms operating on feedback principles, with the goal of creating and maintaining desired conditions. Best known, of course, is his pioneering work on infant attachment, a phenomenon that he viewed in feedback terms. The securely attached child uses its mother as a base. When it feels comfortably secure, it explores. If it's away too long and becomes anxious from the separation (or becomes frightened for some other reason), it returns. If it experiences too much closeness, it pulls away and explores again. The goal is to maintain a desired level of closeness to the attachment figure, neither too little nor (for a securely attached child) too much. Perceptions deviating from the desired level cause change in behavior. Again, although the feedback model provided an organizing principle that was useful, it wasn't a high priority to confirm that this actually is a feedback process.

In later years the functions involved in feedback processes received closer attention. It's now possible to point to studies indicating that feedback processes do occur in at least some kinds of behavioral self-regulation. Some of these studies are our own.

Our Starting Points

The path by which we came to consider the feedback viewpoint began neither with Miller, Galanter, and Pribram nor with Bowlby. We had an interest in phenomena that stem from self-focused attention, an interest prompted by work that others around us were doing at the time (Duval & Wicklund, 1972). Eventually we became convinced that some of these phenomena involved feedback loops.

More specifically, we came to argue that focusing attention on the self is often equivalent to engaging more fully the comparator that's involved in the self-regulation of the activity the person is presently engaged in (Carver, 1979; Carver & Scheier, 1981a). Unbeknownst to us, MacKay had foreshadowed this argument much earlier, writing in 1963 that "an artifact capable of receiving and acting on information about the state of its own body can begin to parallel many of the modes of activity we associate with self-consciousness" (p. 227).

Before we turn to the work that makes this case, we should say a few words about terminology. The term *self-awareness* has a particular meaning here: focusing of attention on an aspect of the self (Duval & Wicklund, 1972; Wicklund, 1975). It doesn't imply a prolonged or penetrating self-examination or self-absorption, nor does it connote self-knowledge beyond the ordinary. *Attention* is selective processing of particular aspects of the informational field available, such that some information is more salient or more fully processed than others. Self-awareness is self-focused attention, selective processing of information about the self.

The word *self-consciousness* also has a specialized meaning here. In colloquial speech, self-consciousness tends to imply embarrassment. Here it doesn't. Fenigstein, Scheier, and Buss (1975) chose this label to refer to individual differences in the propensity to become self-aware. It provided a verbal shorthand to let authors refer to individual differences by one term (self-consciousness) and situationally created states of self-focus by another term (self-awareness) without constantly reminding readers which was which. Other phrases (self-focus, self-directed attention) are used generically to refer to either the disposition or the manipulated state.

As noted earlier, self-focus appears to have predictable consequences, some of which suggest that self-focus engages the comparator of a feedback system managing behavior (Figure 3.1). The earliest, pioneering work on the effects of self-focus was done by Wicklund and Duval (1971; Duval & Wicklund, 1972), who took a different meta-theoretical view than we're taking. They proposed that self-focus leads people to be more conscious of whatever standards for behavior are salient. As people become more aware of a standard, they tend to compare themselves against it. To the extent there's a discrepancy between their present behavior and the standard, the result is often an attempt to alter behavior so it conforms more closely to the standard. These functions are precisely those of a feedback system.

Self-Directed Attention and Comparison with Standards

If self-focused attention does engage a feedback process, the effects should be manifested in several ways. First, greater self-focus is likely

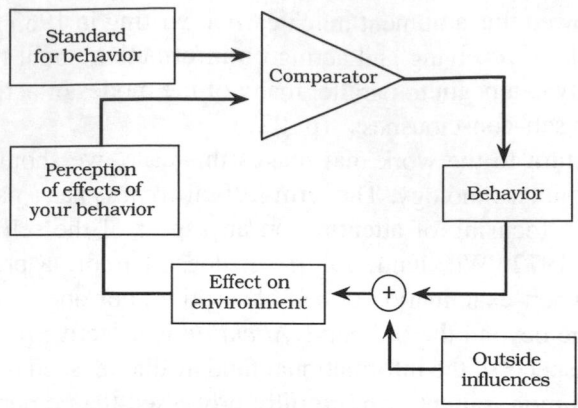

Figure 3.1.   Behavior and perception as elements of a feedback loop guiding human action. In this view, self-focused attention enhances the effects of the comparator.

to be associated with the tendency to compare present self or present behavior against the salient standard. This is hard to verify directly, partly because it's an internal process and partly because it's difficult to separate the comparison function from the broader action of the loop. There is, however, indirect evidence for this assertion.

The studies that provide this support (Scheier & Carver, 1983) created situations with an implicit behavioral standard: to perform well at an assigned task. As a reference value, this is relatively abstract. While you're actually engaged in the behavior that's relevant to this goal, it can be hard to evaluate your progress. If your standard for a day's work is to "be productive," how do you decide at day's end whether you've met your goal? You look at the hard evidence of what you've done, and you look at some concrete comparison point (guidelines provided by a work assignment, or perhaps performances of other people engaged in similar activity). In sum, to compare your behavior against an abstract standard, you often seek out concrete information that facilitates the abstract comparison.

This is the principle behind the studies we conducted. In two studies, we asked people to copy a set of complex geometric diagrams onto paper as accurately as they could. Each diagram was projected for five seconds at a time. While the diagram was visible, the subject could view it but not copy. Only when the diagram disappeared could copying begin (or resume). The subject could view the diagram as often as desired, however, simply by pressing a button. Indeed, subjects were told to view each diagram as often as necessary to copy it as exactly as they could.

The diagram itself was a concrete standard of comparison for subjects' drawings. Looking at the diagram and comparing it to your own drawing is conceptually equivalent to engaging in the comparison assumed in the feedback model in Figure 3.1, at a concrete level. We assumed this process would occur in the service of a more abstract comparison between present behavior and the goal of "accurately duplicating the diagrams," or "performing well at the task." The dependent variable was how often subjects viewed the drawings. Those who did the task in the presence of a manipulation previously shown to increase self-awareness viewed the diagrams more frequently than those who did the task without it. In a second study, subjects whose dispositional tendencies toward self-consciousness were high viewed the diagrams more frequently than those whose self-consciousness was lower.

Two additional studies examined the comparison process with a different paradigm. These studies followed from the idea that one way to judge how well you're doing at a task is to compare your performance against performances of others on the same task. These studies were portrayed as part of a process of establishing norms for new tests of verbal ability. Subjects in one study completed a series of anagrams, calling out the solution for each one to the experimenter, who in turn told the subject how much time had elapsed, which the subject wrote down.

Before starting the task, the experimenter had drawn the subject's attention to booklets on the far end of the table which contained ostensible testing norms from previous semesters. After the anagrams were finished, subjects could consult the norms and compare their solution times against them. The norms thus constituted concrete standards that would facilitate the mental comparison between the abstract standard (performing well) and the performance. As predicted, subjects whose self-consciousness scores were higher consulted more pages of norms than did those whose self-consciousness was lower.

A final study was similar in logic to this one, but subjects had the chance to seek normative information before beginning the task. Participants were told they'd be working on 10 items from a test of abstract reasoning that was being evaluated. They were to choose their 10 items from among 4 categories, 2 of which concerned spatial reasoning, 2 semantic relationships. The item sets also varied (independently) in another way: For 2 sets, normative information was available; for the others, no norms were available. Subjects were to indicate how many items they wanted to work on from each of the 4 sets.

As expected, subjects who completed the form in front of a self-awareness-inducing stimulus chose more items for which norms were available than did control subjects. Presumably, this seeking of normative information occurred in the service of what would later be an attempt to compare abstract performance against a standard.

Self-Directed Attention and Conformity to Standards

If the effect of directing attention to the self in such situations is to engage more fully the comparator of a feedback loop, another thing should also happen, concerning the functioning of the feedback loop as a whole. If the comparison process is more fully engaged, the loop should do a better job of doing what it does: maintaining conformity between its sensed input and the standard. Thus, self-focus should promote closer self-regulation to the person's reference value.

This was, in fact, one of the first effects of self-awareness to be studied. In the first test of this hypothesis, Wicklund and Duval (1971) created a situation in which subjects were given the task of copying prose (printed in a foreign language). They were to copy quickly, and were left alone to work, either in the presence of a self-awareness-inducing stimulus (a mirror) or not. The experimenter surreptitiously timed the subject for a specific period, then interrupted. The question was how much the person copied in that time period. The answer was that subjects copied more when self-awareness was higher than when it was lower.

This is the first illustration of a phenomenon that apparently is sufficiently counterintuitive that it is sometimes misunderstood or ignored (e.g., Ingram, 1990): Increases in *self-focus* can promote increases in *task focus*. In this study, a standard for behavior was made salient: Copy quickly. Subjects with higher self-focus apparently applied themselves to the task more than those with lower self-focus.

This situation, of course, was an extremely simplified one. Further, it made use of one particular kind of standard: an instruction from the experimenter. Is closer conformity to reference values under high self-focus a general phenomenon? It would help to see the effect emerge under a variety of conditions. By this we mean seeing the effect in a variety of behavioral acts (copying prose isn't really the best example of an activity within the broad category "social behavior," though it has the advantage of being easy to measure). We also mean seeing the effect with regard to a variety of types of behavioral standards.

Many types of standards exist. Instructions, social comparison information, the norms of a society or group, a person's attitudes – all these are standards. (Consider attitudes. (A person's belief that something is desirable or undesirable can serve as a point of reference for that person, a value around which to regulate behavior.) The idea that self-focus causes closer self-regulation suggests that when the attitude is salient as a reference value, the person will act in closer conformity to it when self-focus is high than when it's low. (Note that this hypothesis doesn't indicate when attitudes are naturally salient as standards, an issue we'll defer.)

This line of thought provided the basis for another study (Carver, 1975), which used a restricted pool of participants. First they completed a questionnaire expressing their opinion about punishment as a teaching technique. Some favored it (they thought it was effective and they'd be willing to use it); others opposed it (they thought it was ineffective and they'd be unwilling to use it). Weeks later, each participated in an experiment portrayed as a study of concept formation, in which they would teach another person to recognize an embedded visual pattern by a conditioning procedure. As part of that procedure, subjects would reward the learner after correct responses and punish him after incorrect responses. No talking would take place, and even nonverbal communication would be prevented by a partial wall.

Punishment was to be delivered as electric shock to the learner's finger. The punishment could vary in intensity from 1 to 10. Subjects received "sample" shocks to provide a sense of the different levels. They then were told they had freedom of choice over what intensity to administer for any given punishment. The experimenter said that psychologists are unsure about the effects of punishment on learning, and that participants were being asked to use their own opinions as guides. Thus each subject's attitude was made salient as a standard of comparison. For half the subjects in the study a mirror had been placed on the apparatus at eye level; for the other half it was removed.

The learner in this procedure was actually part of the research team. When the experiment began, he opened a door in the apparatus and turned off the shock. He then responded to the problems with a predetermined series of correct and incorrect responses. The punishment levels the subject chose for incorrect trials were recorded.

The results (Figure 3.2) were as predicted. Subjects relied on their attitudes to guide their actions when self-focus was high. Those who favored punishment used intense punishment, those who opposed punishment used very weak punishment. Subjects whose self-focus was low during

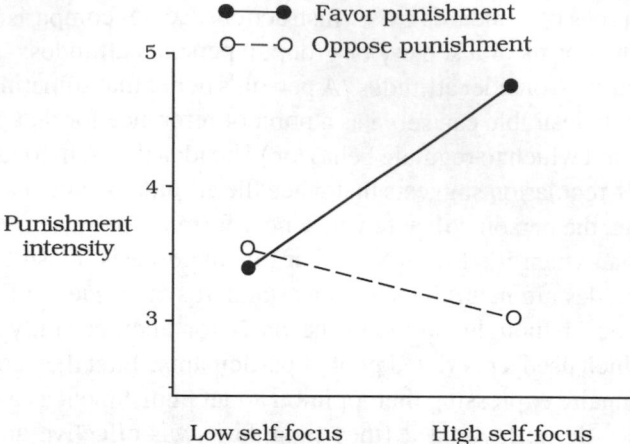

Figure 3.2.   Punishment intensities delivered by subjects who either favored or opposed the use of punishment to produce learning, under conditions of either high or low self-awareness. (Data from Carver, 1975.)

the task apparently didn't use their opinions. There are many possible reasons for this; the one we regard as most plausible is that the task itself demanded a great deal of attention. It would have been easy for subjects to lose track of the fact that they were supposed to be using their attitudes to direct their behavior, unless their attention was periodically directed back to the comparison between what they were doing and what they were intending to be doing.)

The studies just described make the case that self-focus causes closer conformity to salient standards, but they're far from the only studies to make this case. Induction of self-focus has caused effects as wide ranging as these: men conformed more to an implicit social standard of "chivalry" when giving punishment to a woman (Scheier, Fenigstein, & Buss, 1974); students allocating group earnings responded more to equity and equality norms when each was salient (Greenberg, 1980; Kernis & Reis, 1984); students rated erotica more consistently with their own standards (Gibbons, 1978); children in the midst of trick-or-treating conformed more to the instruction to take one (implicitly *only* one) piece of candy from a bowl (Beaman, Klentz, Diener, & Svanum, 1979); people opposed to stereotyping restrained themselves from doing so, whereas those who condoned it stereotyped even more (Macrae, Bodenhausen, & Milne, 1998). Individual differences in self-consciousness also related to improvement in sales performance among salesmen who saw that goal as important (Hollenbeck & Williams, 1987).

We want to emphasize two points about these studies: First, in all cases, self-focused attention caused subjects to conform more closely to the standard that was salient for them in that situation. Second, this effect of self-focus is an influence on a *process*, not a direct effect on the *content* of behavior. That is, being self-aware can make you *less* punitive if the salient standard is nonaggression (Scheier et al., 1974), but it can also make you *more* punitive if the standard calls for it (Carver, 1974, 1975). The content of behavior when self-focus is high depends on the reference value. People often can easily plug in one standard or another, and the effect of self-focus on overt action changes correspondingly.

Brain Functioning, Self-Awareness, and Self-Regulation

Though we have no intention of delving deeply into the nature of the brain's organization and functioning, we do want to address briefly a body of brain research that bears on some of these arguments. In particular, Stuss (1991) has argued that the prefrontal cortex is responsible for phenomena captured by the term *self-awareness* (see also Stuss & Benson, 1986).

Stuss (1991) holds that the frontal cortex has three levels of function. The first involves the ability to organize and maintain information in meaningful sequences. The second is an executive function involved in moving toward goals in novel or nonroutine situations. This control function is divisible into processes such as goal selection, means–end analysis, reflective evaluation of behavioral outcomes, and performance maintenance in light of those evaluations. The third level of frontal function is consciousness itself, the ability to be aware of oneself and one's relationship to the environment.

Much of this argument rests on studies of persons with frontal lobe damage. Stuss (1991) reviewed portions of this literature and (though noting inconsistencies) concluded that several themes can be extracted from it. First, many patients display a dissociation between knowledge and its use – for example, although they can detect errors, they don't use this knowledge appropriately. Second, there's a disturbance of subjective time. Patients with frontal lobe damage often show a loss of the sense of temporal order, a sense that's obviously necessary to implement plans or to experience the continuity of the self (see also Ingvar, 1985; Tulving, 1989). A third theme, more diffuse, is that there are differing levels of awareness of self, with higher levels being more likely to be disturbed by frontal lobe damage.

A very different kind of evidence bearing on a related idea has recently been reported by Gehring, Goss, Coles, Meyer, and Donchin (1993). Subjects in this study performed a long series of simple choices while electroencephalogram (EEG) data were recorded to assess aspects of their brain activity. Of particular interest was what occurred on trials where subjects made errors. The errors were associated with a particular pattern in the EEG, which indicated that a brain mechanism was noting the error even as it was being made. Further, this pattern was also associated with several measures indicating attempts at error correction. Taken together, the data suggest the existence of a brain system that detects errors and attempts to compensate for them.

Although these links between neuropsychology and social–personality psychology are more than just a little tenuous, they are also exciting and encouraging. They suggest that in work such as this there may emerge a better understanding of the physiological mechanisms within which the phenomena described in the preceding sections take place.

How Does Attention Shift to the Self in Ordinary Life?

A question that naturally arises concerning the effects of self-focused attention is how the effects translate to reality outside the lab. What causes attention to shift to the self in the natural course of experience? There are several answers to this question.

One answer is that attention fluctuates naturally back and forth, toward and away from the self, throughout moment-to-moment experience. For example, there's evidence that attention is demanded at decision points in behavior (cf. Norman & Shallice, 1986). Although cognitive psychologists rarely construe decision points in terms of self-focus, the need to make a decision relevant to a present intention would seem to imply that attention is being diverted to the self – more particularly, the aspect of self that's managing the execution of the intention. Thus, natural brief fluctuations in attention to the self probably occur throughout the course of carrying out an intention whose execution is not wholly automatic.

Attention to the behavior-managing aspect of the self also increases if something about your behavior produces an unexpected result (Norman, 1981). For example, if you go to where you parked your car and it isn't there, you check your behavior more closely to see where you walked, to assess whether you went where you intended to go. This sort of event-induced self-focus seems relatively specific to a review of the most recent behavioral output as it relates to the intention, though if this doesn't reveal the error the search quickly broadens.

There are also social stimuli that serve to increase self-focused attention, and others that decrease it. Having an audience looking at you promotes self-focus (Carver & Scheier, 1978), as does spending time writing a story about yourself (Fenigstein & Levine, 1984). Attention to the self diminishes when you're immersed in a crowd (Diener, 1979; Prentice-Dunn & Rogers, 1980) or when you become involved in the story line of a movie.

Aspects of your inner experience can also draw attention inward. The need to make a decision might be considered an inner experience, but more obvious inner experiences can draw attention as well. The experience of physical arousal draws attention to the self (Wegner & Giuliano, 1980). So does the experience of emotion (Carr, Teasdale, & Broadbent, 1991; Salovey, 1992; Wood, Saltzberg, & Goldsamt, 1990), though positive emotion appears to do so less reliably than negative emotion. Although these studies make it clear that inner experiences draw attention, it isn't clear whether the self-focus they prompt shifts to comparison between self and salient standards, or whether it centers only on the state that attracted it.

We should also note that in thinking about self focus in feedback loops (as opposed to other effects of self-focus[2]), the issue isn't exactly what makes attention be self-directed. The issue is what makes attention go to *the comparison between existing condition and reference value*. This comparison can happen if you attend to your "self," but it can also happen if you attend to an intention, task instructions, or some personally held value. That is, thinking about any one of those as a standard tends to make you think about your present behavior in relation to it. Many settings incorporate cues that remind people of their intentions, instructions, and values. These settings thus engage self-focused

---

[2] The self-awareness literature is one of several bodies of work that can be used to discuss how feedback concepts provide a useful model of human behavior. We should note, however, that not all effects of self-focus fit the self-regulatory model we're discussing here. Sometimes self-awareness has simpler effects. Attending to the self can make people more aware of existing affect (Scheier, 1976; Scheier & Carver, 1977) and the *absence* of expected internal states (Gibbons, Carver, Scheier, & Hormuth, 1979; Scheier, Carver, & Gibbons, 1979). Self-focus can cause people to make internal attributions (Arkin & Duval, 1975; Duval & Wicklund, 1973; Ross & Sicoly, 1979), and over time it can cause people to develop more elaborated and firmly anchored self-concepts (Hjelle & Bernard, 1994; Nasby, 1985, 1989a, 1989b). Thus, some of the consequences of self-focus are outside the realm of this discussion.

self-regulation by inducing the comparison process via the standard, rather than via the self more generally.

BROADENING THE APPLICATION
OF FEEDBACK PRINCIPLES

In describing feedback processes in behavior in the preceding sections, we've simplified our description of the nature of the feedback that's available to people. Reality is more complex than we implied, and we need to address that complexity.

Sources and Nature of Feedback
of the Effects of One's Behavior

The feedback that allows you to tell whether a discrepancy exists between the act intended and the act you're doing comes from several sources, and the relative importance of a given source varies from one situation to another. Often, you use several kinds of information at once. In some cases, proprioceptive and efference information is important. These cases tend to be represented more in the domain of motor control than in that of social behavior, but not always. If you're trying to impress someone with your gracefulness or athletic ability, proprioceptive information will be part of your input for judging whether you're doing what you intended to do.

Other sources of information are sight and sound. For example, as an untrained typist types a line of text, he decides whether he's executed each bit of behavior intended by checking to see if the right character or word appears on the computer screen. He also uses the clicking sound of the keys as feedback about whether or not the key has been fully depressed.

With even this many possibilities for feedback, a complex issue begins to emerge. For a feedback system to function properly, the information used as feedback must be relevant to the reference value (Harver, 1994; Langewiesche, 1993). As an absurd example, you could try to regulate typing by attending only to the sounds made by the keys, or (even more absurd) by whether the light coming in the window gets brighter or dimmer as you type. But since these sources of information won't be informative about the consequences of your actions for the intention you're trying to fulfill, they're useless as feedback.

The feedback channels that tell you what your movements have been and whether they were the movements you intended are important. But they aren't the only sources of feedback you use to track your behaviors. Indeed, it could easily be argued that they're the least important sources you use. Most social behavior has consequences that go far beyond the question of whether your act took the form you intended. These more remote consequences are typically the ones you need to monitor, rather than the question of whether the behavior took the form intended.

When you behave in a particular way calculated to make a good impression on someone, part of what you monitor is whether you're acting in the way you intend, but part of what you monitor is *whether you're making the kind of impression you want to make*. The input for this is quite different from the input for monitoring the form of the act. Discerning whether you're making the intended impression involves assessing other people's reactions to you. Your "effect on the environment" in this case means an effect on the other person. The effect is exerted through the filter of that person's preconceptions, interpretations, preoccupations, and distractions (all of which are disturbances). The impact eventually shows up in behavioral cues that he or she emits back to you, implying that he or she has some sort of impression of you.

The additional complexity involved in this kind of feedback raises a number of issues. For example, sometimes the cues you get are clear, but often they have to be interpreted. This means that to have the perceptual input you need in order to tell whether your behavior is appropriately regulated, you need to decode the cues. The process of interpreting the cues isn't easy. Although most people learn to do it fairly well, there are clear differences in how effective they are (i.e., how well their interpretations match normative ones). For example, people high in social anxiety perceive greater rejection from an interaction partner than do people lower in social anxiety, even when the facial cues they see are identical (Pozo, Carver, Wellens, & Scheier, 1991).

The process of interpreting the meaning of other people's behavior has been studied extensively in children by Dodge and his colleagues (Dodge, 1986; Dodge & Crick, 1990). An important difference between inappropriately aggressive children and those who aren't is that the aggressive children don't do a very good a job of interpreting other children's actions toward them. As a result, they're more likely to infer hostile intent and regulate their own actions accordingly. This research makes an important point about self-regulation: Whether you use cues emitted by other people to decide how to act in the first place, or whether you use them to decide how your actions have been received, these cues are critical information.

This sort of interpersonal feedback can also raise another issue, concerning time. Sometimes the cues that tell you the effects of your behavior come immediately, but sometimes not. Often they take some time to accumulate to the point where they can be clearly interpreted. With delays in receiving an interpretable input signal, the problem of lag time arises. As discussed in Chapter 2, effectively functioning feedback processes take into account the fact that feedback isn't always immediate. In such a case it's counterproductive to keep creating output until enough time has passed to determine the effects caused by the initial output (cf. Levine, 1992). Sometimes the lag in providing return input can be speeded up (for example, you can ask other people to tell you what they're thinking), but sometimes it can't.

In sum, the process of creating an input function from the various sources of information available to you is complex. The more abstract the reference value is, the more complex is the problem. As an illustration of the breadth of the problem, consider the use of social feedback as a way of verifying not simply the result of your behavior, but of your very self.

Use of Feedback for Self-Verification

People use social feedback to tell them not only how they're doing in their intended actions, but also to tell them what they're like as people. The information you get from others is sometimes used to fill in missing pieces in your picture of who you think you are (e.g., Cooley, 1902; Mead, 1934), but it also has other uses. It can also be used to verify your self-image (for overviews see Swann, 1990, 1996).

In some cases this use of social feedback works in counterintuitive ways. For example, common sense suggests that people want to be told good things about themselves. It turns out, however, that that's not always true. In particular, people want to be told they're who they think they are, even if they don't think they're very good. That is, someone with a negative self-image apparently wants feedback from others that confirms the negative image, rather than responses that contradict it. These are the cases that seem counterintuitive.

These efforts at confirmation of negative self-images have been shown in a variety of ways. For example, people prefer interaction partners

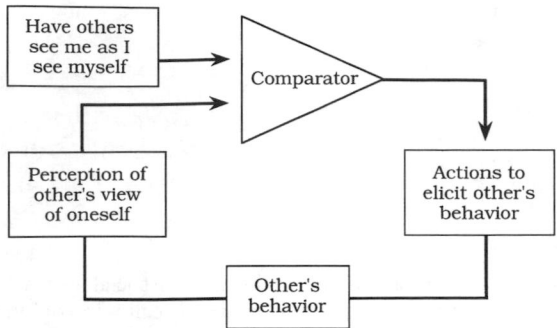

Figure 3.3.   In self-verification, a person acts in ways that elicit responses from others which confirm that they think the actor is the person he thinks he is, even if the characteristics being confirmed are unpleasant ones. (From Swann, 1990).

who give confirming social feedback over those who don't (e.g., Joiner & Metalsky, 1995; Swann, Pelham, & Krull, 1989; Swann, Wenzlaff, Krull, & Pelham, 1992).   Of particular interest at present is the fact that people act in ways that appear calculated to *elicit* the preferred feedback. This tendency is especially strong among people who think their interaction partners already have a misimpression of what they're like (Curtis & Miller, 1986; Swann & Ely, 1984; Swann & Read, 1981) and among those who are confident about what they're like (Pelham & Swann, 1994).

The process of eliciting self-confirming feedback is a feedback process (Figure 3.3). The person acts so as to promote a particular impression in the mind of another person. This behavior also elicits behavior, in return, from the other that confirms the actor's impression of himself. If this doesn't happen (if the cues from the other indicate the desired impression hasn't developed), the actor will modify behavior to try to promote the correct impression in the mind of the other.

It's not that people eliciting negative reactions from others necessarily want to *retain* negative self-views. Rather, they have two kinds of feedback processes occurring at once.   The more pressing process is an attempt to make others' impressions conform to the current self (Figure 3.4). The more hidden process is an attempt to make the current self conform to the desired self. The latter involves creating a closer match between present self-image and a desired self-image. Once this happens, the person will seek out feedback in subsequent encounters to verify the newly altered current self. Until then, however, the more positive feedback will lack confirming value, and won't be sought out.

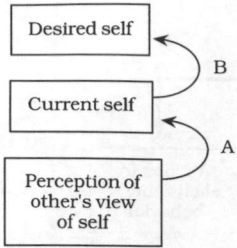

Figure 3.4.   (A) Efforts at self-verification through social feedback from others is an attempt to cause perceptions of social reality to conform to one's current self-image. (B) In many cases there are also (independent) efforts to cause perceptions of one's current self to conform to a desired self-image. Usually, however, these efforts involve different sorts of behavior, because the goals are quite different.

Social Comparison and Feedback Control

Another literature that fits with the argument that behavior follows feedback principles is the literature of social comparison. Social comparison theory (Festinger, 1950, 1954; Suls & Wills, 1991; Wood, 1989, 1996) stems partly from the observation that much of social reality can't be verified objectively. It's easy to measure a room or your weight, but comparable measurement techniques don't exist to tell you whether a painting is good art or whether you have a good life.

Festinger argued that the ambiguity of subjective aspects of the world leads people to search out comparison information from others. Sometimes people use social comparison to validate the levels of their abilities (e.g., Conolley, Gerard, & Kline, 1978; Festinger, Torrey, & Willerman, 1954; Jones & Regan, 1974; Suls, Gastorf, & Lawhon, 1978; Wood, 1989). In other cases people use it to assess whether their attitudes, emotions, or actions are correct or appropriate (e.g., Gerard, 1963; Goethals & Nelson, 1973; Radloff, 1961; Schachter, 1951, 1959). In both cases, ambiguity leads people to seek others and get information from them directly or indirectly, to create a consensual validation of reality. Once a consensus has been reached, there's also an implicit (and sometimes explicit) pressure to conform to the consensually defined value.

Social comparison that pertains to evaluating the appropriateness of attitudes, emotions, and actions bears a striking structural resemblance to the processes we've been discussing. That is, you determine a reference value (the consensually defined standard) and then conform to it. This aspect of social comparison resembles the gravitational metaphor we

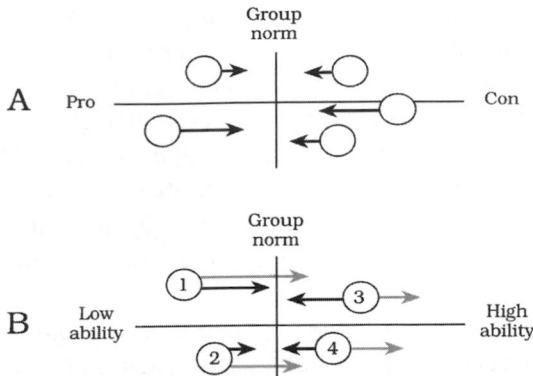

Figure 3.5. (A) Social comparison regarding attitudes involves discerning a group value and moving toward it, regardless of the direction of one's initial deviation from it. (B) Social comparison regarding ability involves a similar pressure to conform to the group's norm, but also a second pressure toward higher ability (gray arrows). These pressures work in the same direction for some people (1 and 2), but in opposing directions for others (3 and 4), causing internal conflict.

mentioned in Chapter 2. The standard of appropriateness provides an attraction point, and the person is drawn to it. Although much of the early interest in social comparison focused on how groups act to enforce conformity, overt pressure isn't required to cause conformity (Asch, 1951, 1956). Indeed, it isn't even necessary that the group be present, only that their views be known (Wicklund & Duval, 1971).

An important contribution of the social comparison model is to point out a way in which reference values for self-evaluation are made salient or, indeed, are created. That is, the first process in social comparison is to determine the standard of appropriateness or correctness. Only then can you conform to it. It's undeniable that a great deal of human social behavior relies on consensual definitions about what's appropriate or correct, ranging from issues of morality to issues of fashion. Social comparison theory highlights the importance of this process. Indeed, this analysis is usually assimilated directly to the discussion of reference groups, groups to which people refer or compare themselves in order to determine the norms to conform to (e.g., Newcomb, 1958).

Social comparison with respect to ability is a little more complex (see Figure 3.5). The information-gathering aspect of the process, prompted by ambiguity, is much the same as with attitudes, but there exist two pressures rather than one (Festinger, 1950, 1954). There's pressure to conform to the group's ability level, but there's also an upward pressure – a desire to have higher ability (represented by the gray arrows). For anyone with ability below the group's norm (persons 1 and 2 in panel B), these two tendencies act in concert with one another, both creating pressure to move higher, more closely approximating the norm. However, for a person with above average abilities (persons 3 and 4), the two tendencies conflict. The group conformity pressure tends to promote a reduction in displayed ability, whereas the upward pressure promotes the opposite.

An illustration of this point is the experiences of a group who play racquetball with one another on a regular basis. There's pressure within the group for everyone to be equivalent in ability, so the games remain enjoyable. Players who are less competent are encouraged to improve, and players toward the top of the group's distribution are discouraged from using their full ability. But there's also pressure to get better, even for the ones at the top. By following this pressure, people sometimes gravitate out of their groups into other ones, where both pressures again work in the same direction instead of promoting conflict.

The term *upward comparison* refers to comparisons made with people who are better off than oneself. *Downward comparisons* are those made with people who are worse off than oneself (Taylor & Lobel, 1989; Wills, 1981). These terms have meaning when applied to social comparison of ability, and also in other contexts that seem to follow the same principle as ability comparisons. For example, suppose you've been diagnosed with a serious disease. How are you doing? To answer this question, you need a comparison group. But what group to use? A group of people who've recovered from the disease would be an upward comparison. Patients with more severe cases of the disease would be a downward comparison.

There's evidence that patients engage in both kinds of comparisons (Helgeson & Taylor, 1993; see also Buunk & Gibbons, 1997). They tend to compare downward in gauging how well they're doing, and they prefer to affiliate with patients who are doing better than they are. This upward comparison can provide them with a sense of hope or motivation to improve, and it can also provide an opportunity to learn more about how to help themselves (Butler, 1992).

For present purposes, what's most important about this illustration is that this kind of upward comparison suggests a gravitational model, a model of pulling oneself closer to a desired point, a model of the conformity tendency that's created by a discrepancy-reducing feedback loop.

When you make adaptive upward comparisons, you think of the better-off group as a goal that's relevant to you, and try to *pull yourself toward it* (see also Collins, 1996; Lockwood & Kunda, 1997). This phenomenon seems very amenable to understanding in terms of discrepancy-reducing feedback processes.

SUMMARY

In this chapter we've outlined a number of phenomena that seem to embody the processes that characterize discrepancy-reducing feedback loops. Some of what we've discussed is at a micro level (evidence of comparisons); some is at a macro level (evidence of conformity tendencies). The research domains have been diverse enough to establish a broad base for the principle that much of human behavior is a matter of isolating a point of reference, then trying to conform to it (and sometimes to convince others of it). Not everything fits this picture, though. For example, social comparison can be upward or downward. Downward comparisons don't fit here. They're about something else. Their story comes next.

4

Discrepancy-Enlarging Loops, and Three Further Issues

In Chapter 3 we talked about efforts to conform to behavioral reference points. Those processes cover a lot of behavior, but not all behavior. Sometimes people want to *attain* particular ends, but sometimes they want to *escape* or *avoid* particular ends. Sometimes people want to *be* specific ways, sometimes they want to *not be* specific ways. The experiences of trying to move toward and trying to move away obviously differ, and they involve different self-regulatory structures.

In this chapter we consider moving-away processes, and a different kind of feedback loop: the discrepancy-enlarging loop. As we said in Chapter 2, some feedback processes act to create a divergence between an input (perception of present condition) and a comparison value. Rather than resembling a gravity field, it looks like antigravity. Rather than a goal, it seems to involve an anti-goal. These loops may be less prominent in behavior than are approach loops. They do, however, play an important role. In this chapter we address that role. Then we turn to some broader questions that transcend the two types of feedback processes.

DISCREPANCY-ENLARGING FEEDBACK LOOPS IN BEHAVIOR

In trying to identify cases of positive feedback in behavior, there are several things to look for. First, positive loops always involve attempts to deviate from a comparison point, efforts to push away from something. Second, it's likely that the distancing from standard is constrained or overridden at some point by the action of a negative loop. To put it differently, an avoidance loop often seems to be operating in the *service* of an approach loop.

In some cases we can provide evidence for the idea that the phenomena we're examining reflect feedback processes. For example, in Chapter 3 we argued that self-focused attention engages the comparator in the loop that's regulating behavior, and we described evidence that self-focus enhances the functioning of discrepancy-reducing loops. It follows that self-focused attention may also enhance discrepancy-enlarging processes. In some of the examples that follow, there's evidence that this does happen.

Downward Social Comparison

At the end of Chapter 3, we described the nature of upward and downward social comparison. We focused there on upward comparisons. Now we turn to downward comparisons.

Downward comparisons occur when people want to confirm they're better off than someone else (see, e.g., Taylor & Lobel, 1989; Wills, 1981; Wood, Taylor, & Lichtman, 1985). Thus, the person that's used as the point of comparison is someone you want *not* to resemble, for one reason or another. For example, someone diagnosed with an early-stage cancer might compare himself to someone with a more advanced cancer. Downward comparison can make people feel better, confirming that they're better off than the comparison group (e.g., Aspinwall & Taylor, 1993; Reis, Gerrard, & Gibbons, 1993; Wheeler & Miyake, 1992).

Although downward comparison is often benign, it can lead to active self-enhancement and even to derogation of others. As Wills (1981, p. 246) noted, derogation increases the psychological distance between the self and those you want not to resemble. This effect of downward comparison suggests a more general theme, which we want to emphasize. When comparing downward, you often don't just want to *verify* a difference between yourself and the comparison group, you want to *emphasize* or *increase* your perception of a difference. Trying to increase the difference fits the idea that a discrepancy-enlarging feedback process underlies downward comparisons.

Negative Reference Groups

The social comparison process can occur in isolated instances, but it also generalizes to the broader case of reference groups. We noted in Chapter 3 that reference groups of various types inhabit people's social worlds. Reference groups help people evaluate the appropriateness of their attitudes and actions. Indeed, reference groups even help people determine their attitudes when preexisting ones are weak or lacking (Newcomb, 1958).

Not all these groups are positive points of comparison, however. There are also *negative* reference groups, groups you dislike and want *not* to resemble. These aren't people you consider irrelevant to your life and therefore disregard. You think about them, actively seek out comparisons with them. You do so to emphasize – and increase – differences between them and you (cf. Brewer, 1979). This process closely resembles the positive feedback process: comparison of a present condition (yourself) with some reference value (the negative reference group) to create larger discrepancies between the two.

Support for this idea comes from research using a subject sample for whom a negative reference group was readily identifiable (Carver & Humphries, 1981). Subjects were Cuban-American students, the negative reference group was the Castro government of Cuba. Most people of Cuban descent in the United States view the Castro government as an army of occupation, despise its leaders, and dream of its demise. Data confirmed that Cuban-American students treat the Castro government as a negative reference group: When opinions on a series of issues were attributed to officials of that government, subjects disagreed with the opinions more than they did otherwise. This finding also confirmed that people respond to the negative reference group by trying to distance themselves from it, which fits the picture of the positive feedback loop.

A second study confirmed that subjects who were higher in self-consciousness renounced the government-linked opinions more than those lower in self-consciousness. Thus, self-focus enhanced the enlargement of a discrepancy between the standard and people's expressed opinions. This is consistent with the idea that higher self-consciousness means more engagement of the comparator of a discrepancy-enhancing loop.

Feared Self and Unwanted Self

Reference groups are social entities external to the self that provide reference points for behavior. Other reference points for behavior are carried around as part of personality. One of these internal standards – a particular mental representation of the self – seems also to reflect the existence of a positive feedback loop.

Markus and her colleagues (e.g., Markus & Nurius, 1986, 1987; Markus & Wurf, 1987) argue that the self-concept consists of more than information about the present and past self. It also incorporates beliefs about the future (cf. Epstein, 1973; Rhodewalt & Agustdottir, 1986), called possible selves. Three such selves are emphasized: the expected self, the hoped-for self, and the feared self (Markus & Nurius, 1986). Expected selves are what people believe they can, or will, realistically become. A hoped-for self is an aspired self, something that feels possible but is more removed than the expected self.

A feared self is a possible self that one doesn't want to become but fears becoming – for example, a drug abuser, a career failure, or a failure in close relationships. Ogilvie (1987) wrote in similar terms about what he called the undesired self. The feared self is held to be an important part of the self-concept because it acts as a motivator, so that the person takes concrete action to avoid that possible self. Because people try to avoid or escape from the feared self, its effect seems to reflect the functioning of a positive feedback loop.

Oyserman and Markus (1990) have argued that the most effective self-regulation occurs when people hold both desired selves and opposing feared selves in a given domain. In their view such a "balance" between the desired and the feared creates an optimal motivational situation, because there's both a goal to strive toward and a goal to avoid. This assertion brings us back to a point we made earlier about discrepancy-enlarging feedback processes.

Positive Feedback Process Constrained by Negative Feedback Process

In thinking about how people respond to feared selves and undesired selves – and negative reference groups and downward social comparisons – we return to an argument about how positive feedback loops work. We said earlier that this loop can be adaptive and functional if its operation is bounded or constrained by a negative feedback loop (see Figure 4.1, which has been adapted only slightly from Figure 2.4). This argument leads us to a position that differs from that of Oyserman and Markus in one respect and resembles it in another.

In particular, an avoidance feedback process always seems to benefit from an approach process constraining it. In this respect we agree with Oyserman and Markus. That an avoidance loop benefits from an approach loop is easily illustrated by reference group behavior. A negative reference group doesn't guide you anywhere in particular (unless the behavioral dimension is occupied at one end by the reference group, which was the case in the 1981 research by Carver and Humphries). Although people do portray and even define themselves

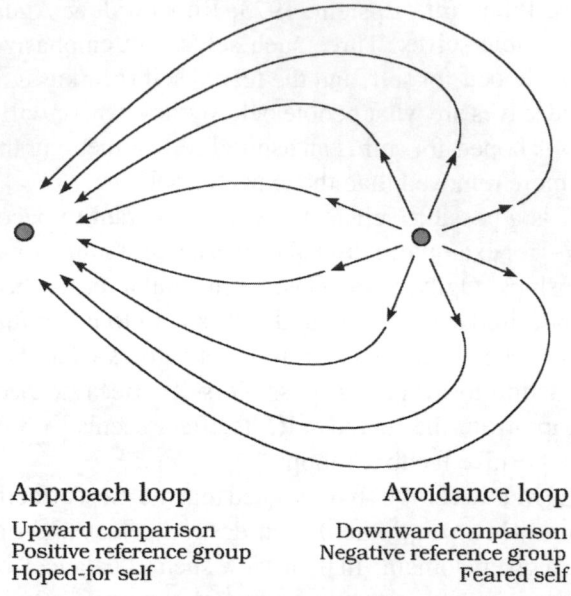

Approach loop

Upward comparison
Positive reference group
Hoped-for self

Avoidance loop

Downward comparison
Negative reference group
Feared self

Figure 4.1. Positive feedback loops (avoidance loops) imply movement away from comparison values, but their action often provides little direction unless constrained by the effects of negative feedback loops (approach loops). We suggest that downward social comparison, negative reference groups, and feared selves serve as reference points for avoidance loops, and that upward social comparison, positive reference groups, and hoped-for selves serve as reference points for approach loops.

partly by differences between themselves and others they dislike, too much reliance on this principle is bad. It produces a person who doesn't stand *for* anything, but only stands *against* things. This isn't much of a basis for a healthy sense of self.

In practice, however, this is rarely what happens. Consider another example of negative reference group behavior. It seems a near universal phenomenon of life in the United States that adolescents want to be different from their parents (thus taking parents as a negative reference group). There are, of course, innumerable ways to be unlike someone else. Although adolescents vary in how they deviate from their parents, positive reference groups typically emerge (other adolescents and various role models). This positive reference group evolves its own norms, to which the adolescent fervently adheres. Thus, it's possible to be a nonconformist by conforming to a different value.

This isn't, of course, a principle of adolescence alone, but a principle of life. To state the principle more baldly, when you're afraid of

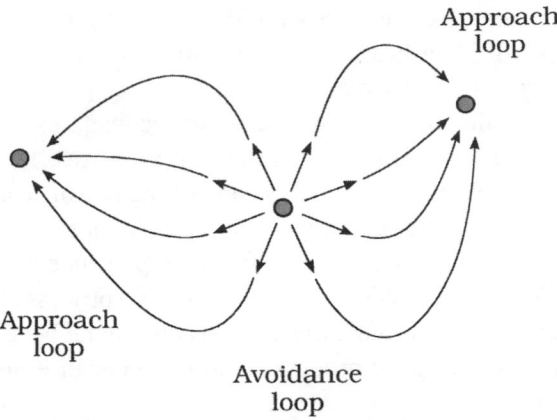

Approach
loop

Approach
loop

Avoidance
loop

Figure 4.2.   Sometimes more than one desired value is available when an avoidance loop is operating. In such a case, some efforts to escape the undesired value will be captured by one desired value; other efforts will be captured by the other desired value. It seems likely that which desired value constrains the moving-away-from process depends partly on which value is closer to a person's preexisting values and partly by the direction in which the person initially moves to avoid the undesired value.

something or repulsed by something, you try to get away from it. But away is just away. Instead of continuing endlessly to get away, you usually find somewhere else that's safe or desirable to go *to*.

In thinking about this point it's worth noting that the situations people confront are often more complex than the one diagrammed in Figure 4.1. Many situations hold several potential attraction points to move toward (Figure 4.2). For this reason, you can't always expect a single positive value to capture all the attempts that people make to avoid the undesired value. Thus, if several people try to deviate from a mutually disliked reference point, they may diverge from one another in pronounced ways. One disgruntled adolescent may gravitate to membership in a rock band, another may gravitate to the army. Presumably, what value is approached will depend partly on the fit between the available values and the person's preexisting values, and partly on the direction the person took initially to escape the undesired value.

This pattern of influences appears to be quite similar to that proposed by Brewer (1991) in her theory of how people use multiple reference groups to achieve two ends simultaneously. She argues that people have a need for connection and similarity to others, and a need to differentiate themselves (be distinct) from others. These goals are achieved by identifying strongly with an ingroup while emphasizing differences regarding an outgroup (or more than one). Social identity and group loyalty are seen as strongest for identifications that maximize the extent of attainment of the two goals at the same time.

Although we see the guidance of a negative feedback loop as nearly indispensable to the long-term effectiveness of a positive loop, unlike Oyserman and Markus (1990) we see no compelling reason to assert that the principle applies in both directions. That is, we're not convinced that the presence of a negative loop benefits from the presence of a positive loop (cf. Elliot & Sheldon, 1997). As long as there's a process that moves the person toward a desired value, there seems no special benefit in also having a potentially disruptive process (disruptive because, in a sense, it's directionless).

The Ought Self

Another example of a discrepancy-enlarging process constrained by a discrepancy-reducing process occurs in what Higgins (1987, 1989, 1996) calls the ought self. Ought selves reflect a sense of responsibility, duty, or obligation. An ought is a self you feel compelled to be, rather than intrinsically desire to be. Although ought selves are positive (people wish to conform to them), the ought self seems to derive from punishment. That is, living up to an ought means being a particular kind of person to avoid others' disapproval or self-disapproval. Thus, self-regulation regarding an ought involves trying to move *toward* the ought, as a way of moving *away from* an unwanted comparison point (see Figure 4.3).

Research by Higgins and his colleagues has confirmed that people whose lives are dominated by ought selves are particularly attuned to the avoidance of negative outcomes. They preferentially encode information pertaining to negative outcomes (Higgins & Tykocinski, 1992). They're also more likely than other people to choose strategies for positive goal attainment based on avoidance of *un*desirable conditions (Higgins, Roney, Crowe, & Hymes, 1994). Such findings have led Higgins (1996) to examine more closely the avoidance aspect of the dynamics of ought-based self-regulation, which had been less prominent in his earlier thinking (see also Higgins, Shah, & Friedman, 1997; Tykocinski, Higgins, & Chaiken, 1994).

Indeed, Higgins has begun to write about what he calls *promotion* and *prevention* focuses underlying behavior (e.g., Higgins, 1996; Higgins et al., 1997). These terms appear to refer to discrepancy-reducing

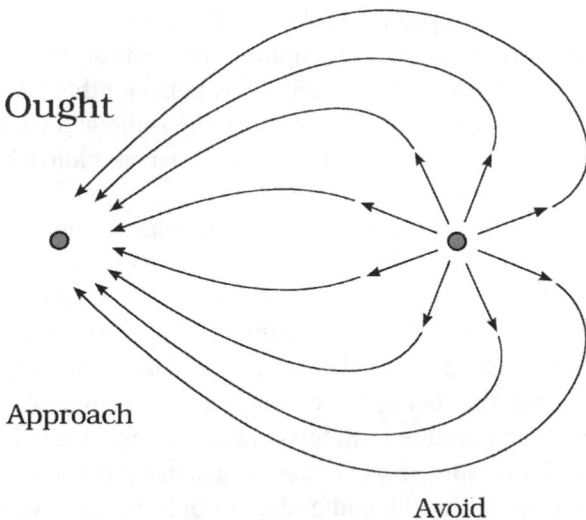

Figure 4.3. Self-regulation with respect to an ought self involves both a desire to move toward a prescribed value and a desire to move away from a proscribed or punished value. The effects of the latter avoidance process are given form by those of the desired ought, which serves as the reference value in an approach loop.

and discrepancy-enlarging feedback processes, respectively, in that they concern attempts to move toward goals versus attempts to move away from anti-goals. Ideal discrepancies evoke primarily a promotion focus; ought discrepancies evoke primarily a prevention focus.

For our present purpose, what's important about the dynamics of ought-based self-regulation is that two processes are involved: one in a sense more basic, the other providing a positive form and direction for the effects of the first. Although there are many ways a person could avoid a feared or disliked self-quality, the desire to escape provides no positive direction for movement (Figure 4.3). A positively valued point is required to provide such direction. This is what the ought self does, thus giving coherent form to self-regulation stemming from avoidance.

Reactance

Another class of phenomena that may reflect positive feedback processes stems from the principle of psychological reactance (Brehm, 1966; Wicklund, 1974). Reactance occurs when you expect some freedom to exist and then experience a threat to that freedom. The threat causes you to try to reassert or regain the freedom. The freedoms here are usually limited in scope: examples are the freedom to choose one action over another, to decide what opinion to hold, or to choose one object from an array of desirable options. The behavior that results from the reactance varies, depending on what freedom is threatened. In many cases, the response involves rejecting an attitudinal position, a behavior, or a choice that's being forced upon you.

Three aspects of this description appear similar to our description of positive feedback loops. First, many reactance effects involve distancing yourself from a value or position – whatever position is being forced upon you. Second, this discrepancy enlargement seems to operate within the framework of a discrepancy-reducing system. That is, pushing away the option being forced on you (or pushing away the attempted infringement on freedom) lets you conform to a self-image (or public image) of a person who exercises self-determination. Third, the reactance effect doesn't go on endlessly, but only to restoration of the freedom. These points fit the notion that the functioning of positive loops is relatively short-lived and occurs in the service of a broader negative loop.

Also consistent with the idea that there are feedback processes at work here (and thus a comparator) is evidence that reactance phenomena are enhanced by self-focus. Some of this evidence comes from research on how coercive attempts to persuade a person influence that person's attitude. Coercive communication causes its recipient to resist the persuasion attempt, even to the point of shifting the opinion in the opposite direction (e.g., Snyder & Wicklund, 1976). This effect is stronger when self-focus is high than when it's lower (Carver, 1977; Carver & Scheier, 1981c).

Another interesting reactance effect occurs when an initial preference for one of several options causes people to feel a loss of freedom of choice. The result of this is a tendency to push away the original preference (making it harder to make a decision). This movement away is stronger among persons high in self-consciousness than among those lower in self-consciousness (Carver & Scheier, 1981c).

In sum, several aspects of the structure of reactance phenomena make it reasonable to suggest that they may involve discrepancy-enlarging feedback processes. In displaying these characteristics, reactance effects join several other phenomena reviewed in preceding sections. Our conclusion from this review of these diverse phenomena is that discrepancy-enlarging loops play an important role in human behavior.

FURTHER ISSUES

We turn now to three issues that pertain to the use of feedback models for behavior. These issues are general ones, bearing on the subject of this chapter and on that of Chapter 3. Two issues stem directly from the idea that discrepancy-reducing feedback loops (and to a lesser extent discrepancy-enlarging loops) are the basic building blocks of self-regulation. The third issue is whether the feedback loop is, in fact, a plausible model at all for the phenomena we address throughout this book.

Feedback Loops in Mutual Interdependence

We've focused thus far on the individual, taken alone. To the extent that we've considered others at all, it's been to view them as sources of feedback about the effectiveness of one's actions. But providing feedback to the actor isn't the only role that others play.

Most of the time when people interact, each interactant has his or her own goals. Any dyadic interaction involves a mutual interdependence between interactants (Figure 4.4). Each individual displays the hallmarks of feedback control – checking on the effects of his or her behavior to see whether desired goals or standards are being met, and altering behavior as needed to move closer to them. Each also acts as a source of feedback to the other, providing information about the other's success in moving toward the value guiding the other's actions.

Thus the two are an interdependent pair of feedback systems, each reliant on the other for critical information, but each with its own agenda (see also Darley & Fazio, 1980). Whenever a dyad interacts, such an arrangement exists. It's possible for the arrangement to be unbalanced, such that the reference value for one interactant is simply the providing of information to the other. But this situation is relatively rare. More commonly, both interactants have their own goals.

The interactants are independent, in a sense (because the goal for each exists in the mind of only one person). In another sense, however, they aren't independent at all. It's often impossible for one person to conform to his or her standard unless the other person acquiesces to the attempt. Often, there will be willing acquiescence only if acquiescence also helps the other person move toward his or her goal. When Harry interacts with Sally, he gets information from her behavior that tells him

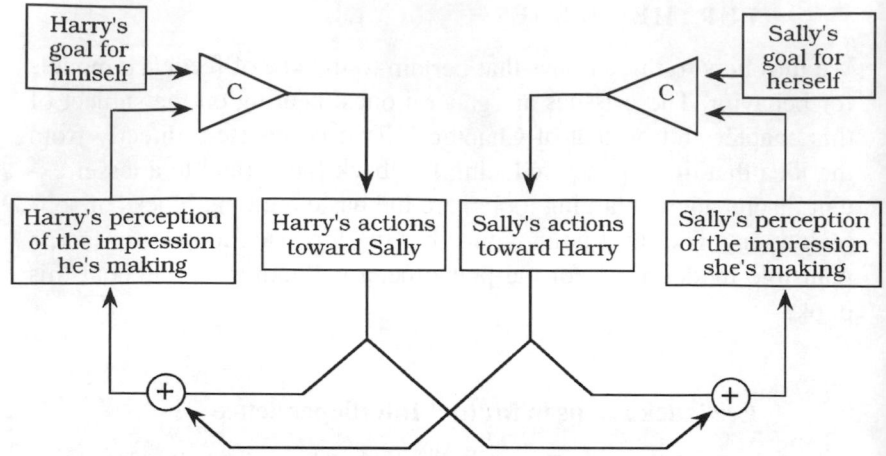

Figure 4.4.   When Harry met Sally, each had a goal in mind in the interactions they had as a dyad. Each acted in such a way as to attempt to attain the goal he or she had in mind. At the same time, each provided information that the other could use to determine whether or not he or she was reaching his or her own goal.

he's doing what he intends to do only if Harry's behavior also tells Sally that she's doing what *she* intends to do.

This portrayal of dyadic interaction is structurally similar to our portrayal in Chapter 2 of the interdependency between a system regulating the temperature of a refrigerator and a system regulating the temperature of the room holding the refrigerator (Figure 2.7). In that example, the output of each system influences its subsequent input (the refrigerator's cooling system decreases the temperature inside the refrigerator). But the output of each system also influences the *other* system's subsequent input (the refrigerator's cooling system increases room temperature outside the refrigerator).

In that example, the effect of each system on the other was labeled a "disturbance," because the effect was unintended, a consequence of the fact that the two systems happened to be in a shared space, with input functions that can be influenced by each other's functioning. In Figure 4.4, the label "disturbance" is omitted, because there's presumed to be an active attempt to use the information contained in the other's behavior as input feedback. In other respects, however, the structure of the two examples is similar.

It's possible, of course, to go far beyond dyadic interaction in talking about relations among interactants with this sort of mutual interdependency (Levine, 1992). The area of thought known as family systems theory (e.g., Bowen, 1978; Bradshaw, 1988; Minuchin, 1974; Papp, 1983; Selvini Palazzoli, Boscolo, Cecchin, & Prata, 1978) is one such extension, considering whole families as interwoven systems. The focus of that theory is partly on the individual, partly on the dynamics that develop as individuals pursue their separate goals within the family unit, and partly on goals shared among the members of the group – in effect treating the group as a feedback system in its own right. When conditions are created that disturb the group's sensed reality, pressures are brought to bear to reestablish the group's equilibrium.

Indeed, there also appear to be feedback processes that occur within even larger populations of organisms. In at least some mammals, processes of this sort control such variables as population densities (Wynne-Edwards, 1964). Although we have less to say about family systems and populations (or even dyads) than about individuals, similar principles do appear to be at work throughout (see also Levine & Fitzgerald, 1992a).

The Search for Discrepancies

We turn now to consider one of the less obvious implications of the feedback concept. The notion that discrepancy-reducing feedback processes are particularly important in behavior suggests a general tendency to be attuned to information indicating a discrepancy between an intended condition and an actual condition.

There's indirect evidence that such a bias may exist (e.g., Kahneman & Tversky, 1984; Pratto & John, 1991; Schwarz, 1990; Taylor, 1991). It consists largely of findings that negative events have a larger impact on people (in a variety of ways) than do positive events (see also Hobfoll, 1989; Rook, 1984; Rusbult, Verette, Whitney, Slovik, & Lipkus, 1991; for discussions of such tendencies in infancy, see Kagan, 1981; Stipek, Recchia, & McClintic, 1992). Indeed, negative information seems to draw attention automatically (Pratto & John, 1991). Situations involving problems are also more likely to stay on people's minds than problem-free situations (Klinger, Barta, & Maxeiner, 1980), and people seem motivated more by the desire to avoid loss of self-esteem than by a desire to enhance it (Tesser & Cornell, 1991). Taylor (1991) has argued that the greater responsiveness to negative events implies a mobilization of effort to minimize their impact, including acting to eliminate the undesired condition.

There's a certain irony in the idea that things being as they should doesn't draw much notice. After all, people want to see things be as they should, and they try fairly hard to make that happen (cf. Friedrich, 1993). Those reviewing the evidence on this point all note what appears to be a reasonable evolutionary basis for this asymmetry: Negative events have potential implications not only for subjective well-being but also for survival. When things are not as they should be, effort must be made to change them. When good things happen, no further action is required, and they therefore elicit less response.

Although negative events aren't quite the same as discrepancies between perceived and desired conditions, there seems enough of a similarity to suggest that the same principle applies to self-regulation. In the process of behaving, something being wrong is more likely to draw your attention than something being right, because (in general) when something's right, you simply move on to the next thing (don't forget that you still have to check in order to know you're right). In contrast, when things aren't right, something else has to be done, adjustments have to be made, before you can move on.

The Issue of Will

The last issue to be taken up in this chapter is a challenge to the notion that feedback processes provide a useful model for self-regulation. The challenge comes from two directions that are quite different from each other, though they have at least one element in common.

An explicit rejection of control theory comes from Locke and Latham (1990a), whose work focuses on work motivation. There's a great deal in their own thinking that resembles the feedback model we're describing in this book. For example, they state that "Goal setting is . . . usually only effective when feedback allows performance to be tracked in relation to one's goals" (Locke & Latham, 1990b, p. 241). Despite this, and despite their nods of approval to other models with similar structures (e.g., Frese & Sabini, 1985), they recoil at the idea that the functions embedded in their theory (and others) reflect the operation of feedback processes.

The crux of their objection seems to be that feedback models are inappropriate because they are mechanistic. Locke and Latham's theory places a good deal of stress on "the causal efficacy of consciousness," a labored way of saying "will." Feedback models are inadequate, in their view, because they don't portray behavior as a series of willful choices. (It's of passing interest that Miller et al. [1960, p. 111] connected the concept of will to the use of inner speech in formulating and executing Plans – essentially the same functions as Locke and Latham emphasize – but postulated this explicitly within the framework of a feedback-based model of behavior.)

A similar issue emerges in the writings of Deci and Ryan (e.g., 1985, 1991; Ryan, 1993; Ryan, Sheldon, Kasser, & Deci, 1996), though apart from this particular similarity their approach has little in common with that of Locke and Latham (see Deci, 1992, for a critique of the latter). Deci and Ryan emphasize the importance of a sense of personal autonomy or self-determination in behavior, arguing that behavior done autonomously (by choice) is different in character from behavior done for other reasons (compliance with explicit or implicit coercion). This raises the question of whether a feedback process can be thought of as reflecting autonomy in any meaningful way. Although this question is a complex one involving many issues, one issue it involves is will.

We've never taken a strong position on this issue, partly because we don't have a strong opinion about it. It may be that the feedback processes about which we're writing operate in service to another set of processes we haven't identified. If so, our account would be incomplete (that is, more incomplete than it is anyway). Nevertheless, it would remain a reasonable portrayal of the functions engaged by whatever is the missing process. As such, it would seem to remain useful and informative. It doesn't seem particularly constructive to insist that control processes can't be involved in the self-regulation of behavior, as Locke and Latham do, when the structure of self-regulation, by their own account, so obviously resembles the structure of a feedback loop.

On the other hand, it may be that what people recognize from introspection as effortful decision making and planning – the things that make it obvious to all of us that we have our own will – is actually self-delusional. Perhaps these patterns of thought are the products of control processes occurring behind the scenes, outside awareness, drawing people toward images of who they might be. If so, the "servicing" of one function by the other would be in the opposite order: consciousness and effortful processing operating to further one's continuing movement toward abstract goals (cf. Dewan, 1976).

Pervin (1992), writing about the Locke and Latham model, expressed considerable skepticism about its rational, volitional view of behavior, based in part on his years of clinical experience. His skepticism derived from the many ways people have trouble exercising will, doing what they wish to do, and refraining from what they wish not to do (for another view on how much trouble these things can be, see Wegner, 1994). Although we have no clinical experience to rely on, we share a measure of Pervin's concern about the question of will. For the time being, then, we will simply continue to assume as a working model that feedback processes are fundamental, and see how far these assumptions will carry us.

5

Goals and Behavior

> You must imagine your life . . . and then it happens.
> (John Updike, *The Witches of Eastwick*)

To say that behavior is regulated by feedback processes is to assume the existence of reference values for behavior. In this chapter we consider reference values and some differences among them. For most practical purposes the term *reference value* is interchangeable with the term *goal*. Life, in this framework, is a continual process of establishing goals and adjusting patterns of behavior to match those goals more closely, using informational feedback as a guide.

GOALS

This emphasis on goals is very much in line with a growing emphasis on goal constructs in today's personality–social psychology (Austin & Vancouver, 1996; Elliott & Dweck, 1988; Miller & Read, 1987; Pervin, 1982, 1989). A variety of labels are used in this literature, reflecting differences in the emphases that various writers place on aspects of the goal construct. The next section briefly reviews a few of these constructs.

An Overview of Broad Goal Constructs

One of the earliest of this generation of goal constructs was Klinger's (1975, 1977) use of the phrase *current concern* to describe goals with which a person is presently engaged. This phrase conveys the sense that the goals are temporary. They occupy the mind for a while but eventually yield to other concerns. The phrase also suggests a sense of mental engagement with an issue or problem, a quality of unfinished business. This sense is certainly compatible with the idea that until a goal is reached it engages the mind in the process of trying to move closer to it.

Another construct that tends to convey a fairly restricted scope is the *personal project* (Little, 1983, 1989). This resembles Klinger's current concern, though its label doesn't convey quite the same sense of urgency or engagement. A personal project is something you want to do, which might be brief (getting ready for an exam) or more extended (finding some good friends).

The sense of engagement seems more implicit in the term *personal strivings*, used by Emmons (1986), and the term *life task*, used by Cantor and Kihlstrom (1987). These constructs are similar in meaning, reflecting broad, overriding goals that can form themes in the structure of a person's entire life. They thus lack the sense of temporal limit suggested by current concern. On the other hand, although broad in scope, strivings or life tasks often vary from one phase of life to another and are sometimes adopted during transitions across phases. For example, the first months at college are typically a time of "trying on" life tasks suggested by a person's initial experiences of the college environment (Cantor & Fleeson, 1991; Zirkel & Cantor, 1990). The same may be said of the first months at a new job.

Miller and Read (1987; Read & Miller, 1989) are among the theorists who simply use the more prosaic term *goal*. They reserve this for the overall goal behind a given set of activities, using *plan* to refer to subgoals and strategies used to attain the overall goal. Miller and Read point out that the carrying out of plans depends on a variety of resources: money, social skills, access to relevant other people, and cognitive resources (Read & Miller, 1989).

In all these conceptualizations there are overall goals and subgoals. There's also room for a lot of individualization. For example, a life task or striving can be achieved in many ways, but each person chooses a path that fits with other aspects of his or her life (people have many current concerns which must be managed simultaneously) and other aspects of his or her personality. Thus, the strategies that people use for pursuing a given life task differ considerably from one person to another (Langston & Cantor, 1989). For instance, a person who's shy will have strategies for making friends that are different from those of a person who's more outgoing.

Another goal construct, mentioned in Chapter 4, which differs in several ways from the ones just listed, is the *possible self* (Markus & Nurius, 1986). This construct is intended to bring a dynamic quality to theory about the self-concept. In contrast to traditional views of the self-concept, but consistent with other goal frameworks, possible selves are future-oriented. They concern how people think of their potential, the kind of person they might become (see also the *self-guide* construct, used by Higgins, 1987, 1996). This view thus involves the self-concept as a goal in the dynamics of behavior, as the person moves from the present toward the future.

Among possibles selves are hoped-for and feared selves. Markus and colleagues thus make explicit that people have avoidance goals as well as approach goals. This variation, however, can easily be applied to all the constructs named earlier. A person can have a personal striving to avoid a bad outcome (e.g., Emmons, 1996); the same is true of current concerns or life tasks. Although the emphasis is usually on the positive, all the goal constructs outlined above potentially imply avoidance as well as approach goals.

Theorists who use the constructs above have their own emphases, but in many respects the points they make are the same. All include the idea that goals energize and direct people's activities in organized ways (Pervin, 1982), that goals serve to engage the activities of those who adopt them. These views implicitly (and sometimes explicitly) convey the sense that goals give meaning to people's lives (cf. Baumeister, 1989). Each of these notions emphasizes the idea that understanding a person means understanding the person's goals. Indeed, it's often implicit in these theories that the self is made partly of the person's goals and the organization among them (which of course is explicit in the possible-self construct).

One difference among these constructs is their breadth. Although all are intended to be flexible, some are more readily applied to discrete and encapsulated transactions (current concerns, personal projects), whereas others seem broader in focus (personal strivings, life tasks, and particularly possible selves).

Task-Specific Goals

Some uses of the goal construct are even more focused than those just discussed. They deal with the nature of the goal a person has in mind in undertaking effort at some particular task. Often these applications are specific to performance or achievement domains, which also reflects a narrower focus than we've taken thus far. An example comes from the work of Dweck and her collaborators (Dweck, 1996; Dweck & Leggett,

1988; Elliott & Dweck, 1988; see also Ames & Archer, 1988; Nicholls, 1984; Ruble & Frey, 1991). Much of this work focuses on children, but its themes are easily generalized to adult behavior.

A fundamental idea behind this research is that task engagement can reflect several possible goals. Sometimes people have the goal of *performing* well to demonstrate or verify they have the skill necessary to perform the task. At other times they have the goal of *learning* from their experiences with the task, to increase their skill. Children with performance goals are vulnerable to deterioration in effort when they aren't doing well at the task, whereas such deterioration doesn't occur among children who approach the task with learning goals.

This particular difference in influences is an interesting one, to which we return in Chapter 11. For the moment, however, what's important about this difference between goal orientations is its very existence. The act of trying a challenging task has two different meanings, depending on which kind of goal is in mind. With a performance goal, the child is trying to demonstrate or verify skill. With a learning goal, the child is trying to acquire skill. These goals are different. An important question is how to conceptualize the difference.

Another literature that's relevant to the discussion of goal constructs in performance domains is work on goal setting (Locke & Latham, 1990a). Studies of goal setting focus on how performances are affected by establishing various goals before people begin to perform. The most frequently noted finding, quite reliable across a range of studies, is that performances are better when a high goal is set than when a lower goal is set or when subjects are told to "do your best."

This finding is usually interpreted in terms of the efforts that people mobilize. A higher goal causes people to make stronger efforts, thereby doing better at the task, than does a lower goal. A "do your best" goal appears never to be taken at face value. Rather, when given this instruction people "satisfice" (Simon, 1953, 1955) – that is, adopt a goal that's less than their best but seems adequate to the situation.

For our present purpose, the importance of this literature is to raise the general issue of standards of performance or of excellence. Performance standards, though not always relevant, are certainly relevant in some circumstances. Indeed, the question of stringency of standards could potentially be applied to any goal construct. A personal project, personal striving, or life task might be viewed not only in terms of content (being nurturant in relationships, performing well in a class, repairing your car, or deciding on whether or not to go to law school) but also in terms of the level of excellence taken as your goal (being the ultimate nurturer, getting a perfect score on the final exam, keeping your car in perfect repair, or making the best possible decision about your professional future).

One implication of the goal-setting literature is that people perform at a higher level if their goals are high than if they are lower or are only vaguely established. It should be noted, though, that there's an important boundary on this effect of high goals. This boundary raises a caution about generalizing the point too far. Specifically, a goal that's *too* high causes lowered performance, apparently because performers fail to adopt the goal and thus don't try. As with the difference between learning and performance goals, we return to this point in Chapter 11.

HIERARCHICAL CONCEPTIONS OF GOALS

Something that's obvious from this brief review of goal constructs is that some goals are broader in scope than others. Exactly what the difference in breadth means isn't always easy to put your finger on. Sometimes it reduces to a difference in temporal commitment to the goal. For example, the personal project of being well prepared for a test may be multifaceted, but this is a goal with a fairly short life span. The life task of being well prepared for business meetings has a longer period of relevance. Sometimes, however, a difference in breadth is more than that. It's a difference in the level of abstraction at which the goal exists.

Basic Premise: Goals Can Be Differentiated by Levels of Abstraction

The notion that goals differ in level of abstraction is easy to illustrate. You might have the goal of being an honorable person, or a self-sufficient person, or a person who always comes out on top when dealing with others. These goals are at a relatively high level of abstraction. You may also have the goal of avoiding contact with the office gossip, or of making dinner for yourself, or getting a good price on a car. These goals are all at a lower level of abstraction. Although the first set of goals may apply for a longer time than the second set, that isn't the only way they differ. The goals of the first set are more abstract in nature than those of the second set. The first set concerns being a particular kind of person; the second set concerns completing a particular kind of action.

You could also think of goals that are even more concrete than the latter set, such as that of walking quietly to your office and closing the door without being heard, or cutting up vegetables into a pan, or keeping your face blank while offering a dollar figure to a salesman. These goals (which some of the theorists cited earlier would call plans or strategies) are closer to specifying individual acts than were the second set listed above, which served more as summary statements about the outcomes of intended action patterns.

How should we think about this difference in abstraction among goals? As you may have noticed, the examples we used for concrete goals (and even more-concrete goals) relate directly to the examples of abstract goals. This was to make the point that there are links between abstract and concrete goals. In this section we consider a way of thinking about the nature of that relationship: the idea that goals are organized in a hierarchy of levels of abstraction.

The notion of "hierarchicality" has been around for a good while. Miller, Galanter, and Pribram (1960) wrote about it, noting that any broad goal can be decomposed into subgoals. You behave honorably by avoiding the office gossip, which you do (in part) by walking especially quietly when you enter your workplace. This, in turn, you do by creating sequences of movements among your limbs. Overall goals are realized by subdividing them into constituent elements, which themselves are realized by mechanisms creating conformity to them. Arguments of a similar form, though differing in many of their particulars, have also been made by a number of other theorists focusing on very different aspects of behavior (see, e.g., Baron, 1987; Broadbent, 1977; Dawkins, 1976; Gallistel, 1980; Toates, 1980).

We won't review in detail the many statements on hierarchical organization. Rather, we pursue this discussion by describing one particular conceptualization we've found interesting and useful over the years. We then turn to a consideration of how this view fits with other goal models.

A Control Hierarchy

In 1973, Powers argued that a hierarchical organization of feedback loops underlies the self-regulation of behavior in living organisms (1973a; see also Powers, 1973b). Since feedback loops imply goals, this argument also constitutes a model of hierarchical structuring among the goals involved in creating action.

Powers took as his own goal describing how a hierarchy of feedback processes might be embedded in the nervous system. He was especially attentive to issues that arise at lower levels of abstraction, where

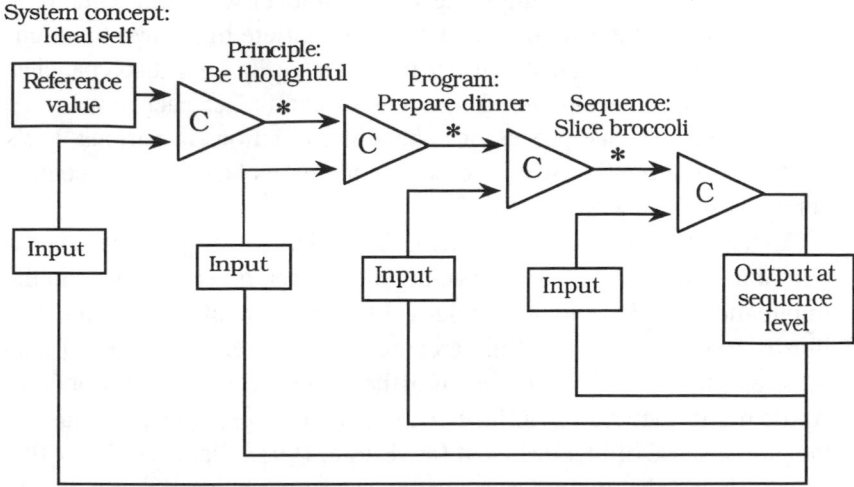

* In each case, this constitutes both an output from the system
to the left and a reference value for the system to the right

Figure 5.1.   Four-level hierarchy depicting the organization of goals and control processes of a person trying to behave in accord with an idealized sense of
self, by behaving in line with a principle of thoughtfulness, which is presently
being realized by the act of preparing dinner for a friend, which involves a
series of action sequences including the cutting up of broccoli for steaming.
(Adapted from the hierarchical model of Powers, 1973a.)

mechanisms had to be postulated for the coordination of movements of
muscle groups. Though he had much less to say about the levels in
which we're most interested, the principles with which he worked can
be generalized fairly readily.

The theory runs as follows: In a hierarchical organization of feedback systems, there are superordinate loops and subordinate loops. The
output function of a superordinate loop consists of the resetting of reference values at the next lower level of abstraction (see Figure 5.1). To
put it differently, higher-order systems "behave" by providing reference
values (goals) to the systems just below them. Presumably, selecting a
particular reference value relies at least partly on associations between
classes of perceptions and classes of actions that have proven to be
discrepancy-reducing at the higher level in similar situations in the past
(cf. Colwill, 1993; see also MacKay, 1956).

The reference values specified as outputs become more concrete and
restricted as one moves from higher to lower levels of the hierarchy.
Control at each lower level regulates some quality that contributes to the

quality controlled at the higher level. Each level within the hierarchy monitors input at a level of abstraction appropriate to its own functioning, and each level adjusts output to minimize its own discrepancies. These functions are assumed to occur in parallel at each level. It's assumed not that one processor is handling functions at various levels of abstraction, but that structures at various levels handle their separate concerns simultaneously.

Powers argued that such a hierarchy underlies the physical execution of actions that people engage in. We've been most interested in the implications of these ideas at relatively high levels of abstraction. The illustration of the nature of hierarchical organization in Figure 5.1 also illustrates the several highest levels in the organization Powers proposed. At the highest level shown (labeled *system concepts*) are such values as the global sense of idealized self (cf. Burke, 1991; Klein, 1987, pp. 65–68). Self isn't the only reference value that might be used there, though it's probably the most intuitive example and may be the most frequently used. Other values include the idealized sense of a relationship (cf. Read & Miller, 1989) or of a society (cf. Markus & Kitayama, 1991).

Goals at this level are very abstract. As one considers the attempt to self-regulate with respect to such values, a reasonable question to ask is what behavioral outputs are even relevant to the attempt. How do you act to minimize discrepancies between these highly abstract values and your behavior? How do you "be" your ideal self? Powers (1973a, 1973b) suggested that the output of this highest system consists of providing goals to the next lower level, which he termed the level of *principle* control. To put it more concretely, you "be" who you want to be by using guiding principles implied by the idealized self to which you aspire. The makeup of the idealized self to which a person aspires obviously differs from person to person. Thus, the principles specified as output will also vary from person to person.

Principles begin to provide some form for behavior, but the form is still pretty vague. Principles are aspects of behavior for which there are names in everyday language – for example, honesty, responsibility, thrift, and expedience (or honor, self-reliance, and dominance, to return to the examples we used earlier). They're the sort of qualities to which people apply trait labels. As such, they're fairly abstract. Just as traits aren't behaviors, but qualities that can be manifest in many ways in particular kinds of situations, principles are specifications not of acts, but of qualities that can be manifest in acts of many types (see also Schank & Abelson's [1977] discussion of meta-scripts). You don't go out and "do" honesty, or responsibility, or thrift, or expedience. Rather, you manifest such qualities in behavior by doing specific activities.

These specific activities, in which behavioral output finally becomes more recognizable as behavior, are *programs* (cf. Schank & Abelson's [1977] script). A program-level goal specifies a general course of action, but one in which there are decisions points and in which many details are left out. The details are unspecified because what's done at any point depends upon the nature of the circumstances encountered at that point. Much of what people do in day-to-day life appears programlike in character. Going to the grocery store, cooking dinner, writing a report, taking a walk – all these are programs. They all have a general, overall goal, but they are incompletely specified because they may entail many decisions along the way.

Principles provide reference values for program-level control in two ways. The first is by suggesting certain kinds of programs as potential goals. For example, one output of the principle of thrift or frugality would be a program involving dinner at home rather than dining out. The second way principles provide reference values concerns choices made within programs. A person who's already committed to the dining-out program might be influenced by the thrift principle to choose an inexpensive restaurant rather than a pricier alternative, or to choose the least expensive dish on the menu and avoid drinks, appetizers, and dessert.

Programs are the sort of activities that people take for granted as "behavior." Although programs sometimes are undertaken to attain relatively abstract goals, the programs themselves are sufficiently concrete and overt that they are easily recognizable as actions. It's easy to describe the actions in a program. Executing programs, however, involves more complexity than may be readily apparent. In the model proposed by Powers (1973a, 1973b), programs act by specifying yet more restricted qualities as reference values to lower-level control structures.

More concretely, you enact a program (partly) by enacting *sequences* of movement. One difference between programs and sequences is that programs involve choice points where decisions must be made (ranging from trivial to important), whereas a sequence is executed all-at-a-piece. When an action becomes sufficiently well learned that its enactment (once begun) is automatic rather than effortful, it can be thought of as having become a sequence rather than a program. Sequences, in turn, are composed of even more restricted qualities, which we won't go into.

Another way of portraying this hierarchy is shown in Figure 5.2. This diagram omits the elements of the feedback processes, simply using

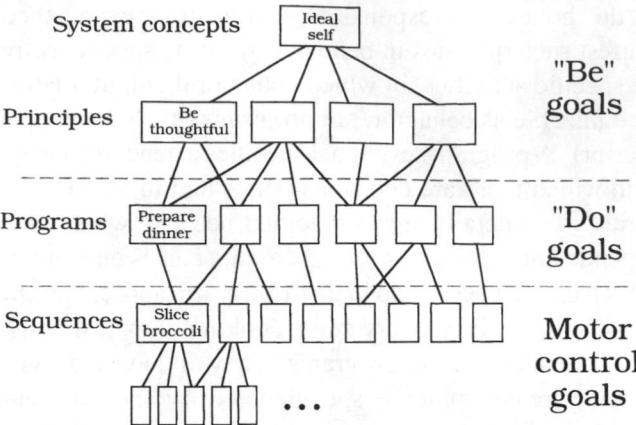

Figure 5.2.   Another way to represent a hierarchy of goals (or of feedback loops), using the same example as in Figure 5.1. Lines indicate the contribution of lower-level goals to specific higher-level goals. They can also be read in the opposite direction, indicating that a given higher-order goal specifies more-concrete goals at the next lower level. The hierarchy described in the text involves goals of "being" particular ways, which are attained by "doing" particular actions.

lines to indicate hierarchical connections among goal values. The lines imply that moving toward a particular lower-level goal contributes to attainment of a higher-level goal (even several at once). Multiple lines to a goal indicate that several lower-level action qualities contribute to its attainment. As indicated earlier, this hierarchy assumes the existence of both goals where the point is to "be" a particular way and goals where the point is to "do" certain things (and at lower levels, goals where the point is creation of physical movement).

The process of specifying high-order, abstract qualities in terms of lower-order, more concrete qualities of action brings to mind the notion of means–end analysis (e.g., Newell & Simon, 1972). The *end* is a higher-level goal; the *means* is a set of lower-level action qualities used to attain it. This phrase was coined in the context of problem solving, to label an active process of dividing a behavioral problem into component steps to resolve it, working from the higher level toward very concrete acts. One might think of a means–end analysis as creating a new program of action, as opposed to using a program that's already familiar.

In general, use of the term means–end analysis implies that the analysis is conscious and effortful. In contrast, this assumption isn't part of the model we're discussing. In the functioning of this hierarchy to guide behavior (as opposed to learning a new behavior), something akin to the outcome of a prior means–end analysis is being evoked from memory, as standards are specified down through the hierarchy. The process is typically implicit and automatic, rather than conscious and effortful. On the other hand, a degree of conscious means–end analysis often occurs at the program level because of the need to choose from several potential strategies within a program of behavior. Indeed, there is evidence that conscious means–end analysis can be helpful in keeping people on track as they manage their day-to-day lives (Gollwitzer & Brandstätter, 1997; Taylor & Pham, 1996).

Hierarchical Functioning Is Simultaneous

It may or may not have been apparent from this discussion that this hierarchical view treats control as simultaneous at all levels of abstraction below the level that's guiding the activity. That is, you don't engage in a high-order action, then stop and wait for lower-level activities to catch up. Nor do you engage in low-level act qualities as preparation for attainment of high-level acts. Rather, the process of carrying out a high-level act *consists of* carrying out low-level acts (see also Vallacher & Wegner, 1985, 1987). For example, if you're conforming to the principle of kindness by doing a favor for a neighbor, the conforming is being enhanced throughout the doing of the favor, not just when the favor is completed.

In this view, exceedingly restricted and concrete behavioral acts (e.g., changes in level of muscle tension, changes in postural orientation) are embedded in the creation of very abstract behavioral qualities (e.g., conveying a certain mood in a piece of art, being gracious to others, delivering a speech with style). To put it differently, whenever some level of control is engaged as functionally superordinate, so are all levels below that one, to permit the carrying out of the action.

One of the strengths of this sort of model is that it links the kinds of activities that are of interest to social–personality psychologists (high-level planning, developing of intentions) to views of how the intentions are carried out physically. To paraphrase Gallistel (1980, p. 287), the problem of motivation becomes a problem of motor coordination as one descends the action hierarchy. Most psychological theorizing at high levels devotes no attention to the processes by which behavior actually occurs. Although the model of action that Powers proposed may be wrong (indeed, the whole family of models to which it relates could be wrong), the effort to make a link between abstract goals and management of physical movement strikes us as important.

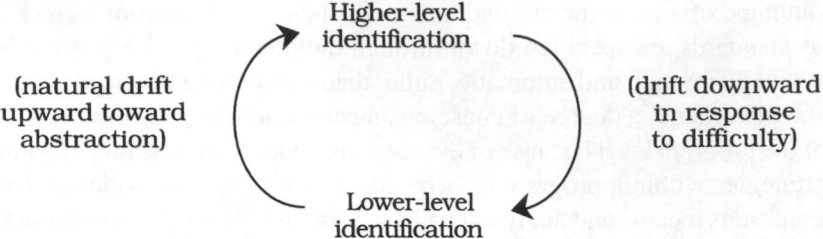

Figure 5.3.   Action-identification theory assumes a natural drift upward in identifying your own actions, so that more abstract identification tends to emerge as you become more comfortable with the behavior. If you have difficulties in maintaining the behavior's identification and regulation at the higher level, there's a complementary tendency to drop downward to more concrete identifications, which function better in handling whatever condition is producing the difficulty.

Action Identification

Although the Powers hierarchy has not been studied empirically, another theory that strongly resembles it – Vallacher and Wegner's (1985, 1987) action identification theory – has received several tests. This model is framed in terms of how people think about the actions they're engaged in, but it also conveys the sense that the way people think about their actions is informative about the goals they're using to guide their actions.

People can identify a given action in many ways. Of particular interest is that act identifications vary in level of abstraction. High-level identifications are abstract (e.g., becoming more cultured), lower-level identifications become more and more concrete (e.g., attending a ballet; listening to sounds and watching people move around while you sit quiet and still). Low-level identifications tend to convey a sense of "how" an activity is done; high-level ones tend to convey a sense of "why."

Vallacher and Wegner posited a natural tendency for people to drift upward to higher levels of identification (a process they term *emergence*), as long as they can successfully maintain them (see Figure 5.3). For example, someone driving across the United States may come to identify the behavior as "relocating to the West Coast" rather than "driving down Interstate 10." When there's difficulty in carrying out an activity as construed at the higher level, the person drops downward to a lower-level identification. For example, a period of frequent traffic hazards may cause this driver to identify the activity as "staying out of accidents" or "maintaining a safe distance from other cars." Consistent with this line of thought, easy and familiar actions occur more smoothly when the person holds a high-level orientation, and more difficult and unfamiliar actions are facilitated by a lower-level orientation (Vallacher, Wegner, & Somoza, 1989; Vallacher, Wegner, McMahan, Cotter, & Larsen, 1992).

Movement from a lower level to a higher level depends on an emergent property at the higher level (a notion that's also tied to the Powers hierarchy). This means that a given lower-level identification can often be absorbed into several alternative higher-level identifications. The availability of many potential higher-level construals, in turn, suggests that the emergence process is vulnerable to influence by transient cues. Consistent with this, subjects placed in a low-level orientation were found to be responsive to cues implying a particular high-level construal of their actions. That is, exposure to the cues made them more likely to adopt that construal, compared to subjects who were already in a high-level orientation and exposed to the same cues (Wegner, Vallacher, Kiersted, & Dizadji, 1986).

As implied by that finding, once a relatively high-level identification is adopted, it tends to be maintained while the action is taking place (subject to forces leading to shifts either upward or downward). To put it differently, people are resistant to putting aside one identification of an ongoing action in favor of another identification at the same level. Shifts in identifying a continuing action are more likely to occur upward or downward.

Although people drift upward and downward as circumstances change, there's also evidence that people differ in the levels they tend to maintain as they think about what they're doing (Vallacher & Wegner, 1989). Some people report typically thinking of their actions in low-level terms; others typically think of their actions in high-level terms. These differences are reflected in a variety of ways. For example, compared with high-level identifiers, low-level identifiers tend to be more impulsive and less planful or stable in their behavior, consistent with the idea that they're especially vulnerable to cues implying different identifications.

In considering the relation between the action-identification model of behavior and the Powers hierarchy, there are two points to make. First, although the Vallacher and Wegner (1985, 1987) model is explicitly hierarchical, it doesn't specify what qualities define various levels. It simply assumes that wherever there's a potential emergent property, there's the potential for differing levels of identification. On the other hand, the examples used to illustrate action-identification processes map quite well onto the levels of the Powers hierarchy: sequences, programs (with variations among smaller-scale and larger-scale programs), and principles. Thus, the work on action identification tends to suggest the reasonableness of these levels of abstraction in thinking about behavior.

COMPARISONS OUTSIDE
PERSONALITY–SOCIAL PSYCHOLOGY

How do these ideas about hierarchicality compare with those of others? We first consider two reference points from outside the field of personality–social psychology. We begin with comments about hierarchicality by Miller, Galanter, and Pribram (1960). Then we briefly examine hierarchical models of motor control.

Hierarchical Plans

Although emerging from its own distinct path of development, the hierarchy proposed by Powers (1973a) turns out to have several interesting similarities to ideas expressed by Miller et al. (1960). Miller et al. argued that a hierarchical organization of goals underlies behavior, that attaining an abstract goal requires it to be broken iteratively into subgoals, until the subgoals are sufficiently concrete that they can be attained by whatever are the body's basic operational mechanisms. Alternatively, understanding the creation of complex activity involves putting feedback loops around increasingly larger and larger segments of behavior. Although Miller et al. made no attempt to specify how many levels might be needed to reach the body's fundamental operational mechanisms, it's clear they regarded such questions as important ones.

Another similarity between the Miller et al. (1960) statement and the Powers (1973a) model concerns the distinction between digital and analog processes and the idea that the two can work in concert within a system. The Powers model is mostly analog in nature (i.e., both feedback and discrepancies are represented continuously and quantitatively). It deviates from that quality only at the program level, where behavior is a digital process (i.e., a linear string of decisions). In the same way, Miller et al. (1960, p. 91) argued that "planning at the higher levels [equivalent to Powers's programs] looks like the sort of information-processing we see in digital computers, whereas the execution of the Plan at the lowest levels looks like the sort of process we see in analogue computers." They went on to suggest that development of a skill is comparable to providing a digital-to-analog converter for the output of a digital machine. Thus, Miller et al. saw the two kinds of systems as compatible. Indeed, their depiction here is very similar to the structure of the Powers model.

Miller et al. also discussed the "roughing in" of movement, the creation of good first approximations to an intended movement prior to the arrival of proprioceptive feedback, a function often labeled feedforward (Chapter 2). They discussed this process in terms of an order generated by the digital device and issued to the analog system for execution. Their implication was that subplans are stored in a distributed fashion and are ready for execution at lower levels, awaiting only a call to do so from a higher level. The more precisely encoded is the subplan, the less the adjustment needed from feedback in order to manifest the action as intended. The sense of this discussion is very similar to the arguments that Powers made about the hierarchy he proposed.

Hierarchical Models of Motor Control

Another useful comparison is to the literature of motor control, in which hierarchicality is used more explicitly than in most areas of psychology. Many of today's conceptions of motor control share with Miller et al.'s statement a tendency to divide the system managing behavior into two levels, a higher level at which central planning takes place and a lower level of motor programs (cf. Greene, 1972). One question at issue in this literature is what form is taken by the lower level.

This question has been addressed in ways that range from explicitly hierarchical (e.g., Keele, Cohen, & Ivry, 1990; Rosenbaum, 1987, 1991b; Sternberg, Knoll, & Turock, 1990; see also Baron, 1987; Greene, 1972) to less so (e.g., Schmidt, 1987). Rosenbaum's approach illustrates a conceptual theme that hierarchical motor control models share with the Powers model. Rosenbaum (e.g., 1991b) argues that programs for movement sequences are structured as a tree diagram of simple segments embedded within larger segments. Higher-level nodes in the tree diagram contain information about how the sequence is broken into segments; bottom-level nodes provide information about the movements themselves. Rosenbaum argues that motor programs aren't simply read from memory as a string of instructions. Instead, information is decoded at several levels of abstraction. This arrangement is held to be functional partly because it permits great behavioral diversity to be assembled from a small number of programs stored in memory (for a discussion of the computational savings created by hierarchicality, see Pinkerton, 1993).

COMPARISONS FROM PERSONALITY–SOCIAL PSYCHOLOGY

We return now to social–personality psychology. We start by considering the relationship of the hierarchical model to goal models reviewed earlier in the chapter. Although none of the theories reviewed earlier makes a point of differentiating among levels of abstraction in the goals they assume, it's possible to infer some variations in that respect among – and even within – theories.

Relations to Goal Models Outlined Earlier

Two theories mentioned earlier appear to focus on goals at the highest level of the Powers hierarchy. One of them is the possible-self construct of Markus and Nurius (1986). The hoped-for self seems a global, coherent entity, corresponding to the idealized sense of self at the top level of abstraction in the hierarchical model. The self-guide model of Higgins (1987, 1996) and collaborators also captures the sense of overall identity within its central constructs. That is, the ideal self and the ought self might be viewed as very integrated goals. The same sense pervades Burke's (1991) model, in which the desired sense of identity is a goal to be regulated against.

Although these models have the conceptual flavor of the top end of the hierarchy, the operationalizations of the constructs in research differ considerably from this. When subjects report on the hoped-for self (or the feared self or expected self), they list several qualities that fit that label. Our experience suggests that it's rare for subjects to write down "complete" hoped-for selves; more often they list several facets of a single hoped-for self. The same is true of operationalizations of self-guides in research by Higgins and collaborators. Subjects write several ideals or oughts, but these qualities typically are facets of a more unitary sense of self.

Neither of these research procedures places constraints on what people can write down. Thus, the responses vary from abstract ("honest person"), to more concrete ("be enrolled in law school"). In practice, however, the responses generally reduce to two types: traitlike statements ("honest," "good looking," "more social"), and statements of places or way stations along some path of activity ("enrolled in law school," "happily married," "have a good job"). It's of interest that these two categories tend to recapture the qualities of principles (*be* goals) and programs (*do* goals) from the Powers hierarchy. Thus, again, it would seem there's a natural decomposition from high-order abstraction (ideal self) to particular kinds of lower-order goals.

As we noted, several theories reviewed earlier in the chapter are harder to pin down regarding their level of abstraction. A life task may be abstract ("acquire wisdom"), but it can also be more concrete ("decide whether to go to law school or graduate school"). A personal striving can be abstract ("help others feel good about themselves") or concrete ("look attentive in class"). As Little (1989) put it, some projects are "magnificent obsessions," others are "trivial pursuits." Once you consider the possibility that people may vary in the levels of abstraction that constitute their goal systems, virtually all these theories can be explored further in these terms.

Consistent with this, Emmons (1992) found evidence that people differ in levels of abstraction they characteristically use when reporting their personal strivings (cf. Vallacher & Wegner, 1989). Some people report strivings that are broad, abstract, and expansive. Others report strivings that are narrower, more concrete, and even superficial. These tendencies are also reflected in moment-to-moment construals of behaviors they're engaged in. When randomly paged and asked to report what they were doing, high-level strivers reported they were engaged in relatively high-level activities; low-level strivers reported they were engaged in relatively concrete actions.

Hierarchicality behind Task Efforts

Another model of goals discussed earlier was Dweck's analysis of children's task behavior. Dweck's view seems to imply a hierarchical organization (Figure 5.4). Task performances sometimes are a means by which children hold onto self-esteem. This is particularly clear in the group Dweck and her colleagues term "helpless" children. These children hold performance goals (goals of demonstrating they have skill) and are experiencing failure. They aren't able to maintain self-esteem with good performances, so they engage in self-inflating verbalizations: talking about skills in domains other than the one pertaining to this task, or boasting of wealth and possessions. Such behaviors seem to reflect a desire to regain threatened self-esteem in domains other than

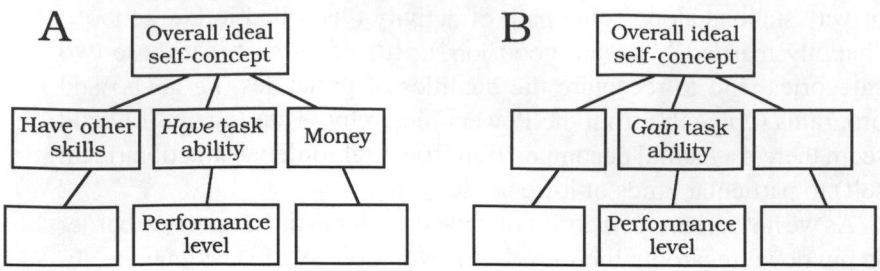

Figure 5.4.   Three-level goal hierarchies of (A) a child who holds a performance goal and (B) a child who holds a learning goal. For the child with the performance goal, performing well creates the sense of having a high level of the ability that's relevant to the task, which contributes to the overall sense of self-esteem. For the child with the learning goal, performing well (eventually, though not necessarily right away) provides evidence of gaining the ability, which contributes to the overall sense of self-esteem. Other qualities, of course, also contribute to self-esteem in both cases. In the case of children with performance goals who were failing at the target task, however, several other contributors to self-esteem were mentioned spontaneously.

the one that's responsible for the threat. This, in turn, suggests a kind of hierarchicality in the child's goals structure, such that many different areas contribute to the overall sense of self-esteem.

Children operating with learning goals (goals of acquiring skill) also have a hierarchy underlying their behavior, but it appears to differ from the hierarchy of children with performance goals. The self-esteem of a child with a learning goal depends partly on acquiring new skills. Attaining this goal doesn't require good performance all the time. Thus, children with learning goals who fail at a task don't display compensatory efforts to look good in other ways. Both orientations have an intermediate-level goal concerning ability, but in the learning-goal hierarchy the intermediate goal is more dynamic in nature (*increase* ability versus *have* or *display* ability).

This difference in dynamic quality becomes even more apparent when the goals are linked to children's views of what ability consists of (Dweck, 1996; Dweck & Leggett, 1988). Children with performance goals think of ability as an entity, something that everyone has to one degree or another, which doesn't change over time and with experience. They try to have it *be* there when they undertake their task efforts. Children with learning goals tend to think of ability as something that's more fluid and volatile, something that can change. They try to figure out ways to *increase* it when they undertake task efforts. Thus, the goals in the hierarchy are more dynamic in one case than in the other (for a somewhat different view, see Ruble & Frey, 1991).

Hierarchicality in Other Models

The notion of hierarchicality is center stage in only a relatively few models in personality–social psychology, but it's implicit in a wide variety of others – more than many people may realize. Here are a few more examples.

Hierarchicality plays a clear role in symbolic self-completion theory (Wicklund & Gollwitzer, 1982). This theory isn't about moment-to-moment construal of action, in the manner of action-identification theory, but about broader construals of the self. It holds that there are ways in which the sense of self can be damaged or incomplete. People try to remedy whatever sense of incompleteness they feel by creating symbolic manifestations of the missing quality.

This theory focuses on the self-presentational, or public, aspects of the self. That is, it assumes that the symbols people create increase their sense of completeness only if those symbols are seen to register on others. By having an impact on others' reactions to the self (causing confirmatory social feedback), the symbolizing activity moves the person toward the goal of creating the desired social construction about the self. Thus, creating the symbol is a lower-order goal that helps attain the higher-order goal of a particular public construal of the self.

The theme of hierarchicality is also implicit in most theories which incorporate the idea that people are motivated to maintain a positive self-evaluation or positive self-image. People make self-serving attributions for outcomes (e.g., Weary, 1980; see also Taylor & Brown, 1988). They go out of their way to create esteem-protective explanations for potential bad outcomes before they occur, though doing so often handicaps their own performances (e.g., Snyder, Higgins, & Stucky, 1983). People bask in the accomplishments of others close to them when it reflects well on them, but avoid such information when it creates unflattering comparisons (Tesser, 1980a, 1986, 1988; Tesser & Campbell, 1983). In sum, people try in a variety of ways to affirm or maintain a positive sense of self (Steele, 1988; Tesser, Martin, & Cornell, 1996).

These effects appear to reflect attempts to prevent discrepancies from arising between a desired sense of self and perceptions of self. In each case, people try to protect a quality that's central to them (to minimize discrepancies at the highest level) by the expedient of taking steps to create certain perceived realities at lower levels. These effects thus seem compatible with the logic of hierarchical organization.

Terror management theory (Greenberg, Pyszczynski, & Solomon, 1986; Solomon, Greenberg, & Pyszczynski, 1991) is another model in which hierarchicality seems implicit. This theory holds that juxtaposing the desire for continuance of life with the knowledge of impending death leads to existential terror. People guard against this by adopting a world view that in one form or another guarantees their continuance into the future, either literally or symbolically. Holding to the world view thus is a means to attain immortality. The world view, in turn, specifies standards that people should uphold behaviorally. In day-to-day life, then, people regulate their behavior according to the specified values. Acting to uphold those values places them in conformity with the cultural world view. The world view, in turn, allows access to the higher-order goal of immortality.

SUMMARY

In sum, many theories in contemporary personality–social psychology make extensive use of goal concepts. Because these theories assume reference points that people try to move toward or away from, the theories fit easily with feedback models of behavior. Many of these models can also be viewed as incorporating notions of hierarchicality, either explicitly or by implication. Thus, we suggest, many of their themes can be integrated into a model of hierarchically organized goals.

The principle of hierarchicality among goals has a good deal of integrative potential. It also raises a number of questions and issues that go well beyond the points we've made thus far. These issues are the subject of the next chapter.

6

Goals, Hierarchicality, and Behavior: Further Issues

In Chapter 5 we discussed the goal construct in personality–social psychology and argued that it's useful to view goals in terms of a hierarchy of abstractness. We focused on a particular view of hierarchicality and its relation to other ideas about goals. For clarity, we skipped a number of issues and questions raised by it. Some issues represent challenges to the model – suggestions that it's wrong. Others are questions about how a hierarchy would function. Questions also emerge from the idea that people typically have several current concerns rather than just one. These issues are the subject of this chapter.

Another matter we've sidestepped so far concerns the nature of the self. We wrote in Chapter 3 about self-directed attention. An important question behind the self-focus construct is what's meant by *self*. This question is touched on here as well.

CHALLENGES TO HIERARCHICALITY

We start by considering a few challenges to the hierarchical aspect of the model outlined in Chapter 5. The idea of hierarchicality has proven useful as a heuristic. But is it really necessary? Is it desirable? Is it even *plausible*?

Hierarchies, Heterarchies, and Coalitions

Some theorists are wary of notions of hierarchicality, preferring ideas such as *heterarchies* or *coalitions* (cf. Broadbent, 1977; Turvey, 1977). There appear to be several bases for this wariness. One of them is a shade of meaning that sometimes attaches to the word *hierarchy*. This word can convey a sense that a command from an executive is carried out verbatim by a single, unified flow down through an organization.[1] As Turvey put it, the term hierarchy suggests the picture of "a detached higher level dictatorially commanding lower levels" (1977, p. 223). One reasonable objection to that picture is that the chain of command *can't* flow so simply or directly – it would be too vulnerable to disruption. An alternative that's sometimes suggested is that action may recruit several parallel streams of management – a coalition among semi-autonomous but cooperating paths which jointly produce the intended behavior.

A second objection concerns the influence of low levels on activities occurring at higher levels. Are higher processes dictatorial, or do they instead ". . . [enter] into 'negotiations' with lower domains in order to determine how the higher representation should be stated" (Turvey, 1977, p. 224)? The latter would imply that information at lower levels can induce a different higher-order understanding than might otherwise be held.

These concerns both have merit. However, we don't think this hierarchical model carries the rigid implications that prompt them. Nothing in this organization prohibits information at lower levels from influencing higher-order perceptions and actions. Nor is there a bias against the involvement of multiple parallel paths of behavior.

Arguments in favor of the term heterarchy sometimes go beyond these concerns, however, to an issue that causes us some wariness of our own. In particular, this term is often taken to imply the absence of an intrinsic ordering of levels. In this view, different qualities can become superordinate to each other at different times, each recruiting the other as a subroutine in turn (cf. Gallistel, 1980, p. 327; Turvey, 1977, p. 221).

Does this really happen? Clearly there can be reversals in the ordering of goals in a program, changing the means–end relationship. For example, you may usually do your work in order to go somewhere with the kids on the weekend, but it's possible for you to go somewhere with the kids on the weekend in order to be able to go do some work. These, however, are both goals in an extended program (or two programs strung

---

[1] Some conceptions of hierarchicality assume there are no cross-links permitting two midlevel elements to work through the same lower-level element (Minsky, 1985, p. 35). That arrangement is very different from our use of the term (see also Gallistel's 1980 discussion of "lattice hierarchies").

together). In terms of the hierarchy we described, they're both at the same level of abstraction. Thus their ordering doesn't involve the issue of hierarchicality at all.

It's *between* levels that the issue of reversal is relevant, and it's there that we experience our wariness. In the Powers hierarchy, the quality that defines a given level simply doesn't exist at the lower levels. It's emergent at the higher level. How could the emergent quality become subordinate to a quality that exists at a lower level?

In sum, we are not convinced that the kind of hierarchicality described here ever reverses itself. It seems to us that cases used to argue for reversibility tend to be cases in which the notion of superordination concerns either prioritization or breadth of inclusiveness. These cases don't actually involve hierarchicality as we've been discussing it.

Are the Qualities of the Proposed Hierarchy the Wrong Sorts?

Another possibility worth considering is that self-regulatory functions are hierarchical, but the qualities in this particular model are the wrong ones. The argument that these qualities are emergent from one level to the next (Powers, 1973a) is just that – an argument. Work on action identification (Vallacher & Wegner, 1985, 1987) tends to suggest that people (or at least college students) tend to *think* in terms of these qualities. Still, this isn't the only set of qualities for which an argument might be made.

Another plausible source of hypotheses is the work of Piaget (e.g., 1963, 1964, 1971). What makes Piaget's work compelling as an alternative is partly that his theory of cognitive development is predicated on the assumption that the cognitive capability defining a given stage is emergent from the capabilities that preceded it. Thus each stage depends on prior stages. Although the possibility of deriving a control hierarchy from these Piagetian concepts thus is plausible (cf. Frankel & Froming, 1992), we know of no data bearing on the question.

Our tentative conclusion, then, is that the qualities in the Powers hierarchy remain what we have seen them as being all along – a useful conceptual heuristic – whether they ultimately turn out to be correct or not.

Responsibility for Details

Yet another question that might be raised about the notion of hierarchical control concerns how such a system functions regarding details of behavior. Occasionally people infer that the idea of hierarchicality implies an executive process that controls all the details of behavior as well as its broad outlines. For this reason, they argue, the hierarchical notion is doomed to failure. This, however, is a straw-man picture, taken from the metaphor of the execution of a program in a sequential processor. There are other ways a hierarchy can function.

As an analogy, consider human groups. An organization such as a university can be run in a variety of ways. The provost might give the entire staff explicit, detailed instructions to follow. Indeed, the provost might micromanage the behavior of even lowest-level staff, checking on the execution of each part of each job. Alternatively, the provost can give autonomy to deans, provided the general goals for their actions are clear and usually attained, and the same autonomy might be given by deans to department chairs.

It would seem apparent that the second strategy – providing goals in general terms to lower-level units that have autonomy and competence in reaching those goals – is the best way to run an organization. Which strategy reflects the way behavior is organized within a person? Here, too, the job is too great for an upper-level executive function to handle the details. Carrying out actions must be decentralized. The real question is what that decentralization entails.

A common characterization of hierarchical systems is that the layers of the hierarchy are only loosely coupled to one another, and that the information flowing down from one to another is fairly general (cf. Baron, 1987; Greene, 1972, 1982). A loop at the program level, for example, might send a message with the equivalent of "walk down this aisle," without specifying anything more than that. The "how-to-do-it" specifications would be dealt with at the next level. Each layer manages affairs at its level of abstraction, relying on lower layers to handle the problems that arise there. Greene (1982) has argued that loose coupling makes a system robust: It diminishes the need for everything to work perfectly in order for anything to work at all. As far as we can see, this characterization is fully compatible with the Powers model.

Certainly people have the subjective sense of loose coupling, especially when behaviors have acquired a degree of automaticity. When something is very routine, only the merest flicker of internal instruction causes the activity's execution. Everything from there on is taken care of, often outside awareness (cf. Minsky, 1985, pp. 56, 169).

FURTHER ISSUES REGARDING HIERARCHICAL FUNCTIONING

The theme of hierarchicality among goals appears robust enough to survive the challenges of the preceding section. It also has a number of implications about the use of goals in behavior that go beyond the points made thus far. In this section we address some of these implications.

Which Level Is Functionally Superordinate Can Vary

In Chapter 5 we described a model in which very abstract qualities, such as the sense of an idealized self, stand as uppermost goals for human behavior. This doesn't imply, however, that such goals are always exerting a directive influence on behavior. Although high-level goals are being used in some circumstances, in many cases behavior is guided not by the superordinate sense of self, but by goals at lower levels – for instance, the level of program control. To put it differently, levels of control below the system-concept level are *functionally* superordinate in the control of action when the person's current concern is at a lower level of abstraction (cf. Klinger, 1975; Shallice, 1978; Vallacher & Wegner, 1985, 1987).

This would appear to be the case, for example, when people engage in the "maintenance" activities of life – shopping for groceries, washing dishes, driving to work. During such activities (aimed at attaining "do" goals) people may lose sight of higher-order aims ("be" goals), as they focus on the concrete elements of the situations confronting them (cf. Norman, 1981). We've also argued that it's common for program control to be functionally superordinate in behavior precisely because of the frequent need for decision making at that level (Carver & Scheier, 1981a).

Though most behavior probably involves at least program control, even this level probably isn't always engaged. States such as deindividuation and alcohol intoxication appear to diminish even program control, sometimes rendering sequence control functionally superordinate. This would be consistent with the impulsive, spontaneous character of actions that occur in those states.

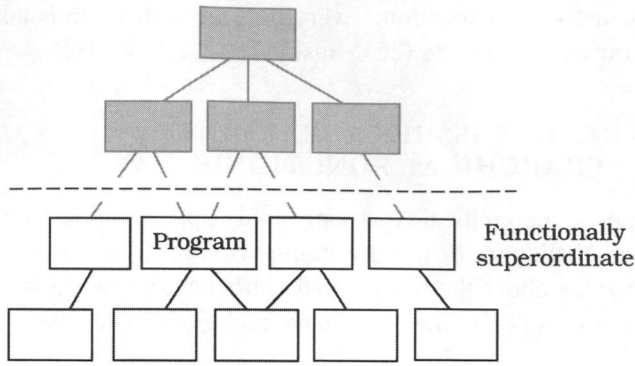

Figure 6.1. When self-regulation at upper levels of a hierarchy has been suspended temporarily (i.e., goals at those levels are presently not in use), one or more goals at a lower level become functionally superordinate in the guidance of ongoing behavior, and higher-level goals may be disregarded. If a program of action (for example, having dinner) is the highest-level goal being used (is functionally superordinate), the person may disregard principles in the process of conducting the program.

We've tended to assume that self-regulation at any level higher than the level that's functionally superordinate is discontinued until attention is refocused on standards at the higher level (Figure 6.1). This does *not* mean, however, that actions taken under low-level control have no *relevance* to higher-level goals. When behavior is controlled at lower levels, it still contributes to the reduction – or creation – of discrepancies at higher levels. Whether higher-level discrepancies decrease, increase, or remain unchanged depends on the consequences of the lower-level activity. The links between the goal qualities at the various levels haven't ceased to exist just because the higher levels aren't being actively used to guide action.

To provide a simple example, a person who's had way too much alcohol and is behaving entirely in sequences (responsive to cues of the moment, rather than to personal values and principles) may happen to behave in ways that embody cordiality, or may behave in ways that embody rudeness. If cordiality somehow emerges – a quality that fits with one of his principles – no discrepancy is created. Indeed, the person is actually living up to the principle. If his behavior is rude (and he later sees it as such), a discrepancy at the principle level is created (or enlarged).

Under an organization in which control is suspended at levels above the functionally superordinate level, effects on high-level discrepancies caused by behavior guided from a low level wouldn't be noted until attention is redirected to the higher level. In the example just above, that might happen in the course of the event, but it would more likely happen the next morning. Only then would the person realize the implications of his actions (whether positive or negative) for the principles he holds.

We should also note, however, that the idea that higher-level control is discontinued in such situations is speculation. It may be that high-level values always exert an influence on behavior, but the influence is simply attenuated when these values aren't focal. If so, the person in the example would continue to have internal pressures to act in ways consistent with his principles, but these pressures wouldn't be strong enough to determine his actions.

Multiple Paths to High-Level Goals, Multiple Meanings in Concrete Action

Although the hierarchy we're discussing is in some ways very simple, it has implications for several problems in thinking about behavior. It's implicit in this approach that goals at a given level can be achieved by a variety of means at lower levels. This flexibility is particularly apparent at the upper levels, where the goals are abstract. This flexibility permits the hierarchical approach to address the fact that people sometimes shift radically the way in which they're trying to reach a goal when the goal itself hasn't changed appreciably. This happens when the quality that is the higher-order goal is implied in several distinct lower-order activities. For example, a person can be helpful by writing a donation check, picking up discards for a recycling center, volunteering at the Special Olympics, or holding a door open for someone else.

Just as a given goal can be obtained via multiple pathways, so can a specific act be performed in the service of diverse goals. For example, you could buy someone a gift to make that person feel good, to repay a kindness, to put the other person in your debt, or to fulfill a holiday season role. The diverse goals can also be at varying levels of abstraction. Walking through a door and closing it behind you may be a mindless *sequence*, it may be part of a *program* of choices (reflecting a decision you've made to go somewhere else), or it may reflect a *principle* (choosing to leave an interaction in which someone is behaving dishonorably).

Thus, a given act can have strikingly different meanings, depending on the purpose it's intended to serve. This is an important subtheme of this viewpoint on behavior: Behavior can be understood only by identifying the goals to which the behavior is addressed. This isn't always easy to

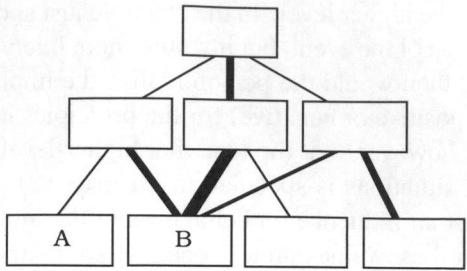

Figure 6.2.   Importance accrues to a given concrete action goal in either of two ways. The action can contribute in a major way to the attainment of a higher-order goal (indicated here by a thicker line), or the action can contribute to several higher-order goals at once (indicated here by a larger number of upward projections). On both of these criteria, concrete action goal A is relatively unimportant, whereas B is more important.

do, either from an observer's point of view (cf. Read, Druian, & Miller, 1989) or from the actor's point of view.

Goal Importance

Another point made by the notion of hierarchical organization is that goals aren't equivalent in importance. The higher you go into the organization, the more fundamental are the qualities found there to the overriding sense of self (or alternative value). Thus, goal qualities at higher levels are intrinsically more important than those at lower levels.

Goals at lower levels aren't necessarily equivalent in importance, either. Just as it's sometimes hard to tell what goal underlies an act, it can also be hard to tell from the act how important is the goal that lies behind it. In hierarchical logic there are at least two ways in which importance accrues to a concrete goal (Figure 6.2). First, the more strongly a given concrete action contributes to a highly valued goal at the more abstract level, the more important that concrete action is. For someone we know, the concrete action of unexpectedly bringing flowers to his wife is the prototypic act serving the higher goal of being nurturant. Nurturance is an important principle in his sense of self. Surprising his wife with flowers thus is an important act to him. Taking out the garbage and washing dishes aren't connected nearly as strongly to nurturance in his hierarchy, and thus are less important to him.

Another way importance accrues to a concrete action is that a given act sometimes relates to more than one goal. An act that contributes

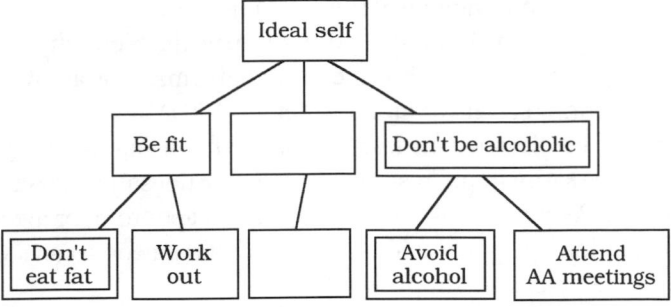

Figure 6.3.   A hierarchy of goals can include anti-goals as well as goals. Anti-goals are indicated here by double boxes. An anti-goal at the principal level means that its attainment – successful avoidance – contributes to the overall sense of self. Such an anti-goal (in this illustration, not living as an alcoholic) can be reached by both approach behaviors and avoidance behaviors at the program level. In the same way, an approach goal at the principal level (fitness) can be reached by both approach behaviors and avoidance behaviors at the program level.

to attainment of several goals at once is more important than an act that contributes to the attainment of only one goal. To continue with our example, bringing flowers to his wife does more than satisfy this man's sense that he's a caring person. It also makes his wife feel special, thereby enhancing their mutual perceptions of their relationship. Thus, importance accrues to this behavior for a second reason as well.

Approach Goals and Avoidance Goals within a Hierarchy

We noted earlier that discussions of the self incorporate a variety of qualities, both positive and negative (Markus & Nurius, 1986; Ogilvie, 1987). It's clear that at principle and program levels, people are guided at least part of the time by the desire to *not*-be, to avoid anti-goals (though we doubt that avoidance self-regulation at the top level is common). What does the mixing of approach and avoidance do to the concept of hierarchicality? Not much, actually.

It's easy to imagine a feared self at a fairly high level of abstraction (illustrated in Figure 6.3 as the anti-goal of alcoholism). This anti-goal can be avoided both via anti-goals at the program level (avoid alcohol and situations involving alcohol) and via approach goals (seek out and attend support meetings). In the same way, a desired aspect of self at a high level (illustrated here as remaining fit) can be approached both via avoidance at the program level (avoid high-fat foods) and via approach (work out regularly). From this point of view, the hierarchy constitutes a web of positive goals with some anti-goals (many or a few) captured within its fabric (see also Van Lange et al., 1997).

It should be clear from these examples that using an anti-goal goal doesn't necessarily imply restraint. Not-*being* doesn't necessarily mean not-*acting*. People can take active steps to escape from, or avoid, undesired conditions (Higgins et al., 1994). Similarly, people can sometimes attain desired goals by simply waiting.

It should also be clear that a given activity can be construed in either approach or avoidance terms (see also Higgins, 1997). A person can have the goal of remaining fit or the anti-goal of avoiding sedentary living. The physical actions these values prescribe may be the same. But the process differs in a fundamental way. In one case the basic self-regulatory tendency is discrepancy-reducing; in the other case it's discrepancy-enlarging. This difference may have very important consequences.

Approach and Avoidance Goals and Well-Being

Some people orient to avoidance more than others. Studies have found that people expressing personal strivings ranged from 0 to about 70% in the proportion of avoidance tendencies they reported (Coats, Janoff-Bulman, & Alpert, 1996; Moffitt & Singer, 1994). These differences also relate to differences in well-being. Emmons (1996) found that people whose lives are dominated by avoidance strivings report more anxiety and more physical symptoms than people whose lives are dominated by approach strivings. Coats et al. (1996) found that avoidance strivings related to pessimism, low self-esteem, and depression. Conceptually similar results have been reported by Elliot and Sheldon (1997) and by Elliot, Sheldon, and Church (1997). Elliott et al. (1997) even found that people with more avoidance goals had poorer well-being prospectively (after controlling for initial well-being) than those with fewer avoidance goals.

How are such findings to be interpreted? One possibility is suggested by the observation that approach is simpler than avoidance (Schwarz, 1990): You have to find only one path to a goal and you're there; to avoid a punisher you have to prevent *all* ways of being confronted with it. Someone dominated by avoidance goals thus is like someone looking for holes in a dike, not knowing where or how many. He can feel successful at avoiding only if many holes have been found and plugged. If he finds no problems, it's hard to feel good because of the feeling that the problems may be present but unlocated. The plugging of holes is itself stressful, because it requires there be a leak to find. People dominated by avoidance goals thus have difficult lives (see also Elliot & Church, 1997).

MULTIPLE SIMULTANEOUS GOALS

Another set of issues arises from the fact that people often have many goals at more or less the same time. Although it's sometimes convenient to think of people as guided by one purpose at a time, this usually isn't true. We don't mean simply that an act managed by a hierarchical system involves both lower- and higher-order goals. Rather, several goals are often salient at once, even within one level of the hierarchy. Several questions can be raised about these multiple demands.

Conflict and Scheduling

Sometimes goals are mutually exclusive. Even short of that, goals often have properties such that moving toward one tends to ensure a lack of movement toward the other. For example, it's hard to be frugal while being a patron of the arts. As many have found, it's hard to make rapid progress in developing your career and also spend large amounts of time with your family. Many conflicts are determined by the constraints of time, others by the mutual incompatibility of the behaviors needed to attain them.

In cases such as these, an act that diminishes discrepancies with respect to one goal can cause discrepancy enlargement with respect to the other goal. This is one way of conceptualizing the nature of conflict. Conflicts such as these, of course, are a major source of dissatisfaction in life (cf. Baumeister, Shapiro, & Tice, 1985; Emmons & King, 1988; Van Hook & Higgins, 1988). The more important are the goals in conflict, the greater the sense of dissatisfaction that results.

An excellent analysis of responses to conflict among goals has been provided by Dodge, Asher, and Parkhurst (1989). They pointed out that although situations sometimes require you to choose one goal and let the other go, more often this is only one of several potential responses to goal conflict. Another common response is to attempt to coordinate the goals. In many cases this becomes an issue of scheduling, so that one goal is temporarily deferred until a more pressing one is attained (cf. Simon, 1967).

Prioritizing can help, but Dodge et al. also point out that it's sometimes ineffective, if the deferred goal gets no attention until the demanding one has been fully dealt with. In such cases, effort often seems best handled by time-sharing, where the person deals with one goal for a while, then with another. Like jugglers keeping many balls in the air at once, people often manage to engage in many kinds of purposive behavior in an almost seamless braid of activity.

Another useful response is to redefine one or both goals, or negotiate changes in the criteria for goal satisfaction, so that conflict diminishes. An example given by Dodge et al. (1989) describes an adolescent who wants to go to the movies with a friend but whose mother wants him to stay home and babysit. The conflict can be reduced if the boy can change his action goal in a way that's still compatible with the higher-order goal of having fun with his friend. A substitute action goal might be to have the friend come over to watch a movie, with the babysitting occurring in a way that no longer intrudes on the two boys' shared fun. This particular example also illustrates the role of hierarchical thinking in certain kinds of goal conflict resolution.

Multiple Goals Satisfied in One Activity

In some cases, the multiple goals that the person has in mind aren't competitors, but potential collaborators. Sometimes it's possible for a pattern of action to cause the attainment of several goals at once. For example, a psychologist who publishes an article in *Psychological Review* may be enhancing a professional reputation, realizing the personal dream of seeing his or her name in that journal, moving in the direction of a big pay raise next year, and becoming more mobile professionally – all simultaneously by the same actions.

As another example, consider a man and woman planning dinner together. Among the goals behind the plan may be an exotic or interesting meal, intellectually stimulating conversation, entertaining and amusing conversation, the chance to display power and status from spending large amounts of money, a sexual interlude after dinner, further development of a positively evolving relationship, the creation of children. Other possibilities exist, of course. Although some goals place constraints on the behaviors that would fulfill them (it would be hard to display status at a fast-food drive-through), it's possible to move toward all these goals with one set of actions.

Action-identification theory (Vallacher & Wegner, 1985, 1987) says that there are many ways to identify an act and that a person holds only one identification at a time. It may be, though, that this is too simple. Perhaps many identities are operational at once, though only one is focal at any moment, with others outside awareness. An interesting question is whether multiple goals influence behavior at a low intensity outside awareness more commonly than people realize. The influence may be expressed in such form as tendencies and preferences that are taken for granted by the actor without question and thus without explanation.

PROGRAMS SEEM DIFFERENT FROM OTHER GOALS

Two more issues pertain to the idea that there's something special about program-level behavior. Aside from the fact that people seem to spend so much of life with that level functionally superordinate (a rather substantial point in itself), there are at least two ways in which behavior at this level seems to differ from behavior at other levels. We note these differences here because we find them interesting (and a little perplexing), but we don't know whether they are simply oddities or more momentous.

Analog Versus Digital Functioning

In Chapter 5 we noted that Miller, Galanter, and Pribram (1960) regarded consciously planful activity (which seems to correspond to what we've been calling the program level of control) as having a digital quality, whereas processing at lower levels has a more analog quality (see also Greene, 1972). What gives program-level functioning its digital character is the sequential decision making that occurs there.

Given the context, it's understandable that Miller et al. didn't address levels of abstraction higher than conscious planfulness. However, there do seem to be levels higher than that to consider. It's of interest that control at higher levels appears to reassume an analog form. Consider principles. Although the sense of a given principle is clear, the quality specified by a principle as a reference value doesn't correspond to a particular act, but rather to a quality that might be reflected in many acts. The psychological sense of how well you've been living up to a given principle is emergent from bits of many events. Further, it seems to be relatively easy to bring this sense to mind, and it tends to emerge with an analog feel rather than a digital feel.

The digital sense seems noticeably stronger at the program level than at levels either higher or lower. It isn't clear, however, what to make of it. Indeed, it isn't entirely clear whether this is really a difference between levels of abstractness, or whether it's really a difference between feedback systems (analog at all levels) and a different kind of function (planner or prioritizer?) that's tied for some reason to the program level.

Opportunistic Planning and Stages in Decision Making

We've been discussing goals and goal-directed behavior as though movement toward goals were continuous and uninterrupted. As long as the final purpose of the intended action is known, action proceeds. There's sketchy evidence, though, that this isn't how programs occur. At least some kinds of action appear to involve developing a partial plan or a subgoal that fits within the framework of the overall plan, executing the partial plan, then stopping and developing a further partial plan (J. R. Anderson, 1990, pp. 203–205). Even attempts at relatively thorough planning appear to be recursive and "opportunistic," changing – sometimes drastically – when unanticipated information becomes known (Hayes-Roth & Hayes-Roth, 1979; see also Gallistel, 1980; Payton, 1990).

In a similar vein, Beach (1993) argues that decision making (a program-level activity) has two separate phases. In the first phase (which he calls screening), a person evaluates available options (e.g., choices of apartments), in terms of the extent to which the options violate criteria pertaining to the eventual decision (e.g., price, size, proximity to work or other destinations). Options that violate too many criteria are rejected; those that don't are retained. Then the person goes to the second phase, the actual choice.

What's odd about the findings reported by Beach is that the process of choice seems to differ from the process of screening. It involves somewhat different criteria and in some cases relies on entirely different information. It's very much as though the person executes one partial plan ("rule out unacceptable options"), then moves to another partial plan ("choose the best of the options that are left").

Such findings suggest that people's plans – even the plans of experts – don't extend nearly as far into the future as people often assume (Gobet

& Simon, 1996). More typically, people have goals where the general terms of the end point are known, but where only the first few steps toward it have been charted. This may reflect a limitation on memory capacity, or it may reflect something basic about the planning process per se (an idea that recurs later on). In any case, the picture created by these findings is one in which more planning of action is done while in the midst of acting than is usually suggested by goal theories.

GOAL HIERARCHIES AND TRAITS

Another set of questions concerns the relation between the goal hierarchy model and the trait concept. In Chapter 5 we noted two characteristics of principles: First, principles act not by specifying behaviors across the board, but by influencing what programs to enter and what decisions to make within programs. Second, principles as qualities of behavior typically are easily described with trait labels. These observations raise interesting questions about whether the trait concept might be merged with the notion of a goal hierarchy.

Traits and Goals

These observations about the nature of principles accord quite well with findings from recent research on how people use trait concepts in describing others. For example, Wright and Mischel (1988) found that when people use traits to describe others, they typically use "hedges": words or phrases that limit the trait term's applicability (e.g., "*sometimes*," "aggressive *when* teased," "shy *when* with strangers"). These hedges imply that the behavior that's seen as reflecting the trait occurs only in particular kinds of situations. Similarly, Shoda, Mischel, and Wright (1989) found that use of trait labels is linked to trait-relevant behavior in particular kinds of situations but not in other (implicitly trait-irrelevant) situations.

More simply, the subjects in these studies don't see traits as applying to behavior in an across-the-board way. Rather, they see traits as relevant to what kinds of situations people enter and to what kinds of responses people make to events encountered there. This portrayal is very consistent with our description of principles: manifesting themselves in choices of what programs of action to enter and in choices of how to respond to behavioral contingencies within a program.

One difference is that, by implication at least, principles are constructions that are adopted as goals, whether through trial and error, verbal transmission, or bootstrapping. In contrast to this picture, at least some traits seem to be determined more directly by biological influences (e.g., Buss & Plomin, 1984). Nonetheless, they often seem to exert their influence in a principle-like way. Perhaps they should be thought of as "implicit" principles. On the other hand, perhaps our depiction of the basis for the existence of principles is wrong. Perhaps people come to know what principles they're following by observing their own behavior and acquiring labels to identify themes they see expressed there.

The notion that traits are goal-based and that they're reflected in certain kinds of actions rather than across the board also appears in other research. Read, Jones, and Miller (1990) found that people see actions as related to traits if the action is also seen as moving the actor toward a goal that's related to the trait. The surface similarity of behaviors to each other apparently isn't as good a clue about whether they reflect the same trait (see also Barsalou, 1985). These findings seem consistent with the idea that situated action sequences link upward to broader goals that take the form of principles. Other findings supportive of this general line of thought have been reported by a number of others (Carlston & Skowronski, 1994; Costa & McCrae, 1988; Park, DeKay, & Kraus, 1994; Werner & Pervin, 1986).

Viewing Others in Terms of Traits versus Actions

The notion that traits are coded in memory at the principle level, but their implications are played out in terms of programs of action, receives a somewhat different twist in research by Dweck and her colleagues. Earlier we described the finding that some people see ability as a fixed entity, whereas others see ability as changeable. There's also evidence that these people differ in how they view traits more generally (see Dweck, Hong, & Chiu, 1993).

Dweck and her colleagues found that these differences in orientation have implications for a variety of decision-making and inference processes. People who hold an entity orientation tend to view others' behavior in terms of broad dispositions. People who hold an incremental orientation tend to view behavior in terms of specific goals and actions, and in terms of situational contingencies (Dweck et al., 1993).

In light of the preceding discussion of traits and behavior, this pattern of findings suggests that some people view reality from the level of principles, whereas others view it from the level of programs (see Hoffman, Mischel, & Mazze, 1981, for discussion of this difference in processing as a function of situational variables rather than individual differences). Earlier we characterized the hierarchies of the entity and incremental viewpoints as differing in terms of the dynamic versus static quality of their goals. Taken together, the points raise a question about possible consequences of viewing the world at different levels of abstraction. It may be, for example, that relying too exclusively on high-level goals as an interpretive framework tends to promote rigidity in thinking about lower-order goals. That is, it may cause people to lose sight of the fact that programs are flexible and modifiable.

Traits and Behaviors in Memory

The preceding discussions of traits and goals, and of individual differences in the tendency to view others in terms of traits versus situated actions, relied on an assumption: that traits are encoded as goal-relevant information at the principle level, whereas situated actions are encoded as goal-relevant information at the program level. In line with this assumption, some support exists for the idea that these different kinds of memory create different sets of stored records.

Klein and Loftus (1993; Klein, Loftus, Trafton, & Fuhrman, 1992) argue that people begin representing knowledge about themselves with memories of behaviors. As the number of trait-relevant acts in memory increases, an abstract representation begins to evolve. Once this happens, a person who's asked about the trait will report from the trait-level structure. Before that structure has come to exist, though, the person will average information from the behavior memories. Klein and Loftus reported a variety of evidence fitting this picture (see also Schell, Klein, & Babey, 1996). Other research has found evidence of a similar division in encoding trait information and behavioral information in forming impressions of others (Carlston & Skowronski, 1986).

The idea of different sorts of storage is also supported by striking anecdotal evidence. Tulving (1993) reported the case of an amnesic patient (with a severe brain injury), who can't recall specific behavioral events from any period of his life, but who can describe his traits in detail and with considerable accuracy. He can do this despite the fact that he apparently has no access to the behavioral exemplars that would permit him to generate a summary report of his traits. This would seem to confirm that he isn't generating the summary, just reporting it.

These sources of data appear to converge on the idea that memory regarding one's own behavior forms a hierarchy of related but distinguishable sets of structures (see also Lichtenstein & Brewer, 1980). This, in turn, is consistent with the idea that goals themselves form a hierarchy.

GOALS AND THE SELF

From consideration of traits, we turn to an even thornier question. What is the self? We focus here on self as "content" (James, 1890). The kinds of theories discussed in Chapter 5 view the content of the self as including knowledge about one's history and knowledge about who one is at present. These can both be conceptualized as working models, accepted and used for the present but in constant evolution (even your sense of your past is amenable to reconstruction). Another aspect of the self is the self-guides or possible selves used to move from the present into the future (which may also be working models). The broad implication of this sort of theory is that the self is partly the person's goals.

A question that's interesting to pose but hard to answer is how many layers of a person's goals should be considered to fall under the label "self"? Most would certainly agree that a person's sense of idealized self belongs to the self, and most would probably say the same for an ought self (though not all would agree about this – a point to which we return momentarily). Since these values so readily translate into principles of conduct, it seems likely that most people would agree that guiding principles are also elements of the self.

But where are the limits? How far down the hierarchy can we go and have it still be sensible? Are the goals that define programs of activity part of the self? Certainly each person individualizes the pattern of goals that make up even such commonly held programs of action as doing the laundry or taking a holiday trip. Furthermore, people differ from one another in what programs they do and don't engage in. But does that make these goal structures part of the self? We have no clear answer.

We do have a stronger sense of the answer to a related question, though: What are the limits to the self that are implied when discussing self-awareness (as in Chapter 3)? Data on self-regulatory effects of self-focus appear to suggest that the effects of self-awareness are exerted on behavior at the principle and program levels. Manipulations that reduce self-focus (deindividuation, alcohol consumption) typically produce effects with characteristics of sequence control (control at a lower level). That is, behavior becomes highly responsive to contextual cues and unresponsive to preplanned programs or principles. Thus, there's some precedent for equating reduction in self-focus with suspension of self-regulation at the program level and higher.

Does this mean there's no self at lower levels? The answer to this question may be a matter of definition. The sequences that are programmed into people's repertoires differ from one person to another, with a distinctiveness that may connote selfhood. On the other hand, these bits of action are so concrete and minimal that it may not be useful to think of them as elements of the self. This issue seems more a matter of preference than a matter of one answer being intrinsically right and the other wrong.

Self-Determination Theory and the Self

Although we think the view on the self outlined in the preceding section will seem reasonable to many, not everyone will agree with all of it. A likely source of disagreement derives from self-determination theory (Deci & Ryan, 1985, 1991; Ryan, 1993; Ryan, Sheldon, Kasser, & Deci, 1996).

This theory holds that self-determined actions are done out of interest in the activity or the belief that the activity is intrinsically valuable. Controlled actions are done for extrinsic reasons, to gain payment or to satisfy some sort of pressure or demand. Behaviors can be controlled even if the control happens entirely inside your own mind. Thus, someone who does something because he knows he'd feel guilty if he didn't is engaging in controlled behavior. Deci, Ryan, and their colleagues argue that conceptions of goals and the self are incomplete unless they address this divergence in the needs that the goals serve. According to this view, goals are not all equivalent, because of these distinct underlying dynamics.

The critical issue in self-determination theory appears to concern the extent to which actions are integrated into the structure of the self (see also McGregor & Little, 1998). The most important distinction is between what's called *introjected* regulation and *identified* regulation. In introjected regulation, the goal has been adopted as a goal but not incorporated into the self. The behavior thus is controlled, though the control is intrapsychic (a sense of guilt or concern about loss of others' esteem). Close examination of self-report items used to assess this tendency (e.g., Ryan, Rigby, & King, 1993, p. 591; see also Ryan & Connell, 1989, p. 752) suggests that introjected values are very similar to *oughts*. They involve moving toward a value in order to avoid disapproval or self-disapproval.

Identified regulation occurs when the behavior is accepted by the individual as personally important and meaningful. Although it began with an extrinsic motive, the person now sees authentic value in it. At this stage the activity has begun to be integrated within the person's coherent sense of self. Such behaviors are self-determined and authentic, reflecting the total involvement of the self.

What's important about this view at the moment is a limitation it suggests on the content of the self. Self in this theory is limited to the integrated values representing the true self. Deci and Ryan wouldn't agree that what Higgins (1987, 1996) calls the ought self is part of the true self. The ought self is a coercive and controlling force, because the person conforms to its values in order to avoid disapproval or self-disapproval. The feared self is even more coercive, for obvious reasons.

The true self, in this view, is restricted to ideals that are integrated with whatever is the person's intrinsic self. Even the role of ideals can be a little tricky, because what you think of as an ideal can actually be controlling, if you use it in a self-coercive way by holding it as a condition of self-worth. The key is whether the behavior is done with self-determination and authenticity.

Are Deci and Ryan right? How to reply appears to depend partly on how you feel about issues of approach and avoidance. That is, the essence of a controlling force on behavior appears to be that at its heart is the engagement of an avoidance tendency. If so, perhaps *any* activity that's done with the ultimate purpose of avoiding an anti-goal fails to involve the true self, by definition. The difference between goals that connect to the true self and goals that don't may reduce to whether the fundamental impulse stems from an approach system or from an avoidance system.

Self-determination theory is one of several theories that cause us to reflect on the balance of forces between self and society. That is, the pressures that Deci and Ryan call "controlling" have their origins in the social matrix. These pressures represent the recurrent clash between the desires of the individual and the needs of society. Whether these pressures connect to the self or not, they certainly are reflected in the arrangements of goals that develop in people's minds as guides for action. For this and other reasons, the distinction between goals that reflect personal desires and goals that reflect the social matrix is an important one. It is the topic of the next chapter.

7

Public and Private Aspects of the Self

> To thine own self be true.
> (William Shakespeare, *Hamlet*)

> What it came down to, stupidly, was a sense of shame. Hot, stupid
> shame. I did not want people to think badly of me.... I would go to
> war – I would kill and maybe die – because I was embarrassed not to.
> (Tim O'Brien, *The Things They Carried*)

The two previous chapters addressed goals underlying behavior. We
made several distinctions there, aimed mostly at conceptualizing differences between long-term and short-term goals, abstract and concrete
goals. In this chapter we address another kind of distinction.

Here we reflect on the fact that some of the goals that lie behind behavior are private and personal. They don't take into account the wishes,
desires, or sometimes even the *existence* of other people. In contrast,
other goals explicitly take into account the wishes and desires of other
people. This chapter focuses on the divergence between these classes
of goals. There are several ways to take other people into account, and
that's part of the story as well.

ASPECTS OF SELF

The themes of this chapter are rooted deeply in psychology – rooted not
in the goal construct so much as in the concept of self. James (1890,
pp. 292–305), discussing the idea that the self is multifaceted, distin-
guished between what he called the *spiritual self* and the *social self*. The
spiritual self is the inner subjective being, the person's dispositions. It's
the part of self that welcomes or rejects experiences. For James, this is
the control center of behavior and perception.

The social self involves recognition and responses from other people.
James noted a great potential diversity within the social self: Because

many people can respond to a given person, he or she can have as many social selves as there are others to respond. James quickly conceded, however, that those others tend to cluster into meaningful groups. Thus, a person might be thought of as having as many social selves as there are *groups* of people whose opinion he or she cares and thinks about.

The distinction between spiritual and social selves was later embellished by Wylie (1968). In writing about the self-concept, Wylie described a matrix of social and private conceptions of the self, both actual and ideal. In her depiction, social and private differ from each other in much the way as was suggested by James, though there's a stronger sense of personal, individualized goals (as opposed to self as center of experience) in Wylie's depiction of the private self. Wylie saw these various aspects of self as contributing to a broader, all-encompassing self-concept.[1]

The conceptual distinction between private and public aspects of self was reemphasized in subsequent work by Fenigstein, Scheier, and Buss (1975). Wylie wrote about the self-concept. Fenigstein et al. were less interested in that than in how the various aspects of the self influence behavior. As we mentioned in Chapter 3, they developed a self-report measure of the tendency to be self-reflective, to be conscious of the self from moment to moment. What we did *not* mention in Chapter 3 is that this measure embodies the distinction between private and public aspects of the self. In essence, Fenigstein et al. said it's too simplistic to talk about the involvement of the self in behavior, because the self has two facets, each of which may influence behavior.

What they called *private self-conciousness*, measured by items such as "I think about myself a lot," is the tendency to be aware of one's thoughts, feelings, private motives, and desires. *Public self-consciousness*, measured by items such as "I care a lot about how I present myself to others" and "I'm usually aware of my appearance," is the tendency to be aware of oneself in relation to others, to think of oneself as a social object to which other people react. Fenigstein et al. assumed that the tendencies to be aware of these different facets of the self (tendencies that vary separately) relate to different aspects of people's experience and action.

---

[1] Although treatment of developmental issues falls outside the scope of our discussion, we note that many perspectives on social development assume developmental shifts in modes of self-regulation (e.g., Kochanska, 1993; Kopp, 1982). Very young children respond to immediate desires and impulses. Later there emerges a responsiveness to external (largely social) contingencies. It seems not too far a stretch to suggest that the former mode of functioning corresponds roughly to self-regulation via the private self, and the latter to self-regulation via the public self (Froming, Moser, Mychack, & Nasby, 1995). The even later shift to internalized rules for self-regulation can potentially reflect either public or private aspects of the self.

Early research demonstrated that this is indeed the case (for more extensive review, see Carver & Scheier, 1985, 1987). For example, private self-consciousness relates to an enhanced awareness of (private) emotional states (Scheier, 1976; Scheier & Carver, 1977), and to an enhanced awareness of the *absence* of anticipated internal bodily experiences (Gibbons, Carver, Scheier, & Hormuth, 1979; Scheier, Carver, & Gibbons, 1979). Public self-consciousness predicted enhanced awareness of an interpersonal snub (Fenigstein, 1979), greater tendencies to use makeup and clothing strategically to influence self-portrayals (Miller & Cox, 1981; Solomon & Schopler, 1982), accuracy in predicting the impressions that would form in the minds of a group of strangers (Tobey & Tunnell, 1981), and the use of reference groups to determine opinions (Carver & Humphries, 1981, discussed in Chapter 4). In general, findings showed that the aspect of self-consciousness that was not expected to relate to these phenomena wasn't related to them. Thus, for example, public self-consciousness was unrelated to awareness of internal states, and private self-consciousness was unrelated to strategic use of clothing and makeup.

Once a literature of self-consciousness phenomena had begun to develop, researchers began to reconsider the idea that experimental manipulations of self-focus have uniform effects. A close examination of the evidence suggested a divergence among manipulations (Carver & Scheier, 1987). Certain manipulations appear to focus attention selectively on the social side of the self – for example, video cameras, the sound of one's own voice, the presence of an evaluative audience. Other manipulations appear to focus attention differentially on the private side of the self – for example, a small mirror image of one's face.

Further Distinctions

The distinction between private and social aspects of the self is an important one, but even greater complexity resides within each of these domains. For example, there are several ways to take other people into account. Sometimes you want to please them, sometimes you want to annoy them (cf. Shibutani, 1961, p. 195). Sometimes you want to share with them, sometimes you want to barter with them (Clark & Mills, 1979, 1993; Mills & Clark, 1982). Sometimes you want only to make a particular impression on them.

Indeed, there are also at least two ways to take *yourself* into account. You can have deep commitment to pursuit of your own values; alternatively, you can be focused on maintaining an acceptable self-image

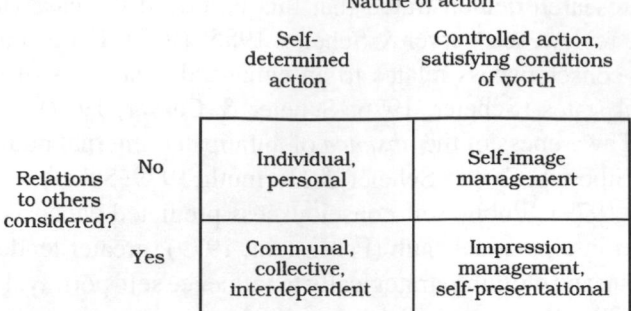

Figure 7.1.   Some goals underlying behavior are purely self-relevant, with the self's own interest as the entire focus (top row); other goals take into account other people and the relation between them and the self (bottom row). Some goals within each of these categories lead to self-determined action (left column); others lead to action that is more controlled, aimed at satisfying some condition of worth (right column).

for your own consumption (Greenwald, 1982). These various distinctions create further complexity in thinking about the goals underlying behavior (see Figure 7.1).

Some classes of goals underlying behavior seem purely self-relevant, since the goal is personal and aimed at an interest that directly concerns only the self (top row of Figure 7.1). These classes of goals correspond to what we've been calling the private side of the self. One of these classes of goals is self-determined and intrinsic (Deci & Ryan, 1985, 1991; Ryan, 1993; Ryan, Sheldon, Kasser, & Deci, 1996). It involves living up to your own personal values or pursuing your own interests. We refer to those here as *individual* or *personal* goals. The other class of self-relevant goals seems more defensive or controlled, involving the creation of a situation that protects self-esteem. We refer to these goals here as *self-image management* goals (after Greenwald, 1982).

The other two classes of goals in Figure 7.1 (bottom row) involve other people in one fashion or another (though more elaborate distinctions can be made among social goals – for example, see Fiske, 1992, and Mills & Clark, 1982 – we won't go into them here). These various goals correspond to what we've been calling the public side of self. One class is self-determined and intrinsic. These goals involve living up to desired images of relationships or mutually shared goals. We refer to those here as *communal, collective,* or *interdependent* goals. The other class appears more controlled (cf. Enzle & Anderson, 1993).

They involve displaying the self to create particular impressions in the minds of others. We refer to those here as *impression-management* or *self-presentational* goals.

Recent Statements

The distinctions we've been discussing here have been in the literature of psychology for a long time. However, recent years have seen a resurgence of interest in them. Many authors have begun to focus on the idea that the self has multiple facets and to consider how the self is involved in social interaction. This resurgence of interest has, for example, inspired recent special issues in the two primary journals of personality and social psychology (Kruglanski, Miller, & Geen, 1996; Miller & Prentice, 1994; see also Baumeister, 1986; Suls, 1993).

A prime impetus to this resurgence of interest appears to have been a growing interest in cultural differences (and a continuing recognition of gender differences; see Brunstein, Dangelmayer, & Schultheiss, 1996; Cross & Madson, 1997; Helgeson, 1994) in how various goals are embedded within the sense of self. Several theorists have proposed models that contrast an individualist cultural orientation with a communal orientation (Brewer, 1991; Landrine, 1992; Markus & Kitayama, 1991, 1994; Triandis, 1989). Western cultures tend to have an individualist focus, whereas Eastern cultures tend to have a collectivist or communal focus. These theorists (and others) have explored in some depth the considerable implications of these differences.[2]

Such differences are reflected in a variety of ways. For example, subjects from collectivist countries show higher levels of conformity in lab settings than do subjects from individualist countries (Bond & Smith, 1996). Spontaneous self-descriptions given by subjects in collectivist societies include more group-linked elements than appear in descriptions from subjects in individualist societies (Triandis, McCusker, & Hui, 1990), and the values that members espouse reflect promotion of group welfare and individual goals, respectively. The personalities ascribed to attractive persons are more socially focused in collectivist societies than in individualist societies (Wheeler & Kim, 1997). There's also evidence that social influence in the two kinds of cultures differs in

---

[2] Rhee, Uleman, and Lee (1996) have shown that even the dichotomy between these two categories of orientation is an oversimplification. Their data reveal both a collectivism and individualism that are specific to kin, and a distinct collectivism and individualism that apply to non-kin relationships.

form: Persuasive messages in individualist countries appeal to personal preferences, those in collectivist countries appeal to ingroup harmony and mutual benefit. Further, messages that match the culture-appropriate pattern are most persuasive (Han & Shavitt, 1994).

Clearly, cultures differ from one another in the balance of influence of self-presentational, collective/communal, individualist/personal, and self-image management goals. Our interest here, however, is not how cultures diverge from one another, but how the qualities that are manifest to different degrees in different cultures are manifest from one time or situation to another in the behavior of a member of *any* culture. To put it differently, cultural differences are of interest here primarily as they illuminate differences among classes of goals that are relevant to all humans.

Aspects of Self and Classes of Goal

The previous sections outlined several conceptual frameworks which assume several potential orientations to experience. The frameworks tend to focus on issues concerning the existence of diverse aspects of the self and the broader question of what the self is (see also Crocker, Luhtanen, Blaine, & Broadnax, 1994; Neisser, 1993). Although these questions are important in their own right, we want to tie them explicitly to the goal concepts of the preceding two chapters.

As we said in Chapter 5, we believe that at a high level of abstraction a person can take several values as goals for self-regulation. These include the idealized sense of self, the idealized sense of a relationship, and the idealized sense of a communal group (cf. Landrine, 1992). There may be an overarching sense of self that incorporates all of these. At a minimum, however, these various sorts of qualities are available for most people for use as positive points of reference for self-regulation.

A central theme of this chapter is that these classes of goals – personal, collective, self-image management, self-presentational – are represented in the self-regulatory potential of all (or at least most) people. Everyone sometimes does things for purely personal reasons. Everyone sometimes does things for mutual benefit with someone else. Everyone sometimes acts in ways calculated to satisfy pressures from someone else or the pressures of a need for self-acceptance. To the extent that each of these categories of goals is represented in the hierarchy that makes up a

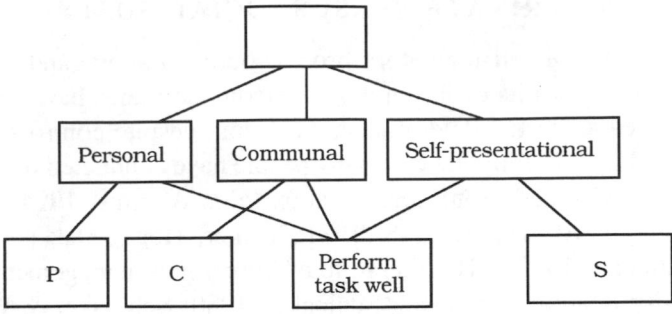

Figure 7.2. Athough some programs entered to satisfy personal goals (P) may be activities different from those entered to satisfy communal (C) or self-presentational goals (S), this is certainly not always the case. Many programmatic actions relate equally well to all such higher-order goals. For example, whether a person wants to perform well on a task to satisfy self-imposed demands or to satisfy social demands, the result is still an attempt to perform well. Therefore, for many concrete actions, it can be very difficult to tell which sort of goal underlies it.

person's self, these goal sets seem to be aspects of the self. Further, to the extent that a given strategy is taken up as an active goal, it will be reflected in that person's behavioral self-regulation.

We take no particular stand on how these goals are organized – with one exception. From the level of program control on downward, the control of a particular action must be virtually identical, whether the goal is personal or communal, intrinsically motivated or self-presentational. Only at a higher level (the level of personal versus communal purposes) does the behavior differ. For this reason, when you observe someone perform a concrete action, it can be very difficult to tell which of these sorts of goal underlies it.

This issue also has an implication for planning research to investigate the role of the private and social facets of the self in behavior: Although some actions are uniquely specified by personal, communal, or self-presentational goals, other actions are not. In the latter cases, attending to the pursuit of any of those goals would yield the same effect. For example, whether you want to perform well on a task in order to satisfy self-imposed demands or to satisfy social demands, the result is still an attempt to perform well (Figure 7.2). Studying such a situation won't provide much information on the relative involvement of different self-aspects.

BEHAVIORAL SELF-REGULATION
AND PRIVATE VERSUS SOCIAL GOALS

Each domain of self-regulatory process outlined above and portrayed in Figure 7.1 has its own literature. Personal attitudes have long been recognized as partial determinants of action, despite controversy over the breadth of their influence. Many people have conducted research on social identity and group identification (e.g., Abrams, 1994; Abrams & Hogg, 1990; Tajfel, 1978, 1981; Turner, Hogg, Oakes, Reicher, & Wetherall, 1987). The literature of impression management is also extensive (Baumeister, 1982; Schlenker, 1980; Schlenker & Weigold, 1992). Discussions of the management of the self-image, though perhaps less common than these others, are not entirely lacking (Baumgardner, 1990; Greenwald, 1982; Greenwald & Breckler, 1985; Leary, 1993; Schlenker, 1980).

It's not our intent here to review these separate literatures. Rather, we want to address the interplay among the processes that underlie each of them. We do so in a framework informed by the goal construct. Simply put, we assume here that when social goals are especially valued by a person or especially salient to the person, social goals will dominate action. When personal goals are especially valued or especially salient, personal goals will dominate action.

Formation of Intentions

One literature in which the mutual and simultaneous influences of personal and social goals has long been recognized bears on the creation of intentions (Ajzen, 1985, 1988; Ajzen & Fishbein, 1980). The Ajzen and Fishbein model of intention formation involves a kind of mental algebra, integrating information and resulting in a probability of doing the behavior. If the probability is high enough, an intention to act forms.

Ajzen and Fishbein suggested that when people are thinking about undertaking an action, they take into account several kinds of information (Figure 7.3). The first is what outcomes the action will produce. The second is how much you personally want those outcomes. These two sources of information integrate to form an *attitude* about the behavior, a personal orientation to the act being considered.

The third and fourth kinds of information pertain to the perceived social meaning of the act. One kind of information is your belief about whether other people who matter to you want you to perform the action.

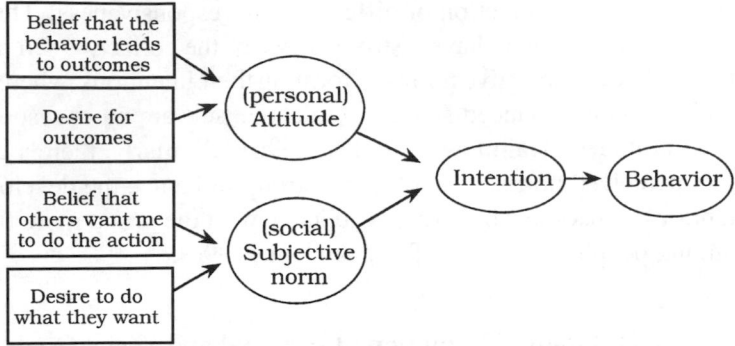

Figure 7.3.   Ajzen and Fishbein's (1980) theory proposes that intentions derive from both attitudes (which reflect personal desires) and subjective norms (which reflect social contingencies), which are weighted separately. Of particular interest is what occurs when the attitude and the subjective norm conflict with each other, and the conflict must be dealt with in forming the intention.

The other is how much you want to do what they want you to do (because you care about them, or to create a good impression, or for whatever reason – the theory doesn't distinguish among these possibilities). These two sources of information integrate to form a *subjective norm* concerning the action.[3]

The final step in forming the intention is to weigh the importance of the (personal) attitude and the (social) subjective norm. From this weighing and integrating comes the *intention*. If the attitude and subjective norm are both positive, you'll form a strong intention to do the behavior. If attitude and subjective norm are negative, you'll form a strong intention not to do the behavior.

The process is more complex (and more interesting) when the attitude and the subjective norm conflict. Sometimes you want the outcome that a behavior will lead to, but you know your friends or your spouse or your boss (or some other significant others) don't want you to perform it (or vice versa). In this situation, your intention depends on which is more important to you – satisfying yourself or satisfying your significant others.

The idea that people vary in how responsive they are to individual and collective goals has important implications for the formation of intentions. The impact of the attitude and the subjective norm on the intention

[3] Ajzen (1985, 1988) added a fifth element to this theory, but for present purposes we can ignore it.

should vary as a function of differences in responsiveness. This seems to be so. People who have a strong sense of the collective self are more responsive to subjective norms in forming their intentions, whereas those with a less pronounced sense of collective self are more responsive to their attitudes (Trafimow & Finlay, 1996). Similarly, there's evidence that perceived norms of a reference group influence the developing intentions of people who strongly identify with the group more than than among people who don't (Terry & Hogg, 1996).

Differential Valuation of Personal and Social Goals

There's no question that people differ reliably from each other in the extent to which they value personal versus social aspects of their identity. Cheek and Briggs (1982) developed a measure of these tendencies, and later expanded it to incorporate a distinction between self-presentational and collective elements in identity (Cheek, 1989).

Individual differences in the valuation of these aspects of the self are related to a number of other differences. For example, consider how people handle issues associated with the development of a sense of identity. Berzonsky (1994) found that people who emphasize the private aspects of self on this measure also report spending time seeking out self-relevant information, trying to develop a set of values that make sense to them. People who emphasize the collective aspects of identity are more likely to rely on norms and expectations and standards held for them by significant others. In dealing with questions of identity they turn to these values, rather than seek out personally meaningful information. People who emphasize self-presentational aspects of identity also report relying on norms and expectations of significant others, but they differ from those who emphasize collective aspects of identity in tending to try to avoid confronting issues of identity at all.

Cheek and Briggs (1982) also found an association between valuing a particular aspect of the self and tending to think about that aspect of self. That is, people who emphasize private aspects of the self are high in private self-consciousness. People who emphasize social aspects of the self are high in public self-consciousness. Similar effects have been reported by several other researchers (Lamphere & Leary, 1990; Penner & Wymer, 1983; Schlenker & Weigold, 1990). In the same vein, Oyserman (1993) found that endorsing individualism as a world view was related to private self-consciousness, whereas endorsement of collectivism as a world view was related to public self-consciousness.

This pattern of associations can be interpreted in either of two ways. It seems consistent with the idea that emphasis on or valuation of a particular aspect of one's identity leads to a search for information bearing on that self-aspect, a search that ultimately focuses partly on that aspect of self. Alternatively, one might argue that the tendency to be absorbed in some aspect of the self leads one to place greater value on that aspect of one's identity.

SELF-CONSCIOUSNESS AND SELF-AWARENESS IN SELF-REGULATION

In either case, a link appears to exist between valuing an aspect of the self and thinking about or attending to it. Recall that self-focused attention produces effects on behavior that appear to reflect the engagement of feedback processes regulating behavior with respect to desired goals. If focus on the *self* causes the engagement of self-regulatory activity, it follows that focusing on different *aspects* of the self may cause the engagement of self-regulatory activity of potentially different sorts. This does not mean different in the sense of different regulatory *functions* (Carver & Scheier, 1987), but different in terms of the *goals* or *reference values* underlying the activities.

This idea cannot be tested indiscriminantly. As we said earlier, in predicting some kinds of behavior, it hardly matters whether the goal is personal, communal, or self-presentational. That is, in some cases, attending to the pursuit of any of these goals would yield the same effect. Of far greater relevance are cases in which the various facets of the self make competing demands, where the pressures they bring to bear conflict with one another (Figure 7.4). These conflicts aren't always present, but when they are, they can be used to illuminate the self-regulatory process. In this section we focus on situations with such conflicting pressures.

Anticipating Interaction

The process of social interaction often begins before the people involved even encounter each other. That is, simply anticipating that you'll be interacting in a casual, nonadversarial way with a stranger often evokes concerns about making a good impression. One strategy that people sometimes use when preparing to interact with strangers is to moderate, or make more neutral, the opinions they'll be displaying to those

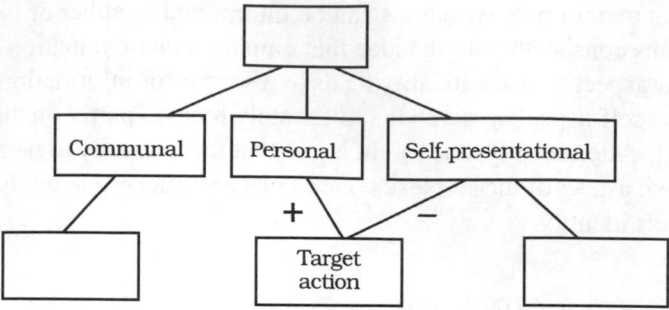

Figure 7.4. Sometimes personal desires and self-presentational pressures conflict with each other, such that one suggests the desirability of behaving in a particular way (+) and the other suggests that this behavior should *not* take place (−).

strangers (e.g., Cialdini, Levy, Herman, Kozlowski, & Petty, 1976; Newtson & Czerlinsky, 1974). This strategy – "smoothing the edges" off your public display – minimizes the chances of offending the other person by appearing to take an extreme or deviant position. For this reason, it's useful in making a good impression.

This tactic clearly takes into account other people's sensibilities. Therefore, this tactic should be linked to focus on the public aspect of self – that is, focus on your existence as a social object to which other people react. It seems likely, on the other hand, that focus on private self-aspects won't prompt sensitivity to those considerations. Indeed, people especially attentive to their private self-aspects may be especially likely to try to portray themselves exactly as they see themselves.

This reasoning was tested in a study in which subjects reported their attitudes on a particular issue at two different times (Scheier, 1980). The first report was made in a preliminary session when self-presentational pressures were expected to be minimal. The second was made during a session conducted separately for each person. Subjects were told they'd be describing their opinions in a brief essay, and later on they'd discuss the same issue with another participant. In reality this discussion never took place. It was mentioned in order to plant the idea in subjects' minds that they'd have to orchestrate a self-presentation a bit later. If anticipation of the interaction caused moderation of opinions, it should have been displayed in the essays subjects wrote.

Focus on the public self was expected to enhance this moderation, and the essays revealed exactly that pattern. Public self-consciousness was associated with expression of more moderated (more neutral) opinions in the essay than had been expressed on the earlier questionnaires. In contrast, private self-consciousness related to a tendency to report opinions very similar to those expressed during the earlier session.

Conformity

The effects of attending to public and private self-aspects while engaging in overt behavior have also been examined. Consider, for example, what may be the most basic self-presentational dilemma of all: that faced by the person who confronts a unanimous group which has taken a position the person thinks is wrong. People often bend to the implicit pressure of groups, even to the point of disregarding evidence provided by their own senses (cf. Asch, 1951, 1956; Crutchfield, 1955). Presumably the conformity that occurs in this research reflects self-presentational concerns. People want to avoid "making waves," or being disagreeable, and therefore go along with the majority even when they believe the majority is incorrect.

This is the sort of effect that should be linked to a sensitivity to one's public display. The more conscious of that display you are, the more likely you are to be concerned about appearing deviant. What would be the effect of attending to the private self in this situation? It seems plausible that this would lead your own personal impression to be more salient to you, and thus cause you to rely on it more than would otherwise be the case. Indeed, it might even cause you to *assert* your own opinion more than would otherwise be the case. Note that these predictions for the effects of focusing on the social and private facets of self are separate predictions, rather than opposite sides of the same coin.

These predictions were tested in a study in which subjects participating in group sessions had to count sets of metronome clicks (Froming & Carver, 1981). After each set, each person in the group was to report via intercom how many clicks there'd been. In reality, all the reports the subject heard over headphones came from a prerecorded tape. On some trials, the voices reported the correct number. On the critical trials, the supposed group members all reported a number that was wrong. The dependent measure was the frequency with which the subjects went along with the group and reported the wrong answer themselves.

As expected, conformity to the incorrect majority was positively related to level of public self-consciousness. Independent of this, private self-consciousness related to greater defiance of the majority (more frequent reporting of the values that subjects' own ears had told them were correct). Thus focusing on the public self appears to promote a tendency to go along with a group; focusing on the private self appears to promote a tendency to ignore the group and go one's own way. Similar findings were later reported by Santee and Maslach (1982).

Schlenker and Weigold (1990) have suggested that the kinds of effects we're describing are mediated at least in part by a process we haven't yet considered. In particular, they argued that people high in private self-consciousness are trying to establish an image (maybe to others, maybe to themselves) of being independent. This interpretation is consistent with the findings we just reviewed, but it suggests greater complexity in the self-regulatory processes associated with private self-consciousness than we've assumed thus far.

Attitudes, Subjective Norms, and Behavior

The Froming and Carver study drew directly from a literature on responses to implicit social pressure. But that surely isn't the only context in which a contrast can arise between social pressure and a person's own beliefs. Earlier in the chapter we described a theory of formation of intentions, in which people weigh their personal attitudes against the social norms they see as held by salient reference groups. Our earlier discussion focused on attitudes and norms as determinants of intentions. Now we consider how these influences apply to overt behavior.

Research on this issue was conducted by Froming, Walker, and Lopyan (1982). They selected as subjects people who satisfied two criteria. First, they had a specific personal opinion about the use of punishment as a technique to promote learning (either favoring or opposing its use). Second, they also reported the belief (as a subjective norm) that "most people" hold the opposite opinion. These participants later came to individual sessions in which they were instructed to teach a concept to a supposed co-subject. An apparatus was used to present stimuli, determine the correctness of responses, and deliver punishments. Every time the learner made an incorrect response, the subject punished him, choosing from among 10 levels available. The supposed co-subject, however, was actually making a preplanned series of "correct" and "incorrect" responses, and was recording the punishment intensities.

Froming et al. didn't examine the effects of individual differences in self-consciousness in this research. Rather, they varied subjects' attentional focus by experimental manipulations. In one condition, a small mirror was suspended from the apparatus in front of the participant,

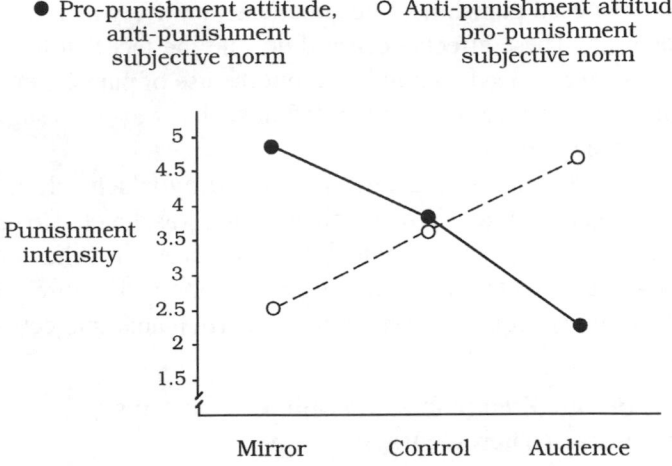

Figure 7.5. Some participants opposed the use of punishment but believed (as a subjective norm) that "most people" favor it. Others favored the use of punishment for learning but believed (as a subjective norm) that "most people" oppose it. Both types of participant later came to a laboratory, where they tried to teach a concept by punishing incorrect responses. Compared to a control condition, the presence of a small mirror caused the behavior of both types of subjects to conform to their attitudes, and the presence of an evaluative audience caused them to conform to their subjective norms. (Based on data from Froming et al., 1982, combining data from experiments 1 and 2.)

above the control panel. In another condition, an audience of evaluative observers was standing next to the apparatus while the subject was trying to teach the concept. These two manipulations were both expected to direct subjects' attention toward themselves, but toward different *aspects* of the self – private and public, respectively. This was predicted to cause heightened responsiveness to personal attitudes in the first group, and to subjective norms in the second group.

The results of the research supported this reasoning (see Figure 7.5). Compared to a control condition, the presence of the mirror caused subjects to behave in a fashion that was more consistent with their personal attitudes. That is, subjects who opposed the use of punishment as a teaching tool used *less* punishment if the mirror was there; subjects who favored punishment used *more* punishment if the mirror was there.

The presence of an evaluative audience – as predicted – had precisely the opposite influence. Rather than promoting conformity to attitudes, the presence of the audience promoted conformity to subjective norms. Subjects who thought "most people" favored punishment became more punitive when the audience was present; those who thought "most people" opposed punishment became less punitive when the audience was present. These effects occurred despite the fact that the audience members never voiced an opinion about the use of punishment, and the fact that the audience was not labeled in such a way as to suggest they held a particular opinion.

Thus, overt action was greatly influenced by which self-aspect was focal in subjects' minds. When their attention was directed to the private side of the self, personal attitudes were reflected in behavior. When attention was directed to the public side of the self, entirely different qualities emerged, qualities reflecting the participants' subjective norms.

Private Preferences and Subjective Norms Vary in Their Content

The pattern displayed in this research allows us to point to a more general theme that characterizes this literature. It's a relatively subtle point, but an important one: Specifically, neither the private side of the self nor the public side of the self is intrinsically linked to a particular content quality of behavior. That is, whatever value is held as a personal attitude is what emerges in a person's behavior when that person's attention is directed to that private goal for action. For some people, the private self specifies punishment as good; for others the private self specifies punishment as bad. Thus, for some people in the research conducted by Froming et al., focusing on the private self resulted in reduced punishment; for others, focusing on the private self resulted in increased punishment.

In the same fashion, subjective norms can vary from person to person, or even from context to context. Whatever behavioral value is held as a subjective norm (or is created in the context as a subjective norm) is what will emerge in behavior when attention is directed to the social side of the self. Thus, for some people in the Froming et al. research, focusing on the social self resulted in reduced punishment; for others it resulted in increased punishment.

This conceptual point is also illustrated by a set of studies on distributive justice (Greenberg, 1982; Kernis & Reis, 1984). This work examines how people allocate rewards when more than one person has contributed to the outcome prompting the reward. The context in which the allocation occurs can vary in many ways. Self-presentational pressures can be created to favor use of an equity norm (reward proportional to input) or to favor use of a parity norm (equal reward). In the same manner, situational cues can evoke a private sense that allocation should be equal or a private sense that allocation should be proportional.

In the studies by Greenberg (1982) and by Kernis and Reis (1984), subjects whose attention was directed to the social self conformed to the value that had been evoked as a self-presentational standard. However, the salient self-presentational value varied from study to study. Thus, attention to the social self moved behavior in opposite directions (toward equity and toward equality) in the two projects. In the same way, when attention was directed to the private self, subjects conformed to the value that was evoked as the private standard. But these values also varied from study to study. Thus, attention to the private self also moved behavior in opposite directions in the two projects.

In sum, a single process can shift behavior in opposite directions, depending on what value has become plugged in as the reference value for the feedback loop. To the extent that different values are elicited in people's minds as communal goals (or self-presentational goals) in different contexts, focusing on the social side of the self will cause behavior to shift in divergent directions in those contexts. To the extent that different values are elicited in people's minds as personal goals in different contexts, focusing on the private side of the self will cause people's behavior to shift in divergent directions.

More generally, of course, focusing on the private versus public aspects of the self is nothing more than taking one package of goals as salient, rather than another package of goals. In either case, the goals that are taken up and attended to are the ones that become manifest in actions. Thus, what can appear to be vast differences between people, and even cultures, really reflect a common set of functions, but using different goals for guidance.

8

Control Processes and Affect

> It is the striving toward the known goal that confers unity,
> not the successful arrival.
> (Gordon Allport, *Personality: A Psychological Interpretation*)

> And later, much later, he realized it was the going itself,
> not the arriving, for which he cared.
> (Jeffrey A. Carver, *Panglor*)

Much of human behavior is accompanied by feelings, good and bad.
During an average day most people experience brief (and sometimes
more extended) periods of anxiety, sadness, irritation, and happiness.
Often there are also passing moments of guilt, shame, joy, envy, jealousy,
and relief. Although most people go through occasional periods in which
emotions are relatively absent, affect is an important part of life. Our
feelings color our experiences in ways that make those experiences three-
dimensional. In doing so, feelings tell us critical things about those
experiences.

In this chapter, we consider feelings and their origins. Many theorists
have analyzed the kinds of information feelings provide and the kinds
of situations in which they come to exist (e.g., Frijda, 1986; Izard, 1977;
Lazarus, 1991; Ortony, Clore, & Collins, 1988; Roseman, 1984; Scherer
& Ekman, 1984). The question we address here is a slightly different
one, however: What's the internal mechanism by which good and bad
feelings come to arise?

What creates affect? This is a deceptively simple question. Some
would say good feelings come from getting what you want – goal
attainment – and bad feelings come from failing to get what you want,
or from exposure to punishers. There's some truth to these observations,
but it seems to us that something's wrong with this view – something
incomplete, or something not taken properly into account. For example,
this view doesn't seem to deal well with the fact that affect sometimes
arises on the way to goals, rather than at their attainment (or the failure of

their attainment). Nor does it fit the fact that negative affect sometimes occurs when goals are close or even attained, and that positive affect sometimes occurs when goals are far away.

Prompted in part by issues such as these, we've proposed a different answer to the question (Carver & Scheier, 1990a). The reasoning behind our answer deals with the fact that feelings exist on the way to goals, and the fact that feelings while on the way can be either good or bad. It also suggests a reason why goal attainment sometimes prompts sadness rather than happiness. This model of the source of affect is the subject of this chapter.

GOALS, RATE OF PROGRESS, AND AFFECT

In Chapter 3 we characterized self-regulation as a process of monitoring the results of ongoing actions and comparing what we see to salient reference values, making adjustments as necessary to minimize discrepancies. Think of this feedback process as *monitoring*. We suggest there's a second kind of feedback process that builds on this, builds in a sense very different from the notion of hierarchical organization. This second process operates simultaneously with the monitoring function and in parallel to it, whenever monitoring is occurring. The second feedback system serves what for lack of a better term (and we've tried hard to think of one) we'll call a *meta-monitoring* function.

Discrepancy Reduction and Rate of Reduction

In trying to describe this second function, an intuitive way to begin is to say the meta loop is checking on how well the action loop is doing at reducing the discrepancies it's trying to reduce. More specifically, the perceptual input for the meta loop is a representation of the *rate of discrepancy reduction in the monitoring system over time*. (For the present, we focus exclusively on discrepancy-reducing loops; we turn to discrepancy-enlarging loops later.)

What's important to the meta loop isn't merely *whether* discrepancies are diminishing at the action loop, but how *rapidly* they're diminishing. If they're reducing rapidly, the action loop's progress toward its goal (perceived by the meta loop) is high. If they're reducing slowly, the action loop's rate of progress is lower. If they aren't reducing at all, the action loop's progress is zero. Any time a behavioral discrepancy is *enlarging*, of course, the action loop's progress is inverse. (For convenience, we'll treat as equivalent such phrases as "progress of the action loop" and "rate of discrepancy reduction in the action loop.")

We find an analogy useful here (an analogy that may also have more literal implications): Because action implies change between states, consider behavior as analogous to distance (construed as a vector, because perception of action incorporates both the difference between successive states and the direction of the difference). If the monitoring loop deals with distance, and if the meta loop assesses the progress of the monitoring loop, then the meta loop is dealing with the psychological equivalent of velocity (also as a vector). Velocity is the first derivative of distance over time. To the extent the physical analogy is meaningful, the perceptual input to the meta loop should be the first derivative over time of the input used by the action loop.

Although this input is important, we don't believe it's responsible for affect by itself, because a given rate of progress has different affective consequences in different circumstances. Accordingly, we've proposed something a little more complex: that the meta process is a feedback loop. The sensing constitutes an input, but no more. As in any feedback system, this input is compared against a reference value (cf. Frijda, 1986, 1988). In this case, the reference value is an acceptable rate of behavioral discrepancy reduction. As in other loops, the comparison process checks for a deviation from the standard. If there's a deviation, an output function engages to reduce it.

We suggest that the outcome of the comparison process at the heart of this loop (the error signal generated by the comparator) is manifest phenomenologically in two forms. The first is a hazy and nonverbal sense of expectancy. The second is affect, a feeling quality, a sense of positiveness or negativeness.

When sensed progress in the action loop conforms to the reference rate of progress, the meta system registers no discrepancy (see Table 8.1, example 1). With no discrepancy at the meta level, affect is neutral. When the action loop is making progress toward reducing its discrepancy but its rate is slower than the meta system's reference value, a discrepancy exists for the meta loop (Table 8.1, example 2). The result should be a degree of negative affect and doubt, proportional to the size of this discrepancy. When the rate of discrepancy reduction in the action loop is higher than the meta loop's reference value (Table 8.1, example 3), a positive discrepancy exists at the meta loop, an overshoot of the reference value, reflected in confidence and positive feeling.

It's clear that the action and meta systems are related to each other, but we've argued that only one creates affect. Table 8.1 shows why. In the

Table 8.1. *Five Examples of Behavior over Time, the Situation That Exists at the Level of the Action Loop, How Each Situation Would Be Construed at the Meta Loop, and the Affect That Theoretically Would Be Experienced*

Behavioral situation	Situation at action loop	Construal at meta loop	Affect
1. Progress toward goal, at a rate equal to the standard	Discrepancy reduction	No discrepancy	None
2. Progress toward goal, at a rate lower than the standard	Discrepancy reduction	Negative discrepancy	Negative
3. Progress toward goal, at a rate higher than the standard	Discrepancy reduction	Positive discrepancy	Positive
4. No progress toward goal	No discrepancy reduction	Negative discrepancy	Negative
5. Movement away from goal	Discrepancy enlargement	Negative discrepancy	Negative

Source: Adapted from Carver and Scheier (1990a).

first three examples in Table 8.1, there is a discrepancy at the action loop and discrepancy reduction is occurring in that loop. However, the affect experienced differs across examples. Affect can be neutral, negative, or even positive (examples 1, 2, and 3, respectively), depending on how fast discrepancy reduction is happening. This is why we believe the monitoring loop doesn't determine affect.

This isn't to say that predictions from the two systems never coincide. Table 8.1, example 4, shows a case with no behavioral movement; example 5 shows a case where there's movement *away* from the goal. Both have negative discrepancies at the meta level, and both lack behavioral discrepancy reduction. Both cases should have negative affect, both from our perspective and from a perspective in which behavioral discrepancies themselves produce affect.

From our perspective the size of the discrepancy at the action loop doesn't determine the input to the meta loop. A large discrepancy – even a *very* large discrepancy – at the action loop can be related to either abundant progress or little progress. A large behavioral discrepancy thus can be tied to either confidence or doubt, and to either positive or negative affect. The same is true when behavioral discrepancies are small. If the meta system senses an abundant rate of movement forward, there should be positive affect and confidence. If it senses inadequate movement, there should be negative affect and doubt.

Thus, it should be possible for a person with a large discrepancy at the action loop to feel better than a person with a small discrepancy at the action loop. If the first person is perceiving better progress than the second (and both have the same rate-loop reference values), the first person will feel better. In terms of the physical analogy, the first person is more distant from the goal but is moving forward faster.

Progress Toward a Goal versus Completion of Subgoals

Our view on affect emphasizes progress toward goals across time, rejecting the idea that affect arises from attainment per se. We take this position partly because affect can arise on the way to goals, rather than simply at goal attainment. It's reasonable to ask, though, why not assume affect arises from attainment of subgoals? If a subgoal's attained, there's a cause for positive affect, even though the ultimate goal hasn't been reached. The more subgoals attained, the more positive the affect (cf. Wyer & Srull, 1989, chap. 12).

We have two reactions to this. First, it seems to provide little guidance about what experience should exist in the absence of attaining a subgoal. Should there be negative affect, because the subgoal hasn't been attained? If so, when will the person ever experience a condition of neutral affect when a goal is in mind? Affect would always be either positive or negative with respect to that goal, and we don't think that's correct.

Second, and perhaps more important, even this view ultimately must take into account the passage of time. That is, attainment of a subgoal in 30 seconds must generally be more pleasing than attainment of the same subgoal across a span of 30 minutes. Absence of subgoal attainment across an hour must generally be more distressing than absence of attainment across 10 minutes. As the time dimension is taken into account, however, the subgoal analysis becomes a first approximation of our model, just as a difference equation provides a first approximation to a differential equation (Figure 8.1).[1] As the subgoals are sliced

---

[1] Mentioning a difference equation brings to mind the idea that people retrospectively evaluate affectively relevant experiences in terms of the peak intensity and end intensity of the experience (Kahneman, Fredrickson, Schreiber, & Redelmeier, 1993), with the experience's duration given little weight. Thus, if a very painful period has a period of lesser pain added on, the entire experience is seen as having been less aversive than if the final period was omitted (this is true despite the fact that the final period contributed additional time in pain, albeit less intense pain). Thus, people's affective judgments seem particularly sensitive to changes – changes which in our view signify progress, in this case progress toward absence of pain.

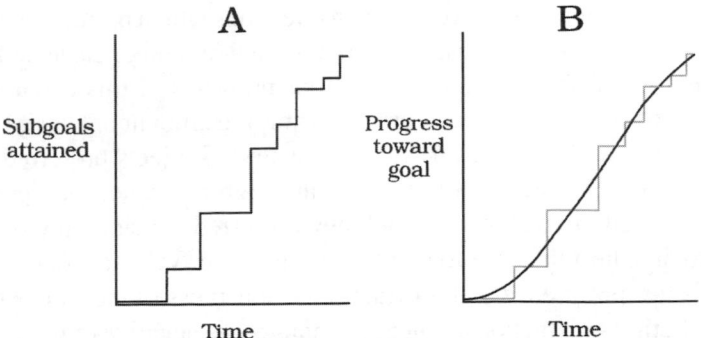

Figure 8.1. One might think of affect as arising from the attainment of sub-goals, but ultimately the passage of time must be taken into account. (A) An analysis in terms of subgoal attainment then represents a first approximation of (B) an analysis in terms of continually assessed progress toward the overall goal.

thinner and thinner (it's somewhat arbitrary, after all, what constitutes a subgoal), the subgoal analysis becomes a closer and closer approximation of a derivative. The models ultimately reduce to the same thing. The difference between them pertains primarily to the assumption one makes about whether the affect occurs in chunks according to a step function (from attainment of subgoals) or whether it's created continuously. We see the process as continuous.

EVIDENCE ON THE AFFECTIVE CONSEQUENCES OF PROGRESS

At least a little evidence has accumulated that supports aspects of the idea that affect originates in a rate or velocity function. Several projects are outlined in the following sections.

Hsee and Abelson

Two studies were reported by Hsee and Abelson (1991), who came independently to the idea that a velocity function relates to affect. Hsee and Abelson examined the relation between velocity and satisfaction. In one study, subjects read descriptions of paired hypothetical scenarios and indicated which outcome they'd find more satisfying. For example, would you be more satisfied if your class standing had risen from the 30th percentile to the 70th over the past six weeks, or if it had done so over the past three weeks?

Each participant answered seven questions which paired outcome scenarios. The questions tested the role of final outcome, distance changed, direction of change, and velocity. For purposes of this discussion, the effect of velocity is most interesting (holding amount of change constant and varying the time over which it occurs). Subjects preferred *improving* to a high outcome over a constant high outcome; they preferred a fast velocity to a slow one; and they preferred a change involving high velocity/short distance to one involving slower velocity/longer distance (this last preference demonstrates the robustness of the time element in predicting satisfaction). When the change was negative (e.g., salaries got worse, indicating a downward velocity), subjects preferred a constant low salary to a salary that started high and fell to low; they preferred slow falls to fast falls; and they preferred large–slow falls to small–fast falls.

In a second study, subjects viewed an outcome actually changing in time. They watched a computer display a bar moving vertically on a scale portraying changes in hypothetical outcome (e.g., the price of a stock the subject had invested in). This time subjects had a reference scenario given a satisfaction level of five on a nine-point scale. They were to make ratings in comparison to the reference scenario. In this study, distance of change was held constant; direction, final outcome, and velocity were varied. Study 2 replicated the findings in study 1, yielding a significant velocity effect. Subjects preferred a fast velocity when outcome was improving and a slow velocity when outcome was declining.

Lawrence, Carver, and Scheier

A limitation of the Hsee and Abelson research is that the outcomes were hypothetical. Although subjects were asked to imagine themselves experiencing the outcomes, it's hard to be sure they experienced them as having personal relevance. It remained uncertain whether the same effects would occur while people actually engaged in goal-related behavior. In part for this reason, we felt it desirable to conduct additional research on the matter.

The study we conducted (Lawrence, Carver, & Scheier, 1997) used a paradigm in which feedback of progress toward a goal could be manipulated over an extended period. The experiment was disguised as a study of social intuition, in which subjects made a long series of ambiguous judgments. The project ostensibly was investigating the ability to sense the meaning of words from obscure foreign languages (actually nonsense words). On each trial the subject viewed a word and indicated

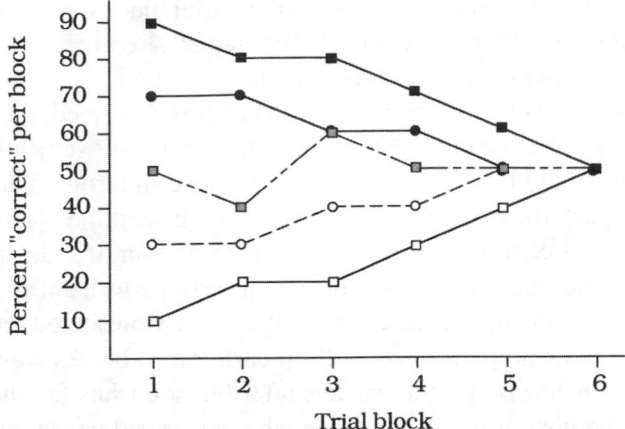

Figure 8.2.   Pattern of feedback across trial blocks given to subjects in each of 5 experimental conditions. Some subjects began with good performances and got worse; others began with poor performances and got better; a control condition consistently performed at an average rate. (From Lawrence et al., 1997.)

whether it meant the same as a comparison English word. To engage their involvement, the subjects were told that this intuitive skill could be very important in the broader social world.

Subjects were also told many factors influence performance on this task, including mood fluctuations. To control for such factors, assessments would occur periodically during the course of the session. Mood was assessed (on an 11-point scale ranging from "very positive mood" to "very negative mood") before the task began and at the end of the sixth block.

Each block of 10 was followed by feedback about performance on that block (the conceptual equivalent of a stock price from the study by Hsee & Abelson, 1991). Subjects received one of 5 patterns of feedback (Figure 8.2), converging across blocks such that feedback on block 6 was identical for all subjects, at 50% correct. Subjects in a neutral condition received a 50% score on the first and last block, and 50% on average across all blocks. Two groups had positive changes in performance (positive velocities), starting poorly and gradually improving. One had a relatively large change (from 10% to 50%), the other more moderate (from 30% to 50%). The final two groups had negative changes (negative velocities), starting well and gradually worsening. Again, one change was large (from 90% to 50%), the other more moderate (from

70% to 50%). Thus, considered across the 6 trial blocks to that point, at the moment the 5 groups were told they had 50% correct for block 6, they were experiencing 5 different velocities.

In contrast to velocity, operationalized as just described, distance to the goal can be viewed in either of two ways. First, all subjects scored 50% on the final block. If you think of distance in terms of adequacy of current performance (equivalent to a stock price), the 5 groups are at that moment equidistant from their goal. However, it's also possible to think of the task as a whole, in which case performances prior to block 6 also influence distance from the goal. Considered from this angle, subjects who performed well on earlier trial blocks would have the smallest behavioral discrepancies after block 6 (thus far, they were closest to the goal overall), and those who performed poorly on earlier blocks would have the largest behavioral discrepancies after block 6 (thus far, they were farthest from the goal overall).

When viewed in this way, subjects with positive velocities – whom we expect to have positive change in mood – are precisely those for whom discrepancy from the behavioral goal (doing well) is actually greatest at the end of block 6. If behavioral discrepancy is what matters, these subjects should be in the worst mood. Similarly, subjects in the conditions with negative velocities – whom we expect to have negative change in mood – are those for whom discrepancy from the behavioral goal is smallest at the end of block 6. If behavioral discrepancy is what matters, these subjects should be in the best mood.

The results favored velocity. Subjects whose performances improved across blocks displayed positive shifts in mood at the end of block 6 (somewhat constrained by a ceiling effect, as everyone began in a generally positive mood); those whose performances decreased displayed negative shifts in mood (Figure 8.3). Subjects whose mood had become more negative were those with the *best* cumulative performance; those whose mood had become more positive were those with the *worst* cumulative performance. This pattern is consistent with the analysis portrayed in Table 8.1, in which affect is related to rate of discrepancy reduction rather than to the size of the behavioral discrepancy.

Brunstein

Another study that appears to bear on this view of affect, although not conducted with this purpose in mind, was reported by Brunstein (1993). This study examined influences playing themselves out over a period of

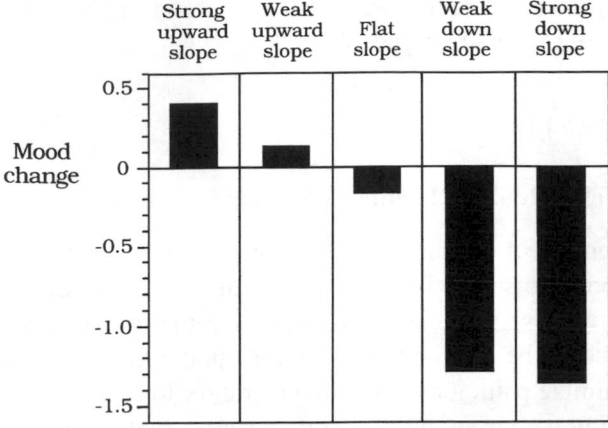

Figure 8.3.   Mood change from pretask to after trial block 6. (Data from Lawrence et al., 1997.)

months rather than minutes. It examined subjective well-being among college students over the course of an academic term, as a function of several goal-related perceptions, including perceptions of progress toward goals.

At the start of the semester, subjects generated a list of six long-term personal goals (goals pertaining at least to the full semester). They also made a series of ratings on items intended to assess their commitment to their goals (their determination and willingness to work at goal attainment and the urgency the goal had for them) and their perceptions of the attainability of the goals. At subsequent measurements (4, 10, and 14 weeks later), subjects reported their perceptions of progress toward the goals, and their subjective well-being. Of greatest interest at present is the fact that perceived progress at each measurement point was strongly correlated with concurrent well-being. Progress was also related to subsequent well-being.

Affleck and Colleagues

Similar results in a very different domain have recently been reported by Affleck et al. (1998). These researchers studied fibromyalgia patients, who experience a good deal of daily pain from their disease. Subjects in this study rated their pain and fatigue, and also their mood, several times a day across a 30-day span. These patients also made daily ratings of their progress toward a social–interpersonal goal (of their own choosing). Daily progress toward this goal proved to be associated with increases in positive mood and decreases in negative mood, independent of that day's levels of pain and fatigue.

QUESTIONS

Is This Really a Feedback System?

Our view on affect is that it results from a comparison process in a feedback loop. This view has a counterintuitive implication. If affect is created the way we say it is, it's a signal that the rate of progress isn't right and should be adjusted. This implies that although the organism tries to minimize pain, it does *not* in general try to maximize pleasure.

Minimizing pain is straightforward. Negative feelings reflect a negative discrepancy in rate, indicating a problem. Things aren't moving forward fast enough. The normal response is to try harder. If this happens, the negative affect ceases to exist. Thus, people strive to minimize pain.

Positive feelings reflect a positive discrepancy in rate. This is good in at least two senses: It means things are going better than they need to, and the experience feels good subjectively. To a system whose goal is to control sensed rate, however, a discrepancy is still a discrepancy, and discrepancies are to be reduced. If what we're discussing is really a feedback loop of the sort we've proposed, neither negative *nor* positive affect is a state the system wants to see. Either quality of affect (either deviation from the standard) would represent "error" and lead to changes in output to reduce it.

If the meta loop is truly a feedback system, an overshoot of the reference value should lead to a self-corrective attempt to return to the reference value. Put more concretely, people who exceed the desired rate of progress should slow subsequent efforts in this domain of behavior. They'll "coast" for a while. The result in the person's subjective experience would be that the positive affect from the overshoot isn't sustained for very long. This is particularly true if the person turns to another arena of behavior (Erber & Tesser, 1992).

Why should there be a built-in tendency to cause positive feelings to be short-lived? A plausible basis can be found in the idea that behavior is hierarchically organized, with multiple current concerns. People typically are working toward several goals more or less simultaneously. To the extent that movement toward goal attainment is more rapid than expected in one domain, it lets the person shift effort toward strivings in another domain, at no cost. To continue an unnecessarily rapid pace in the first domain may increase positive affect, but by diverting efforts from other goals it may create the potential for negative affect in other domains.

Further, there's at least some reason to believe that extremes of positive affect can be as problematic as extremes of negative affect. For example, people experiencing manic states make bad decisions, ignoring information about risk they'd ordinarily be attentive to. Being in very positive feeling states within a more normal range may make people momentarily complacent, and thus slower to mobilize themselves in the face of a threat. In a dangerous world, too much positive feeling can render people vulnerable.

These ideas are speculation. Indeed, this aspect of the model raises a number of questions that we can't readily answer. For example, sometimes people enjoying their activities seem to take the positive feeling as a sign to continue, rather than as a sign that they can now turn to something else. The questions of when and why positive feelings cue one response versus the other (cf. Martin & Stoner, 1996) deserve more attention than they've yet had.

We will, however, add one further speculation in this respect. It may be that normative subjective experience takes the error signal from the comparator, and adds a constant that for most people is an optimistic adjustment (Figure 8.4). This would yield slight positive affect when progress matches the reference value, absence of affect when progress is below it, and negative affect only when the negative discrepancy is more extreme. Keeping the assumption that rate is the controlled quality, rather than affect per se, this would also result in continued effort in conditions of mild positive affect. Reduced effort would occur only when affect became more positive.

This line of thought would fit with the idea that people in general appear to have positive biases about their situations (Taylor, 1989; Taylor & Brown, 1988). It also suggests a way of thinking about individual differences in baseline affective tone (differences that may be genetically determined [Lykken & Tellegen, 1996]): Such differences would reflect differences in the constant that's added to the error signal. Perhaps this constant relates to serotonin levels, with individual differences in baseline affect relating to differences in serotonin (cf. Kramer, 1993).

Does Positive Affect Lead to Coasting?

Does positive affect actually lead people to reduce effort? We don't know of much information on this question. Melton (1995) found that people

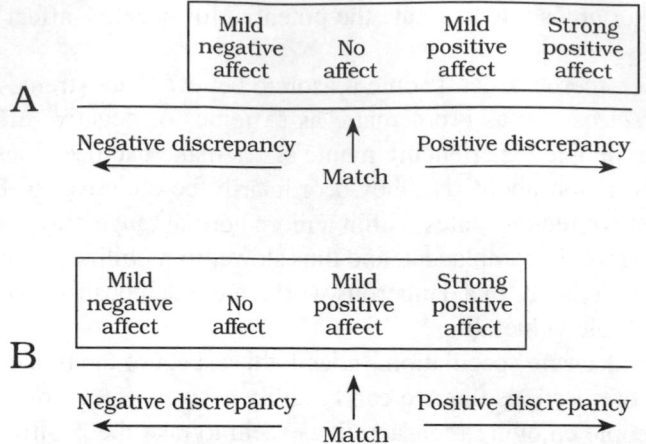

Figure 8.4.   (A) Thus far, we've assumed that a match between input and standard in the meta loop yields no affect, with deviations in either direction creating affect. (B) Another possibility is that normative subjective experience takes the error signal from the comparator and adds a constant positive adjustment. This would have the effect of displacing the array of subjective affect in comparison to the range of possible discrepancies.

in a good mood performed worse than control subjects on syllogisms. A variety of ancillary data led him to the conclusion that the people in good moods did worse because they were exerting less effort on the task.

We also found a study that hints of such an effect at the group level, though the evidence is ambiguous. This study (Mizruchi, 1991) examined the performances of professional basketball teams in playoff games across a span of 35 years. Mizruchi argued that prior success decreases the urgency of further success, leading to a letdown and risk of future failure. In a complementary way, failure increases the urgency of success, leading to stronger efforts.

Mizruchi employed a variety of controls in analyzing the data, including controls for home court and for the teams' relative strength (computed from records up to that point in the season). Given these controls, the data revealed a significant tendency for the team that won the preceding game to lose the current game. The ambiguity stems, of course, from the fact that it's impossible to tell whether the prior winner relaxed, the prior loser tried harder, or both.

Informal observers of athletic contests often see such patterns in the ebb and flow of individual games. When one team gets ahead, it's common for that team to lose momentum. The mechanism behind such phenomena is unclear (and these observations are subject to the same problem of not knowing which team creates the momentum shift – the one that's behind or the one that's ahead), but it seems likely that loss of concentration is a contributor.

A Cruise-Control Model of Affect

It took us a while to realize it, but this model of the origin and consequences of affect is essentially a "cruise-control" model. That is, the system we've postulated functions much the same way as the cruise control on a car. If you're going too slowly toward some goal, negative affect arises. You respond to the insufficient progress by putting more effort into your behavior, trying to speed up (cf. Cervone, Kopp, Schaumann, & Scott, 1994). If you're going too fast, positive affect arises, and you respond by coasting. The car's cruise control is very similar. You come to a hill, which slows you down. Your cruise control responds by injecting more gas into the engine's cylinders, to bring the speed back up. If you come across the crest of a hill and are rolling downhill too fast, the system pulls back on the gas and drags the speed back down.

The analogy is intriguing in part because it concerns mechanical regulation of the very quality we believe the affect system is regulating: velocity. It's also intriguing to realize that this analogy incorporates a similar asymmetry in the consequences of deviating from the set point. That is, both in your car and in your behavior, going too slow requires investment of greater effort and resources. Going too fast doesn't. It requires only pulling back. That is, your cruise control doesn't apply your brakes, it simply cuts back on the gas. In this way it permits you to coast back to your velocity set point. In the same fashion, you don't usually respond to positive affect by trying to make it go away, but simply by easing off.[2]

CHANGES IN RATE: ACCELERATION AND DECELERATION

Our model addresses rates of progress. It should be obvious, however, that the rate can itself change. Change in rate is subjectively manifest

---

[2] The cruise-control metaphor also suggests an image for individual differences in overall emotional tone. People whose psychic cars are light and high powered, who blast over the crests of hills, are people who frequently experience positive emotion. People whose psychic cars are heavy and underpowered, who slow down whenever there's a steep grade, are people who frequently experience negative emotion.

not as affect, but as *change* of affect. Increases in rate cause shifts toward more positive feelings, with the precise quality of the experience depending on the initial and final rates. When the change is from a rate far below the meta standard to one that's higher but still below the standard, affect should change from very negative to mildly negative. If the change is to a value that exceeds the standard, affect will change from negative to positive.

In the same manner, downward changes in rate also yield affective shifts. Again, the quality of the experience will depend on the initial and final rates. When the change is from a rate above the meta standard to one below the standard, the affect change should be from positive to negative. When the change is from just below the standard to far below the standard, the affect change would be from mildly negative to very negative.

Subjective Experience of Acceleration and Deceleration

Shifts in rate can be gradual or abrupt. The more abrupt an increase in progress, the more the subjective experience includes a rush of exhilaration, reflecting the sharpness of the contrast between the more negative feeling and the more positive feeling (cf. the description of "sentimentality" by Frijda, 1988, p. 350). The more abrupt a *decrease* in progress, the more the experience should incorporate a kind of "de-exhilaration." This is the well-known "sinking feeling," when affect suddenly shifts toward the negative.

We suggested earlier that the quality of experience the meta loop senses as input is analogous to velocity. To carry the analogy one step further, what we're now addressing is acceleration, the second derivative of distance over time. Given that people apparently are equipped to sense that experience, the analogy suggests that some neural processor is computing a second derivative over time of the information input to the action loop.

In the same way that distance and velocity are independent, both are in principle independent of acceleration. (An object moving forward at 20 feet per second can at that instant be accelerating or decelerating, or its velocity can be constant; the same is true if the object is moving at 80 feet per second.) We've argued for the same independence on the other side of the analogy (Carver & Scheier, 1990a): that the rush of exhilaration associated with acceleration is distinct both from the size of the discrepancy at the action level and from the rate of discrepancy reduction there. In this model, then, exhilaration is distinct from the sense of positivity–negativity. The latter we regard as affect; the former we regard as something different.

Consider as an example a slice in time: a person with a large project at work that will occupy him for the next two months. With so far yet to go, he's experiencing a large discrepancy at the action level. He's experiencing positive affect if the rate of discrepancy reduction is greater than needed – if he's made a lot of progress in the hour before we happened upon him. This positive affect will be free of exhilaration if the high rate of discrepancy reduction has been constant. If the rate is instead shifting upward at this moment (he's just had a huge insight about how to solve a major problem), the positive feeling will be accompanied by a sense of exhilaration. The more sudden the shift, the stronger the sense of exhilaration.

Surprise

The literature of emotion holds suggestive support for the notion that the sense of exhilaration–de-exhilaration from abrupt change in rate is distinct from the affective tone of positiveness versus negativeness. The concept in this literature that's closest to the quality we're discussing is surprise. Surprise is a special case in this literature, for at least two reasons.

First, historically there has been a lack of consensus as to whether to consider surprise an emotion. For example, although Izard (1977) included surprise as a fundamental emotion, he also said "Surprise is not an emotion in the same sense as joy or sadness is" (p. 277), and "In some respects surprise is not a real emotion like the other fundamental emotions considered in this book" (p. 281). Tomkins (1984) said that surprise "is ancillary to every other affect" (p. 171). Second, at least two projects (Fehr & Russell, 1984; Shaver, Schwartz, Kirson, & O'Connor, 1987) have found that adults don't treat words indicating surprise the same as they treat other emotion-relevant words, leading Shaver et al. (1987) to express reservations about surprise as an affect.

Also of interest is that surprise is in itself apparently neither positive nor negative (e.g., Izard (1977, p. 283); Ortony et al., 1988, p. 32). Rather, its tone is a product of the experiences associated with it. Roseman (1984, p. 31) identified surprise as co-occurring with both positive and negative emotions. Several studies have found empirically that surprise either is unrelated to a pleasantness dimension (e.g., Ellsworth & Smith, 1988; Tesser, 1990) or is related equally well to independent dimensions of positive and negative affect (Moffitt & Singer, 1994). Such findings suggest that surprise is free of positiveness or negativeness, but can be combined with either of these qualities.

This pattern is precisely what one would see from a quality that's related to affect but not quite the same as affect. This is essentially what we're proposing about the quality resulting from the perception of acceleration or deceleration (which may *be* surprise). That is, we're arguing that it's derived from the experience of affect change, though not an affect itself. Though theorists tend to think of surprise as an absolute rather than having a directional value, we think there's a difference between positive surprise and negative surprise (acceleration versus deceleration). Perhaps the relative lack of words to refer to the two divergent qualities reflects the fact that the entire experience is one step farther removed from behavior than is affect (at least in our view), and thus is less accessible to intuition or amenable to verbal description.

Research

Although there's indirect support for our position on acceleration in the literature, some data also suggest our view may be incorrect. On the other hand, these data are not without ambiguity. The evidence comes from a study by Hsee, Salovey, and Abelson (1994, experiment 2). In this study subjects watched a number that indicated the price of a stock they owned. The number changed repeatedly over a 45-second period representing the passing of 3 months. Subjects were to make a continuous record of their satisfaction with the stock, using a pointer on a 15-point scale. The stock price was varied between subjects in several ways, the key differences being shifts that established group differences in acceleration toward the end of the 3-month period while maintaining equivalence of velocity during the final month.

Portions of the data appear to support the idea that satisfaction was responsive to both velocity and acceleration. However, there are problems of interpretation. To create acceleration differences while holding final velocity constant, Hsee et al. had to use very different starting values (stock prices) for the curves. Yet at the beginning of the 3-month run, the "satisfaction" pointer was always placed for the subject at the scale's midpoint, thereby establishing that stock value as a middle value on the satisfaction scale. In reporting the findings, the authors focused on the final satisfaction rating, ignoring the differential anchor. The differential anchor, however, makes the absolute values of subjects' self-reports hard to interpret.

Nonetheless, consider the results. In half the conditions a moderate rate (gain or loss) shifted to a more extreme value. In these conditions, satisfaction ratings tracked the rate values quite well, consistent with a view in which velocity matters but not acceleration. In the other conditions a high rate of change (increase or decrease) moderated rather abruptly, though it did not reverse. Satisfaction ratings, however, reversed direction. If only velocity mattered, the ratings should have leveled off, not reversed. This aspect of the findings appears to indicate a link between satisfaction and acceleration.

Aside from the anchoring problem, a second difficulty in interpreting the findings concerns the concept of "satisfaction." Thus far we've treated this quality (the outcome variable in this study, as well as in the research by Hsee & Abelson, 1991) as equivalent to positive versus negative affect. This may be so, but it's also arguable that the two differ. It might be that satisfaction implies both affect and the accompaniment of exhilaration or de-exhilaration. (This issue indicates more generally how hard it is to sort out psychological elements in events of this sort.)

Let's be clear here about what we believe. We think the subjective quality tied to the experience of acceleration and deceleration is important. We believe it's often created simultaneously with new affect (it arises when affect is shifting). We believe, however, that what it contributes to the experience is something different from what is contributed by affect per se (cf. Izard, 1977; Tomkins, 1984).

AFFECT FROM DISCREPANCY-ENLARGING LOOPS

When we began describing this conceptualization of affect, we said we were going to restrict ourselves at first to discrepancy-reducing loops, where the person has a desired goal. Thus far we've done that, dealing only with issues that arise in the context of approach. Now we turn to the part we've left aside, attempts to distance oneself from a point of comparison, attempts to "not-be" or "not-do," discrepancy-*enlarging* loops.

It should be apparent from earlier discussions (Chapters 4 and 5) that avoidance behavior is just as intelligible as approach behavior. But what are the affective accompaniments to avoidance loops? Our response to this question derives from several sources, including insights from Higgins and his colleagues (see Higgins, 1987, 1989, 1996). For clarity, we present our own position now and defer until Chapter 9 a comparison between it and the ideas developed by Higgins.

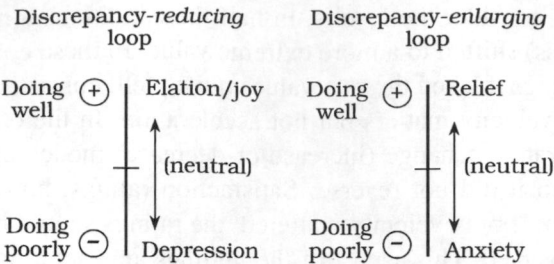

Figure 8.5. Two sorts of meta-level systems and the affective dimensions we believe arise from the functioning of each. Discrepancy-reducing systems yield sadness or depression when progress is below standard and happiness or elation when progress is above standard. Discrepancy-enlarging systems yield anxiety when progress is below standard and relief or contentment when progress is above standard.

Doing Well, Doing Poorly

The affect theory presented in this chapter rests on the idea that positive affect results when a behavioral system is making rapid progress in *doing what it's organized to do*. The systems considered thus far are organized to close discrepancies. There's no obvious reason, however, why the principle shouldn't apply just as well to systems organized for the opposite purpose. If the system is making rapid progress doing what it's organized to do, the result should be positive affect. If the system is doing poorly at what it's organized to do, the result should be negative affect.

That much would seem to be fully comparable across the two types of systems. We see, however, one difference between the two: a difference in the affective qualities involved (see Figure 8.5). In each case there's a positive pole and a negative pole, but the positives aren't quite the same, nor are the negatives quite the same.

Following the lead of Higgins, we suggest that the affect dimension relating to discrepancy-reducing loops is (in its purest form) the dimension that runs from depression to elation. The affect dimension that relates to discrepancy-enlarging loops is (in its purest form) the dimension that runs from anxiety to relief or contentment. As Higgins and his colleagues note, dejection-related and agitation-related affect may take several forms, but these two dimensions capture the core qualities. The connections drawn in Figure 8.5 between affect quality and type of system are compatible not only with the Higgins model, but also with other theories. For example, Roseman (1984, p. 31) has argued that joy and sadness are related to appetitive (moving-toward) motives, whereas relief and distress are related to aversive (moving-away-from) motives.[3]

Activation Asymmetry between Dimensions

It's of interest that the two dimensions in Figure 8.5 are asymmetrical regarding the degree of activation in the affects at the opposing poles. Anxiety is an energized affect; relief (the opposite pole) is not. Elation, joy, and enthusiasm are energized; sadness and depression (the opposite pole) are not.

This asymmetry is consistent with the idea that the two affect dimensions arise from functioning of systems with different types of goals (the argument we've made). In effect, the pole with activation is tied to the "business end" (the reference value) of the behavioral system to which it relates. Activation in an approach loop occurs when, by doing well, one is closing in on a desired goal – when the situation invites pouncing. Activation in an avoidance loop occurs when one is closing in on a match to an anti-goal – when the situation is dire (cf. Riskind, Kelley, Harman, Moore, & Gaines, 1992). Pouncing and escaping dire straits are, in effect, what these two kinds of behavioral systems are about.

These observations regarding activation also fit the idea that the two affect dimensions relate to two different kinds of behavioral tendencies (approach and escape), which have different dynamics and thus different energy mobilization needs. The notion that there are ties between particular qualities of affect and functioning of systems that regulate behavioral approach versus avoidance has been suggested for varying reasons by a number of theorists (e.g., Davidson, 1992a, 1992b; Depue & Iacono, 1989; Gray, 1981, 1990; Tomarken, Davidson, Wheeler, & Doss, 1992). We examine this work more closely in Chapter 9.

---

[3] Human feelings range well beyond those we've focused on here. Although we won't address them all, we note that some affects appear to imply blends of feeling qualities, with multiple goals being relevant; others reflect variations in the circumstances under which movement with respect to a goal is facilitated or impeded. The latter sort of variation is discussed in attributional terms by Weiner (e.g., 1982, 1986a, 1986b); an approach that emphasizes appraisals rather than attributions has been developed by Smith and Ellsworth (1987; Smith, Haynes, Lazarus, & Pope, 1993; Ellsworth & Smith, 1988).

AFFECT AND BEHAVIOR

Although our focus in this chapter is on the mechanisms we think underlie the creation of affect, we also want to examine aspects of the relationship between affect and behavior. In what follows, we consider how affect can come to exist in the absence of behavior, and we address the implication of hierarchical organization for affective experience. Then we consider a linkage of affect to behavior that we think connects control theory with the concept of motivation in a very interesting way.

Affect in the Absence of Action

The model in this chapter focuses on a particular kind of coupling of behavior and affect. Recall that feedback models don't require behavior to occur in order for goals to be attained – goals can be attained by disturbances from outside the system. Nor does the affect model require action to occur in order for for affect to be created. Events other than your own actions – outside disturbances – can also influence the sensed rate of discrepancy reduction.

It's quite possible to be making very rapid progress toward goal attainment without acting, if other forces in the world are operating to create a situation fostering the attainment of your goal. For example, knowing that a powerful friend is taking care of a problem for you can create pleasure (presuming the goal doesn't intrinsically require self-sufficiency). This line of reasoning also accounts for happiness via religious beliefs, another case where perceived movement toward a desired end comes from forces outside the self.

Negative affect, of course, is even easier to create without action than is positive affect. Having a goal for which there's a meta-level standard and not trying to move toward it as time passes should in itself generate negative feelings.

It's also possible for negative feelings to be created by events in which you don't participate, but which somehow change your status vis-à-vis others. People who are the object of someone's romantic interest but don't reciprocate often feel guilty over the the other person's suffering (Baumeister & Wotman, 1992). Similarly, people feel guilty over inequities that benefit them over others (for a review see Baumeister, Stillwell, & Heatherton, 1994).

Our interpretation of these cases is that they involve closing in on an undesired condition. That is, a person who feels guilty over a beneficial inequity sees himself as unworthy, or fears that others see him as unfair or greedy. The person who feels guilt over failing to respond to another's attentions sees the other person (and perhaps a wider audience) viewing him as heartless and unfeeling. These are cases in which discrepancies are perceived to be changing in an undesired way due to forces other than the person's own actions.

Affect from Recollection or Imagination

Thus far we've focused on the experience of affect in the course of moment-to-moment experience. The model also suggests a mechanism whereby affect can be created from the processing of information from memory, or from imaginary experiences.

Sometimes people play mental scenarios in their minds (e.g., Taylor & Pham, 1996), recalling past experiences or imagining new ones (or imagining past experiences with new endings). If you think of a past event involving an affective experience, that affective quality will come to mind (cf. Bower, 1981, 1991). That's not our point here. Rather, there's a basis for arguing that the meta process can be engaged whenever a person plays out a scenario mentally (as opposed to simply recalling the occurrence of an event).

Thus, by mentally reliving a past event, a person can renew feelings (as opposed to simply recalling them). The more vivid the reliving, the stronger the affect (see also Frijda, 1988). In such a case the affect wouldn't simply be retrieved from memory, it would be regenerated. By playing through experiences that haven't happened, a person can create affect for events that are imaginary. In the same way, a person can feel hope or despair over the anticipated course of an event that hasn't yet begun to unfold (cf. Markus & Nurius, 1986).

Potential for Affect and Levels of Abstraction

Just as the monitoring of action can take any of several levels in a hierarchy as superordinate, so should the meta system be able to function at any of several levels. It seems certain, however, that meta discrepancies have more emotional impact when they concern a central element of self than when they bear only on a peripheral goal. Failure sometimes has a big impact on people's feelings and sometimes not (Dweck & Elliott, 1983; Dweck & Leggett, 1988; Elliott & Dweck, 1988; Hyland, 1987;

Locke & Latham, 1990a, p. 229; Srull & Wyer, 1986). The difference between cases may be partly the level of abstraction at which the person is focusing (Frijda, 1988; McIntosh & Martin, 1992; Wyer & Srull, 1989). That is, failure to conform to the idealized sense of self, or to follow a principle that's implied by that ideal self, or to perform a specific act that relates to your ideal self, should cause more distress than failure to remember all the items on your grocery list.

Indeed, people may realize this intuitively and use the knowledge tactically to guide the flow of their behavior. For example, Wegner and Vallacher (1986) have suggested that criminals may avoid moral concerns raised by their acts (and negative feelings that can thereby result) by focusing on low-level details of the actions they're taking. Similarly, people in evaluative exams can avoid (at least temporarily) the emotion-inducing aspect of the experience by focusing fully on the nuts and bolts of answering one item at a time.

Merging Affect and Action

This chapter has focused on ideas about a mechanism whereby affect might be created during the flow of experience. Thus far we've said little about how this mechanism influences behavior. This is an important consideration. After all, affect matters in part (maybe in large part) because it serves as a signal pertaining to the current consequences of action. How, then, does the affect loop influence *action*?

A more basic question (which leads to the same end point) is this: We've treated affect as the error signal of a meta loop, but what's the *output function* of that loop? If the input function is a perception of rate of progress, the output function must be an adjustment in rate of progress. In some cases an adjustment is straightforward – go faster. Sometimes it's less straightforward. The rates of many "behaviors" we're interested in (higher-order activities) aren't defined in terms of literal pace of motion. Rather, they're defined in terms of choices among actions, or even potential *programs* of action. For example, increasing your rate of progress on a reading assignment may mean choosing to spend a weekend working rather than playing. Increasing your rate of kindness means choosing an action to perform that reflects that value. Thus, adjustment in rate must often be translated into other terms, such as concentration or reallocation of time and effort.

It should be apparent from this discussion that the action system and the rate system work in concert with one another (see Figure 8.6). Both

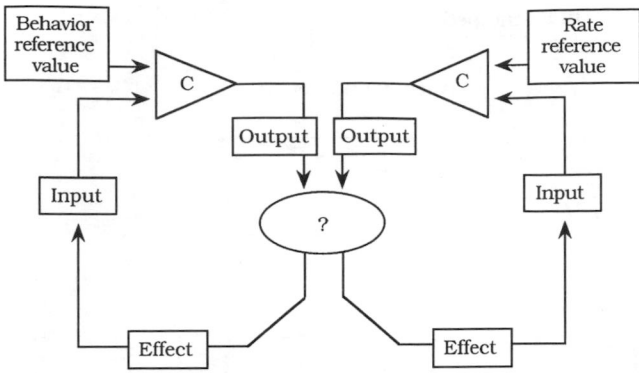

Figure 8.6.   The feedback loop that manages action and the loop that manages rate work in concert with one another. Though they influence different *aspects* of action, both are involved in the flow of action. Given the fact that adjustments in rate sometimes occur by the reprioritization of actions, there must also be some interweaving of their function. Exactly how to conceptualize that interweaving, however, is not clear.

are involved in the flow of action. They influence different *aspects* of the action, but both are always involved. Indeed, the fact that the rate system can affect what programs of action are undertaken implies that they're even *more* interwoven in operation than is indicated in Figure 8.6.

The functions we've just described are roughly comparable to the set of functions typically ascribed to motivation. In effect, we seem to have arrived at saying that the action loop handles most of what's sometimes called the *directional* function of motivation (choosing some behavior from among many options, keeping the action as intended), and that the affect loop handles the *intensity* function of motivation (the vigor, enthusiasm, effort, concentration, or thoroughness with which the action is pursued). Our linking of affect with the intensity aspect of motivation is a consequence of the structural assumptions we started with, rather than a principled decision. However, this link is certainly consistent with statements of many theorists who have emphasized the intimate connection between emotion and motivation.[4]

---

[4] A question some readers may have is this: Does it make more sense to see the meta loop as regulating rate or as regulating affect (since the two may be completely confounded) – or even as regulating confidence, which is also tangled up with both of them? In some respects, it doesn't really matter. Rate discrepancy is isomorphic to affect. But there's one respect in which it seems to be more useful to think of regulation in terms of rate than in other terms. Specifically, there's a formal relation between distance and rate, which facilitates discussing them together, as we've done in this section. Thinking in terms of regulation of affect removes that relation, and thus tends to interfere with that aspect of the discussion.

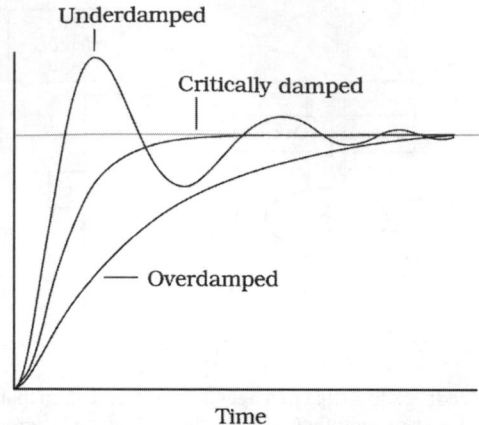

Time

Figure 8.7.   Deviations of a position-regulating system from its desired value as a function of three sensitivities of a second-order (velocity-regulating) system. In the overdamped case, the system responds slowly, but eventually settles in on the reference value (the gray line). In the underdamped case, the system responds quickly, but it overshoots, then oscillates, before eventually settling in on the reference value. In the critically damped case, the system responds moderately quickly, and reaches the reference value without overshooting or oscillating. In all three cases the system eventually reaches the reference value, but does so after different patterns of "behavior." (Adapted from Clark, 1996.)

Two Systems in Concert: Other Applications

We know of two other occurrences of the idea of position and velocity loops working in concert. One of them is in control engineering, where this arrangement is commonly used to produce quick-yet-stable responses in mechanical and electronic devices (Clark, 1996; Ogata, 1970). Clark (1996, chaps. 7 and 10) points out that a velocity loop can have several different consequences for a position loop. The influence depends on the degree of "damping" the second-order (velocity) system places on the response of the first-order (position) system (chap. 7 of Clark, 1996). Damping varies with the second-order system's sensitivity.

In what's termed an *overdamped* case, the position system responds sluggishly to a perturbation, moving to its goal value slowly (see Figure 8.7). In an *underdamped* case, the position system responds very quickly but overcompensates, overshoots its goal, then oscillates around it, gradually closing in on it (cf. Figure 2.3 in Chapter 2). The ideal case, termed *critically damped*, is a compromise between these two. It creates a relatively rapid response (though not as rapid as the underdamped case) with little or no overshoot. Thus, when the velocity loop is properly "tuned," responses are comparatively quick but also stable (i.e., without oscillations).

These cases appear to parallel the influence of individual differences in emotional reactivity in people. The overdamped case corresponds to a person who is emotionally very unreactive. It takes this person's behavior a long time to return to its reference point after a perturbation away. The underdamped case corresponds to a person who is emotionally very reactive. The strong emotional impact of a perturbation for this person results in behavioral overcompensation. If this person is "behind" (sad or anxious), he speeds up sharply; if he's "ahead" (happy or relieved), he may stop trying altogether. Each of these responses then leads to deviations in the opposite direction, provoking the opposite emotional response.

The ideal case, critical damping, corresponds to a person who is emotionally reactive, but not *too* reactive. This person responds fairly quickly to the perturbation (the function of emotional responsiveness is to promote quick responses), but he doesn't overrespond in such a way as to throw himself into behavioral oscillation (the moderate damping keeps his responses fairly stable).

This critically damped arrangement presumably is the norm in the human population. It's fairly easy to see why evolutionary pressures would favor this pattern. Too little emotional reactivity yields behavioral responses that are too lethargic to avoid danger. Too much emotional reactivity yields behavioral responses that may render the person vulnerable to danger by virtue of their instability.

Another depiction of position and velocity loops working in concert, one bearing on behavior, comes from the literature of movement control (indeed, this application is what led us to examine the engineering discussion). McIntyre and Bizzi (1993) addressed a point of dispute in the motor control literature about whether purely feedback models were adequate to account for the execution of rapid arm movements. They argued that if separate control loops were assumed for position and velocity, the coupled system works as well as the alternative (more complex) models. One reason this position-plus-velocity model seemed plausible to them was its frequent use in control engineering. They reasoned that if adding a velocity loop produces quick-yet-stable responses in artificial devices, perhaps it does the same in human movement control. Simulation data supported this hypothesis.

There are interesting parallels between the coupled systems discussed by McIntyre and Bizzi (1993) and the coupling between affect and action systems we've suggested here. In both cases, the velocity system manages rapid adjustment, and (when properly tuned) does so in a fashion that ensures stable functioning. This parallel also raises interesting questions. What's the error signal of the velocity system handling motor movement? Does it create affect? We wouldn't want to go that far. However, the conceptual parallel does cause us to wonder whether systems at those lower levels create sensations analogous to affect (perhaps a sense of sharpness versus sluggishness in movement control), which we notice but rarely think about.[5]

BREADTH OF APPLICATION

In closing this chapter we wish to be explicit about our intended scope. The examples we used came mostly from domains of achievement and instrumental activity. However, the model isn't just about achievement-related affect. Those domains simply provide easy illustrations of the logic. The model is intended to apply to *all* goal-directed behavior. This includes attempts to attain goals that are amorphous and poorly specified, and for which construing rates of progress isn't easy. It includes goals for which the idea of rates of progress might at first seem odd. Human goals such as developing and maintaining a sound relationship, being a good mother or father, dealing honorably and graciously with acquaintances, seeing someone you care about experience happiness and fulfillment, having a full and rich life, even becoming immersed in the flow of fictional lives in a novel or film are amenable to analysis in these terms. These are all qualities of human experience toward which people try to move, goals that evolve or recur across time, as do most goals underlying human action.

At the moment you see and act on an opportunity to behave honorably, you're making rapid progress toward that recurring goal in your life and

---

[5] In principle, there's no limit to the number of loops that might be working in concert, each handing yet a further derivative across time. This begs a question: Is there a limit on how many regulators exist? Is some particular number optimal for some reason? Apparently a two-regulator arrangement, simple as it is, goes quite a long way. Indeed, in yet another very different area of work (concerning the nature of habituation), Staddon and Higa (1996) found that the best fit to real data came from a simulation model with feedback loops in two time scales. Is this recurrent adequacy of two layers coincidental, or might it have some meaning as yet unrealized?

you feel good. When you sense that you've just done the right thing in an interaction with your child, you've made progress in manifesting that principle in your life, and you feel good. When you enter a room and see a painting that has qualities you've learned to like (or when the band hits the section of the song that says something special to you), you've just lurched toward the goal of sensing beauty, and you feel good.

To the extent that progress toward goals such as these is taken as important, to the extent that people are invested in experiencing these qualities in their lives sooner rather than later, the meta loop produces positive and negative feelings, as progress is faster or slower. Sometimes pacing toward such goals matters little, sometimes it matters a lot. In the latter circumstances, we suggest, these events yield affect.

9

Affect: Issues and Comparisons

Our description of the affect model in Chapter 8 was intended to convey the essence of its ideas without letting you be distracted too readily into side issues. But questions naturally arise in thinking about those themes. Some questions pertain to the model itself and how it works, others pertain to the relation between this model and other approaches. In this chapter we address some of these matters, starting with questions about the model itself.

META-LEVEL STANDARDS

Consider first reference values at the meta level. Several questions can be raised about these values.

Meta-Level Standards Vary in Stringency

Most basically, what reference value does the meta system use? It depends on what behavior the person is engaged in. We assume the meta system can implement standards that vary widely across contexts. Sometimes the standard is demanding, sometimes less so. Sometimes it's imposed from outside (as when work has a deadline for completion), sometimes it derives from social comparison (as when people are in competition), sometimes it's self-imposed (as when someone has a personal timetable for career development). Regardless of origins, of course, the standard must be adopted by the person in order for it to have affective consequences.

An example where the meta standard is both stringent and externally imposed is degree programs in medical or law school. Even continuous behavioral progress (increments in mastery of material) is adequate only if it occurs at or above the rate required by the degree program. Thus, as the person tries to attain the action goal of becoming a doctor or lawyer, the meta-level reference value is stringent. Though it is externally imposed, most people entering this situation build the requirement into their understanding of the situation they're in; it's now their requirement as well.

The stringency of the standard used at the meta level for any given activity has straightforward implications for the person's emotional life. If the pace used as a reference point is too high, it will rarely be matched, even if (to an outside observer) the person's rate of progress is extraordinarily high. This person will experience negative affect often and positive affect rarely. If the reference point is low, progress will more frequently exceed it. This person will experience positive affect more often and negative affect more rarely. The stringency of the standard thus matters a good deal to the person's subjective experience.[1]

Influences on Stringency

What influences the stringency of the meta-level standard? Obviously a critical determinant is the extent of time pressure on the activity. Some actions are clearly time-dependent (you have a presentation at 10 o'clock tomorrow), others are more vaguely so (it's about time to fertilize the lawn), and time dependency for others is even hazier (you want to go to China someday). When an activity has demanding time constraints, the meta-level reference value is stringent. With a relative lack of time pressure, a lax standard is more likely.

Though time dependence is most easily illustrated by situations that require a rapid pace, there is also a second sort of time dependence: for activities that people wish to have *done* but no desire to *do* (a common view of chores). Such goals are highly time-dependent, in the sense that people wish their attainment to be instantaneous. This wish puts the meta-level reference value at a high level. Because the rate of

---

[1] An issue that's separate from the stringency of a standard is the sensitivity of the system doing the regulating. In Chapter 2 we noted that control systems can regulate closely (if the system has precise error detection) or they can be sloppy (if the system doesn't detect deviations until they're large). This can also be true of the affect system. A person with good error detection will be prone to emotional fluctuation, as small deviations are noted. A person whose error detection isn't very sensitive won't experience emotion until the rate of change has deviated much farther from the standard. Differences in error sensitivity are one way of thinking about individual differences in emotional temperament.

progress therefore cannot meet the standard, positive affect is nearly impossible and aversiveness is almost inevitable whenever such activity is engaged in.

On the other hand, the intensity of this affect is proportional to the importance of the activity, which is often low. Indeed, a common way of dealing with chores is to focus on their concrete aspects, thereby rendering the acts even less important (lower in the action hierarchy). As you focus on a concrete facet of the activity, the aversiveness of the experience diminishes. To put it differently, drudgery is drudgery only when you treat what you're doing at a higher level of abstraction.

The issue of time dependence has further implications, one of which we note briefly. Sometimes passage of time causes a goal that once was only vaguely time-dependent to become more explicitly time-dependent. For example, consider a scientist who has the goal of doing an important piece of work sometime in his or her career, or the person who wants to have children "someday." Early on, there's little pressure to make progress, since the time available stretches far into the future. The passage of time, however, removes degrees of freedom (cf. Kirschenbaum, 1985). The result may be an increased sense of time dependence as the years go by. This sense, with respect to the issue of having children, is known as "hearing one's biological clock ticking."

Changing Meta-Level Standards

Not only do meta-level reference values differ across categories of behavior and across time, but they can also respond to accumulation of experience (cf. Lord & Hanges, 1987). That is, as people accumulate experience in a domain, adjustments can occur in the pacing they expect and demand of themselves. There's a kind of recentering of the system around the past experience, by changing the reference value.

Sometimes the adjustment is downward. For example, a researcher experiencing difficulty in meeting his personal timetable for career development may gradually use less stringent standards of pacing. One consequence of this is a more favorable balance of positive to negative affect across a given time span. In other cases the adjustment is upward. Someone who gains work-related skills may undertake greater challenges, requiring quicker handling of action units. Upward adjustment of a rate criterion has the side effect of decreasing the potential for positive affect and increasing the potential for negative affect.

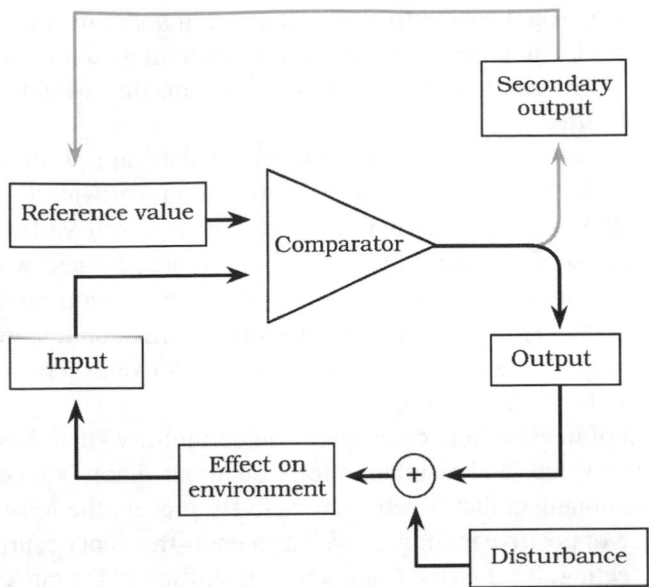

Figure 9.1. A feedback loop (in this case, the postulated meta loop) acts to create change in the input function, to shift it toward the reference value. Sometimes an additional process occurs as well (gray line), which adjusts the reference value in the direction of the input. This process is presumed to be weaker or slower; thus, the reference value is stable, relative to the input value.

These changes don't happen quickly or abruptly. Shifting the reference value downward isn't the first response when you have trouble keeping up a demanding pace. First you try harder to keep up. Only more gradually, if this fails, does the meta standard shift to accommodate. Similarly, an upward shift isn't the immediate response when your rate exceeds the standard. The more typical response is to coast for a while. Only when the overshoot is frequent does the standard shift upward.

We believe that such adjustments in meta standard occur automatically, but slowly. Such adjustments *themselves* appear to reflect a self-corrective feedback process, as the person reacts to insufficient challenge by taking on a more demanding pace, or reacts to too much challenge by scaling back (see Figure 9.1, which duplicates Figure 2.9). This feedback process is slower than the ones we've focused on thus far. The shift accumulates gradually.

Assume for the moment that a signal to change standard occurred every time there was a signal to change output, but much weaker. Given this, it would take a long time to for the standard to change. Indeed, as long as the person deviated from the standard in *both* directions (under and over) with comparable frequency, the standard wouldn't change at all. It's only repeated deviation in one direction that would yield an appreciable effect.

The idea that changes in a meta-level standard are produced by a slow-acting feedback system may help to account for why it's so hard to shift voluntarily. That is, you can easily change self-verbalizations ("stop being so demanding of yourself – be more satisfied with what you're accomplishing"), but this sort of self-verbalization rarely takes effect immediately. If a shift in meta standard relies on a slow-acting feedback loop, that would account for why subjective experience tends to lag behind self-instruction.

It's also of interest (and once again counterintuitive) that these shifts in reference value (and resultant effects on affect) imply a mechanism within the organism that functions to actively prevent the too-frequent occurrence of positive feeling, as well as the too-frequent occurrence of negative feeling. That is, the (bidirectional) shifting of the rate criterion over time would tend to control pacing of behavior in such a way that affect continues to vary in both directions around neutral, roughly the same as it had before.

Such an arrangement for changing meta-level standard thus wouldn't result in maximization of pleasure and minimization of pain. Rather, the affective consequence would be that the person experiences more or less the same range of variation in affective experience over extended periods of time and circumstances (cf. Myers & Diener, 1995). The organization would act as a gyroscope that serves to keep you floating along within the framework of the affective reality you're familiar with. It would provide a continuous recalibration of the feeling system across changes in situation. To use a different image, it would repeatedly shift the balance point of a psychic teeter-totter, so that rocking in both directions remains possible. What we're describing here resembles in some respects what Solomon (1980; Solomon & Corbit, 1974) described as the long-term consequences of the operation of an opponent process system.[2]

---

[2] Although we believe this is the normal experience for most persons, this shift is not inevitable. Indeed, for some people negative feelings appear to lead to further sensitization and vulnerability to negative feelings (cf. Suomi, 1991). It's almost as though the adjuster of the meta system were acting as a positive feedback loop. It is unclear why this should happen, but it seems an important phenomenon to understand.

FURTHER ISSUES

There are several further issues to raise which aren't so readily cata-
logued into groups. We consider them in the following section, in no
particular order.

Stress as the Disruption of Goal-Directed Activity

The conceptual analysis of affect in Chapter 8 is a view on affect, not
on stress. It does, however, offer a window on the experience of stress.
From this frame of reference, stress occurs when goal-oriented efforts
are interfered with or threatened (see also Burke, 1991; Carver, Scheier,
& Pozo, 1992; Thoits, 1991). This is true whether the effort is disrupted
by situational threats, chronic external impediments, or personal inade-
quacies. As goal-directed efforts are disrupted, progress toward the goal
is slowed and negative feelings arise. The more disruption (and the more
central is the threatened goal to the overall sense of self), the greater the
distress.

Indeed, it can be argued that the experience of stress is disruptive not
only because it inherently fosters creation of negative affect, but also because dealing with a problem in one domain tends to interfere with other
aspects of life as well.[3] This is a natural consequence of having multiple
current concerns: There's only so much time and attention to be used.
If too much has to go into one domain (because it's demanding or because it intrudes at unpredictable and inopportune times), concentration
is necessarily removed from other domains. As attention is pulled from
other domains, progress in those domains begins to suffer and negative
feelings arise with respect to *those* current concerns. Stress thus breeds
more stress.

The effects of disruption of behavior on distress are well illustrated
in a study by Millar, Tesser, and Millar (1988). They started from a
viewpoint similar to the one assumed here: that the self is partly a set of
goals manifest in ongoing behaviors, many of which are activities shared
with other people. Their study took advantage of the natural interruption
of shared activities which occurs when starting college. They assessed
how many activities shared with a significant other were disrupted by
the transition to college. They predicted and found that more disruption of activities predicted more depression and more thought intrusions
about the person formerly sharing the activities. If the behaviors were

---

[3] We thank Arthur Stone for drawing our attention to this point.

somehow continued, however (e.g., with another person), these effects were greatly diminished.

These disruptions seem to represent both disruption of desired behavioral activities and the disruption of an ongoing relationship. Our interpretation is that interference with both types of goals contributed to distress, and that interference with the relationship led to thought intrusion about the relationship. The pattern of findings Millar et al. obtained is quite consistent with the observation that the death of a spouse disrupts many aspects of a person's ongoing life, and that the disruption of the activities shared between the persons may be responsible for some of the distress that results (Stroebe, Stroebe, Gergen, & Gergen, 1982).

These findings are also consistent with data from a number of other sources. For example, a study of the experience of overload among police dispatchers (Kirmeyer, 1988) found that sheer volume of work influenced perceptions of overload only indirectly, via the number of interruptions per hour of work. Other studies have found that social hindrance of goal-directed activity is linked to distress (Ruehlman & Wolchik, 1988; see also Manne & Zautra, 1989; Rook, 1984). Several influences probably contribute to the adverse consequences of interruption in goal-directed efforts, such as cognitive fatigue from holding many unfulfilled intentions in mind (e.g., Cohen, 1980). Nevertheless, we'd argue that these consequences are also determined partly by the negative feelings resulting when movement toward a desired goal is interfered with.

Goal Attainment and Negative Affect

Successful goal attainment usually produces positive feelings. From our point of view, this is because you're often closing the gap rapidly at the point of goal attainment. However, this rapid progress doesn't always precede goal attainment. Nor is it true that reaching a goal always produces strong feelings of pleasure.

There are two aspects to this. One concerns the final period of approach to the goal, and the velocity that characterizes that period. If your velocity is low as you approach the goal, the final approach shouldn't feel very positive. This is the experience you have when the last stages of finishing a project involve a lot of struggle, so the forward motion feels like swimming in Jell-O. This is the experience you have when a significant other finally does something you've been asking for, but after so much time it hardly seems notable. In a word, when progress slows before goal attainment, the attainment sometimes feels anticlimactic.

The other aspect of this issue concerns the relation between this goal and other goals. Paradoxically, goal attainment sometimes produces bad feelings. A great deal depends on the context in which the success is embedded. Sometimes the success opens up the possibility of other goals to move toward. In such cases, the success is progress in two senses – progress toward the initial goal and progress toward new goals. Sometimes, however, the goal that's attained is a dead end, leading to no further possibilities, in a domain that you value. In such a case the success leads to an abrupt *halt* in progress. Such a success feels truly empty. This sort of goal attainment may be followed (or even accompanied) by feelings of dysphoria rather than elation.

Others have described this view on the consequences of goal attainment more vividly. Pervin (1992) wrote ". . . if positive affect is derived only from the process of striving for the goal, then we are forever on the precipice of being disappointed as we achieve what we have most wanted. Having achieved our goal, we are left with the choice of setting a higher or different standard, or being left with nothingness" (p. 163). In a newspaper column, author Ran Henry put it more bluntly, as well as more pessimistically: "The worst moment in your life is when you attain your goal." Given the context of his writing, Pervin wasn't happy about drawing this conclusion about goals and affect (and we'd have to infer that Henry wasn't either). Yet, this conclusion seems to be implied by this model.

We believe that success is most likely to lead to sustained positive feelings when the attainment of one goal slides smoothly into a sense of progress toward other goals. In this model people are the psychological equivalent of sharks. Just as the shark must always move forward to stay alive, positive feelings seem to require continuously or repeatedly having the sense of moving forward toward your goals.

Conflict and Mixed Feelings

Our discussion thus far has focused on the existence of one feeling at a time. However, it's entirely possible for a single event to produce more than one feeling quality if the event has implications for two (or more) distinct goals.

For an event to have such implications is not at all uncommon. The goals in the hierarchy of a person's self-definition aren't always perfectly compatible with each other at a given moment. As we noted in Chapter 6, sometimes conflicting goals become salient at the same time (Emmons,

1986; Van Hook & Higgins, 1988). For example, you may want career advancement and time with your young children, but the 24-hour day makes it hard to reach both. Sometimes the very actions that permit progress toward one goal (working extra hours) simultaneously interfere with progress toward the other. If both goals are salient, the result is mixed feelings – positive feelings from the career advancement, negative feelings from failure to spend enough time with your children.

Even the process of experiencing a particular emotion can arouse another emotion. Consider a person who's been taught that pride over accomplishment isn't good, because his happiness causes others to feel bad and inferior (not an unusual lesson, in some cultures). Upon experiencing rapid movement toward a goal, this person experiences happiness and pride. Upon realizing that he's feeling happy and proud (thus deviating from the cultural standard), he feels shamed. The result is mixed feelings.

The idea of multiple simultaneous goals thus provides a simple explanation for mixed feelings. People making rapid progress on one current concern and poor progress on another are likely to have positive feelings about the first and negative feelings about the second.

We're assuming here that meta-monitoring takes place for more than one goal at a time. We assume it happens even for goals that are largely outside consciousness. Perhaps one factor causing affect to seem so mysterious over the years is that people can have feelings, even strong feelings, without a clear grasp of their source. This would happen when for some reason the goal relevant to the feelings isn't readily accessible. This inaccessibility doesn't mean the goal isn't there, and it doesn't mean the person isn't trying to self-regulate toward it, even though being unaware of doing so (Bargh, 1997).

A person with more than one goal in force, one of which is inaccessible to awareness, can have feelings that seem inappropriate or inappropriately strong. We share with many the belief that these feelings arise because of the relevance of a current experience to some important goal that's being monitored out of awareness. In this respect we find ourselves in agreement with psychodynamic models of human functioning.

Time Windows for Input to Meta-Monitoring Can Vary

Another issue concerns the input to the meta system. We described the model in terms of distance, velocity, and acceleration at a given slice in time. However, the values computed internally as velocity and

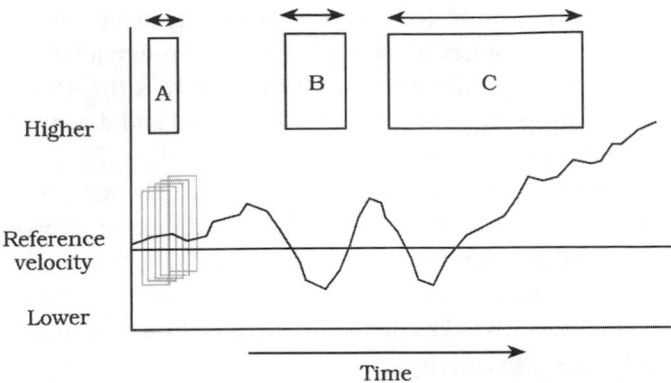

Figure 9.2.   Input to the meta system can reflect data aggregated across a span of time, rather than data from a single instant. An instant-by-instant computation of velocity would track the graphed line exactly. If computation used data from a brief window of time (span A), each successive instant's computation would take into account data from the preceding window (adding and omitting an instant each time). This would have the effect of smoothing and dampening the curve. The temporal window may also vary from brief (A) to longer (B and C), with longer windows yielding more dampening.

acceleration depend on information drawn not just from that instant, but from some period preceding that instant. We assume that the time span used for this computation can vary, from a very brief span to one that may be fairly long. Whether the input is merged over a short or a long period can have important implications for the resulting subjective experience.

Consider the person whose velocity toward a goal over time is illustrated in Figure 9.2. This person is moving forward throughout, but the movement is erratic in pacing. Velocity is fairly high in some periods and low in others (this illustration assumes an arbitrary, constant reference value). Instant-by-instant computation of velocity would track exactly the line in the figure. If computation instead used data from a brief window of time moving continuously forward, computation (and affect) would still occur at each instant. However, each computation would take into account the events of the preceding window (merging across preceding instants). What would emerge would be a "moving average" rather than a point-by-point account. This would have the effect of smoothing and dampening the curve. The temporal window may also vary from quite brief (span A) to much longer (span C). The longer the window, the more the curve is dampened.

What impact does this have on affect? If the input to the meta system is based on a brief window of time, periods of widely varying velocity will cause the person to feel good across some spans and bad across others. If the same series of events is viewed through a longer window, the affect that's experienced while moving across the span will vary, but be more moderated. The deviations upward and downward will be blunted by the aggregation process.

The moderating effect of a longer window might seem to imply that it's desirable to have a broad view. There is, however, a potential disadvantage to this. Merging data over a very long window can create insensitivity to what actually are meaningful changes. Thus, there's a tradeoff. Too brief a window yields emotional lability; too long a window yields affective insensitivity.

This general line of reasoning suggests a possible process basis for the fact that people differ in how variable their moods are (Diener, Larsen, Levine, & Emmons, 1985; Larsen, 1987; Penner, Shiffman, Paty, & Fritzsche, 1994; Wessman & Ricks, 1966). Perhaps differences in emotional variability reflect differences in the window of time used to create input to the meta system.

Are There Other Mechanisms that Produce Affect?

Our focus in Chapter 8 was on a mechanism that we believe underlies the creation of affect in the normal flow of experience. It's clear, however, that affect can be induced in ways other than by direct operation of this mechanism. Affect is responsive to feedback from facial musculature, from patterns of vocalizations, and from postural and movement patterns (see, e.g., Ekman & Davidson, 1993; Ekman, Levenson, & Friesen, 1983; Hatfield, Cacioppo, & Rapson, 1993; Levenson, Ekman, & Friesen, 1990; Stepper & Strack, 1993). How do such findings fit the model we've suggested?

Our speculations here will not do justice to the complexity of the problem, but a small degree of speculation is in order. Let's assume that the various behavioral qualities noted above are closely linked in the functioning of the nervous system with the experience of affect (an assumption that's consistent with positions of theorists who emphasize the role of muscle activity in emotional experience). Two possibilities are suggested by these close connections.

One possibility relies on the idea that links between the phenomenological experience of affect and the facial, postural, and vocal qualities are well elaborated in memory. It may be, then, that creation of the muscle patterns pulls the affective-tone information from long-term storage into working memory, yielding the phenomenology of affect. The other possibility is that the muscle feedback and meta systems are mutually entrained, such that the action of either pulls the functioning of the other into line with it. If this were so, the creation of specific patterns of muscle movement might influence the action of the meta system in some unknown fashion, such that the experience of affect is created anew.

In either case, we aren't inclined to a view in which facial, vocal, and postural muscle activities have primacy in the creation of affect over an internal evaluator of some sort. On the other hand, such motor activity may well be bound up in a multimodal affective response, perhaps even as a co-equal with the subjective experience of the affective quality. Our model implies no particular stand on that question.

RELATIONSHIPS TO OTHER THEORIES

At this point we turn to brief comparisons with several other viewpoints on affect. This is not a comprehensive survey of alternative theories. However, there are several views to which we think comparisons are particularly useful or interesting.

Affect and Reprioritization

Some years ago, Simon (1967) proposed a view on affect that was intended to show how affect functions within the framework of cognitive and motivational processes. He suggested that affect, particularly negative affect, causes people to interrupt their behavior (see also Sloman, 1987) and consider the possibility that an alternate goal (not presently focal) should have a higher priority than it now has. The stronger the emotion, the stronger the message that the less attended goal should receive high priority, replacing the goal that's presently focal. Thus a potential function for the negative emotion is to cause a reconsideration and reprioritization of one's goals.

Simon's analysis seems compatible with the ideas we're proposing, but his view on reprioritization rests on a point we've thus far considered only superficially. Specifically, his analysis seems to require that discrepancies with respect to at least two different reference values can be monitored (and meta-monitored) simultaneously – one focally, the other less so. The emotion that calls for reprioritization is being generated by what's occurring with respect to the *less focal* value. The call for reprioritization is a call to upgrade the priority of that second value.

The easiest illustration of this argument is what occurs when anxiety arises while the person is engaged in goal-directed effort. Consider, for example, the anxiety that arises when a person with a snake phobia tries to approach and pick up a snake. In such a case, the rate of progress toward the focal reference value – the concrete behavioral goal that the person is trying to attain – is not itself the source of the anxiety. Rather, the anxiety is produced by something happening with respect to a second reference value (cf. our earlier discussion of conflict).

This second reference value may be concern about physical harm (in the case of the phobic person). In other cases it may be the desire to maintain a positive self-portrayal, the desire for approval, or even holistic personal integration (cf. Rogers, 1980). As the person attempts the intended action, that second value (whatever it is) is threatened. The farther the person goes in the attempted action, the greater is the threat to that second goal. If self-regulation is going poorly with respect to that second goal, the result is negative feelings. If the second goal is an avoidance goal, the feeling will be an agitation-related affect such as anxiety. If it's an approach goal, the feeling will be frustration or eventually a dejection-related affect such as sadness or depression.

The threat that creates distress in these cases is a by-product of the attempt to do something else. The snake phobic is trying to approach a feared stimulus, but doing so is creating perceptions of diminishing safety. The fear thus signals that he should be devoting greater attention to the goal of staying away from danger than the goal of holding the snake. As with all self-regulation, action isn't necessary for the effect to occur. Affect can arise if environmental disturbances, or even the passage of time, cause changes in discrepancies regarding a nonfocal goal. For example, imagine you have four errands to do, one at a store that closes at 5 o'clock. As the afternoon wears on, the completion of that errand – which otherwise wasn't as important as the others – begins to be threatened. Affect may arise, causing you to reprioritize, moving it up in line.

This view on reprioritization assumes that reference values are often monitored outside awareness until discrepancy changes are detected, at which point the value intrudes on awareness. This view also suggests a way of thinking about cases in which an affect arises without a clear source. That is, perhaps the signal for reprioritization has reached awareness, but for some reason the behavioral goal itself hasn't. Obviously many questions are unanswered here about how often, and to what extent, such parallel processing of multiple goal values takes place in human behavior (cf. Bargh, 1997).

Though anxiety is perhaps the easiest emotion to address in terms of Simon's analysis, other emotions can be assimilated to it. For example, guilt occurs when behavior creates a discrepancy regarding a moral standard, or reduces a discrepancy regarding an undesired self. Shame seems to result when an action moves a person closer to social disapproval (Tangney, 1990; Tangney, Wagner, Fletcher, & Gramzow, 1992). Each of these emotions can arise from behavior that perfectly matches your action intention. In each case, the emotion seems not to concern the value toward which you're trying to move behaviorally. Rather, it's a by-product of that movement, occurring because the action has consequences in addition to those intended.

Simon's ideas about reprioritizing apply most readily to negative affect, with the interrupting condition always being a demand to accord higher priority to some nonfocal goal. This asymmetry raises again the more general issue of people being more responsive to negative than positive information. Several researchers have pointed to the biological necessity to be more alert to pain than to pleasure (Hansen & Hansen, 1988; Pratto & John, 1991; Taylor, 1991). Negative events have potential implications not just for emotional well-being, but for survival. Thus it's especially important to note them. Simon's analysis of affect as a call for reprioritization seems very compatible with this line of argument (cf. Pratto & John, 1991, p. 380).

Self-Discrepancy Theory

Another useful comparison relates our ideas to the theory proposed by Higgins and colleagues (Higgins, 1987, 1989, 1996; Higgins, Bond, Klein, & Strauman, 1986; Strauman, 1989), which we've already mentioned at several points in the book, called self-discrepancy theory. It holds that certain emotions occur as the result of discrepancies between pairs of psychological entities called self-guides.

The theory focuses on two kinds of discrepancies. The first is between the perceived actual self and the ideal self (actual–ideal discrepancies). The second is between the perceived actual self and the ought self (actual–ought discrepancies). As noted earlier, an ideal self is a desired self to which one aspires. Living up to the ideal means attaining something desired. An ought self is a duty or obligation, a self one feels compelled to be rather than desires to be (similar to what Ryan and Deci call introjected values – see Ryan et al., 1993, table 1). Living up to an ought means doing something to avoid disapproval (including self-disapproval).

Each person has ideals and oughts (which may be interwoven or distinct), and the perceived actual self can be compared to each reference point. According to this theory, discrepancies between ideal and actual yield depression or other dejection-related feelings (see also Finlay-Jones & Brown, 1981). Discrepancies between actual and ought yield anxiety or other agitation-related feelings.

Three differences between self-discrepancy theory and our model deserve mention. First, self-discrepancy theory holds that affect is produced by a discrepancy between two representations of the self. To us, the discrepancy that matters concerns rate of progress toward goals, including idealized representations of the self. Thus, from our point of view, a person who's discrepant from the ideal but has the perception of moving toward it rapidly enough is likely to experience positive rather than negative affect.

A second difference is also implicit in this last statement. Our model addresses both positive and negative affects. Self-discrepancy theory was proposed as a theory of negative affect. It's less clear how to think about positive affect in that framework in a way that permits the existence of positive, negative, and no affect under varying circumstances. In including a clear basis for the existence of positive feeling qualities, our model thus seems to add something important.

The third comparison is perhaps the most interesting. It concerns the distinction between ideals and oughts, the most novel and innovative aspect of the Higgins analysis. This distinction provides a conceptual basis for differentiating anxiety from depression, an important and difficult differentiation between two qualities that tend to co-occur in human experience. The theory has been quite successful in predicting a unique association between actual–ideal discrepancies and dysphoria, and a unique association between actual–ought discrepancies and anxiety.

As we said in Chapter 4, we think there's a structural difference between oughts and ideals. Ideals seem to require only approach goals (with discrepancy-reducing loops). In contrast, oughts seem inherently to involve two self-regulatory processes at once (see Figure 9.3, which duplicates Figure 4.3). Oughts seem to involve trying to move toward a positive goal and simultaneously trying to escape from an anti-goal (a discrepancy-enlarging loop).

Which loop matters most? From our viewpoint, if an avoidance loop is doing poorly at avoiding, the result is anxiety. This view suggests

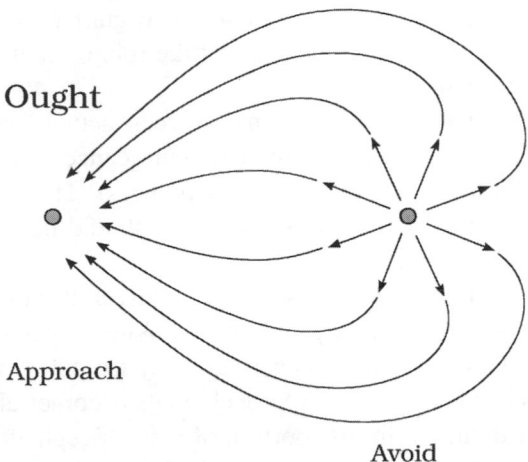

Ought

Approach

Avoid

Figure 9.3.   Self-regulation with respect to an ought self-guide can be viewed as involving both a desire to move toward a prescribed value and a desire to move away from a proscribed or punished value. The effects of the latter avoidance process are given form by those of the positive ought value, which functions as the reference value in an approach loop.

that the source of anxiety in an actual–ought discrepancy may be an ineffective effort to avoid the feared or undesired self more than an ineffective effort to attain the ought self (see also Higgins et al., 1997).

We recently conducted a study to explore this idea (Carver, Lawrence, & Scheier, in press). Subjects generated lists of ought selves, ideal selves, and feared selves. They then rated how closely their actual selves resembled each self-guide. Actual–ought, actual–ideal, and actual–feared discrepancies were computed by summing the differences reported. These were then correlated with later reports of several kinds of affects.

In the full sample, the patterns of associations tended to indicate that the feared self plays an important role in agitation-related affects, preempting the role of discrepancies from the ought self. Somewhat to our surprise, the feared self also played a role in prediction of dejection-related affects. It didn't preempt the role of the ideal self but added to it.

Perhaps the most interesting findings, however, came from analyses testing interactions between proximity to the ought self and proximity to the feared self. Significant interactions emerged for the agitation-related affects – anxiety and guilt. Among subjects who were relatively near their feared selves, discrepancy from the ought self played no role. That proximity to the feared self was all that mattered. Among subjects farther from the feared self, however, anxiety and guilt were strongly predicted by actual–ought discrepancies, and the role of actual–feared discrepancies diminished.

In contrast to this pattern, interactions between actual–feared and actual–ideal discrepancies did not approach significance as predictors of dejection-related affects (depression and happiness). This appears to indicate that the dynamic behind these latter affects did not vary as a function of closeness to the feared self.

This pattern for agitation-related affects is consistent with the dynamic of the analysis suggested by Figure 9.3. When a person is too near the feared value, what matters is getting away from it. Only when some distance has been attained do approach goals become salient and thus more relevant to affect. In that portion of the self-regulatory map, distance to the desired goal begins to matter, and the oughts assert their affect-relevant properties with more clarity.

In sum, the data appear to fit a picture in which being near the feared self causes people to orient to the feared self. In that zone, the actual–feared discrepancy is what matters. This fits the notion that evolution places a great premium on avoiding danger. The second force (the move-toward force) is less pressing. When there's distance between the actual and the feared self, there's less reason for concern about danger. In this zone of self-regulation, people can attend more closely to the desired values that ultimately are important in guiding behavior.

In Chapter 4 we noted that discrepancy-enlarging feedback processes appear to be functional only when somehow constrained by negative feedback processes. That principle also seems to apply to feared selves. Although there are many ways in which a person could escape from a given feared self, the mere desire to escape provides no positive guidance. It requires a positive goal to provide such direction. This is what the ought self does (Figure 9.3). The ought self thus gives coherent form to self-regulation that has escape and avoidance as its impetus.

Positive and Negative Affect

Another comparison worth considering concerns our position that approach and avoidance loops yield two bipolar dimensions of affect (a view strongly influenced by self-discrepancy theory). Figure 9.4 (identical to Figure 8.5) is a reminder of our position. In this section we compare this view to that discussed under the labels *positive* and *negative affect* (Watson & Tellegen, 1985; Zevon & Tellegen, 1982; see also

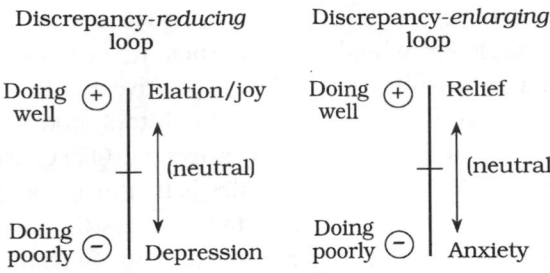

Figure 9.4.   We assume a discrepancy *reducing* meta system yields affective qualities of sadness or depression when progress is below standard and happiness or elation when progress is above standard. We assume a discrepancy *enlarging* system yields anxiety when progress is below standard and relief or contentment when progress is above standard.

Diener & Emmons, 1984; Diener & Iran-Nejad, 1986; Warr, Barter, & Brownbridge, 1983).

The view identified with the terms positive and negative affect (and their dispositional counterparts, positive and negative affectivity) has become quite prominent in recent years. We would argue, however, that these labels are misleading (see also Larsen & Diener, 1992). They convey the sense that each dimension is unipolar, running from neutral to positive feeling and from neutral to distress, respectively. In reality, despite the labels, each dimension has both positive and negative indicators. Each dimension thus has both positive and negative poles.

Indeed, early on Watson and Tellegen (1985) labeled them as bipolar. More specifically, in reanalyzing several sets of mood data, Watson and Tellegen (1985) found two dimensions of affect, but sometimes there were negative indicators of positive affect and positive indicators of negative affect. Of particular interest, the few descriptors of depression (e.g., blue, sad, downhearted) loaded on *positive* affect. The few terms reflective of relief (the closest being calm, carefree, placid, and satisfied) loaded on *negative* affect. These loadings are quite consonant with the model in Figure 9.4. In sum, the data sets reviewed by Watson and Tellegen (1985) fit well to the dimensions we've argued for on different grounds.

This resemblance would be harder to identify, however, from later discussions of positive and negative affect. In developing scales to measure positive and negative affect (the PANAS), Watson, Clark, and Tellegen (1988) chose not to include any item implying either depression or relief-serenity. Their item choices ensured that each dimension was represented only by items with the valence appropriate to the scale's label. In so doing, however, they obscured the question – left hanging by the earlier research – of why descriptors such as "sad" and "down" should be part of a dimension with the label "positive affect."[4]

The PANAS has become popular as a research tool, both in a situational format and in an individual-differences format. One consequence of this popularity and the names of the scales is that many people have come to assume that all negative affect is more or less the same. This, we think, is an error, particularly regarding depression and anxiety (see also Endler, Cox, Parker, & Bagby, 1992). As noted above, Watson and Tellegen (1985) found that depression-related items relate to the positive affect dimension. There's also evidence that depression and anxiety have different cognitive concomitants (e.g., Ahrens & Haaga, 1993; Clark, Beck, & Brown, 1989; Dalgleish & Watts, 1990; Greenberg & Alloy, 1989; Greenberg & Beck, 1989; Mineka & Sutton, 1992; Strauman, 1989; Wickless & Kirsch, 1988; Young, Fogg, Scheftner, Fawcett, Akiskal, & Maser, 1996). Further evidence that these qualities are differentiable comes from the entire literature of self-discrepancy theory.

Certainly there are many circumstances when an impending failure to attain a desired goal is confounded with an impending failure to avoid a punisher. For example, failing to have a desired romantic liaison may co-occur with receiving cues of rejection or disapproval. In such situations people may experience both sadness and anxiety, and in such situations the distinction may be of little practical importance. However, there's a conceptual difference between failure to attain something desired and failure to avoid something undesired. We believe it's important to note this difference, and we suspect there are circumstances in which the distinction is of practical value as well.

Biological Models of Bases of Affect

Another important theoretical comparison pertains to a group of theories that are biological in focus. The research base of these theories ranges

---

[4] Cacioppo and Berntson (1994) have argued that the evaluative space in which attitudes exist is two-dimensional, corresponding to the dimensions of the Watson et al. model. We see the evaluative space as two-dimensional, but we see each dimension as extending beyond the neutral point to bipolarity. Thus, a summary attitude is more than an amalgam of elements of liking and disliking. It can reflect associations of the attitude object with (at a minimum) happiness, sadness, fear, and relief – the four anchors of the two dimensions under discussion.

from animal conditioning and behavioral pharmacology (Gray, 1972, 1977, 1978, 1982, 1987b) to neuropsychological studies of brain activity (Davidson, 1992a, 1992b, 1995; Davidson & Sutton, 1995; Tomarken et al., 1992). The various theories are quite similar in important ways, but in other ways they differ.

These theories all incorporate the idea that two systems (sometimes more) are involved in the regulation of behavior (cf. Konorski, 1967; Schneirla, 1959; Thayer, 1989). One system deals with appetitive motivation, approach behavior. This system is variously called a behavioral activation system (Fowles, 1980; Cloninger, 1987), behavioral approach system (Gray, 1981, 1987a, 1990), behavioral engagement system (Depue, Krauss, & Spoont, 1987), and behavioral facilitation system (Depue & Iacono, 1989). The other deals with aversive motivation, withdrawal or avoidance. This system is usually called the behavioral inhibition system (Cloninger, 1987; Gray, 1981, 1987a, 1990), though it's sometimes termed a withdrawal system (Davidson, 1992a, 1992b).

The two systems are generally regarded as independent, because they're believed to be regulated by different brain mechanisms. Thus, their functions can be enhanced (or diminished) separately by situational cues. Activity in one system doesn't imply the absence of activity in the other. A second sort of independence concerns the fact that individuals presumably differ from one another in how sensitive the biological systems are to stimuli that engage them. These sensitivities should be independent from one system to the other (cf. Carver & White, 1994).

In sum, these models assume two systems, one concerned with approach of desired goals, the other concerned with withdrawal from antigoals. At least some of the theories assume further that the two systems underlie affect. In situations with cues of impending reward, the activity of the approach system creates positive feelings. In situations with cues of impending punishment, the avoidance system creates feelings of anxiety.

Data from a variety of sources fit this picture. Of particular interest are findings from Davidson and his collaborators. These findings are of interest partly because so many of them come from human subjects. This research examines EEG recordings, assessing changes in activation in response to affective inducing stimuli and assessing the possibility of individual differences in susceptibility to the experience of particular affective qualities.

Among the findings are these: Subjects exposed to films inducing fear and disgust (Davidson, Ekman, Saron, Senulis, & Friesen, 1990) and confronted with possible punishment (Sobotka, Davidson, & Senulis, 1992) show elevations in *right* frontal activation. In a similar vein, but with a different measure, anti-anxiety medication reduced metabolic rate in the right occipital and frontal cortex in subjects with anxiety disorder (Buchsbaum et al., 1987). In contrast, adults with an opportunity to obtain reward (Sobota et al., 1992) and smiling 10-month-olds viewing their approaching mothers (Fox & Davidson, 1988) showed elevations in *left* frontal activation, as have adult subjects presented with positive emotional adjectives (Cacioppo & Petty, 1980).

Resting asymmetries have been viewed as reflecting differential susceptibility to affect. Higher relative left frontal activation (at rest) related to reports of higher levels of trait positive affectivity (Tomarken, Davidson, Wheeler, & Doss, 1992) and to the tendency to experience stronger responses to films eliciting positive feelings (Wheeler, Davidson, & Tomarken, 1993). Higher relative resting levels of right frontal activation related to stronger negative affect in response to films eliciting anxiety and disgust. Self-reported emotional *reactivity* to incentives and threats shows even stronger relations to relative left and right frontal resting activation, respectively (Harmon-Jones & Allen, 1997; Sutton & Davidson, 1997). On the basis of findings such as these, Davidson (1992a, 1992b, 1995) concludes that specialized neural substrates for approach and withdrawal systems (and thus positive and negative affect) are located in the left and right frontal areas of the cerebral cortex, respectively.

The logic of these models thus far resembles the logic of our model (and also that associated with the dimensions of positive and negative affect). All agree on the sources of elation and anxiety. At this point, however, the theories begin to diverge. They diverge regarding the impact of *failure to attain reward* and *successful avoidance of punishment,* the conditions producing the affects represented in the bottom left and upper right portions of Figure 9.4.

Gray (1977, 1978, 1981, 1987b, 1990, 1994) holds that the avoidance system is responsible for negative feelings in response to cues of punishment and cues of frustrative nonreward. He holds that the approach system is responsible for positive feelings in response to cues of reward and cues of escape from (or avoidance of) punishment. In his view, then, each system is responsible for affect of one hedonic tone, positive in one, negative in the other (see Figure 9.5). This view is consistent with

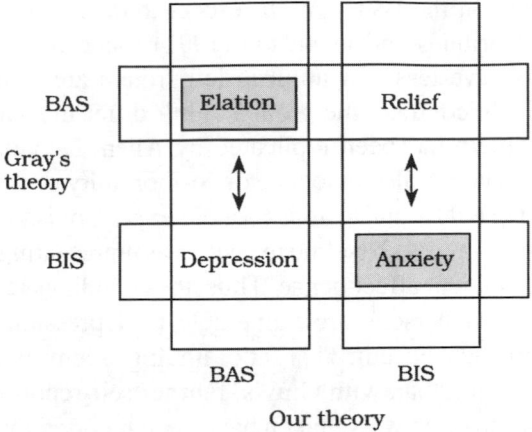

Figure 9.5.   Gray's view of affect (horizontal groupings) ties positive affects to the behavioral activation system (BAS), as results of occurrence of reward and avoidance of punishment. It ties negative affects to the behavioral inhibition system (BIS), as results of frustrative nonreward and occurrence of punishment. Our view (vertical groupings, as in Figure 9.4) ties the dimension of elation–depression to the BAS and the dimension of anxiety–relief to the BIS.

a picture of two unipolar affective dimensions, each linked to a distinct behavioral system.[5] A similar position has been taken by Lang, Bradley, and Cuthbert (1992).

Our position, detailed earlier, argues for two bipolar dimensions, one related to an approach system, the other to an avoidance system (Figure 9.5). We think the disappointment and eventual depression that result from failure to attain desired goals involves the approach system (for similar predictions see Clark, Watson, & Mineka, 1994, p. 107; Cloninger, 1988, p. 103). Sadness and depression involve *reduced* activity in the approach system, as the pursuit of goals diminishes. A parallel line of reasoning suggests that relief, contentment, tranquility, and serenity relate to the avoidance system rather than the approach system, reflecting low levels of activity in that system.

Less information exists about neurophysiological bases of these affects than about anxiety and happiness. With regard to relief-tranquility,

---

[5] The core issue is not which system produces which affect, so much as which system is responsive to the particular stimulus situation in question. Gray says the avoidance system is responsive to frustrative nonreward. Given that presumption, assignment of responsibility for negative affect in frustrating circumstances to the avoidance system follows directly.

we know of no data on the issue. With respect to depression, limited evidence exists. Henriques and Davidson (1991) found that clinically depressed subjects have less activation in left frontal areas than non-depressed controls. In contrast, the groups didn't differ in right frontal activation. This pattern has been replicated by Allen, Iacono, Depue, and Arbisi (1993). There's also evidence of co-morbidity of depression with stroke involving left frontal lesions (Gruenberg & Goldstein, 1997).

Recall that Davidson views baseline measures as representing suscep-tibility rather than ambient affect per se. Thus, these findings tentatively suggest that depressed persons are vulnerable to depression through deficits in their approach system. This set of findings seems more com-patible with our position than with Gray's. Further self-report data that seem to support the position we've taken have been reported by Higgins et al. (1997, study 4); behavioral data consistent with this position have been reported by Henriques, Glowacki, and Davidson (1994).

In sum, the available evidence, limited though it is, appears consistent with a model in which an approach system that's very active displays a propensity to experience happiness while goal-engaged, and an approach system that's hypoactive displays a propensity to experience sadness and dejection when goal attainment is frustrated.

In future research attempting to separate these theoretical views, it will be important to create situations in which only one affect quality is created at a time. This is easier to say than do. It will also ultimately be important to assess physiological change from baselines in each hemi-sphere, as opposed to relying entirely on hemispheric asymmetries. Such comparisons are necessary in order to be sure which hemisphere (and thus which behavioral system) is involved in a given effect. It will be very interesting to see the results of such research as it proceeds.

10

Expectancies and Disengagement

> But they did find their mountain. And they did climb it. . . . And for a
> while they *thought* they would get up to the top. And while they
> *thought* they could, they were happy.
> (Virginia Axline, *Dibs: In Search of Self*)

> Whether you think you can or think you can't, you're right.
> (Henry Ford)

People sometimes talk as though feelings and thoughts were totally
distinct, but that's not true. Sometimes feelings are directly linked to
thoughts. Sadness connects to doubt, and happiness to confidence, hope-
fulness, and optimism. In Chapter 8, we suggested that a single mechanism yields two subjective readouts. The first – affect – was the subject of the rest of Chapter 8. The second, we said, is a hazy sense of
confidence versus doubt. We turn now to that experience, confidence
versus doubt – expectancies about what will happen in the immediate
future.

We start with evidence of a link between affect and expectancy, then
consider the fact that repeated experience can cause expectancies to become more solidified in memory. In judging what will happen next,
people sometimes rely on those memories as much as (or more than)
their current experience. Later we consider the idea that expectancies (or the experiences that give rise to them) create a divergence between two classes of behavior, a divergence with a great many implications.

AFFECT IS LINKED TO EXPECTANCY

A basic premise is that the mechanism underlying positive versus negative affect also gives rise to a sense of confidence versus doubt. This hazy
sense of expectancy is more cognitive than is the affect, but we're not

suggesting that these expectancies are carefully thought out, or that they appear in consciousness as probability estimates. Rather, they're a non-verbal sense of optimism versus pessimism about whatever behavioral goal they derive from (or are connected to).[1]

The premise of a common origin implies a link in experience between feelings and expectancies. Several studies seem to make such a case – some directly, others more indirectly.

Feelings and Confidence

Some of the evidence linking affect to confidence is fairly direct. Studies have found that a bad mood causes bad events to seem more likely; a good mood makes good events seem more likely (Erber, 1991; Forgas & Moylan, 1987; Johnson & Tversky, 1983; MacLeod & Campbell, 1992; Mayer, Gaschke, Braverman, & Evans, 1992; Salovey & Birnbaum, 1989). Depressed people (e.g., Beck, 1972; Lewinsohn, Larson, & Muñoz, 1982; Pietromonaco & Markus, 1985; Pietromonaco & Rook, 1987; Youngren & Lewinsohn, 1980) and anxious people (Dewberry & Richardson, 1990) see negative events as more likely than do comparison groups. Evidence from the literature of coping also indicates that confidence and affect covary (Carver & Scheier, 1994).

Wegener and Petty (1996; see also Wegener, Petty, & Klein, 1994) extended this simple effect of mood to show it can influence how people react to persuasive messages. Subjects received messages arguing that changing their opinion would cause a good outcome. Those placed in good moods beforehand saw the good outcome as more likely (were more confident of it) than people placed in bad moods. Being more confident of the good outcome's occurrence, they were more persuaded. Indeed, mediational analyses indicated that the greater confidence was *why* they were more persuaded. The finding had a boundary condition: It happened only among people who are prone to think things over. But it fits the idea that positive feelings make people a bit more optimistic, whereas negative feelings make people a bit more pessimistic.

---

[1] In Chapter 8 we noted that one might conceptualize the meta process as controlling either rate, affect, or confidence. In past years we sometimes assumed that confidence is most basic and that behavior and affect follow from that (Carver & Scheier, 1981a). We now believe that the initial sense of confidence versus doubt stems from the same processing mechanism as affect. As a given experience plays itself out, though, it seems likely that the affect and confidence a person experiences can reciprocally influence and entrain each other.

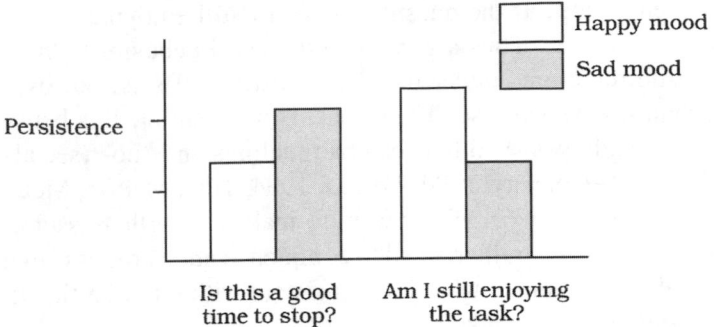

Figure 10.1.   Persistence among subjects who'd been placed in either a happy or sad mood, and who were told to ask themselves periodically whether it was a good time to stop or whether they were still enjoying the task. Mood had differing effects in these instructional conditions, consistent with the idea that being in a happy mood made people more likely to decide "yes" whereas being in a sad mood made people more likely to decide "no." (Adapted from Martin, Ward, Achee, & Wyer, 1993, experiment 2.)

Mood and Decision Making

Another finding that makes a similar point, but with a different twist, comes from research by Martin, Ward, Achee, and Wyer (1993; see also Martin & Stoner, 1996). Martin et al. gave people an ambiguous task, under varying instructional sets. In one experiment, some subjects were told to continue the task until they could reach a conclusion, others were told to continue as long as they still felt like it. In a second experiment, some subjects were told to continue until they felt it was a good time to stop, others were told to continue as long as they still enjoyed it (subjects were given specific questions to pose to themselves, to help them decide).

The outcome was how long subjects stayed with the task. Figure 10.1 shows the findings of the second experiment. Among subjects asking themselves "Is this a good time to stop?," those who'd been put in good moods beforehand stopped sooner than those in bad moods. Among subjects asking themselves "Am I still enjoying the task?," those in good moods stopped later than those in bad moods. The other experiment produced a similar pattern.

Here's the interpretation: When people asked themselves the question they'd been given, the tendency to answer "yes" or "no" was influenced by their mood. Good mood biased the person toward yes; bad mood biased the person toward no. If the question is "Is it time to stop?," yes means stop. If the question is "Am I still enjoying the task?," yes means continue. Thus a given mood caused behavior to be pushed in opposite directions under the two instructional sets, but by the same mechanism in each case. The mechanism is a simple link between good feelings and "yes" and between bad feelings and "no" (see also Clore, Schwarz, & Conway, 1994; Forgas, 1994; Hirt, Melton, McDonald, & Harackiewicz, 1996). If one were to make the further assumption that "yes-ness" is generally related to confidence and "no-ness" to doubtfulness, this mechanism would be consistent with our assertion that affect and confidence are linked.

The Martin et al. (1993) research is particularly interesting because yes-ness versus no-ness was reflected in continuing versus stopping. The linking of confidence to action is an especially important connection in its own right, to which we return shortly.

Confidence and Brain Function

Another source of indirect support for the idea that expectancies are linked to affect comes from research on brain function and expectancies. Recall from Chapter 9 that evidence links affective qualities to activation of the frontal lobes (Davidson, 1992a, 1992b). Greater activation of right frontal areas is tied to the experience of negative affects such as anxiety and disgust. Greater activation of left frontal areas is tied to the experience of positive feelings.

There's also evidence that links frontal asymmetry to people's expectations for their future. This evidence, however, involves a *manipulation* of activation, rather than its assessment. This research derives from evidence that having people attend to stimuli in one direction causes greater activation of the opposite hemisphere (for review and explanation, see Drake, 1984). Drake used this manipulation to increase activation in one side or the other (in different groups), after which he asked subjects to make ratings of the likelihood that various events would happen to them.

Subjects manipulated to activate the left hemisphere made ratings that were more optimistic about their future than subjects manipulated to activate the right hemisphere. This finding has been replicated using another manipulation of attention (Drake, 1987). This difference in processing has also led people to make differentially optimistic recommendations about risky decisions (Drake, 1985).

The findings of this research regarding expectancies displays a strong parallel to findings discussed in Chapter 8 regarding affect. Left hemisphere activation induced optimism (whereas in the research discussed earlier it was linked to positive feelings); right hemisphere activation induced pessimism (whereas in the other research it was tied to negative feelings). This parallel between sets of findings hints that the expectancies and affect were produced by similar mechanisms.

INTERRUPTION AND FURTHER ASSESSMENT

Although a link between feelings and expectancies seems very likely, it's obviously far from perfect. People's conscious expectancies for an outcome don't rest entirely on their currently noted rate of progress toward that outcome. Although adversity yields a sense of doubt, the transient sense of doubt is often modified substantially by further thought. This further thought probably entails at least a momentary interruption of behavior.

Interruption

We've often suggested that when people experience adversity in trying to move toward their goals, they periodically experience this sort of interruption of efforts and assess the likelihood of a successful outcome (e.g., Carver & Scheier, 1981a, 1983, 1986b, 1990a, 1990b). In effect, people suspend the behavioral stream, step outside it, and evaluate in a more deliberated way than occurs while acting. This may happen once, or often. It may be brief, or it may take an extended period.

What circumstances *induce* this interruption? It seems probable that the negative affect and sense of doubt arising from the meta processor is part of the stimulus to interruption. The experience of deceleration may also play a role. We argued in Chapter 8 that deceleration is manifested subjectively as a shift toward a more negative feeling. It seems reasonable that a discernible shift toward more negative feelings is often precisely the cue that triggers the interruption of action and causes people to consciously judge the chance of their eventual success. This is consistent with characterizations of surprise, which we argued is related to the acceleration–deceleration experience. For example, Tomkins (1984) has said that surprise represents sort of a "circuit breaker or interruptor mechanism" (p. 171).

One might contrast the experience of interruption with the experience of "flow" (Csikszentmihalyi, 1990). Flow is a condition in which behavior is never interrupted for an expectancy assessment. Perhaps the flow experience reflects a velocity function that's smoothly tracking its reference value. This is consistent with descriptions of the flow experience that emphasize the close fit between the demands of the environment and the person's competencies, such that the person is fully engaged in behaving but is never pressed to wonder whether the behavior can be successfully maintained.

People certainly vary in the tendency to interrupt their action and undertake expectancy assessment. Some are by disposition prone to lapse repeatedly into assessment (cf. Kuhl's, 1981, 1994b, concept of state orientation). These people would have a great deal of difficulty having a flow experience. Others only rarely stop to wonder whether an outcome is likely.

These differences in susceptibility to interrupting and assessing seem at least partly tied to the individual's preexisting levels of confidence. A fundamental effect of confidence seems to be to *preempt* the question of whether or not an action will be successful (see also Csikszentmihalyi, 1990, p. 39). The question is simply less likely to come up for a confident person than for a doubtful person.

Descriptions of the effects of serotonin reuptake inhibitors suggest that they act to reduce exactly the kind of hesitancy in action that seems to reflect repeated or extended expectancy assessment (e.g., Kramer, 1993). It may be that by changing the person's ambient level of implicit confidence, such medications tend to preempt the assessment question in the same way as does naturally occurring confidence.

Our interest here is on interruption during tasks, but we should note that something very similar to this interruption often happens before action even begins (cf. Gollwitzer, 1990). This is especially likely if the person knows the task will be hard. One element evaluated in such contexts is the likelihood of success. Indeed, the judged likelihood of success may be a critical determinant of the decision to undertake the behavior.

Assessment of Expectancies

The interruption of action in the face of adversity is tied to a deliberative assessment of the likelihood of success, given continued efforts. In more consciously assessing the probability of the desired outcome, people presumably depend heavily on their memories of prior outcomes in similar situations. They may also consider other issues – for example, additional resources they might bring to bear on the problem (cf. Lazarus, 1966; MacNair & Elliott, 1992) or alternative approaches to the problem. People also make use of social comparison information (e.g., Wills, 1981; Wood, 1989; Wood et al., 1985) and attributional analyses of prior events (Peterson & Seligman, 1984; Pittman & Pittman, 1980; Wong & Weiner, 1981) in assessing what the eventual outcome might be.

Many questions may be weighed and information drawn from several sources. Some influences on this assessment stem from variations in the situation. Others stem from personality. Dispositions can influence expectations, even when the situation confronted is the same for all. For example, the disposition of optimism versus pessimism is a dimension of generalized expectancies about the occurrence of good versus bad outcomes in one's future (Scheier & Carver, 1985, 1992; Scheier, Carver, & Bridges, 1994). Other circumstances being equal, people who are optimistic by nature are more likely to emerge from expectancy assessment with a greater sense of confidence than people who are pessimistic.

Irrespective of whether the influences are situational or dispositional in origin, the point remains the same: The thought-out and verbalizable expectancies that people generate when they interrupt their efforts and think about their likely outcomes can be influenced by a wide range of information.

In some instances the processing that occurs here is very simple. It may entail no more than retrieving a summary memory about prior outcomes in this class of situations (e.g., "I'm terrible at standardized tests"; "People never seem to like me"). It may involve engaging in self-exhortation ("You can do it – try harder" [Baggett, Saab, & Carver, 1996]). Other instances involve a search of diverse memories, or a more extensive analysis of possibilities. This would be true whenever people consider such questions as whether additional information is obtainable, whether others might provide help, or whether important aspects of the situation are likely to change soon enough to matter.

When people retrieve "chronic" expectancies from memory in summary form, the information already constitutes expectancies. Presumably these memories are accumulations or consolidations of products of meta-monitoring during previous instances of behavior. When brought from memory, this information would contribute directly to a subsequent sense of confidence or doubt. Since these memories may also link to memories of affect, they may also directly influence subsequent affect (cf. Mayer & Gaschke, 1988).

For cases involving more thorough processing, however, people typically bring to mind scenarios regarding the situation. For the scenarios to influence subsequent expectancies, their likely consequences must be evaluated, perhaps by playing them through mentally (see also Armor & Taylor, 1998; Taylor & Pham, 1996). Playing the scenarios out should lead to conclusions that influence the expectancy. ("If I try approaching it this way instead of that way, it should work better." "This is the only thing I can see to do, and it will only make the situation worse.")

As we suggested in Chapter 8, it seems reasonable that this mental simulation process engages the same mechanism that handles the meta process during overt behavior. When your progress is temporarily stalled, playing through a scenario that's confident and optimistic indicates a higher rate of progress than is currently being experienced. The meta loop thus will yield a more optimistic assessment than is currently being derived from overt action. If the scenario is doubtful and hopeless, it will indicate a further reduction in progress, and the meta loop will yield an assessment of deeper doubt.

Thus, expectancy-relevant rumination can either reduce or increase hesitancy and doubt, depending on what scenario comes to mind. We suggest, though, that the influence on subsequent expectancies (and affect, as well) may involve the same mechanism that produces more momentary effects on expectancies during the actual flow of behavior. This process can precede action, as well as happen in the midst of action (Strathman, Gleicher, Boninger, & Edwards, 1994). Thus a person can also feel hope – or despair – over the anticipated progress of an event that hasn't yet begun (cf. Markus & Nurius, 1986).

Generality and Specificity of Expectancies

While we're on the topic of expectancies and their assessment, we should also note that expectancies vary in specificity (Armor & Taylor, 1998; Carver & Scheier, 1989), in a hierarchy of inclusiveness. Any goal involving "doing" or "being" can have an expectancy. People can have expectancies about specific acts (hitting a ball with a golf club, making a good pot of coffee), about domains of activity (test taking, social interaction, athletic performance), and even about the broad scope of important life outcomes (optimism versus pessimism). Some discussions emphasize situational expectancies (e.g., Bandura, 1982, 1986).

Others emphasize expectancies about domains that are broad but still well delineated (such as test anxiety or social anxiety). Yet others emphasize generalized expectancies (optimism versus pessimism; Scheier & Carver, 1985, 1992; Scheier et al., 1994).

Clearly these various expectancies exist. But what are the relations among them? Which ones matter in what circumstance? The answers to these questions aren't entirely clear. Consider the relations among expectancies. One might assume that expectancies about specific activities in a given domain aggregate to create a domain-specific expectancy (e.g., expectancies about the various skills involved in playing baseball might aggregate to form an expectancy of success at baseball). Undoubtedly there's some truth to this, but reality may be more complicated (cf. Marsh, 1993; see also Dutton & Brown, 1997). For example, there may be differential weightings of contributors (specific baseball skills) according to their perceived importance to the broader domain. Indeed, expectancies at a given level of abstraction might even be created with respect to the quality that's *emergent* at that level of abstraction, and be relatively disconnected to qualities at lower and higher levels (except inasmuch as success at one level tends to be associated with success at the other levels). In such a case, an expectancy would be specific to a goal at some particular level of the hierarchy discussed in earlier chapters.

Which expectancies matter? Again, there isn't too much evidence on the question. However, two possibilities seem plausible. The best prediction may come from the expectancy that matches the outcome variable in level of specificity (cf. the finding that attitudes predict behavior best when levels of specificity match [Heberlein & Black, 1976; Weigel & Newman, 1976; Weigel, Vernon, & Tognacci, 1974]). That is, a specific expectancy would best predict a specific outcome, and a general expectancy would best predict a broader outcome. Alternatively, the best prediction may come from assessing multiple expectancies. That is, perhaps expectancies at several levels of abstraction influence the performance of specific acts.

As an illustration of these possibilities, imagine a college student who's moderately pessimistic about life, who also has doubt about academic outcomes as a domain, but who feels relatively confident about multiple-choice exams in particular. If you wanted to predict a general outcome – for example, success at coping with life during a difficult period during the school year – you might do better by using the student's general pessimism as a predictor than by using expectancies about academic outcomes or multiple-choice exams. If you wanted to predict academic performance across several courses, you might do best by using expectancies for academic outcomes. If you wanted to predict performance on a specific multiple-choice exam, you might do best by using the specific expectancy.

On the other hand, it isn't altogether clear that you wouldn't be best off thinking about the student's behavior in even the specific case as influenced by "layers" of expectancies. Even as the student enters the exam room, his generalized sense of pessimism (which derives in part from domains of life that are irrelevant to the exam) may be coloring how he's construing the situation (cf. Blaney, 1986; Clark, Milberg, & Ross, 1983). His doubts relevant to the academic domain may be at work simultaneously, as well as the confidence that comes from knowing that at least the exam is multiple-choice instead of essay.

Indeed, the level of abstraction at which the student is focusing while taking the exam may also influence how these various expectancies influence behavior. If he focuses on the fact that the exam is multiple-choice, he may be disproportionately confident. If he focuses on higher-level qualities of the experience – the fact that the exam is just one more manifestation of his life's bad karma – he may be disproportionately pessimistic.

We aren't the first to suggest the possibility that behavior may be best predicted by an expectancy whose level of specificity matches that of the behavior itself, or by a combination of expectancies of varying specificity (see Lefcourt, 1976; Rotter, 1954). But these possibilities have not yet received as much research attention as they deserve. Thus they remain a matter of speculation.

EFFORT VERSUS DISENGAGEMENT

Although the processes of creating expectancies and locating expectancy-related information in memory are of interest in their own right, of even greater importance is what *follows* from assessment of expectancies.

Theory

The result of expectancy assessment is reflected in the behaviors that occur subsequently (Figure 10.2). If expectations of success are sufficiently positive, the person returns to efforts toward the goal. If expectations are sufficiently negative, the result is an impetus to disengage from

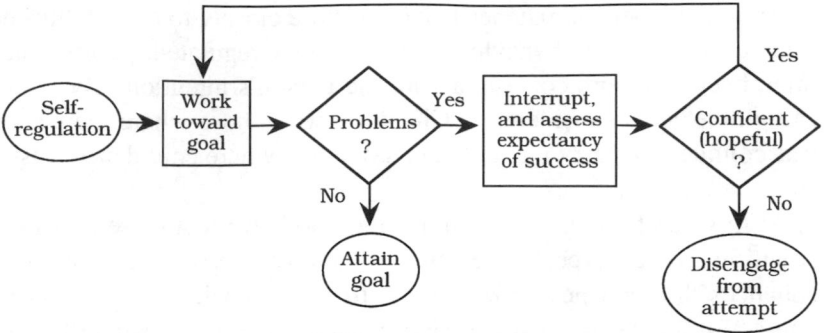

Figure 10.2.   Flowchart depiction of self-regulatory possibilities, indicating that action sometimes continues unimpeded toward goal attainment, that obstacles to goal attainment sometimes induce a sequence of evaluation and decision making, and that if expectancies for eventual success are sufficiently unfavorable the person may disengage from further effort. (Adapted from Carver & Scheier, 1981a.)

further effort, and potentially to disengage from the goal itself (Carver & Scheier, 1981a, 1983, 1986b, 1990a, 1990b; see also Klinger, 1975; Kukla, 1972; Wortman & Brehm, 1975).

There's a subtle but important point to be emphasized here. This principle doesn't mean that when people become frustrated or afraid when they're trying to do something, they invariably quit trying. Frustration and fear *are* signs of situational expectancies shifting toward the negative. But, as described above, this situational influence (the current lack of progress) isn't the only determinant of the expectancies people take back to their task. Evidence exists that a momentary sense of impediment to movement – situationally deteriorating expectancies – can be overridden by a more firmly established sense of confidence. Thus, when negative affect goes up (along with the sense of doubt), people sometimes overcome this disruptive influence to continue their efforts. This ability to rely on more well-established expectancies is one of the ways in which people's elaborate cognitive capabilities can serve to remove them from the press of the situational forces of the moment. Such effects aren't inevitable (cf. Duval, Duval, & Mulilis, 1992), but they do occur on some occasions.

Another element of theory to mention here concerns self-focused attention. We argued in Chapter 3 that self-focus engages the comparison process in the feedback loop monitoring whatever behavior the person is consciously regulating. In general, this means that when self-focus is increased, the person matches behavior more closely to the established standard or goal. As behavior is more closely regulated, performance often becomes more consistent with the person's intention. By implication, the cases considered in Chapter 3 were those where the person was confident of carrying out the behavior (or where confidence wasn't an issue).

At this point, however, we must add another effect of self-focused attention. When expectancies are sufficiently *unfavorable*, self-focus enhances the tendency to *disengage* from the goal. Thus, there's an interaction between self-focus and expectancies, such that self-focus increases the impact of both confidence and doubt on behavior. The interactive effects of self-focus and expectancies are displayed in a number of ways, which are described in the following sections.

Research: Comparisons with Standards

In Chapter 3 we said that self-focus enhances the functioning of the feedback loop's comparator. In making our case, we described evidence that people engage more in comparison between their present behavior and the reference value when self-focus is higher than when it's lower (Scheier & Carver, 1983). One such comparison involved seeking out information about test norms. By choosing to work on items for which norms were available, people high in self-focus were better able to compare their upcoming performances to relevant standards of comparison.

Although this increase in comparison is the usual result of self-focus, sometimes the opposite occurs. Subjects in another study (Carver, Antoni, & Scheier, 1985) were given a similar opportunity to choose test items from among sets with norms available and sets with no norms. In this case, however, subjects' expectancies about how well they'd do on this task were manipulated by a previous success or failure on a closely related task. In this study, self-focus interacted with the manipulation of expectancy. Among subjects who expected to do well, self-focus enhanced the tendency to seek out items for which norms were available, just as in the earlier studies. Among those who expected to do poorly, however, self-focus led them to avoid items for which norms were available. In this way, they were showing evidence of disengaging themselves from the goal of performing well compared to other people.

This is one of several instances in which unfavorable expectancies have been shown to cause people to turn away from goal-relevant information. Another case involved a different level of expectancy: optimism versus pessimism. This study examined experiences of men undergoing coronary artery bypass surgery (Scheier, Matthews, Owens, Magovern, Lefebvre, Abbott, & Carver, 1989). On the day before surgery and 7 to 10 days afterward, they were asked questions about what they were thinking about (and doing) and also questions about what they were trying *not* to think about. Before surgery, optimistic men said they were thinking ahead to the period after the operation; afterward they reported seeking information about the weeks ahead. In contrast to this, pessimistic men reported they were trying to *avoid* thinking about the future and what it would be like. Again, doubt seemed to promote an attempt to reject information pertaining to a comparison between a goal and a present condition.

Research: Responses to Fear

Turning away from goal-relevant information isn't the only consequence of doubt. There are also effects on overt behavior. The idea that self-focus interacts with confidence to influence action has been tested in several ways. One of these studies helps establish the point that the temporary, ephemeral doubts associated with negative affect can be overridden by a more firmly established sense of confidence about the ultimate outcome. This study examined people who reported that they were moderately fearful of snakes (Carver, Blaney, & Scheier, 1979b). The level of fearfulness was identical for all. They differed, however, in how they thought they would react if asked to pick up and hold a nonpoisonous snake. Some of them (confident) chose the response "I'd do it, but I'd feel a little queasy about it," whereas the others (doubtful) chose "I'm not at all sure that I'd do it."

Naturally enough, that's exactly what they were asked to do, in individual sessions later on. The snake (a three-foot-long boa) was in an aquarium at the end of a hall. Self-focus was increased among half the subjects. Nine levels of approach had been predefined, and an observer (outside the subject's view) determined how far in the approach sequence the subject got before stopping and returning. Subjects then made self-reports concerning their "contents of consciousness" during the task.

Two aspects of the findings are important. First, although self-focus made all subjects more aware of their situational fear, that was the only fear difference among groups. More specifically, *confident subjects reported experiencing just as much fear as doubtful subjects*. In contrast, self-focus and confidence had an interactive effect on approach behavior.

Self-focus caused doubtful subjects to quit sooner in the approach sequence, but it tended to *enhance* the performances of confident subjects. Analysis of postexperimental reports revealed that self-focus caused confident subjects to attend more to comparisons between their behavior and their goal (picking up and holding the snake), whereas it caused doubtful subjects to attend less to that comparison. Instead, self-focus made the doubtful subjects attend more to signs of fearfulness inside themselves.

These findings indicate that residual confidence provided one group of subjects the wherewithal to overcome the fear they were experiencing – very real fear – in order to stay focused on the behavior they intended to execute. Thus, one of the points of this study is that the increased fear levels among the confident subjects failed to impair their task concentration. The other group, lacking this confidence, turned their attention away from the task. This response – avoidance of the behavior–goal comparison – is very similar to the pattern described in the previous section on information seeking.

Research: Persistence

Other research examined persistence at task-related efforts as a function of self-focus and expectancies (Carver, Blaney, & Scheier, 1979a). Subjects were told they were participating in a project evaluating several tests of abstract reasoning currently under development. Each was to work on portions of two tests. The first one was a set of anagrams, presented along with bogus norms indicating that the anagrams were relatively easy. In reality, however, they were extremely difficult and in some instances impossible. As a result, all participants performed poorly. The experimenter noted the poor performance, ensuring that it was salient.

By now, there was a substantial discrepancy between subjects' desired and actual performance. At this point, the experimenter manipulated expectancies for future success by remarking that the second task tended to produce scores that were either very similar to or not very similar to scores on the anagrams. The subject then was taken to a second room, where another experimenter took over. The second task was a line-tracing problem originally developed to measure persistence (Feather, 1961). The first problem was impossible to solve according to the rules. The measure was how long the subject tried to complete it before going to the next problem, determined unobtrusively from outside the subject's

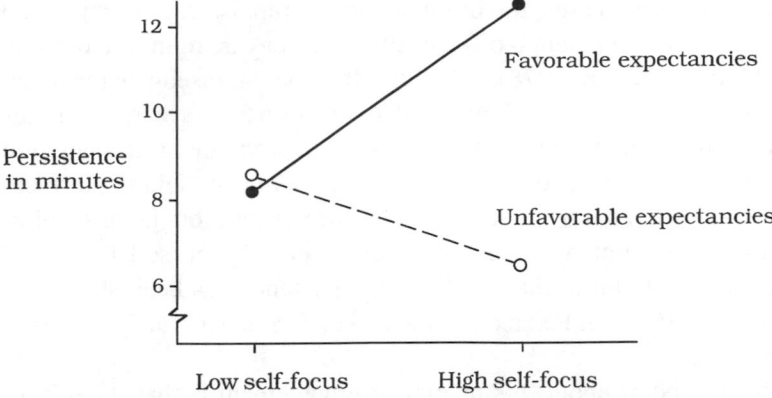

Figure 10.3.   Persistence at an impossible problem as a function of performance expectancy regarding the task and self-directed attention. (Adapted
from Carver, Blaney, & Scheier, 1979a, combining data from experiments 1
and 2.)

view. Subjects attempted the task at a table where they either did or
didn't face a mirror.

An interaction emerged between the manipulations of expectancy
and self-focus (Figure 10.3). Self-focus enhanced persistence among
subjects who thought they'd be able to make up for their earlier failure.
This finding conceptually replicated the many cases in which self-focus
has caused enhanced conformity to standards. In contrast, self-focus
led to reduced persistence among subjects who'd been induced to have
doubts about doing well on the second task.

Subsequent research by Duval, Duval, and Mulilis (1992) conceptually replicated this pattern regarding persistence, but added an interesting
and important qualifier. In their studies, self-focus led to enhanced persistence among subjects who'd been led to perceive themselves as able
to close a relatively small discrepancy between present condition and
standard of comparison. But among subjects with very large discrepancies, even the perception of constant movement toward the goal didn't
lead to persistence under self-focus. Only when the rate of progress was
seen as adequate – relative to the discrepancy – did the facilitation occur.

Mental Disengagement, Impaired
Task Performance, and Negative Rumination

Although people sometimes can disengage behaviorally from task goals,
sometimes this isn't easy to do. For example, social constraints may

prevent it. In such cases, the disengagement impulse can be expressed in mental disengagement – off-task thinking, daydreaming, and so on (cf. Diener & Dweck, 1978). Although this mental disengagement can sometimes be useful (for example, self-distraction from a feared stimulus may permit anxiety to abate), it can also create problems. If the situation is one with time pressure, mental disengagement can yield impairment of performance, as time is spent on task-irrelevant thoughts instead of the task. Consistent with this, an interaction between self-focus and expectancies similar to that shown for persistence has been shown for performance (Carver, Peterson, Follansbee, & Scheier, 1983; Carver & Scheier, 1982).

A further point about this mental disengagement is that it can't always be sustained (Figure 10.4). Mental disengagement may remove you psychologically from the situation, but life is often structured in ways that cause this removal to be temporary. For example, a person in a performance setting continues to reconfront the unfinished task. Daydreaming won't make the task go away. As the person reconfronts the task, there may be briefly renewed effort, which (given little progress) quickly gives way to expectancy reassessment and renewed awareness of the doubts that prompted the disengagement impulse in the first place. This reconfrontation with doubt may be experienced as a phenomenology of repetitive negative and often self-deprecatory rumination (cf. Carver, 1996a; McIntosh & Martin, 1992; Wine, 1971, 1980).

Remember also the implications of the affect model that's linked to this discussion. That model holds that negative affect is created by failure to make progress toward goals. The person who's experiencing the cycle of brief effort, disengagement, and reconfrontation with the current failure and the more sustained doubt is likely also to be experiencing a continuing rise in negative feelings. Being stuck in a corner and unable to back out, the person becomes helpless and miserable (cf. Abramson, Metalsky, & Alloy, 1989; Seligman, 1975).

Self-Focus, Task Focus, and Rumination

As just noted, adversity sometimes leads to a phenomenology of continuing or repetitive negative rumination, which often focuses on self-doubt and perceptions of inadequacy. We wish to be quite explicit here about our view on the nature and source of this phenomenology. A number of writers – both from an earlier tradition of cognitive–attentional theories of anxiety (e.g., Sarason, 1975; Wine, 1971, 1980) and some more

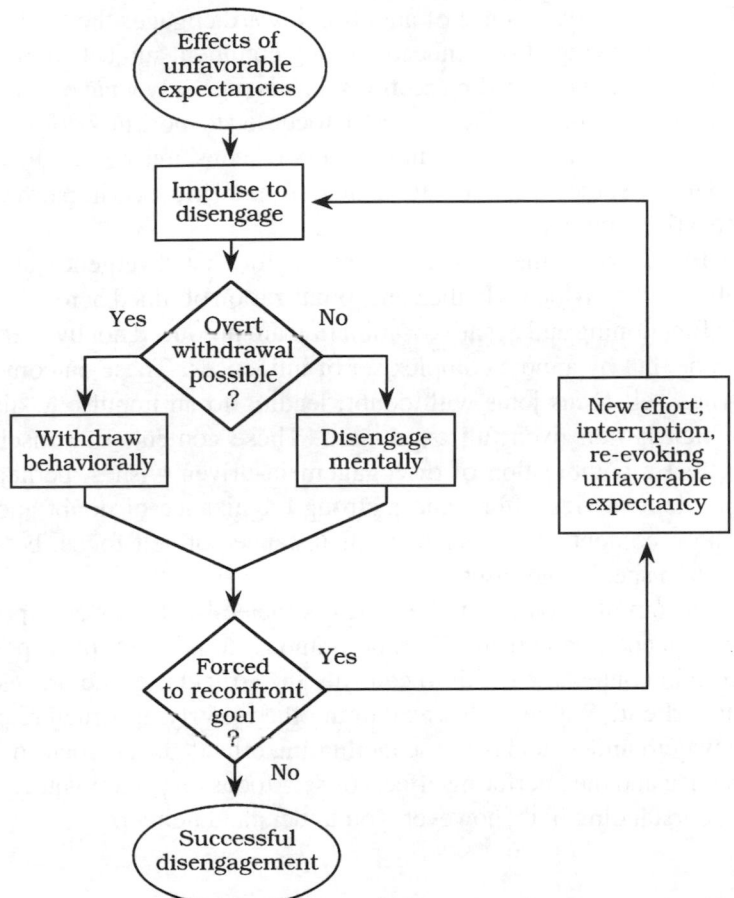

Figure 10.4. Sometimes behavioral withdrawal or mental disengagement succeeds in separating people from the goals they're doubtful about moving toward. Sometimes, however, the structure of the situations people are in forces them to reconfront the goal. This may induce new effort, but if it continues to meet with difficulty, the result is likely to be fresh interruption, a renewed awareness of the doubts, and a renewal of the attempt to disengage.

recent (Ingram, 1990) – have equated this phenomenology of negative rumination with the term *self-focus*. We think that using that label here is a mistake, because it creates a misleading picture of what's going on (see also Pyszczynski, Greenberg, Hamilton, & Nix, 1991).

Why is the label self-focus misleading here? Because self-focus doesn't always produce interference. As described earlier in this chapter and in Chapter 3, self-focus is in many cases associated with *task* focus, as the experience of attention inward engages the feedback process underlying effort. Indeed, among confident subjects in the studies reviewed in the preceding sections, this is precisely what occurred, even under conditions of adversity. Self-focus led to more task effort, as manifest both in behavior and in contents of consciousness. Only among doubtful subjects did self-focus lead to performance impairment or to negative rumination.

In our view, there's a good reason for that divergence among the effects of self-focus. In the conceptualization outlined here, impairment in functioning and negative rumination are produced not by "self-focus" alone, but by a more complex set of influences. These outcomes occur when self-focus joins with doubt, leading to an impulse to disengage which is not given full expression. These contents of consciousness reflect a combination of disengagement-driven wishes, perhaps some problem-solving effort, and a strong cognizance of doubt and worry. These contents don't occur in all instances of self-focus, but only in certain specifiable cases.

In sum, it's possible to become distracted by the surface appearance of a phenomenon (self-absorption among certain groups of persons in certain contexts) and fail to consider the structure of the processes that underlie it. We think that examining the underlying structure provides a way to understand both the facilitating effects of self-focus on performance and the interfering effects of self-focus on performance. Without understanding both, however, you understand neither.

EFFORT AND DISENGAGEMENT: THE GREAT DIVIDE

Much of what we have to say in this book stems from the premise that people are goal-directed creatures. People take up goals, intentions, values, wishes, and try to make these qualities manifest in the experiences of their lives. But this doesn't always work. It isn't always possible for people to reach their goals. When things are going poorly, people confront a decision: Keep trying or give up? Many of the important issues of life turn on the choice between these two behavioral options (cf. Klinger, 1975). Which choice occurs at any given fork in the road of life can have enormous implications for subsequent behavior. There is a great divide – a watershed – between the two categories of response. It follows that the boundary between confidence and doubt is a critically important one.

Is Disengagement Good or Bad?

A question that must be raised about the dichotomy between effort and giving up concerns the adaptive value of the two tendencies. Is disengagement good or bad? The answer is that it's both and neither. On the one hand, disengagement (at some level, at least) is an absolute necessity (see also Petroski, 1997). It's a natural and indispensable part of self-regulation. If people are ever to turn away from efforts at unattainable goals, if they're ever to back out of blind alleys, they must be able to disengage, to give up and start over somewhere else.

The importance of disengagement is particularly obvious with regard to concrete, low-level goals: We must be able to remove ourselves from literal blind alleys and wrong streets, give up plans that have become disrupted by unexpected events, and spend the night in the wrong city if we've missed the last plane home. Disengagement is also important, however, with regard to higher-level goals. A vast literature attests to the importance of disengaging and moving on with life after the loss of close relationships, through both dissolution and bereavement (e.g., Cleiren, 1993; Duck, 1982; Orbuch, 1992; Stroebe, Stroebe, & Hansson, 1993; Vaughan, 1986; Weiss, 1988). People sometimes must even be willing to give up goals that are deeply embedded in the self if those values create too much conflict and distress in their lives.

As with most processes in self-regulation, however, the choice between continued effort and giving up presents opportunities for things to go awry. It's possible to stop trying prematurely, thereby creating problems for oneself. It's also possible to hold onto goals too long, thereby preventing oneself from taking adaptive steps toward new goals. We return to these points later. For now, however, our point is this: Continued effort and giving up are both necessary parts of the experience of adaptive self-regulation. Each plays an important role in the flow of behavior.

11

Disengagement: Issues and Comparisons

If I can't win, I won't run.
(Chariots of Fire)

Chapter 10 described a division between two classes of responses to difficulty in moving toward goals. A sense of confidence leads to renewed effort, and a sense of doubt leads to giving up. These classes of response are both integral parts of the system of self-regulation that keeps people adapted to the world.

Once again, the conceptualization raises questions and issues. Some of them concern disengagement as an event: what it is, alternative ways to view it, whether in fact disengagement per se actually occurs. Other issues arise in considering how this theory relates to other models of the phenomena under discussion. Another point concerns the fact that issues of engagement and disengagement arise in many literatures, some quite unexpectedly.

SCALING BACK GOALS
AS LIMITED DISENGAGEMENT

By now we've described several variations on the theme of disengagement: diminishing effort, leaving the behavioral context, mental disengagement (daydreaming and off-task thinking), and the bind between having the impetus to disengage and being unable to express it.

In this section we consider another potential reflection of disengagement. Sometimes progress toward a goal is going poorly, expectancies of success are dim, and you want to quit. Rather than quit altogether, you trade this goal for a less demanding one – a kind of limited disengagement. You've given up on the first goal at the same time as you're adopting a lesser one (cf. Miller et al., 1960, p. 171). This limited disengagement has an important positive consequence: You remain engaged in the general domain you'd wanted to quit. By scaling back the goal (giving up in a small way), you keep trying to move ahead (thus *not* giving up, in a larger way).

As an example, a student who wants an A in a course, but who's struggling ineffectually to attain high exam scores, may decide that an A is out of the question and lower his sights to a B or C. Given the change in goal, exam scores in the B or C range will represent better progress than they would have represented toward the initial goal. The result is that the student keeps plugging along, completes the course adequately instead of dropping it, and may feel satisfied with a C.

Small-scale disengagement happens all the time in the context of moving forward in a broader way. As another example, consider the behavior of a researcher trying to develop a career. Some of her projects are working out well, others aren't. She steps away from unproductive lines of work (small-scale disengagements) to focus more closely on productive ones, with the overall aim of fostering progress toward the broader goal of career development.

Another example comes from research on couples in which one partner is becoming ill and dying from AIDS (Moskowitz, Folkman, Collette, & Vittinghoff, 1996). Some healthy subjects initially have the goal of overcoming their partners' illness and continuing to have active lives together. As the illness progresses and it becomes apparent that this goal won't be met, it's not uncommon for the healthy partners to scale back their aspirations. Now the goal is to do more limited activities during the course of a day, for example. Choosing a goal that's more limited and manageable ensures it will be possible to move successfully toward it. The result is that even in these difficult circumstances, the person experiences more positive feeling than would otherwise be the case and stays engaged behaviorally with efforts to move forward.

Problems with Limited Disengagement

A potential problem with the limited-disengagement strategy stems from the fact that goals are often interrelated. It may be fine in principle to lower your grade aspirations from an A to a C. But if a high grade here is a prerequisite to another goal – for example, admission to medical school – the limited disengagement works only temporarily. The same issue will likely recur later on, with respect to the broader goal to which this one leads.

In some cases, this bind isn't easily resolved. If medical school is your ultimate educational goal and your grades are bad, some rearrangement of the ultimate goal is going to be necessary. In other cases, the bind seems more manageable, despite requiring rearrangement of goals. If your life partner's health is getting worse instead of better, you can find satisfying activities other than those you might have planned. Broad goals about how to spend your time may have to change (e.g., actual travel may give way to learning about interesting parts of the world), but this adjustment seems less disruptive (at least for a while) than the adjustment of choosing a new career path.

The difficulty of rearrangement depends on a further issue about the interrelation among goals. If the blocked goal relates to a higher-level identity and the person has no alternate paths to express that identity, adjusment will be harder. The person unable to get into medical school who can say to himself that becoming a physician was just one way to live a life of service to others can develop another career path that serves the higher end. The person for whom being a physician was an end in itself will have more difficulty.

Scaling Back Goals as Changing
Velocity Reference Value

How does this scaling back take place? In Chapters 2 and 9 we noted that if the output function of a feedback loop is inadequate at moving the input in the direction of the standard, a second (slower-acting) process sometimes moves the standard in the direction of the input. This is illustrated, in terms of the student example, in Figure 11.1 (adapted from Figure 9.1). The scaling back of goals seems to reflect such a change of standard.

This viewpoint raises another question. We've been treating the behavioral goal (and changes in it) as the relevant issue. Attaining a C requires learning less than does attaining an A. Attaining a grade implies behavior. However, there's also a sense of velocity here. Bert, who's shifted to a lower goal, will be more pleased by a B on the next exam than Ernie, who's held onto the higher goal. Why? Because Bert's velocity standard has dropped (he now has to master less material in a given time frame in order to reach his more limited action goal). He now perceives an actual velocity that exceeds his standard.

In Chapter 8 we argued that the action loop and the affect loop work in concert with each other. They're interconnected in influence and functioning. We have no strong basis for saying that one matters more than the other. Our own view has sometimes been that behavior has primacy,

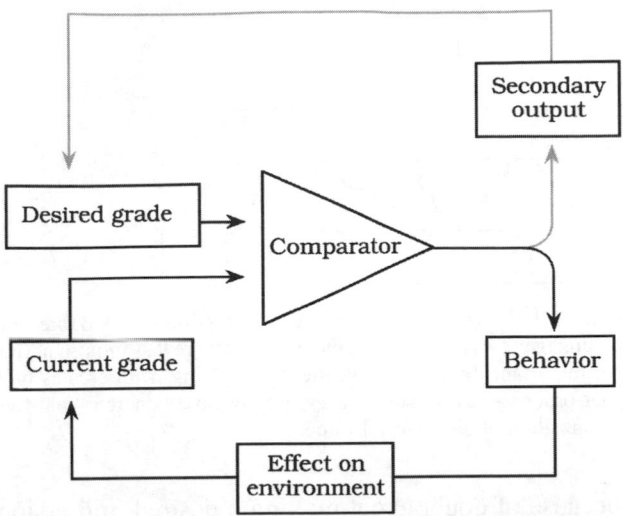

Figure 11.1. The feedback loop with dark lines behaves to create changes in the input function (attained grade), to shift its value toward the reference value (desired grade). An additional process may also be in place (gray lines) which works to adjust the reference value in the direction of the input.

but others see it differently. Perhaps the behavior and affect loops work in close coordination, but which *seems* more important phenomenologically depends on individual or contextual differences that are not well understood.

WHEN GIVING UP IS NOT A TENABLE OPTION

We said above that limited disengagement – scaling back – doesn't always work (accepting mediocre grades creates a problem getting into medical school). The inability to disengage actually occurs more often than in the scaling-back context, and we should address this issue explicitly. What do people do when they want to give up but can't? What *gives rise* to this bind?

Hierarchicality and Importance
Can Impede Disengagement

We said in Chapter 10 that constraints sometimes keep people from abandoning goals they want to give up. Sometimes these are social constraints. For example, a shy person might want to escape from a social

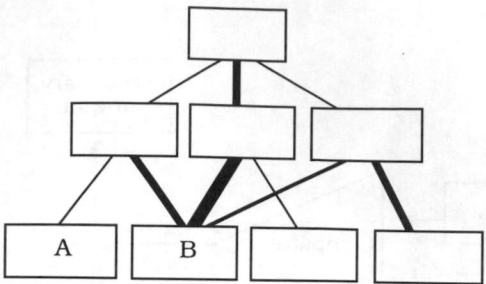

Figure 11.2.   Concrete goals that are very important (box B) are more difficult to disengage from than are concrete goals that are less important (box A). The more important the lower goal, the more giving it up creates problems for higher-order values. In some cases, giving up a concrete goal forces major reorganization of higher-level values.

gathering because of doubt about making a desired impression. However, running from the room would occasion embarrassment (by conflicting with another goal concerning social display), so it isn't tenable. Similarly, test-anxious students aren't usually the first to leave an exam, though their most common thought during the exam may be the desire to be elsewhere (Galassi, Frierson, & Sharer, 1981).

It's not only situational constraints that prevent disengagement. A larger part of this problem stems from the notion of hierarchicality. Disengaging from values low in the hierarchy is often easy. Indeed, disengagement from subgoals in programs is quite common, even while you continue to pursue the program's overall goal. For example, if you go to buy something and the store is closed for inventory, you'll leave this store and head for another one.

Lower-order goals vary, however, in how closely they're linked to values at a higher level, and thus in how important they are (Figure 11.2, which duplicates Figure 6.2). To disengage from low-level goals that are tightly linked to high-level goals causes discrepancy enlargement at the higher level. The higher-order qualities are important, some even central to your life. As implied in the previous section, you can't disengage from them, disregard them, or tolerate large discrepancies regarding them, without reorganizing your value system (Carver & Scheier, 1986b; Kelly, 1955; Kling, Ryff, & Essex, 1997; McIntosh & Martin, 1992; Millar et al., 1988). In such cases, disengagement from concrete goals can be difficult.

To put it differently, the model we're discussing is a member of the family of expectancy–value models of motivation (e.g., Atkinson, 1964;

Feather, 1982; Vroom, 1964). Its dynamics depend not just on expectancies, but also on value – the goal's importance. The more important it is, the harder it is to disengage from.

Now recall again the affective consequences of being in this situation. The desire to disengage was prompted in the first place by unfavorable expectancies. These expectancies are paralleled by negative affect. In this situation, then, the person experiences distress (because of an inability to make progress) and is unable to do anything about the distress (because of an inability to give up). The person simply stews in the feelings that arise from irreconcilable discrepancies (see also Martin & Tesser, 1989). This situation – commitment to unattainable goals – is a sure prescription for distress.

Inability to Disengage and Responses to Health Threats

The reasoning that it's hard to disengage from important goals, and that the result of failure to disengage is distress, has many implications. For example, we've applied it to the subjective experiences of people diagnosed with life-threatening illness (Carver, Scheier, & Pozo, 1992; Carver et al., 1993). The diagnosis represents a threat to the continuation of the activities that make up the person's life (Scheier & Bridges, 1995). People who are doubtful enough about their future experience the tendency to disengage. In this case, however, the threatened goals constitute the person's whole life-space. They're far too important to be abandoned. Giving up here means giving up on your life. The result is that people confronting a serious illness are especially vulnerable to distress, to the extent they have doubts about their future.

We've found support for several facets of this portrayal among breast cancer patients (Carver et al., 1993). Expectancies were measured as optimism. Compared to optimistic women, those who were more pessimistic were more likely to report feeling the tendency to give up, and trying to deny the reality of the experience – to push it away from them. They were also more distressed throughout the year postsurgery, even controlling for previous levels of distress. Finally, there was evidence that differences in distress were mediated by differences in mental responses to the situation. In effect, the optimistic women accepted the new situation but remained goal-engaged – life-engaged. The pessimistic women were more likely to experience the sense of giving up, but giving up on goals that they *couldn't* give up.

Helplessness

Discussions of giving up inevitably touch on one of the most widely known terms in the vocabulary of psychology: helplessness. This concept derives from the finding that exposure to painful and unavoidable shocks made it harder for dogs to learn an avoidance or escape response when doing so became possible (Overmier & Seligman, 1967; Seligman & Maier, 1967). This finding led to a flood of studies on human subjects. The typical study of human helplessness examines effects of prolonged failure on later performance (e.g., Hiroto & Seligman, 1975; Miller & Norman, 1979).

The first explanation for the helplessness effect was based, somewhat loosely, on conditioning principles. As analogous research was done on people, however, the theory became progressively more cognitive, involving expectations of future noncontingency (Abramson, Seligman, & Teasdale, 1978) or expectations of being unable to control outcomes (Wortman & Brehm, 1975). In simple terms, helpless people develop the idea that they can't obtain good outcomes because the outcomes are unrelated to their actions. Helplessness is of interest outside the learning lab largely because it's been viewed as a useful model of depression (Abramson et al., 1978; Peterson & Seligman, 1984). As people become helpless, they show motivational deficits, cognitive interference (Sedek, Kofta, & Tyszka, 1993), and depressed feelings.

The emphasis on expectancies in models of human helplessness (and their successor, the hopelessness theory of depression put forward by Abramson, Metalsky, & Alloy, 1989) resembles the emphasis we've placed on expectancies here. Although the labels for the constructs differ, one overall point is much the same from theory to theory: People who feel doubtful enough about being able to move toward their goals stop trying, whereas more confident people keep trying.

We'd like to add two points about helplessness. The first concerns the fact that phenomena termed helplessness are sometimes viewed as though they represent a unique domain of behavior. They really don't. Helplessness occupies one place in a broader and more elaborate pattern of motivational phenomena. Extreme helplessness is one particular reflection of a giving-up response. But conceptually it's related in important ways to other, more benign – even *necessary* – kinds of giving up.

The second point is more important. An understanding of helplessness is incomplete without including a conceptual element that's rarely noted.

The person (or dog) displaying helplessness is manifesting a giving-up response in one or more ways (e.g., performance deficit, cognitive interference). But the expression of the giving-up response is *incomplete*. The element that's usually left out is this: In helplessness, the goal for which the giving up is occurring is one that cannot easily be abandoned. Thus the goal remains in place. There's a giving up of effort, but not a giving up of the goal.

Why? Because in cases of real helplessness the goal is too important, and there's no available substitute. If the goal is trivial, you give it up and turn to something else. But if the goal is important and there's no alternative to turn to, you can't fully disengage. This combination of circumstances represents another instance of commitment to an unattainable goal, leading to an absence of goal-directed effort and presence of emotional distress. Unless you remain committed to the unattainable goal, however, there's no obvious reason for distress.

WATERSHEDS, DISJUNCTIONS, AND BIFURCATIONS AMONG RESPONSES

Another issue concerns the divergence of the behavioral and cognitive responses to favorable versus unfavorable expectancies. Within an expectancy-based view of action, there are many ways in which confidence might relate to behavior. The relationship doesn't appear to be a linear one, such that as confidence deteriorates, effort gradually diminishes. But what *is* the relation?

We've long emphasized the idea that there's a psychological watershed among responses to adversity – that responses diverge (Carver, 1979; Carver & Scheier, 1981a). One class of responses is continued comparisons between present state and goal and continued efforts. The other is disengagement from comparisons and disengagement of effort. Just as rainwater falling on a mountain ridge ultimately flows to one side of the ridge or the other, so do behaviors ultimately flow to one of these classes.

Our initial reasons for taking this position stemmed largely from the work we reviewed in Chapter 10. In particular, the findings that self-focus creates diverging effects on information seeking and behavior (as a function of expectancies) suggest a bifurcation among responses. We aren't the only ones to have emphasized a disjunction among responses, however. Several others have done so, for reasons of their own.

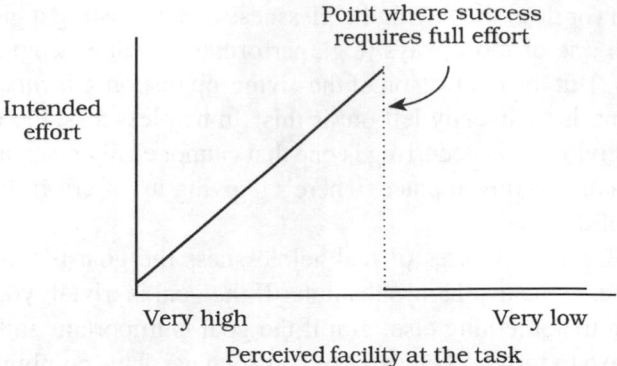

Figure 11.3.   Kukla's theory regarding the relationship between effort and perceived ability (and thus, we infer, expectancy of success). (Adapted from Kukla, 1972.)

Other Disjunctive Motivational Models

A relatively early model that emphasized a disjunction in behavior was proposed by Kukla (1972). His was an attempt to integrate expectancy theory with attribution theory applied to achievement behavior. Kukla depicted effort as a function of perceived task facility (a construct not so different from expectancy of success). When ability at the task is high, not much effort will be expended, because it isn't needed. As facility at the task falls off (or as expectancy of success becomes lower), effort rises (Figure 11.3), because more is needed (Kukla noted that although his figure depicted this as a linear decrease, linearity isn't a necessary assumption). When facility is such that your maximum effort should yield a success, you'll exert maximum effort. Given tasks for which you think that even maximal effort won't produce success, effort falls off abruptly. Of greatest interest at present is that this model assumes an abrupt shift from maximal effort to virtually no effort – a disjunction between two very different responses.

Another model that bears on this issue is the integration between reactance and helplessness offered by Wortman and Brehm (1975). They argued that reactance and helplessness both stem from problems with control, but differ in the extent of the perceived problem. Threats to control, in which control isn't lost, are said to produce reactance and an attempt to regain or reassert control. Perceptions that control is lost produce helplessless. Wortman and Brehm fit these ideas together by assuming a disjunction between two responses (reassertion of control

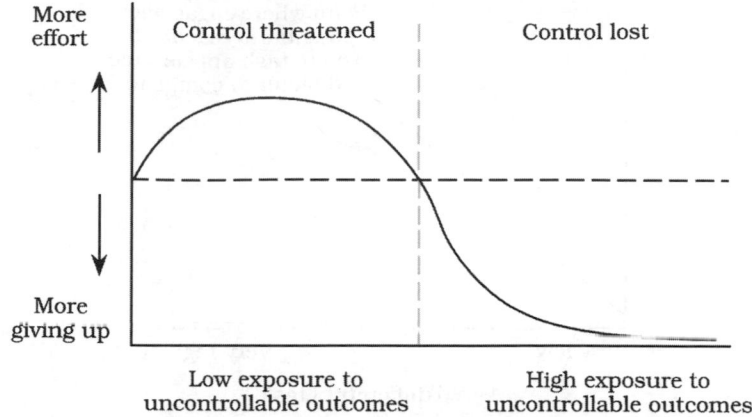

Figure 11.4.   Wortman and Brehm's integration of the principles of reactance and helplessness. When control is threatened by exposure to uncontrollable outcomes, the result is reactance and enhanced effort to regain control; when control is seen as lost, the result is helplessness and a giving-up response. (Adapted from Wortman & Brehm, 1975.)

and giving up) at the point where a threat to control becomes a perception that control is lost (Figure 11.4). Again, this is a watershed model.

Brehm and his collaborators (Brehm & Self, 1989; Wright & Brehm, 1989) have more recently developed an approach to effort intensity, or task engagement, that resembles in many respects that of Kukla (1972). In this view, a person puts effort into behavior to the extent that effort is needed to complete it successfully. If the task is easy, requiring little effort, little effort will be expended. As the task becomes harder, more effort is required to complete it, and more effort will be expended (Figure 11.5). (This analysis actually has a good deal in common with the logic underlying feedback processes: It isn't necessary to exert maximum effort to do something small – no need for a sledge hammer to swat a fly.)

At some point on the difficulty dimension, you're exerting your maximum effort. If the task gets any harder, you'll see it as beyond your capacity. There's no point in investing effort in a task that's impossible. Thus, at this point you withdraw your effort (Figure 11.5). Once more, there's an abrupt disjunction between two classes of response (see Wright, 1996, for a review of literature stemming from this theory). For our purposes, this model appears virtually identical to that of Kukla (1972). The principle behind it (and Kukla's) is captured in the idea that

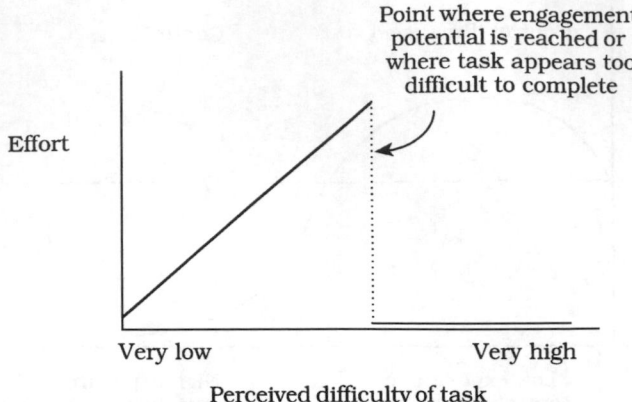

Figure 11.5.   Brehm's analysis of task engagement, in which effort expands to fill the *need* for effort up to the point where the task is too difficult to complete even with maximum effort. (Adapted from Wright, 1996.)

you exert only as much effort as you need to succeed, and if no amount of effort will work, you quit.

As this brief sketch makes clear, there's considerable theoretical basis for the belief that a disjunction exists between two classes of response – effort and disengagement. The two responses don't necessarily shade gradually into one another. Rather, one appears to give way to the other, with some degree of abruptness. This is a very interesting idea, to which we return later.

DOES DISENGAGEMENT IMPLY AN OVERRIDE MECHANISM?

The idea that people's efforts give way to disengagement as expectancies become more negative raises another issue. How does this characterization mesh with the conceptualization we presented earlier in the book? If behavior operates by feedback control, shouldn't people try endlessly to reduce discrepancies, however ineffectively? Why shouldn't the negative affect and doubt simply persist or intensify? What permits the person to disengage from one behavior and turn to something else?

Our initial response to this question (Carver & Scheier, 1990a) was that in normal self-regulation there must be an override of some sort that's capable of taking precedence over this feedback system and cause disengagement from the reference value that's currently in use. In dated computer jargon, this would be a *break* function (today a *cancel* command),

A Variations in motive strengths

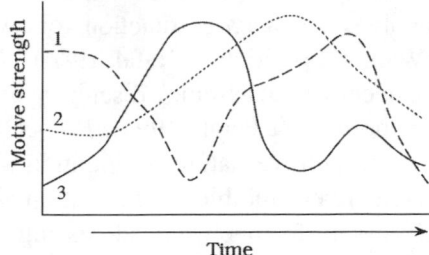

B Topography of behavior across time

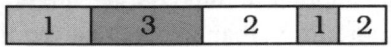

Figure 11.6. (A) Many traditional models of competing motives assume that all active motives vary in intensity over time, as a function of several variables, including the recent occurrence (or not) of behavior that temporarily satisfies the motive. (B) The motive that is most intense at a given time is presumed to be reflected in behavior. Thus behavior shifts in character over time.

suspending or abandoning ongoing computation. Disengagement similarly frees the person to turn to the pursuit of substitute or alternative goals.

Disengagement, or Competing Motives?

There's reason to believe, however, that this assumption isn't necessary. Another view stems from the idea that people have many motives, all competing for access to consciousness and resources for action (e.g., Atkinson & Birch, 1970; Murray, 1938). There are many determinants of how motives are reflected in behavior. Most discussions focus on the passage of time since a motive was satisfied (Figure 11.6). However, another influence might be the person's confidence or doubt about its satisfaction.

That is, perhaps the tendency to continue exerting effort toward the focal goal simply fades (compared to tendencies to exert effort toward other goals) as expectancies for success fall. In this view, there's no need for a break function. Another behavior simply becomes prepotent at some point, and the person turns from the previous behavior to the newly focal one. Disengagement would be isomorphic to engaging the newly focal goal.

Interestingly enough, an analogous issue has arisen in analyzing how people turn attention from one visual stimulus to another. It's been believed that this shift involves a *disengage* function followed by an *engage* function (Posner, Walker, Friedrich, & Rafal, 1984). Recent evidence suggests that it's not necessary to assume a disengage mechanism (Cohen, Romero, Servan-Schreiber, & Farah, 1994). Rather, the effect may be attributable to the competitive nature of attention allocation: Attention devoted to one area creates inhibition of attention elsewhere.

That case isn't quite the same as the one we're addressing. It's about how people are distracted from one stimulus location to another. In contrast, we're asking how a person leaves a "stimulus location" behind without necessarily having another in mind. Nonetheless, the similarity is provocative. Perhaps more often than people realize, disengagement from a goal really is *distraction* from it, rather than voluntarily withdrawing from it.

Thinking about disengagement in terms of competition for attention suggests further implications. Spreading-activation models of memory assume that many areas of partial activation compete continuously for access to consciousness. Most discussions of information in and out of consciousness focus on perceptual or cognitive events, but there's no obvious reason why the arguments don't apply to goals and goal striving (Bargh, 1997; Wegner & Bargh, 1998). It seems likely that many goals are partially active and engaged in people's minds most of the time (perhaps all the time) – out of awareness but competing for access. Whichever goal has temporarily become active enough to reach the top of the priority list is the one you're aware of (see also Minsky, 1985).

There may well be a continuum of degrees of engagement (thus degrees of access to consciousness). A person who's struggling behaviorally to overcome impediments to a goal has the goal and the self-regulatory attempt fully in consciousness. A goal that's near the top of the list, but too low to keep the person actively engaged in its pursuit, may prompt thought intrusions (Martin & Tesser, 1996). A goal that's drifted yet lower on the list no longer prompts intrusions. It may not be gone – some part of the mind may still be grinding away at resolving the blockage. But at present it's no longer sufficiently potent to obtain access to attention.

Is a goal that's far down on the priority list doomed to stay there, or can it regain access to attentional resources? A possible facilitator is a sudden step toward resolution of the blockage. If the internal problem solver that's slowly picking at the problem suddenly lurches forward, doubt diminishes. If, as speculated just earlier, doubt causes a goal to drop in priority, confidence may do the opposite. Thus, an out-of-awareness partial resolution of the problem might cause the goal to rise in priority, perhaps even to pop into the person's mind unbidden.

For many years, how to integrate the interrupt and disengagement aspect of the conceptual model with its feedback aspect has been a vexing puzzle to us. The disengagement facet has always had something of an ad hoc feel to it. However, the view that people have multiple current concerns and the idea that shifts in allocation of attention depend partly on levels of confidence would integrate these two aspects of the model more fully. The phenomenology of disengagement wouldn't change, but the event would be construed more in terms of which goals retain which positions on a priority list.

Loss of Commitment

An implication of this view of multiple current concerns is that goals people have disengaged from retain an attraction. This isn't altogether surprising. It's long been known that uncompleted activities exert a pull on people (Zeigarnik, 1927). However, this idea also connects to a deeper issue: Abandoning *behavioral* effort doesn't mean that the person has abandoned *commitment* to the goal. In the preceding section we discussed views of disengagement of effort and goal salience. But what about removal of commitment?

Detaching yourself from goals to which you've had strong commitment can be quite difficult (Klinger, 1975). How does it happen? A possibility is suggested by our earlier discussion of scaling back as limited disengagement. There we suggested that a slow-acting back-door feedback process may gradually move the reference value closer to present input (Figure 11.1). Perhaps that process constitutes reduction in commitment. If so, spending an extended time with no behavioral effort toward a given goal would yield a continuing loss of commitment to it. This reasoning seems plausible in cases where people abandon a higher goal for a lower one. It's less apparent whether this reasoning applies when people simply put aside goals and never try again to reach them.

Does commitment ever go away entirely? It's not clear. Indeed, today's views on learning hold that extinction doesn't remove the link between cue and behavior tendency, but only dilutes it (see, e.g., Bouton, 1993, 1994). Perhaps there's always a trace of attraction to goals you've once held, even if you've successfully turned your back on them.

FURTHER THEORETICAL COMPARISONS

Two further theoretical comparisons deserve comment with regard to the effect of expectancies on behavior. The first is the relationship between our model and Bandura's (1977, 1982, 1986) analysis of efficacy expectancies.

Efficacy Expectancy and Expectancy of Success

Bandura's theory began as a way of understanding behavior change. Bandura (1977) argued that people with problems generally know exactly what actions are needed to attain their goals. Just knowing what to do, however, isn't enough. People must also be confident of their ability to *do* the behavior. The perceived ability to carry out a desired action is what Bandura terms self-efficacy expectancy. According to Bandura, when therapy works, it's because it restored the person's sense of efficacy, or confidence in the ability to carry out actions that earlier were troublesome.

We agree fully with certain aspects of that model. Clearly, the bottleneck in behavior often is the person's lack of confidence about having the capacity to perform it. On the other hand, there are also situations in which personal capability is not the central issue. By emphasizing the role of personal capability to the exclusion of other factors, Bandura removed from the theory's purview situations in which expectations of outcomes derive from other sources of influence. For example, if a cancer patient believes her prescribed medical regimen will cure her, it hardly seems sensible to say that her optimism about survival (and her careful following of the doctor's instructions) rests on perceptions of self-efficacy.

In Bandura's efficacy model, expectations of personal efficacy are always the critical element. We've long felt this is misleading. Judgments about the likely impact of other causal forces also influence people's belief that continued action will yield good versus bad outcomes. In our view, perceptions not only of personal capabilities but also of causal factors outside the person matter in determining behavior.

What ultimately matters is the *emergent expectation of success or failure*, which derives from assessment of both kinds of factors. In some cases, the role of personal agency is paramount. In other cases, it's minimal. As we said earlier about feedback loops, sometimes the action of the output function is what produces the desired effect, but sometimes an external perturbation does so. Whether personal agency is paramount or not so important, what matters is whether the person remains engaged with the goal to which the behavior is oriented.

We also suggest that Bandura's emphasis on the role of personal agency has clouded the extent to which he takes other factors into account implicitly. He *has* discussed alternative sources of futility (1982, pp. 140–141), but not comparable sources of success expectancies. Clearly these influences matter as well. Imagine a collegiate wrestler who knows he's moderately good at offensive maneuvers, very good at defensive ones, and moderately good at evoking his best efforts in the heat of competition. From these and other considerations he derives a sense of self-efficacy with respect to wrestling (or even specific efficacy expectancies for different situations in a match). He has a particular vision of his capabilities, his competencies. Given a specific opponent (with a given set of perceived capabilities), he also has a sense of the likelihood of prevailing.

Now imagine he learns this opponent has severely sprained an ankle, cannot use it without great pain, and therefore cannot even attempt certain important maneuvers. Surely this news will increase his confidence of success. Is that because his sense of self-efficacy has increased? Some would say yes. Yet how can that be? His knowledge of the extent of his own skills hasn't changed. How could the sense of self-efficacy increase if self-efficacy is a judgment of one's *capability*?

We think self-efficacy researchers often measure more than people's judgments of their capabilities. The measures used to assess the influence of the self often assess other influences indirectly, though the result is always labeled *self*-efficacy. Thus, although the discussions always focus on the self, the *situations* the self confronts are a partner in the assessment.

The Sense of Personal Control

Another construct that merits mention here is the sense of control. Many people believe that perceived control is an important determinant of successful adjustment to stressful events (Baltes & Baltes, 1986; Heckhausen & Schulz, 1995; Skinner, 1996; Taylor, 1983, 1990; Taylor & Brown, 1988; Thompson & Spacapan, 1991; Weiner, 1985). Indeed, the idea that people deal better with stressors when they have a sense of control is a recurring theme in the stress literature.

Does the sense of control really confer benefits? The answer isn't as simple as it might seem (see Aldwin, 1994; Averill, 1973; Thompson, 1981; Thompson & Spacapan, 1991). Some studies suggest that perceptions of control help. For example, among newly diagnosed breast cancer and lymphoma patients (Burgess, Morris, & Pettingale, 1988), those with an internal locus of control (the belief they have control over important outcomes in their lives) had less depression and anxiety and a more positive coping style than those with an external locus of control (the belief that control rests outside themselves). Another study found that cancer patients with a sense of control in specific domains reported less distress than those whose control perceptions were lower (Thompson, Sobolew-Shubin, Galbraith, Schwankovsky, & Cruzen, 1993). Particularly beneficial was the sense of control over symptoms and emotional reactions.

In contrast to this, in some situations personal control apparently is detrimental (Affleck, Tennen, Pfeiffer, & Fifield, 1987; Burger, 1989; Folkman, 1984; Thompson, 1981). In a review of research on the sense of control, Burger (1989) identified several conditions that might cause people to relinquish control or to experience distress when having control. Of particular interest is his assertion that control is undesirable when it reduces the likelihood of a desired outcome (or increases the chances of an undesired outcome). This assertion is of interest because it implies that what matters most is the anticipated *outcome* rather than the path by which it will occur.

Support for this view comes from several sources. For example, Burger, McWard, and LaTorre (1989) found that most subjects who were asked to give a blood sample relinquished control over this procedure to the experimenters, who were more experienced. Apparently this occurred in an effort to avoid pain, an undesired outcome. A similar principle seems to underlie results reported by Miller (1979). Subjects thought they were being tested for reaction speed. Each was paired with a partner, and only one of them could respond on a given trial. Subjects were told they'd be shocked each time the reaction failed to occur within a specified time. Students who thought their partners had faster reactions than they did relinquished control, again to avoid a painful outcome.

Work in health psychology also suggests that personal control can increase distress in some circumstances. Rodin (1986) suggested that as individuals age and their physical problems become more chronic, perceived control over these problems can cause more stress, worry, and self-blame. Affleck et al. (1987), studying patients with rheumatoid

Sense of personal causal responsibility

		Yes	No
Good outcome	Yes	A	B
	No	C	D

Figure 11.7. If perceptions of control are beneficial, people in the left-hand column should experience less distress than people in the right-hand column. If perceptions of control are beneficial when associated with good outcomes but detrimental when associated with bad outcomes, A should be better off than B and C should be worse off than D. The effect of perceived control per se cannot be evaluated, however, by comparing cell A with cell D, which is what many studies have done.

arthritis, concluded that a sense of personal control in situations with few opportunities for actual control leads to coping difficulties. Similarly, Eitel, Hatchett, Friend, Griffin, and Wadhwa (1995) recently found that control over treatment among patients with end-stage renal disease led to poorer adjustment.

As a group, the studies just discussed suggest the conclusion that control is desirable (and may diminish distress) when it makes a desired outcome more likely, but that having control is undesirable (and may exacerbate distress) when it makes a desired outcome less likely (see also Law, Logan, & Baron, 1994). This conclusion challenges the importance of the sense of control per se. The powerful factor, instead, would be expectancies about the outcomes, consistent with our conceptualization (Figure 11.7).

It's important to note that a good deal of prior research on perceived control confounds two qualities: the perception that good or bad outcomes *depend on what you do* (personal control) and the anticipation that successful outcomes *will occur* (positive outcome expectancies; for a broad discussion of issues in control, including this one, see Thompson & Spacapan, 1991). For example, earlier we mentioned a study by Thompson et al. (1993) that appears to indicate the value of perceived control. However, Thompson et al. combined subjects' ratings of the amount of *control* they perceived in a given domain with their ratings of the *effectiveness* of their control efforts (i.e., successes) in that domain. This makes it impossible to know whether it was the control perception that mattered or the perception of success. As another example, items measuring internal locus of control also turn out to imply greater confidence that good outcomes will occur (Carver, 1997c).

The suggestion that the sense of control is not in itself beneficial will be counterintuitive to many people, for whom the importance of personal control is something of an article of faith. It's often noted, for example, that patients who find they cannot control the course of their disease turn to aspects of their situation that they can control, such as their daily activities or their emotions (e.g., Taylor, 1983; Thompson et al., 1993). This suggests that patients engage in a continuing search for control, which is shunted in other directions when control in one domain becomes unlikely.

In our view, however, this pattern isn't a search for control but a search for good outcomes. Indeed, we believe that people shift to more limited domains precisely *because* these are domains where positive outcomes still occur. Such shifts can be thought of as small-scale disengagements and retrenchment. Instead of continuing to focus on a part of life in which expectancies are negative (e.g., having a terminal cancer go into remission), the person turns to a part of life in which good outcomes are more likely (e.g., continuing to have enjoyable interactions with friends). As a result, there's more opportunity to experience positive feelings and less distress.

A final note on control: Some have suggested that control can be exerted vicariously. Thus, the perception that others (e.g., medical caregivers) have control over stressful events should work in the same way as the expectation of personal control: If someone working for your benefit has control, you are likely to have less distress. In our opinion, this stretches the concept of control past recognition. Invoking the concept of vicarious control is a virtual admission that what matters is the expected outcome, not the perception of having control over the outcome. Interestingly enough, Thompson and Spacapan (1991) concluded that vicarious control yields positive effects when good outcomes are expected, and adverse effects when poor outcomes are expected, much as Burger (1989) argued for personal control. This conclusion is consistent with the view presented here.

ENGAGEMENT AND DISENGAGEMENT IN OTHER LITERATURES

In discussing research on expectancies and disengagement in Chapter 10, we focused on several studies of our own. A vast literature addresses these matters, however, from points of view that resemble ours in some ways but differ in others. We didn't originate the idea that expectancies have an influence on behavior (e.g., Tolman, 1932, 1938). We've simply discussed it as it fits into the picture of self-regulation we're sketching in this book (see also, e.g., Bandura, 1994; Feather 1982, 1989).

Before leaving the topic of expectancies, though, we want to point to several places where we think expectancies matter. As a way of illustrating the breadth of the theme's applicability, we focus here on conceptually diverse cases, including cases where the principle emerges in surprising ways.

Goal Setting

One literature to which the dichotomy between effort and disengagement seems readily applicable is the literature of goal setting (mentioned in Chapter 5). The central finding of this literature is that performances are better with a high goal than with a lower goal or when people are told to do their best (Locke & Latham, 1990a). This finding is usually interpreted in terms of the efforts that people mobilize. A higher goal causes people to try harder, and thereby to do better.

We noted earlier that this effect has an important boundary condition. This boundary is of special interest here: Specifically, a goal that's too high impairs performance rather than enhancing it. This finding is usually discussed in terms of commitment to, or acceptance of, the goal (Locke & Latham, 1990a, chap. 6). People who fail to adopt the goal (or who fail to remain committed to it) withdraw effort, causing poorer performance. This effect emerges when the goal is too far out of their reach. To frame this principle in our terms, people who doubt their ability to reach the goal disengage from its pursuit.

Social Facilitation

The literature of social facilitation is one of the oldest in social psychology (Triplett, 1897). The findings are of two sorts: Presence of other people (as observers, competitors, or co-actors) when one person performs a task causes performance to improve. Sometimes, however, the presence of others causes the opposite, an impairment of performance.

This contradiction stood unreconciled until Zajonc (1965) proposed an integration in terms of drive theory: He argued that presence of other people causes an increase in drive, which causes an increased emission of dominant responses. When the situation is one in which the dominant response is also correct, the result is performance facilitation. When the dominant response isn't appropriate to the situation, performance is impaired. Thus, facilitation typically occurs when the task is easy; impairment typically occurs when the task is hard.

There are, however, other ways to look at these phenomena. We think facilitation is a product of increased self-focus, caused by the presence of the other people (Carver & Scheier, 1981c). As the comparator of the feedback loop is more fully engaged, behavior matches more closely to the standard. What of performance impairment? We believe impairment occurs when the person has doubt about performing adequately and starts to disengage from the attempt (or mentally disengage, creating cognitive interference). Hard tasks tend to produce such doubt; thus hard tasks yield the impairment effect.

Evidence from at least two sources tends to support this view. Bond (1982) had subjects work on a task with one of two forms: Some people had mostly simple items with a few complex ones mixed in; other people had mostly complex items with a few simple ones mixed in. Drive theory predicts that facilitation will occur for simple *items*, impairment for hard *items*. Bond argued, however, that people working on hard items are likely to realize after a while that they're doing poorly. This realization is likely to interfere with performance on even simple items. Though Bond didn't say so, we'd regard this as reflecting mental disengagement from the task. This pattern is exactly what he found. Further and more elaborated support for an expectancy-based dichotomy between effort and disengagement in the social facilitation setting has since been reported by Sanna (1992). In sum, the social facilitation context is another setting in which effort versus disengagement may be an important explanatory principle.

Upward and Downward Social Comparison

Early in the book we described various aspects of social comparison processes. The recent literature of social comparison emphasizes the difference between upward comparison (to those who are better off than you) and downward comparison (to those who are worse off than you). We said that upward comparison can provide people with a sense of hope or motivation to improve (Wood, 1996). Downward comparison can help people confirm that they're better off than others (see, e.g., Taylor & Lobel, 1989; Wills, 1981; Wood, Taylor, & Lichtman, 1985) or even enhance their perception of being better off.

Although both of these results can happen, the literature of findings is more varied than these statements suggest. Sometimes upward comparison is beneficial, but sometimes it creates distress. Sometimes downward comparison is beneficial, but sometimes it's threatening. What's responsible for the divergence between these sets of findings?

We argue that the divergence rests on people's confidence or doubt regarding the goal to which the comparison relates. When you make an upward comparison, you make the better-off group a goal, an aspiration for yourself. You want to pull yourself up to where this group is. This is adaptive, if you're confident enough about being able to get there. But if you doubt you can pull yourself up (you see insufficient progress), the comparison is painful. When you make a downward comparison, you're making the worse-off group an anti-goal. You want to push yourself away from them. This is adaptive, if you're confident you can escape their situation. But if you fear you're slipping in their direction, the comparison is painful. The concepts of confidence and doubt thus bring order to a mixed set of findings.

Self-Verification

The principle of doubt leading to disengagement may also play a role in the literature of self-verification (Swann, 1990), which we also touched on earlier. Recall that people seek out social feedback confirming their view of themselves – indeed, they will go out of their way to elicit such feedback. What's made this literature so interesting is partly that the effort to "find feedback that fits" occurs even when people hold negative views of themselves. These people would rather hear confirming information than positive information.

Sketchy evidence suggests that efforts to self-verify show a kind of disengagement under conditions promoting doubt about being able to attain the desired goal (the confirmation of the self-view). Specifically, married people with negative self-views whose spouses saw them more positively reported less commitment to the relationship than did other married people (Swann, Hixon, & De La Ronde, 1992). In effect, they acted as though they were withdrawing because they couldn't convince their spouses of their true natures. Other analyses showed that people whose spouses held discrepant views of them felt less intimacy in the relationship than did people whose spouses' views echoed their own (Swann, De La Ronde, & Hixon, 1994). Although subject to other interpretations, these findings hint that people withdraw psychologically from relationships when they are unable to instill the view they have of themselves.

Performance Goals and Learning Goals

The doubt and disengagement principle seems to be challenged, in one case we want to consider. In Chapter 5 we discussed work by Dweck and her collaborators (Dweck, 1996; Dweck & Leggett, 1988; Elliott & Dweck, 1988) on goals underlying achievement-related behavior. An idea behind that research is that people engaged in a task sometimes have the goal of *performing* well on it, to show or verify that they have the skill required to complete the task. At other times, people have the goal of *learning* from their experiences with the task to in order increase their skill.

These goals have different consequences. Children with performance goals are vulnerable to deterioration in effort when they aren't doing well; this doesn't occur among children with learning goals. Adults with performance goals are inclined to self-handicap (Rhodewalt, 1994), which doesn't happen in adults with learning goals. In both cases, it appears that tasks threaten those who hold performance goals. Both phenomena (helplessness in children, self-handicapping in adults) look like disengagement from efforts because of doubts about the final results. Findings by Butler (1993) also fit this picture. Butler found that subjects with ego-involving goals (comparable to performance goals) were more likely to ask for performance norms than were those with skill-acquisition goals – *but only if they were high in ability*, and therefore doing well. If they were low in ability, and therefore doing poorly, they stopped asking for the norms.

This evidence seems to suggest that disengagement follows from failure and doubt regarding performance goals, but that the disengagement can be put off by instituting a learning orientation (Dweck & Leggett, 1988). This principle hints that expectancies of success can be made not to matter. It's important, though, to be clear about what the findings do and do not show.

Remember that people with learning goals do have goals – but goals of a different type. It's possible for doubts to develop about moving toward the learning goal, just as for the performance goal. What isn't known yet is whether doubt about *being able to increase ability* will reinstitute the deficits. That is, having a learning orientation doesn't imply acquisition of the skill – only the belief that the skill is acquirable. You can hold this view as long as increments occur periodically (cf. Trope & Neter, 1994) – a little failure doesn't imply an inability to learn. But what if failure is extensive? It seems likely that this would create doubt about extending the ability, and that it would yield disengagement. When people don't succeed at least some of the time, even learning goals will be undermined.

In short, although it appears clear that the shift to a learning orientation is facilitative of continued efforts, we don't think this shift gets entirely around the problems that result from doubts. Rather, it puts the doubts off, because they take longer to develop.

Curiosity

Curiosity is very different in content from any area we've addressed thus far, but even this concept seems to have a role for the disjunction between engagement and disengagement. Loewenstein (1994) has argued that curiosity stems from a perception of a gap in knowledge. Reviewing Hebb, Piaget, Hunt, and Berlyne (among others), he concluded that curiosity involves a comparison of one's present information against a reference point. Curiosity occurs when the reference point is higher than present knowledge. He argues that people must experience a contrast between these elements in order to experience curiosity.

Although people are always ignorant of many things, they aren't always curious. Loewenstein argues that whether curiosity arises or not depends on the size of the discrepancy. A too-large disparity (which by implication raises doubt about closing it) dampens curiosity. In effect, people feel overwhelmed and disengage. Indeed, he argued that before people expose themselves to a curiosity-inducing situation, they estimate the likelihood that their curiosity will ultimately be satisfied. If the chances are too slim, most people won't expose themselves to the situation. Thus, curiosity represents an engagement aimed at discrepancy reduction, and avoiding the unknown represents a disengagement.

This distinction, which seems to fit our conceptualization quite well, is not entirely new in the literature of curiosity. Loewenstein (1994) quotes both Hebb and James on the idea that some lack of correspondence between current knowledge and a reference point has a stimulating effect, whereas too much has a disruptive effect.

Stress and Coping

Another literature to which the distinction between engagement and disengagement pertains concerns stress and coping. The theory of Lazarus, Folkman, and their colleagues (Lazarus, 1966; Lazarus & Folkman, 1984) dominates discussions of these phenomena. It holds that the experience of stress is a dynamic transaction between person and environment. In this view, particular kinds of appraisals – the perception that a situation involves challenge, threat, or loss – engage a process of selecting and carrying out coping responses.

Stress follows mainly from negative appraisals (we ignore challenge here – the possibility of gain – because there's less agreement about its stressful character). Threat is an appraisal of doubt about being able to attain a desired end. Loss is the appraisal that there is no possibility of attaining the desired end. Coping is the various ways in which people respond to these perceptions of adversity.

These considerations have led us to suggest that the experience of stress and coping isn't really a distinct category of phenomena. Rather, stress is embedded in the structure of self-regulatory processes (Carver et al., 1992). Stress is the condition that exists when something is interfering with movement toward desired goals (or away from anti-goals). Coping is what people do in response to that perception.

Coping responses are typically divided into several categories, according to their aims and functional characteristics. What Lazarus and Folkman (1984) called *problem-focused* coping aims at changing the situation to make it better. This clearly reflects continued engagement with goals that the stressor is threatening. In effect, this category of coping constitutes taking steps to keep those goals alive and active. Although active coping can also dampen distress (Valentiner, Holohan, & Moos, 1994), that's not its main purpose. Reducing distress is the purpose of *emotion-focused* coping.

Another category, often termed *avoidance* coping (e.g., Billings & Moos, 1984; Cronkite & Moos, 1984), is attempts to avoid further contact with, or contemplation of, the stressor. Avoidance coping includes wishful thinking (Bolger, 1990; Felton, Revenson, & Hinrichsen, 1984; Folkman & Lazarus, 1985), self-distraction (Carver, Scheier, & Weintraub, 1989), overt denial (Carver et al., 1993), escapism (Rohde, Lewinsohn, Tilson, & Seeley, 1990), actually giving up on the threatened goals (Carver et al., 1989, 1993), and use of alcohol or drugs to cope (Carver & Scheier, 1994; Wills, 1986).

Avoidance coping has a great deal in common with disengagement responses. In all avoidance coping, one consequence is a temporary removal from considering the threatened goals (see also Tobin, Holroyd, Reynolds, & Wigal, 1989). Much stress research examines situations in which disengagement from goals cannot be successfully sustained for long. As a result, avoidance coping often yields more distress than other types of coping (e.g., Carver et al., 1993).

We've argued that giving up is a functional aspect of behavior – when it occurs in the right circumstances. Perhaps avoidance coping can be functional – provided it moves the person to an adaptive disengagement. The adaptive value of disengagement can be illustrated by situations involving losses that cannot be redressed. Such a loss (e.g., death of a loved one) renders one or many desired goals unreachable (e.g., continuing activities once engaged in with that person – cf. Millar et al., 1988). At first, one remains committed to those goals. Over time, however, one is better served by disengaging from them rather than holding onto them (cf. Tait & Silver, 1989).

The view on stress and coping we're proposing has a number of implications. Most broadly, it implies that when you think about stress and coping in a particular context, you should also think about the relevance of principles of self-regulation. Two aspects of these principles seem worth exploring. First, given a severe enough stressor, one can expect to see a dichotomy among responses to it, based on confidence versus doubt. Some people will struggle to overcome the obstacle (cf. Roth & Cohen, 1986); some will be overwhelmed and will experience a tendency to give up what's threatened (see also Aldwin, 1994; Aldwin & Stokols, 1988). Second, when a person is doubtful enough to want to give up something that cannot be given up, that person can be expected to display deep distress.

SUMMARY

The disjunction between confidence and doubt, effort and disengagement, appears to have relevance to a wide range of issues. The examples discussed here by no means exhaust the applications of this principle in personality–social psychology. Other candidates for discussion in these terms include the tendency of reference groups to discard members who deviate too much from the group's values (and vice versa), perhaps based on doubts that those members will conform; division of persuasive appeals into latitudes of acceptance and rejection, perhaps based on doubt about the recipient's ability to assimilate the message, given his or her current attitude; and division of initial negotiation offers into those that are worth discussing further and those that are not, perhaps based on doubt about being able to reach the desired resolution level. In all these cases and probably more, there's a pull toward some goal, but at some point in the confidence range the goal is abandoned.

12

Applications to Problems in Living

If you don't run, you can't win.
(*Chariots of Fire*)

You got to know when to hold 'em, know when to fold 'em.
(Don Schlitz, *The Gambler*)

Our main interest is in the structure and processes of normal behavior. However, any view on normal behavior also suggests ways that functioning can go awry. The conceptualization we've presented here is no exception. It suggests several angles on dysfunctional behavior, which we examine in this chapter and the next. In them we consider ways in which processes outlined earlier can go off track, leading to difficulties (for views that are related to this but also differ in some ways, see Baumeister & Heatherton, 1996; Baumeister, Heatherton, & Tice, 1994; Hamilton, Greenberg, Pyszczynski, & Cather, 1993; Kirschenbaum, 1987). In keeping with our overall strategy, we begin simply and then elaborate. The issues treated in this chapter are straightforward; Chapter 13 treats matters of greater complexity.

Some of the problems in people's lives stem from relatively simple snags in the self-regulatory process. These snags involve only the feedback loop and ways in which the effects of that loop can be disrupted. The problems are simple in structure, but not trivial in consequence.

REGULATING WITH THE WRONG FEEDBACK

Ours is a view in which people self-regulate their actions in order to keep on track in moving toward desired goals or intentions. We pointed out earlier that it's crucial to use the right feedback to self-regulate, or you won't be producing the behavior you intend to produce. Even when you keep very close track of an input channel, if the channel you're monitoring is irrelevant to the intention, self-regulation will be faulty. You may even go in directions that *contradict* your intention.

For example, we know a couple in which the woman acts happy all the time. Indeed, she does so whether her partner is behaving in ways that please her or not. He attends to her facial expressions to assess whether he's behaving as desired, assuming they will tell him what he wants to know. Since she always looks happy, he always concludes he's doing fine. Periodically, she makes it known that he's wrong, and it always takes him by surprise. He's monitoring a channel that's actually uninformative about the adequacy of his actions (see also Swann, Stein-Seroussi, & McNulty, 1992). He's confused because this channel does provide relevant information in other cases. In this case, though, it doesn't. For this woman, the pertinent information comes verbally, on request, rather than through her facial expressions. Unfortunately, the man hasn't adjusted his information-seeking to take this into account, and he continues to check the wrong channel.

From the literature of health psychology comes another example of reliance on misleading feedback. Hypertension has no reliable symptoms. Yet people who enter treatment for hypertension quickly conclude that they can tell when their blood pressure is up (Baumann & Leventhal, 1985; Meyer, Leventhal, & Gutmann, 1985). Indeed, the longer they're in treatment, the more confident they are. More than 90% of people in treatment for more than three months claim to be able to tell (Meyer et al., 1985).

Can they? Generally, no (Baumann & Leventhal, 1985). However, because they're monitoring what they think is a symptom of hypertension, they often use it to tell whether to take their medication. If they think their blood pressure isn't up (because there's no symptom), they don't take the medication. If there's no symptom over time, they may stop treatment altogether. This can lead to serious medical problems – all because they're relying on irrelevant feedback information to guide their actions.

Automatic Distortion of Feedback

Sometimes, then, people simply use the wrong information to self-regulate. Sometimes they do use information that's relevant, but they rely too much on automatic interpretations of it, based on their preconceptions. Sometimes people distort feedback to make it closer to what they *want* to see (Swann, 1990). Sometimes people distort feedback to make it closer to what they *expect* to see. For example, socially anxious people, who expect others to react negatively to them, perceive rejection even when it isn't happening (Pozo et al., 1991).

In broad scope, this problem sometimes receives the label *mind-reading*. You read nonverbal cues in order to get cues about how others are responding to you. Frequently this tells you what you want to know. But often – maybe more often than most people realize – the cues are ambiguous. Often others aren't trying to communicate how they see you. Instead, they're attending to their own concerns, influences you aren't aware of. For example, a person's frown may be about something that happened earlier in the day and is still in mind, not about what you're saying. In interpreting cues from others, most people assume a lot. They know what it means when someone smiles or goes silent. They read the other person's mind and know what that person's thinking. Sometimes, though, people are wrong, and the feedback isn't informing them about the actual effects of their behavior.

GOALS OPERATING OUT OF AWARENESS

Automatic distortions of input aren't the only automatic influence on behavior. An idea that's occurred a couple of times in earlier chapters is that people have goals they're monitoring outside their awareness. Research summarized by Bargh (1997) makes it clear that there's automaticity in a lot of human social behavior. This means there's minimal awareness of what's taking place, or even of what stimuli are cueing the behavior.

The idea that people have goals that influence their actions outside awareness means they can be actively trying to do things they don't realize they're doing. These attempts at goal conformity simply blend into the backdrop of the personalized sense of normalcy that the people take for granted. Some aspects of behavior are automatic because they're biologically engineered in (e.g., danger avoidance, interest in potential sexual partners). Pursuit of other goals may be automatic because the goals were particularly important early in life. Thus efforts to attain them were overlearned, and became automatized to the point where they're no longer noticed.

For example, many people think the attachment pattern formed in infancy – and the issues reflected therein – reverberate in adult behavior, though the actor may be unaware of it (see Bartholomew & Perlman, 1994; Hazan & Shaver, 1994; Parkes, Stevenson-Hinde, & Marris, 1991).

That is, people may orient to new relationships in ways that derive from how they managed their earliest relationships. Presumably a particular manner of attaining relationship-relevant goals was overlearned during early attachment, and has now become automatic.

Thus, a child who learned that his caregivers couldn't be relied on to provide comfort may become an adult who automatically assumes the need to be responsible for his own well-being, and who shuts others out of his life without realizing it. A child who was clingy and angry because caregiving was inconsistent may become an adult who insists on a high degree of consistency and emotional availability from partners. Both of these people may be easily captured by and drawn into – and vulnerable to the negative consequences of – situations with a structural resemblance to their early life experiences. They may respond particularly badly to rejection and inconsistency, respectively, without a clue as to why they're overreacting, or even *that* they're overreacting. They experience difficulties in life that they may not understand, or may ascribe to other sources. In theory, however, the difficulties are arising from responses they're making to goals that have slipped out of awareness.

If this portrayal has any validity, it presents a challenge for anyone seeking to understand human behavior. This portrayal, though consistent with a self-regulatory model, implies that determining the goals that constitute any person's self-structure will involve a lot of guesswork. If people's goals aren't always accessible to the observer or the actor, it will be hard to know what they are. Somewhat to our surprise, we find ourselves in the position of saying that it can be hard to know what motives underlie behavior, including one's own behavior. This is a point of contact between self-regulatory and psychodynamic models that we wouldn't have expected 20 years ago.

DOUBT AS A ROOT OF PROBLEMS

The problems we've discussed thus far concern the functioning of simple feedback processes. Other problems relate to another aspect of the model: confidence versus doubt about attaining goals, and how these qualities influence people. Put simply, many problems in living stem in one way or another from doubt that continued effort will yield desired outcomes.

Some problems deriving from issues of confidence and doubt are simple in structure; others are more complex. A very simple problem related to these issues returns us to the theme of automaticity. When confronting adversity, many people tend to turn automatically to previously encoded sources of information about expectancies.

Automatic Use of Previously Encoded Success Expectancies

As noted in Chapter 10, difficulty induces a hazy sense of doubt, which may promote a more conscious deliberation on the chance of success. That deliberation potentially involves mental simulation ("If I do it this way, what will happen?") and social comparison ("How would Don handle this?"). Often, though, it's just a quick check of consolidated records of prior experiences ("I usually do pretty well at this") or even a single exemplar ("Oh, not this again!"). When the person's had a lot of experience in some domain, the memories are encoded with a great deal of redundancy, whether consolidated into a verbal summary or not. When things get difficult, people often overrely on those memories to inform them about the likely outcome of what's happening now.

Sometimes this works to people's advantage. As we showed in Chapter 10, people who think they can overcome a particular kind of adversity can use that residual sense of confidence to help them overcome the doubt occasioned by rising anxiety. This residual sense of confidence thus is often a good thing to have. On the other hand, this sense of confidence can potentially lead you astray. A continuing unrealistic and inaccurate optimism can cause you to waste time, energy, and effort on goals that are simply out of reach.

Too often, though, the residual sense isn't confidence, but doubt or inadequacy. If that residual sense is strong enough, or redundantly encoded enough, the person will experience the impulse to give up at the first signs of adversity. When doubts are deeply ingrained, you may not even attend well to what's *going on* in the current situation. Being convinced that the situation will end badly, you fail to realize that the present difficulty is minor, and easily resolved. You give up trying, and the doubt increases.

This automatic overreliance on heavily encoded doubts can be overcome, but it's easier to say than do. The person needs to learn to attend to the actual situation for information relevant to expectancies instead of relying on preconceptions. Indeed, a tactic in cognitive therapies is to train the person to identify the cue that now leads reflexively to accessing the preconception, and to use that cue instead as a reminder to stop and process relevant information more effortfully.

PREMATURE DISENGAGEMENT OF EFFORT

Whether doubts are retrieved automatically from memory or are derived from ongoing experience, they have consequences. Doubts can cause scaling back of goals or giving up on goals. It's bad for this to happen too readily. A person who gives up whenever things get difficult will have trouble reaching any goal in life. Disengaging too fast keeps you from trying your best, and short-circuits what could be successes.

Sometimes people who disengage quit completely and go on to something else. Such a lack of persistence, moving the person endlessly from goal to goal to goal, is a potentially serious problem. However, we focus here on a more subtle pattern. It involves disengagement of *effort*, but continued *commitment* to the goal. This pattern may be reflected in several ways, including self-distraction, off-task thinking, even temporarily leaving the scene. Despite this, however, the goal hasn't been abandoned. But any attempts to move forward are sporadic, disrupted repeatedly by this withdrawal of effort and off-task thinking.

That this is a problem of disengagement is often disguised by the fact that the withdrawal is mental rather than behavioral. Mental withdrawal is hard to observe. It's reflected indirectly, though, in experiences with labels such as *cognitive interference* (Sarason, Pierce, & Sarason, 1996). This term refers to unwanted thoughts that intrude on a person's activities, often producing performance impairment. Among these intrusive thoughts are thoughts about things other than the present task.

Our view is that what underlies these interference effects is the following flow of process (Figure 12.1): An interruption is caused by task difficulty or stressful context, and the person's doubts prompt disengagement, which is deflected into mental disengagement. It can't be maintained, because the person hasn't given up the goal and eventually must reconfront it. The reconfrontation leads to a reengagement of effort, which may quickly lead to reevoking of doubts and a renewal of the impulse to disengage. As we said in Chapter 10, this cycle is experienced as repetitive negative rumination with self-deprecatory overtones (Carver, 1996c; McIntosh & Martin, 1992; Wine, 1971, 1980). Because there's commitment to the goal but no movement toward it, the person also experiences distress.

Test Anxiety

The dynamic just described appears to be a key factor underlying the experiences of people with test anxiety (Carver, 1996a; Carver, Peterson,

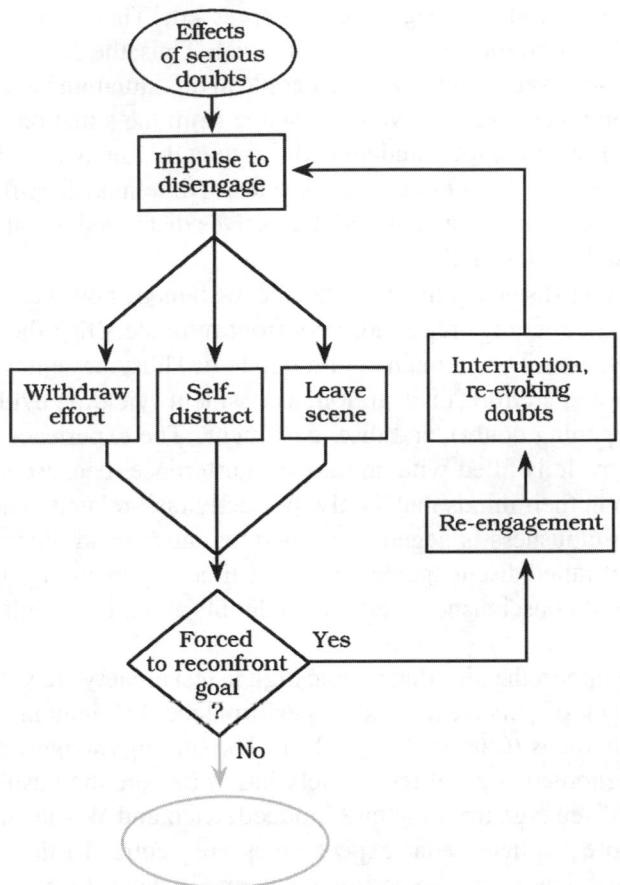

Figure 12.1.   Doubts lead to a disengagement impulse, which can be expressed in several ways – as withdrawal of effort, self-distraction, or even
leaving the scene. In some cases the disengagement is complete, and the
person turns to other pursuits. In the case depicted here, this doesn't happen.
Rather the person eventually is forced to reconfront the goal about which
the doubts exit. The reconfrontation leads to a reengagement of effort, which
may be followed quickly by reevoking of the doubts and a renewal of the impulse to disengage. The overall experience incorporates a sense of cognitive
interference, often accompanied by self-deprecation.

Follansbee, & Scheier, 1983; Carver, Scheier, & Klahr, 1987). In essence, we think that test-anxious people have grave doubts about being
able to do well in performance settings. (Other problems may also characterize them, such as study-skill deficiencies, but we focus on the role
of doubt because we view it as pivotal.)

We think that when people high in test anxiety encounter adversity during an exam, they turn to their preconceived doubts, and the

disengagement tendency begins to be expressed. The settings for test taking tend to discourage physical withdrawal. Thus, the disengagement isn't expressed overtly, but covertly. People in this situation have trouble concentrating, because they want to escape from the situation (Galassi et al., 1981). Test-anxious students don't typically run away. They just sit in their seats and *wish* to escape (see also Nottelman & Hill, 1977). They daydream, fantasize, and find themselves distracted by other stray thoughts, sights, or sounds.

This mental disengagement cannot be sustained, however. People in performance settings repeatedly confront reminders that the task remains unfinished. They remain committed to it. Thus, they enter into the cycle of sporadic effort, interruption, assessment (yielding evidence of further deepening doubt), and disengagement. The experience of people in this cycle is filled with cognitive interference, because so much is going on in their minds that's only indirectly task-related. Their content of consciousness is negatively toned, as they spend more time in this cycle of failed disengagement and less time daydreaming. Because the content of consciousness pertains to doubts about their abilities, it's self-deprecatory.

Studies support the idea that people high in test anxiety are vulnerable both to a lack of persistence and to performance deficits under conditions of self-focus (Carver et al., 1983). The findings suggest strongly that the phenomenology of test anxiety has at its core the unsuccessful attempt to disengage from the task. Indeed, Rich and Woolever (1988) showed more explicitly that expectancies are central to this pattern: When expectancies were experimentally manipulated to be favorable among highly test-anxious subjects, self-focus caused *enhancement* of performance rather than the usual impairment.

Social Anxiety

A dynamic similar to this seems to be involved in the experiences of people high in social anxiety. One difference is the goal about which the doubts exist. In social anxiety, people have doubts about being able to create and maintain desired self-presentations (Schlenker & Leary, 1982; Smith & Sarason, 1975).

Many social interactions are stressful and difficult for most people, not just the socially anxious. Meeting someone for the first time, speaking your mind before a group of strangers, knowing you have to make a good impression on someone in a job interview – these situations are hard for most people. Different people respond in different ways, though. People with doubts about being able to create desired self-presentations are likely to experience the impulse to disengage from the effort.

Social settings are often such that overt disengagement is difficult, resulting in a phenomenology of negatively toned self-deprecatory cognition, which itself interferes with self-presentational efforts. People who are vulnerable to this experience will have thoughts of self-doubt even when anticipating stressful social interactions. These doubts may cause them simply to avoid entering situations where they anticipate adverse outcomes. Such avoidance can be thought of as disengagement that occurs before the behavior begins. It's of some interest, in this regard, that avoidance of social encounters is the very hallmark of social anxiety.

Evidence to support this line of thought comes from several sources. One study (Burgio, Merluzzi, & Pryor, 1986) examined self-presentations made by college men to a young woman. Subjects were men chosen as moderately high in social anxiety, but as varying in expectancies. Some expressed confidence about being able to create a good impression in a brief telephone interaction, others expressed doubt. Each later made a phone call to an undergraduate woman (an accomplice of the researchers) to get acquainted. Half did this in front of a TV camera (high focus on the public self). The woman was instructed to be moderately positive to all callers, and to try to form an impression of them. As predicted, self-focus interacted with expectancies. Confident subjects were seen as friendlier and more socially skilled than doubtful subjects – but only if they'd been self-focused during the call.

Another study examined what went through the minds of people waiting for a similar interaction (Carver & Scheier, 1986a). Subjects were high or low in social anxiety. Independent of that, some were high and some low in their dispositional tendencies to be focused on their social self-aspects. Subjects were led to anticipate a getting-acquainted conversation, left alone briefly, then asked to list the thoughts that had come to mind in the interim. Consistent with the data from Burgio et al. (1986), people lower in social anxiety reported fewer negative self-related thoughts and more positive self-related thoughts than those higher in social anxiety. These differences were reliable, though, only among subjects who were also relatively high in self-focus.

Another study (Hope, Heimberg, & Klein, 1990) examined the ability of people high and low in social anxiety to recall concrete information from a social interaction they'd just engaged in. Among those low

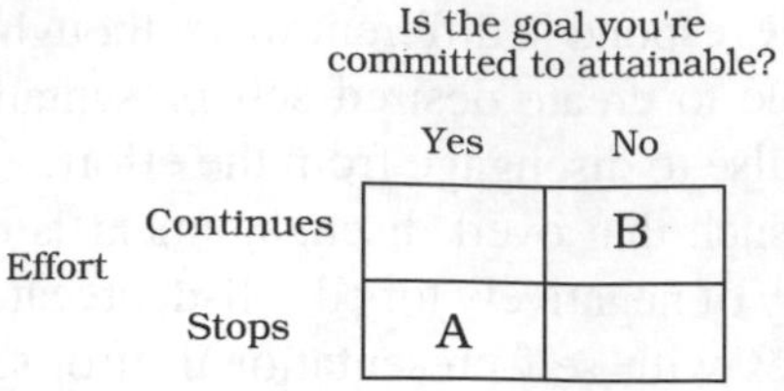

Is the goal you're
committed to attainable?

	Yes	No
Continues		B
Stops	A	

Effort

Figure 12.2.   Two kinds of self-regulatory problems in which people remain committed to a goal. In one case – cell A – the person withdraws effort too soon from a goal that's actually attainable. This person hasn't fully disengaged from the goal, though. Although the trying has stopped, the commitment remains. In the other case – cell B – the person perseverates mentally and perhaps behaviorally on a goal that's unattainable. The person may even realize the goal is unattainable, but be unable to disengage from it. In either of these cases, one result is distress.

in social anxiety, feeling more self-focused during the interaction was associated with better recall and fewer errors. This suggests that self-focus caused these people to become more engaged in the interaction. Among those high in social anxiety, in contrast, more self-focus related to more *errors* of recall, suggesting that they were less engaged in the task.

FAILURE TO DISENGAGE COMPLETELY
WHEN DOING SO IS THE RIGHT RESPONSE

Just as there are drawbacks to withdrawing effort too quickly (cell A in Figure 12.2), there are also drawbacks to continuing to struggle toward goals that are unattainable (cell B in Figure 12.2). We said in Chapter 10 that giving up is an indispensable part of self-regulation, because people need to be able to retrace their steps, back out of corners, free themselves to go elsewhere. Giving up, then, can be good. To be good, though, it must be relatively complete.

Some problems reflect a failure to disengage at times when disengagement is the right response – when the goal is unattainable and the person knows it. Without disengaging, the person continues a cycle of sporadic effort (or mental effort), interruption of effort, the distress that comes from no progress, and reconfrontation with the unattainable goal. It's important to get beyond failures, to put them behind us and move on. Sometimes moving on means scaling back. Sometimes it means giving up completely on something. Whichever the case, moving on isn't possible unless the unattained goal fades into the background.

The inability to give up a lost love is probably the easiest example of this kind of problem. It can lead to personal torment, and it prevents the person from moving forward to a potential new relationship. It's not hard to bring to mind other examples with the same structure – for example, educational or occupational goals that are out of reach for one reason or another. There are also cases of entrapment in conflicts, in which people become committed to escalating struggles and are unable to step away from them (e.g., Brockner, Shaw, & Rubin, 1979).

This sort of problem has three general consequences (as does failure to give up because of unrealistic optimism): Continued commitment to a goal that's unattainable wastes resources in futile efforts. It prevents the person from taking up new, viable goals, and it prevents the person from noticing, recognizing, or responding to new opportunities (cf. Baumeister & Scher, 1988; Feather, 1989; Janoff-Bulman & Brickman, 1982). It also causes distress (Carver & Scheier, 1990a; Klinger, 1975; Pyszczynski & Greenberg, 1992a). The person who's unable to move forward but is unable to let go is condemned to suffer. These consequences suggest how important it can be to accept the reality of a permanent change in one's situation (Carver et al., 1993).

"Hanging On" Is Related to Distress

Consistent with this general line of thought, there's evidence that an inability (or unwillingness) to disengage relates to depression. Depression has been linked to indicators of failing to disengage mentally from experimentally created failures (Kuhl, 1984, 1985; Pyszczynski & Greenberg, 1985, 1987), to self-reports of a tendency to obsess on failures (Carver, La Voie, Kuhl, & Ganellen, 1988), and to ruminative thoughts during forced suspension of valued activities (Millar et al., 1988). Mental perseveration among depressed people isn't limited to major life goals, but occurs even for transient and relatively trivial intentions (Kuhl & Helle, 1986). Thus, there's evidence that depression is bound up with a general failure to disengage mentally from goals. Indeed, this failure may be a core element in the dynamics of depression (see also Klinger, 1975; Pyszczynski & Greenberg, 1992b).

We've said several times already that the surest prescription for distress is having a continued commitment to a goal you believe you cannot attain. This highlights the importance of actually disengaging from a goal when it's out of reach. Sometimes people *appear* to have given up, but the quitting isn't complete (see also Snyder & Frankel, 1989). The effort has stopped, but the self-regulatory apparatus of the mind is still engaged with the lost goal. This person is in the self-regulatory bind just described. This, we think, is the source of depressed affect. If the goal can be relinquished, the source of the affect also goes away.

WHEN *IS* DISENGAGEMENT THE RIGHT RESPONSE?

In the preceding sections we described two classes of situations that share an important structural characteristic. In both cases, the person remains committed to a goal. In one case, the goal is attainable, but doubt causes reduction in effort. In the other case, the goal is unattainable. When we juxtapose these cases, we return to these questions: When is giving up the right response? How can one recognize when it's the right response?

It's easy to address this question by example, but there's a sizable gray area in which the answer is far from clear. When a goal is truly unattainable, you should let it go. When a loved one dies, there's little to be gained by yearning for the rest of your life to reestablish your relationship with that person. When the goal is potentially realizable, on the other hand, even the limited giving up of withdrawing effort can be a mistake. It can keep you from reaching the goal and can solidify your doubts about attaining similar goals in the future.

A key question in life is knowing when to keep trying and when to give up, when it's right to keep "hanging on" and when "letting go" is the right response (Pyszczynski & Greenberg, 1992a). As the lyric that begins this chapter puts it, you have to know when to hold 'em and know when to fold 'em. Distinguishing between these alternatives can be hard, but the ability to do so is a very important life skill (see Feather, 1989, pp. 87–88). Another important skill would seem to be the ability to give up completely – to *really* let go – on occasions when giving up proves necessary. The combination of these two skills yields flexibility, permitting the person to recognize and step out of intractable situations while maximizing efforts in situations that are amenable to change.

LIVES OUT OF BALANCE

We've talked at length about doubt and the giving up of effort that follows from doubt. Now let's consider some of the broader ramifications these phenomena have for the sense of self.

The hierarchy of goals making up the self includes many values. It usually includes both instrumental goals, and goals pertaining to relationships with others. Many theorists have argued that health and completeness require a degree of balance between these domains (see Guisinger & Blatt, 1994). Clearly, though, some lives are out of balance. Some people work long hours and have no social existence outside of what's needed to sustain the work. Some people are totally social animals and wouldn't work a day in their lives if they could possibly avoid it.

The balance between involvement in these classes of goals probably depends in part on pressures of biology and socialization (cf. Brennan & Morris, 1997; Guisinger & Blatt, 1994). However, it's likely that imbalance is also fostered by experiencing failures in some areas of life and successes in others. These experiences can produce increasingly firm expectancies about future performances in the respective areas. It seems likely that people tend to spend most of their time doing things they think they can do fairly well. Given enough perception of failure in some life domain, the person will disengage – stop making effort in that domain. The result, eventually, is what some would regard as a withered branch of the self.

The strong area (or areas) may become even stronger over time, for three reasons. First, the person may make a conscious effort to compensate for the lack of success in the problem domain by doing well in the stronger one. Second, if the person does have skills here, this aspect of the self will naturally develop in a positive way even without an attempt to compensate. Third, given that satisfaction accrues from successful activities, people may bury themselves in the success domain as a way to avoid thinking about the other domain. If both domains of life are really necessary, though, the result is still a life out of balance.

Living a life out of balance may be bad intrinsically. It also poses a risk, should performance in the successful domain begin to falter. Dodge et al. (1989) described the problem: "Many adults think it better to focus virtually all of their attention on a central achievement goal, even when that has meant sacrificing goals in many other domains. . . . Certainly the unrelenting pursuit of a single central goal is a risky business. It allows high levels of attainment, and when the individual is successful, that individual is honored and rewarded. . . . But when it leads to failure, the individual has little else to serve as a source of meaning or satisfaction" (p. 124).

Complexity of the Self

Linville (1985, 1987) has made a related point regarding the complexity of the self. She found that people low in self-complexity – whose goals form a network that's not very elaborated – are vulnerable to extreme emotional reactions and shifts in self-esteem after failure. Low self-complexity also makes people more vulnerable to depression and illness in response to life stress (Linville, 1987). Niedenthal, Setterlund, and Wherry (1992) found that the complexity of anticipated *future* selves dampens emotional reactions to *anticipated* failures. Why? When things go badly in one domain, if the self has only limited differentiation there's no alternative self-aspect to turn to for a stabilizing sense of satisfaction. It's unclear what fosters self-complexity, but a history of successes in diverse areas of experience is a likely candidate.

In the same vein, Pelham (1991) found that people who are depressed typically have a self-aspect that's positive, but too narrow and restricted. These people remain free of depression when the positive self-aspect is center stage, but it's hard to stay free of depression because negative self-aspects too often are salient. Pelham didn't determine how these people came to have a low number of positively valued self-aspects, but again the dynamics of successes and failures over an extended period provide a plausible mechanism by which patterns of this sort might emerge.

RUMINATION

People with problems often find their minds occupied by those problems. This preoccupation, or rumination, is sometimes considered a problem in its own right, especially when the preoccupation is undesired. Sometimes rumination even creates vulnerability to more distress (Lyubomirsky & Nolen-Hoeksema, 1993, 1995; Nolen-Hoeksema, 1996; Nolen-Hoeksema & Morrow, 1993). How are these experiences to be understood?

Martin and Tesser (1996) proposed a view of the nature and functions of rumination that has a lot in common with the self-regulatory model described in this book. They define rumination as recurrent thoughts that emerge in the absence of an immediate situation requiring them. They argue that rumination is produced by discrepancies. Some discrepancies are between perceptions and mental models (e.g., when events are hard to interpret or to see meaning in). Mostly, though, the discrepancies are between desired progress and current progress toward important goals.

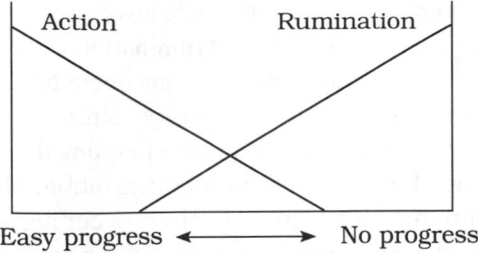

Figure 12.3. When a person is self-regulating with respect to a goal and progress is relatively easy, action and the thoughts that accompany action dominate the discrepancy-reduction effort. When progress is thwarted, rumination dominates. (Adapted from Carver, 1996c.)

More simply, rumination occurs when you want to attain something and you're stuck (see also Clark, Henry, & Taylor, 1991).

Rumination as Problem Solving and Attempted Discrepancy Reduction

Martin and Tesser argued that frustration of goal-directed effort sets in motion a set of cognitive processes aimed at unblocking the path to goal attainment. They don't always do so directly, nor are they always successful, but that's their aim. Martin and Tesser see rumination as an attempt at discrepancy reduction – implicit problem solving – even when it isn't doing so successfully.

The argument that rumination is aimed at discrepancy reduction implies a functional similarity between rumination and goal-directed action (Carver, 1996c). Goal-directed action is (obviously) also aimed at discrepancy reduction – indeed, the same discrepancy reduction to which rumination is directed. Action, and the thoughts that accompany action, dominate the discrepancy reduction effort when obstacles aren't encountered, or when obstacles are minimal or manageable (Figure 12.3). In contrast, rumination dominates the effort when the action is fully thwarted.

Keeping track of the priority of information is a critical issue for a self-regulating organism (Lord & Levy, 1994; Martin & Tesser, 1996). Conscious experience is commonly viewed as reflecting the end result of a series of preattentive decisions that some information matters more than others. What matters most at the moment is what winds up in consciousness. According to this view, when rumination occurs – when thoughts about a problem appear in consciousness unbidden – it implies that the goal behind the rumination is (preattentively) being judged as important – indeed, as more important than whatever the person is already doing. More specifically, emergence of rumination seems to imply that an alternative goal is being judged as important enough that the lack of progress toward it is forcing a temporary priority shift.

This line of thought resembles Simon's (1967) argument, discussed in Chapter 9, concerning affect as a call for reprioritization. Martin and Tesser (1996) said that rumination is more likely to occur regarding important than unimportant goals, which also fits Simon's argument. In Simon's model, reprioritization isn't called for when *any* goal is threatened, only when an *important* goal is threatened. The more important the goal, the stronger the affect, the stronger the call for reprioritization, and (as Martin and Tesser assert) the more likely that rumination will occur regarding the goal.

As we said earlier, however, this last step assumes the unavailability of an action to resolve the threat. If an action is available, reprioritization occurs, and the action – instead of the rumination – takes place (Figure 12.3).

Rumination as Dysfunctional

Although we think the idea of rumination as implicit problem solving has considerable appeal, not all instances of rumination have an obvious problem-solving character. Nor does everyone agree that the term rumination should be applied to this sort of thought process. Nolen-Hoeksema (1996) has suggested that the label rumination should be left to thought processes that *don't* have a clear problem-solving quality. She and her colleagues have studied this latter set of processes in a variety of contexts.

A common procedure in this research is to induce either rumination or distraction in subjects who are dysphoric or not. The rumination induction usually has subjects think about their current emotional states, their personalities, and how their life is going. One result of this induction is that dysphoric people become more dysphoric.

A particularly important study (Lyubomirsky & Nolen-Hoeksema, 1995) found that the rumination induction caused dysphoric subjects to generate *poorer-quality solutions* to hypothetical interpersonal problems than after a distraction manipulation. Unstructured rumination among sad people thus may actually interfere with their ability to solve problems. (On the other hand, not only did the rumination fail to have an adverse effect on nondepressed subjects, it actually improved their performances on one measure, consistent with the Martin and Tesser analysis.)

Nolen-Hoeksema's (1996) interpretation of the findings for depressed people is that when people are in a depressed mood, the rumination induction causes them to attend to that mood. It thereby activates associated information (also negative) in memory. This in turn has an adverse impact on how they process the tasks in front of them, causing performance to deteriorate. It also enhances dysphoria. This kind of rumination thus is problematic for depressed people. A pattern of findings similar to this also emerges from individual differences on a measure of ruminative response style (Nolen-Hoeksema, 1991; Nolen-Hoeksema, Parker, & Larson, 1994).

Do these findings challenge the idea that the processes behind rumination are oriented to problem solving and ultimately discrepancy reduction? We think not. What they *do* show is that problem solving doesn't always occur optimally. When people are in disengagement mode (which is more likely among depressed than nondepressed people), problem solving is inefficient. In such cases, problem solving is competing with a mental tendency to give up. There's no question that some approaches to problem solving are more effective than others (Nolen-Hoeksema, 1996) and that being depressed can adversely bias the approach a person takes. But this doesn't mean that a problem-solving tendency isn't somehow woven into the mechanism leading to the rumination.

13

Hierarchicality and Problems in Living

> The secret of juggling is inner harmony and knowing how to let go.
> (Robert Fulghum, *From Beginning to End: The Rituals of Our Lives*)

The last chapter described several potential contributors to people's problems which seem to be implied by the self-regulatory model presented earlier in the book. The issues we addressed there were relatively straightforward. In this chapter we continue to consider problems, but we turn to issues that are more complex. In one fashion or another, these issues all relate to the notion of hierarchicality.

LINKS BETWEEN CONCRETE GOALS AND THE CORE VALUES OF THE SELF

Several potential problems stem directly from the idea that there are hierarchical links between action goals and the core principles and values that make up the self.

Hierarchicality as an Impediment to Disengagement

One of these problems concerns the expression of the disengagement impulse. In Chapter 12 we described difficulties in which doubt causes a person to experience an impulse to disengage from some goal but the person can't do so. We managed to avoid saying much there about *why* people are sometimes unable to give up. The test-anxious person remains committed to passing the exam, the socially anxious person remains committed to making a good impression, the mourning spouse remains committed to the lost relationship. Why can it be so hard to give up?

In considering this question, we restate a theme from Chapter 11: The nature of a goal hierarchy can make disengagement hard. Sometimes goals form a chain, such that attainment of one (acing chemistry) is

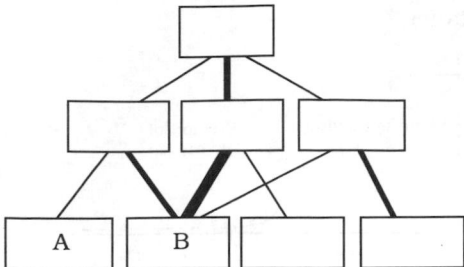

Figure 13.1.   Concrete goals that are very important (box B) are more difficult to disengage from than those that are less important (box A). The more
important it is, the more giving it up creates problems for the higher-order
values. In some cases giving up a concrete goal forces major reorganization
of values at the higher level.

necessary before another can be taken on (getting into medical school).
Some goals that are relatively concrete (doing well on an exam) are
closely linked to higher-order goals a (self-image as an intellectually
competent person). The more important or valued a goal – the more directly it relates to the core sense of self (Figure 13.1) – the harder it is to
disengage from it (see also Pyszczynski & Greenberg, 1992a, 1992b).

When you think about giving up in terms of hierarchical organization,
it becomes more apparent why it can be hard to abandon even goals that
don't themselves seem very profound. It's obvious that a person can't
disengage from the core sense of self, or ignore it, or tolerate large
discrepancies within it, without somehow experiencing considerable reorganization of the self (Kelly, 1955; McIntosh & Martin, 1992; Millar
et al., 1988). But what's sometimes less obvious is that concrete goals
sometimes connect closely to those deeply embedded values. When they
do, disengagement from the concrete goals also becomes very difficult.

Another way to envision how hard it is to give up goals that connect deeply to the sense of self is to think in terms of the watershed
between effort and giving up. A question we also sidestepped earlier
is where the watershed falls on the dimension of confidence. It seems
likely that where the watershed is depends on the goal's importance (see
Figure 13.2). If the goal doesn't matter, when you encounter difficulty
and doubt starts to build, effort gives way to disengagement easily (as
shown in Figure 13.2A). When the goal's really important, you presumably will hang on longer, even when doubts are high (Figure 13.2B).
Thus, another way of thinking about this issue is that it's hard to give
up on important goals – even concrete ones – because the threshold for
quitting is high (Lewin, 1948).

A Low importance

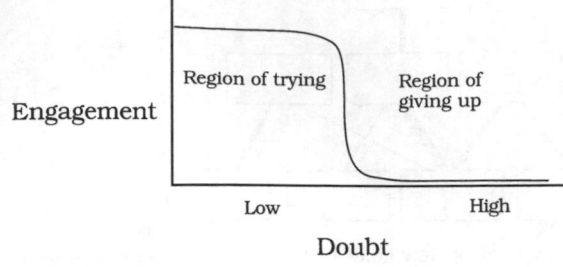

Doubt

B High importance

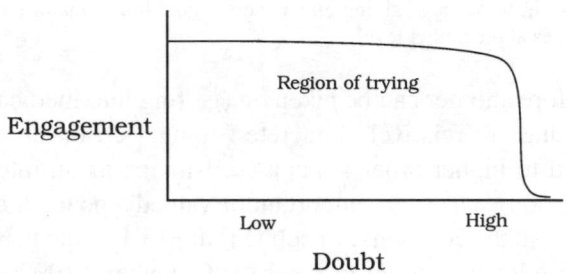

Doubt

Figure 13.2. Where the watershed between effort and disengagement falls depends partly on the importance of the goal. (A) When the goal doesn't matter, effort gives way to disengagement at lower levels of doubt. (B) When the goal is very important, people presumably will persevere even when their confidence is very low.

Problems as Conflicts among Goals

Another way in which problems can arise derives from the fact that people's hierarchies sometimes incorporate the potential for conflict between goals. Conflict occurs when you are committed to two goals that can't be attained easily at the same time (e.g., being a successful attorney while being a good wife and mother; having a close relationship while being emotionally independent). You may alternate between goals, but this can be exhausting. It's hard to keep the conflict from reemerging. Another solution is to decide that one goal contributes more to your higher-order values than the other, and to reorganize or reweight your hierarchy accordingly.

There's evidence that conflict among goals does create problems for people. Emmons and King (1988) asked subjects to report the personal strivings that motivate their lives and then make some further ratings about those strivings. These included ratings of the extent to which success in one striving tended to create problems in achieving another one. The researchers found that conflicts between personal strivings were tied to psychological distress and physical symptoms. This outcome contrasts with the finding that people who value their strivings and see them as important express greater satisfaction with their lives (Emmons, 1986; see also Lecci, Okun, & Karoly, 1994).

Problems as Absence of Links from High to Low Levels

Yet another idea suggested by the hierarchical model is that people sometimes see abstract goals as important but don't know how to reach them. That is, if behavior is hierarchically organized, people regulate toward high-level values by specifying values at the next lower level, and so on. If specifications are missing at some level, self-regulation falls apart. Thus many people want to be "happy," "popular," or "head of my own company" – many even have more concrete goals, such as "not arguing with my wife" or "being more assertive" – but they don't know how to go about reaching them. They can't specify concrete acts that would move them in the right direction, so they can't make progress and become distressed.

In the same vein, Dodge et al. (1989) have noted that children who lack certain social competencies aren't totally inept socially. They make goal choices that are functional with respect to low or midlevel goals. They seem not to realize, though, that decisions they can make at that lower level can be helpful at implementing desired goals at a broader or higher level. It seems as though the children simply don't see the relevance of the decision they're currently making to the higher-order value. (The same is sometimes true of adults.) This failure seems to reflect the absence of a link between action goals and higher-order goals.

Reorganization of the Self

Implicit in several of the preceding sections is the idea that the self is sometimes forced to undergo reorganization. Links need to be created from higher values to lower-level actions. Conflicts need to be sorted out. Giving up on a concrete goal can mean rethinking the relevance of a higher goal. The self as an organization of values is relatively stable (Greenwald, 1980). As long as it functions more or less adequately, it retains its form. Reorganization is hard and painful (and thus resisted), but it can happen (cf. Crocker & Major, 1989; Heatherton & Nichols, 1994).

When one value or set of values is put aside, another is usually available to take its place, and the person moves on as a different person. As an illustration, it's common in the college years for students to change majors (even several times), and to redefine for themselves (sometimes in major ways) their future occupational and interpersonal roles in life. However, sometimes there isn't an alternative readily available to take the place of the value being abandoned. It's arguable that the resulting vacuum can lead the person to adopt dysfunctional values, if those are the only ones salient. For example, an adolescent living in a troubled neighborhood might reorganize his sense of self by adopting the values of gang life.

Thus, reorganization of the values that make up the self doesn't always foster better long-term adaptation. New adaptive values must be readily available as reasonable and feasible options if the reorganization is to lead to a good outcome.

MAKING LOW LEVELS
FUNCTIONALLY SUPERORDINATE

Another potential source of problems has connections to the broad theme of hierarchicality, and it also reflects a failure of the feedback control process that differs from those discussed in Chapter 12. More precisely, it reflects a relative absence of control at high levels of the hierarchy (Carver & Scheier, 1996b).

Remember that the process of feedback control implies a comparison between the sensed input regarding current behavior and some reference value. The comparison has to be *made* if it's to influence self-regulation. Sometimes people have the reference values and input available but don't use them. The comparison at that level of abstraction simply isn't taking place. The result is that lower levels become functionally superordinate.

Our examination of these phenomena begins simply, with evidence that such failure to self-regulate at high levels does occur, and indeed occurs in contexts that are fairly familiar to most people. The picture then becomes more complicated, as we consider *why* people might abandon higher-level control.

Reduction of High-Level Control
by Deindividuation and Alcohol

As indicated in Chapter 3, we've linked the comparison process of the feedback loop to self-focus. High levels of self-focus cause more

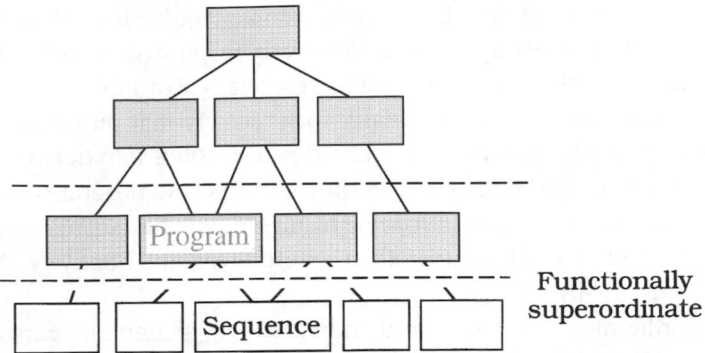

Figure 13.3.   When self-regulation at upper levels of a hierarchy has been temporarily suspended (the goals at those levels are not being attended to), goals at a lower level become functionally superordinate in guiding overt behavior.

comparison, and thus cause behavior to be better regulated. It follows that reduced self-focus should cause behavior to become more *poorly* regulated. But what does poor regulation mean? It doesn't mean the person ceases to act altogether. It means that the behavior is more likely to fluctuate, to become more random and impulsive, less carefully thought out.

Two bodies of research have studied effects of lowered self-awareness. Their origins differ, but the effects they've revealed are strikingly similar. One group of studies bears on deindividuation, an experience that people have when they become immersed in a group. In so doing, they appear to lose their sense of personal identity. This loss, in turn, makes them more likely to use obscenities (Festinger, Pepitone, & Newcomb, 1952), to be aggressive (Mullen, 1986; Prentice-Dunn & Rogers, 1980, 1982), and to engage in childish and uninhibited acts (Diener, 1979).

Deindividuation creates reduced self-awareness (Diener, 1979; Mullen, 1986; Prentice-Dunn & Rogers, 1982, 1989). Thus it's easy to see the effects of deindividuation as reflecting poorer self-regulation with respect to the programs and principles that normally guide behavior. Given poorer self-regulation at that higher level, there's a greater tendency to act impulsively, to respond to cues of the moment, rather than to use well-thought-out plans. In terms of the hierarchical analysis, behavior is limited to a string of sequences rather than being guided by higher-order values (see Figure 13.3).

A second literature bearing on the loss of self-focus concerns the effects of alcohol. Many effects of alcohol intoxication are remarkably similar to those of deindividuation. People who've been drinking often are inappropriately aggressive and overly responsive to cues of the moment. Alcohol is widely regarded as a releaser of inhibitions – indeed, it's sometimes used intentionally for precisely that purpose. Taken as a group, the behavioral characteristics of alcohol intoxication reflect a reduction in careful self-regulation with respect to programs and principles. As with deindividuation, the result seems to be a string of sequences of spontaneous acts, rather than carefully planned activity (Steele & Josephs, 1990).

Furthermore, as is true of deindividuation, alcohol appears to act on behavior (at least partly) by reducing self-awareness (Hull, 1981; Hull & Rielly, 1986; Ito, Miller, & Pollock, 1996; see also Shibutani, 1961, p. 203). As self-awareness diminishes, you stop monitoring your values and intentions. As a result, behavior becomes more disorganized, impulsive, and fragmented (Steele & Josephs, 1990). There's also neuropsychological evidence that alcohol disrupts the functioning of the prefrontal lobes (Peterson, Rothfleisch, Zelazo, & Pihl, 1990), which is consistent with this interpretation of alcohol's effects.[1]

It's important to remember that the absence of attention to higher-order standards doesn't mean the standards cease to exist. Behavior during periods of intoxication or deindividuation may in fact be *quite* relevant to higher-order values. When the higher value is eventually attended to, the person may be mortified at what he or she has done while intoxicated or deindividuated. For this reason, periods of loss of higher-level control are potentially quite problematic.

In the cases we've just described, lower levels of control became functionally superordinate because the higher-level control was lopped off by an experimental manipulation. In one case it was removed by deindividuation, in the other by the effects of alcohol. Given the loss of higher-level control, all that was left was the lower levels. These literatures thus illustrate involuntary effects of deindividuation and alcohol consumption.

In life outside the lab, there doubtlessly are instances in which natural versions of these manipulations impinge on people and influence their behavior. You can be swept up in a group or be handed a drink

---

[1] These effects of alcohol and deindividuation also suggest that low self-focus (or absence of self-regulation at high levels of control) may facilitate so-called acting-out problems. Such problems are characterized by impulse expression, which seems partly attributable to a lack of self-focus at higher levels, and thus a lack of principled override of impulses of the moment. In many cases, the impulses would conflict with the persons' higher-order goals, but because the higher goal isn't consulted, the impulses aren't overridden (Steele & Josephs, 1990).

without any particular motive to seek out either experience. Yet people sometimes *choose* to relinquish or abandon high-level control. Why?

Relinquishing or Abandoning High-Level Control as Escape from the Self

A reason for abandoning high-level control follows from the fact that people sometimes are experiencing difficulties at high levels. Important things sometimes are going badly in people's lives. Focusing on a situation in which things are going badly is aversive. The greater the importance of the problem (the closer it is to the core sense of self), the greater the aversiveness. Doing something to impair your ability to focus at that higher level can reduce the aversiveness. Thus relinquishing functioning at the higher level (stepping downward to a lower level of control) can be a way of distracting yourself from the pain of staring at something that's not working.

This line of reasoning fits with the idea that people use alcohol strategically to interfere with higher-level thought to avoid focusing on unpleasant life situations (Hull, 1981). This effect of alcohol represents a kind of mental disengagement from the higher-level value. In such cases, stepping downward to a more concrete level of functioning protects the person (at least temporarily) from awareness of higher-level discrepancies within the self.

Such abandonment of high-level control need have no point other than reducing high-level awareness of unresolved problems. Sometimes, however, the situation is more complex, involving competing tendencies at high and lower levels. On some occasions the person is trying to restrain a lower-level impulse via control at the higher level, and is having difficulty doing so. Sometimes the person in this situation abandons self-regulation at the higher level and lets the lower-level impulse be expressed.

Baumeister and Heatherton (1996) have called this sequence *self-regulatory failure* (see also Kirschenbaum, 1987).[2] An example of this sequence is the events leading to binge eating. The binge eater wants to

---

[2] Baumeister and Heatherton (1996) restricted their use of the term self-regulation to cases in which the person (the self) acts to override or suppress another action tendency that has developed at a lower level of abstraction. The literature as a whole has used the term more broadly than this, however, to refer to a wide range of attempts to fit sensed qualities to reference values. In our view, the cases discussed by Baumeister and Heatherton are more appropriately labeled *self-control*, a term that has a long history of referring to the restraint of impulses.

eat (concrete impulse) but also wants to restrain the desire (higher-level programmatic or principled self-regulation). Self regulatory failure occurs when the person stops trying to restrain the desire to eat, lets himself go, and binges.

In characterizing the decision to quit trying to exercise self-restraint, Baumeister and Heatherton noted that although restraint is hard work, quitting rarely depends on total exhaustion. Rather, there's a point where the person says "Enough," and stops trying to control the lower-level impulse. How does the person decide when to give up? We suggest that the answer is bound up in the person's level of confidence about resisting the impulse. The person who's very confident continues to struggle. The person whose confidence has sagged far enough is more likely to give up. Subjectively, the latter experience is the sinking feeling of being swallowed up by doubt (followed by an effort to obliterate that feeling).

Baumeister and Heatherton characterized the step downward as an "escape from the self," implying that the person's higher-order values constitute the self (see also Hamilton et al., 1993). Indeed, they've suggested that a wide range of activities (including sexual masochism and binge eating) are efforts to escape from the self in this sense (Baumeister, 1988, 1991; Heatherton & Baumeister, 1991). The activities they've analyzed in these terms all involve immersion in one or another kind of sensory experience, forcing the relative exclusion of higher-level thought, or even impairing the ability to engage in such thought. Thus the feeling of failure is removed from mind.[3]

Relinquishing or Abandoning High-Level Control as Problem Solving

It's apparent that more is involved in problems of this type than a simple loss or lapse of high-level control. High-level control can be abandoned in this dysfunctional way, but it can also be temporarily relinquished in a way that's adaptive. Earlier in the book we described a model of multiple levels of functioning that's relevant to this issue: Vallacher and Wegner's (1987) action-identification theory. That theory casts a very different light on why a lower level is rendered functionally superordinate.

---

[3] It should be clear that this represents escape from the self only in a specific sense; the sensory experience is the self's experience, but the experience is at a level of abstraction that is low enough to minimize the involvement of other, higher-order aspects of the self.

Interestingly enough, the step downward in this model is also occasioned by a problem at the higher level. As we said in Chapter 5, Vallacher and Wegner hold that two forces determine what level is functionally superordinate. First, people tend to organize, identify, and construe their actions at the highest level they can maintain coherently. Thus there's a general drift upward. Second, if there's difficulty in carrying out an act identity, people are pulled to a lower identification of the same action. Stepping to the lower level lets people focus on the nuts and bolts of the action and deal with whatever is making it hard to manage at the higher level. Thus, going down a level can get the person through a difficult period in carrying out a desired action. This makes the stepping-down response adaptive in nature.

Note, however, that if the person gets through the difficult period, there's a gradual drift back to the higher-level identification. The shift downward in this model clearly presumes the capability and desirability of returning upward. As such, this stepping down a level doesn't comport well with deindividuation or alcohol, or any other immersion in low-level sensations intended to impair higher-order thought. Those tools for reducing high-level control aim at making it hard to return to the higher level. There's a big difference between stepping down temporarily to deal with a problem while retaining access to the higher level, and stepping down *by diminishing access* to the higher level.

Consider how these two ways of stepping to a lower level might be manifested in an instance of impending self-regulatory failure, in which a person is having difficulty exercising restraint over eating. To engage the problem-solving function, the person could step to a lower level and try to implement the self-control attempt concretely. For example, rather than "try to resist temptation," the person might pick up a magazine and "read and turn the pages," might "try to follow a TV program carefully," might "focus on the elements of a conversation," might focus on "politely declining the host's repeated offers of food" – all as concrete ways of accomplishing not-eating. To engage the escape-from-the-self function, the person would stop trying to restrain and would immerse himself in the concrete sensations of a binge, to withdraw awareness from the higher value of restraint.

Further Comparisons

There are several further points worth making about this divergence between two types of lower-level responses in this situation. First, though they have certain processing similarities, they have radically different purposes. In one case the stepping down is an *attempt to reach* a higher goal – it occurs *in the service of* effort at the higher level. The other case is an attempt to *escape* from thinking about higher goals – it's part of a *disengagement from* the higher-order value.

As indicated earlier, an important variable underlying the divergence seems to be confidence about being able to carry out the desired behavior. In the cases Vallacher and Wegner focused on, people who step down believe they can be successful in resolving the problem they've encountered and can complete the intended act (which, by the way, suggests a boundary condition for the stepping-down effect in the Vallacher and Wegner model). In the cases Baumeister and Heatherton focused on, people who step down a level do so precisely because they *don't* believe they'll be successful at the high level. The stepping down is *itself* an expression of abandoning effort at the high level.

A third point concerns the implementation of the giving-up response in cases of self-regulatory failure that lead to binge eating or drinking (and perhaps other dysfunctional behaviors as well). As we noted earlier, a person may binge to escape thoughts about *any* disliked aspect of the self (or *any* unresolved problem). But in many cases examined by Baumeister and Heatherton, the self-aspect that's being escaped concerns the very behavior that's taking place. That is, often binges occur because people feel they've already failed to keep the binge-related behavior in check, and they now wish to obliterate their awareness of that fact. Thus for a dieter or an alcoholic a lapse can easily become a relapse.

In these events a single act has two simultaneous, though distinguishable, functions. That is, immersion in the binge constitutes *both the violation of the higher-level value and the means by which the person escapes from thinking about it.* These cases are unusual in the fact that the same activity serves both functions. That they occur simultaneously in the same activity can make it difficult to keep them separate conceptually.

The notion of hierarchicality suggests one further point in this context. Escape from the self usually is temporary.[4] In many cases, the person will eventually reconfront the discrepancy at the higher level. If

---

[4] This isn't always true, of course. The ultimate disengagement – the ultimate escape from the self – is suicide (Baumeister, 1990). This particular escape from the self is quite permanent.

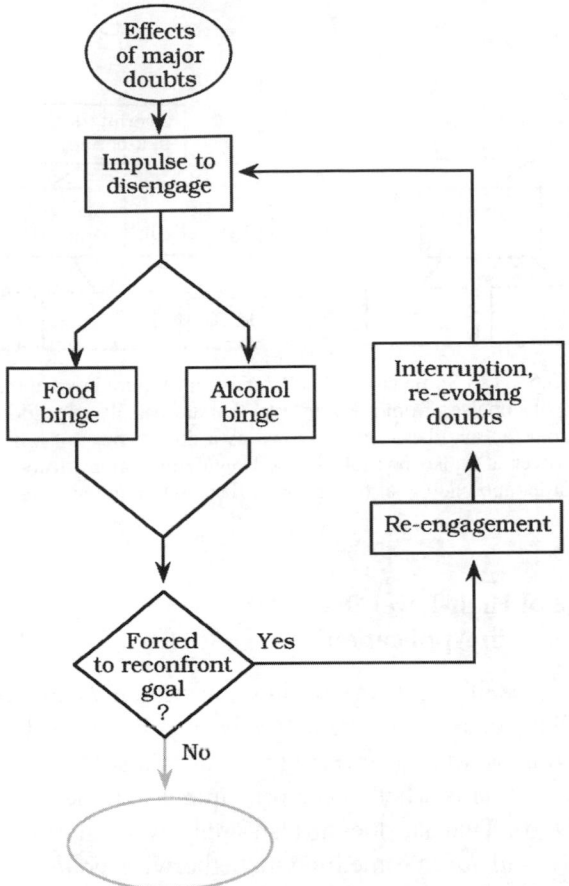

Figure 13.4.   Doubts about conforming to a value lead to a disengagement impulse. Sometimes the impulse is expressed through activities such as binge eating or drinking. Though these activities can provide temporary escape, the person eventually reconfronts the value for which the doubts exist. The reconfrontation leads to a reengagement with the goal value, which may be followed by reevoking of the doubts and a renewal of the impulse to disengage.

the activity performed violates higher-order values (which is true of the case just discussed), reconsideration of the values is likely to reinduce negative affect and further intensify doubt about being able to conform to the higher values effectively. The longer-term result may be a cycle of abandoning the attempt to uphold the higher value (perhaps by repeated binges), punctuated by being reminded that one holds that value and spo-radic efforts to live up to it, a pattern we described in more general terms in Chapter 12 (see Figure 13.4, which is an adaptation of Figure 12.1).

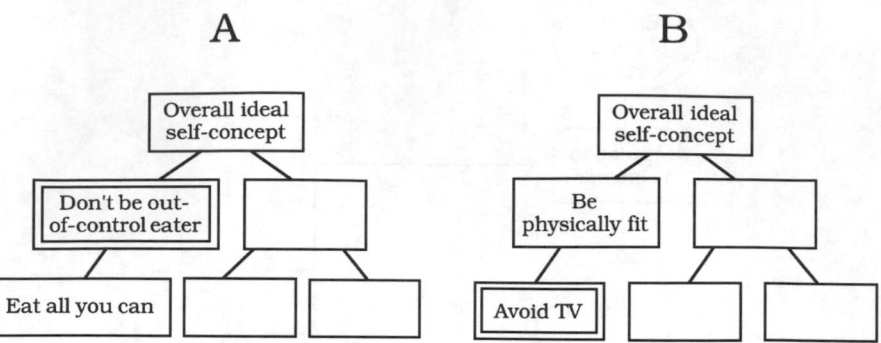

Figure 13.5. (A) Some cases of self-regulatory failure involve the overt expression of impulses from a lower level that are usually overridden by a restraint goal (an avoidance goal, shown as a double box) at a higher level. (B) However, it's also possible for self-regulatory failure to occur when a higher-order approach goal fails to override a conflicting avoidance goal at a lower level.

Failure of High-Level Override: Symmetry in Application

The examples of self-regulatory failure on which Baumeister and Heatherton (1996) focused involve lapses in impulse control. It's intuitive to think about loss of high-level regulation in those terms. However, an interesting question is whether the principle is symmetrical (Carver & Scheier, 1996b). That is, does it also apply when the higher-level override would entail *doing* something that otherwise *wouldn't* be done, rather than restraining an impulse? In principle, there should be cases in which removing upper-level control fosters *in*action, cases where it would take an override to overcome low-level inertia and put the person in motion.

It is, in fact, fairly easy to bring to mind cases that fit this depiction. Consider, for example, the person who has the goal of being physically fit but hasn't done anything about it, spending his free time instead in the mindless distraction of watching TV (Figure 13.5). For him to engage in exercise would require that the loop regulating the higher goal override the inaction. Consider the person who has a comfortable but boring job, who wants a sense of fulfillment from her work but hasn't taken steps to try to find a job that would provide it. For her to move toward a more satisfying career would require the higher goal to override the inertia. The same principle seems at work in the person who hasn't brought himself to leave a moribund relationship. These cases all seem to suggest that the notion of override from higher levels is indeed symmetrical. If so, then failure of a higher-level override to overcome quiescence is just as much self-regulatory failure as is the failure to restrain an impulse.

The expression of quiescence has a very different surface appearance than does the expression of an impulse. Nonetheless, it seems that the person who can't get himself to turn off the TV, the one who remains in the boring job instead of striking out on a more interesting path, and the one who stays in the lifeless relationship are also displaying a self-regulatory failure of the sort Baumeister and Heatherton focus on: a failure to override.

RESIDING TOO MUCH AT HIGH LEVELS

This discussion of the perils of removing high-level control suggests that maintaining high-level control is good. There are, however, reasons for questioning whether that's always true. It can also be bad for you to spend too much of your time trying to exert control at those higher levels.

We return again to the implications of the theme of hierarchicality. A person working on a task – as a *task* – must sometimes deal with setbacks in the effort to perform well. A person who's working on a task as a way of trying to maintain a sense of self-worth (a higher-level goal) has a bigger job when performance falters. When self-esteem is on the line, a poor performance (or a poor period of performance within a task) is more threatening than it is when the task is just a task. The greater the implication for the overall self-image, the bigger the potential threat. The person trying to control behavior from too high a level will experience a poor performance at lower levels not as a task failure, but as a failure of the self.

Now consider what happens when the impulse to disengage arises for the task that isn't going well. If the task doesn't matter, disengagement is relatively easy; the person quits this activity and moves on to something else. The more the task matters, the harder it is to disengage and to sustain the disengagement. When the person is actively trying to control the sense of self, it's impossible to disengage without in effect renouncing the desired self. The more a task matters to the sense of self, the more the person is immersed in the phenomenology of being stuck in a loop that's not moving forward but can't be released. This is what can happen when a person resides too much at high levels of abstraction.

The idea that some people attempt to self-regulate from the top level on downward suggests an interesting interpretation of another problem, the tendency to generalize from a single bad occurrence to the broader sense of self-worth (Beck, 1967; Carver, 1998; Carver & Ganellen, 1983; Carver, La Voie, Kuhl, & Ganellen, 1988). When something bad happens to a generalizer, it isn't experienced simply as a bad event – it's a failure of the self. Generalization from bad outcomes is reflected in cognitions about broad personal inadequacy, rather than inadequacy in some particular domain. Such cognitions interfere with further efforts to perform – not only in this context, but more widely (Epstein, 1992). As such, they can be debilitating. It should be no surprise to learn that generalization is related to depression (Carver, 1998; Carver & Ganellen, 1983; Carver et al., 1988).

The tendency to generalize is also reminiscent of the psychological circumstance that precipitates self-regulatory failure (Baumeister & Heatherton, 1996). That is, it's a tendency to broaden a given failing into a general sense of *being* a failure. An interesting question is whether people prone to generalization are, for this reason, especially vulnerable to the impulse to escape from the self. Alternatively, it might be that generalizers' tendency to try to control everything from the top down causes them to be especially resistant to such an impulse. Hamilton et al. (1993) have suggested that at least some people experience an "upward reverberation," in which failure leads to a high-level focus rather than a low-level focus – the opposite of the escape-from-the-self response (and the opposite of the action-identification analysis). The high-level focus fosters a drawn-out consideration of the implications of the failure for superordinate goals. Perhaps this is what generalizers do.

We noted in Chapter 5 that Emmons (1992) has studied the levels of abstraction at which people focus their personal strivings. Some people appear to be chronically high-level strivers and others appear to be low-level strivers (he verified this by paging them periodically for reports on what they were doing). He also found that the difference in striving level has implications for the person's emotional life. In particular, high-level strivers are more vulnerable to negative affect – especially depression – than are low-level strivers.

There are two ways of viewing this finding that we think deserve mention. The more obvious is the one we just described. Higher-level strivings are goals that are closer to the core sense of self. If you think about the majority of your day-to-day actions as having implications for your core self, and if you're struggling with any of them, it's no wonder you feel distressed. If you think of your behavior in ways that are more peripheral from the core self (lower-level strivers), the behaviors are less important and there's less chance of experiencing negative affect.

A second way of viewing these findings (which is complementary to the first, rather than contradictory) concerns a point that's implicit in the logic of hierarchical feedback systems. Higher-order systems intrinsically have longer lag times for discrepancies to be reduced. This greater time lag must be taken into account in evaluating the system's success at reducing the discrepancies. People may not be terribly adept at taking this fact into account, however, until they've had a lot of practice (and maybe not even then). This may result in negative affect due to the application of overly stringent standards at the meta level. All other things being equal, longer lag times make negative affect more likely to occur because changes take longer to occur.

If it's bad to try to run things from the top down, and it's bad to escape higher-level failures by bailing out and controlling action at lower levels, what's the best thing to do in the event of serious high-level discrepancies? The answer suggested by the studies (and ideas) reviewed here is that it may be desirable to step downward in level of abstraction, but to do so in *problem-resolving* mode. Not escape from the self, not obsessive preoccupation with the high-level failure, but a focus on untangling problems at the lower levels, in an effort to clear the way to making better progress again at the higher level.

14

Chaos and Dynamic Systems

Many people are coming to believe that the world is filled with chaos and catastrophe. We're not referring to war, famine, hurricanes, and earthquakes here, but to two sets of ideas in scientific thought. In this chapter and the next we explore these ideas as they bear on self-regulation. Both chaos theory (or dynamic systems theory) and catastrophe theory have implications for behavioral self-regulation. Our treatment here isn't technical, and implications go well beyond the points made here (see Beer, 1995; Kelso, 1995; Nowak & Vallacher, in press; Port & van Gelder, 1995; Smith & Thelen, 1993; Thelen & Smith, 1994; Vallacher & Nowak, 1994; van Geert, 1994). However, even this brief treatment suggests points of contact between these ideas and those in earlier chapters (see also Vallacher & Nowak, 1997, and the commentaries that follow it).

DYNAMIC SYSTEMS

Chaos theory, or dynamic systems theory, has been heralded as a new science by some (Gleick, 1987) and regarded more skeptically by others. Several introductions to it are available (e.g., Alligood, Sauer, & Yorke, 1997; Barton, 1994; Brown, 1995; Field & Golubitsky, 1992; Gleick, 1987; Ruelle, 1991; Stewart, 1990; Thelen & Smith, 1994; Vallacher & Nowak, 1994, 1997; Waldrop, 1992). Rather than present a complete overview, we describe several focal themes, then indicate places where we think these themes apply to subjects of our interest.

Although these ideas have been attached in many people's minds to the term *chaos*, chaos is in some ways a misleading label. This is one reason some prefer the term dynamic systems theory (cf. Kelso, 1995) or the term complexity. The view attached to all these labels is deterministic. It holds that the behavior of a system is a reflection of the forces operating on (and within) the system. Despite this, predictability of a complex system's behavior over anything but the very short term isn't very good.

There are several reasons for this. First, observers never know all the influences on a system with total precision. What you *think* is happening may not be quite what's happening. And that difference, even if it's small, can be very important. Further, the behavior of the system may not be influenced in a simple linear way by the forces operating on and within it, but may be influenced in nonlinear and interdependent ways. Thus the behavior of the system – though highly determined – can give the appearance of randomness. This determinism in principle but unpredictability in practice underlies the label *chaotic*.

Here's another way to think of it. Brown (1995) characterized chaos as an "irregular oscillatory process." An oscillatory process is a process with recurrences (e.g., movements of a pendulum). A surprising number of events are oscillatory, including human behaviors. Some oscillations are fairly regular: the waking–sleeping cycle, the inspiration–expiration cycle, the start of the major league baseball season. Other events cycle, but more irregularly: putting gas in the car, doing laundry, the point in the baseball season at which the Red Sox fold. Other events oscillate with an even more irregular pattern: the love life of an avoidant introvert, compliments to your spouse. Chaotic events are events with a high degree of irregularity. Thus, although they do recur, their occurrence is hard to predict.

Why the irregularity? One contributor is that influences are sometimes nonlinear. Another is that small differences now sometimes make a huge difference later. These contributors are discussed in the next two sections.

Nonlinearity

An important theme in dynamic systems thinking is that many relationships between variables are nonlinear. Many people are accustomed to thinking of important relationships as linear. That's the principle on which most statistical procedures are based (though nonlinear tests do exist). When you look for a correlation between two variables, you're looking for a linear relationship.

In contrast to this, nonlinearity occurs when the effect of some variable differs across different parts of its range. For example, a quadratic or cubic effect in a regression analysis is a nonlinear effect. A step function is a nonlinear effect. A common illustration of this point

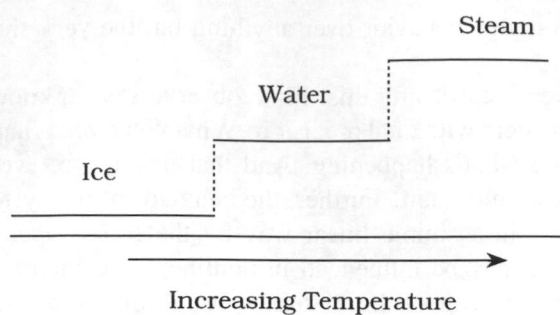

Increasing Temperature

Figure 14.1.   The chemical compound H_2O behaves in different ways as a function of temperature. This behavior displays a nonlinear character, shifting abruptly from a solid to a liquid, and shifting abruptly again from a liquid to a gas.

(e.g., Newtson, 1994; Ruelle, 1991, chap. 20) is the behavior of H_2O as a function of temperature (Figure 14.1). At low temperatures, H_2O is a crystallized solid – ice. Up to a point, increasing temperature has very little effect on this aspect of its behavior. It remains crystallized and solid. As temperature continues to rise, however, there's a sudden and dramatic change. Ice becomes a liquid. This change is nonlinear. As the temperature shifts toward the melting point, ice doesn't gradually lose viscosity to become water. If the temperature is below this point, ice remains ice. If the temperature is held at the melting point, though, all the ice becomes water – not instantaneously, but without a further rise in temperature.

Continuing to increase the temperature changes the behavior of this liquid very little, for another extensive range on the temperature dimension. The water molecules move around more as they absorb heat, but the hot water remains a liquid up to another critical temperature. When water reaches its boiling point, it changes character again, to a gas. Again the transition between states is rather abrupt – nonlinear. The change from one state to another is called a *phase transition*.

It's sometimes said that traditional ways of thinking in psychology have no place for nonlinear thinking. It's sometimes asserted that the dynamic systems approach is a completely new way of thinking (and a more accurate one, since many physical systems display nonlinearities). However, there's reason not to conclude too fast that it's all new (Carver, 1997b). Several kinds of psychological phenomena that are taken completely for granted reflect nonlinearities (Vallacher & Nowak, 1997). For example, consider *threshold* effects, in which an increase in a predictor has no effect on an outcome until a critical level is reached, after which an effect occurs, sometimes as an abrupt step function. There are also *ceiling* effects, in which an increase in a predictor has an influence on an outcome only to a certain point, past which further increases in predictor fail to yield changes in outcome. These effects are well known to personality and social psychologists, and both illustrate the principle of nonlinearity.

Nonlinearity in our literature goes far beyond these effects, however. Nonlinearity is illustrated every time a study shows that two predictor variables *interact* to create an outcome (Carver, 1997b). An interaction means the effect of one predictor on the outcome differs as a function of the level of the second predictor. Thus the effect of the first predictor on the outcome is not linear. The nature of the effect depends on the state of the second predictor. The second predictor is thereby acting as what's sometimes called a *control parameter* – a factor "that hold[s] potential for changing the intrinsic dynamics of a system" (Vallacher & Nowak, 1997, p. 77).

As an illustration of this principle, consider the interaction between self-focused attention and level of test anxiety on performance (Carver, Peterson, Follansbee, & Scheier, 1983). Subjects high and low in test anxiety tried to solve a set of fairly hard anagrams, under fairly stressful conditions, with either high or lower self-focus. As shown in Figure 14.2A, self-focus facilitated the performances of subjects low in test anxiety, but tended to impair those high in test anxiety (the pattern expected – see Chapter 10). This finding shows that the effect of self-focus on performance isn't linear. Rather, it's discontinuous, its nature depending on level of test anxiety. At high levels of test anxiety self-focus is disruptive, but the effect reverses at some point in the continuum of test anxiety to become facilitative (Figure 14.2B). Vallacher and Nowak (1997) point to such reversals in sign as being a particularly interesting aspect of nonlinearity.

Obviously the diverging interaction in Figure 14.2 is far from unique. Indeed, many psychologists think in terms of interactions much of the time. In our opinion, people accustomed to thinking in terms of interactions as determinants of behavior are already accustomed to thinking in nonlinearities. To that extent, the emphasis that dynamic systems thinking places on nonlinearity is not only congenial but even *familiar* to many psychologists.

Threshold effects and interactions are nonlinearities that are taken for granted, though perhaps not usually viewed in those terms. Looking intentionally for nonlinearities reveals others. For example, many developmental psychologists now think many developmental changes

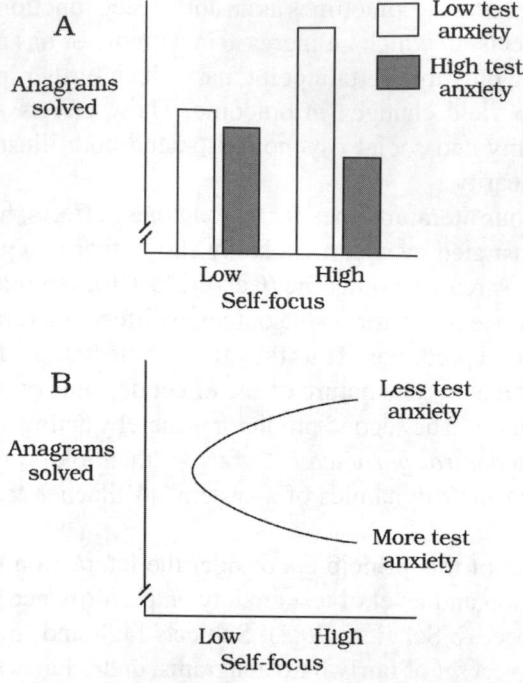

Figure 14.2.   (A) Enhanced self-focus facilitated the anagram-solving performance of subjects low in test anxiety, but tended to hamper the performance
of those higher in test anxiety. (B) Thus, the effect of self-focus on task performance was not linear, but curvilinear. (Adapted from Carver, Peterson,
Follansbee, & Scheier, 1983.)

are dynamic rather than linear (Bertenthal, Campos, & Kermoian, 1994;
Siegler, 1994; Thelen, 1992, 1995; van der Maas & Molenaar, 1992).
Developmental changes in the motor coordinations of young children
seem to have a nonlinear path (Freedland & Bertenthal, 1994): There
seems to be increased variability, followed by relatively rapid emergence and stabilization of the new coordination (e.g., hands-and-knees
crawling). There's also evidence that physical development in the brain
follows a pattern of discontinuous growth spurts (Fischer & Rose, 1994;
and perhaps so does evolution – Ager, 1995).

Sensitive Dependence on Initial Conditions

Another theme in the dynamic systems literature, often taken as a hallmark of potentially chaotic systems, is identified with the phrase

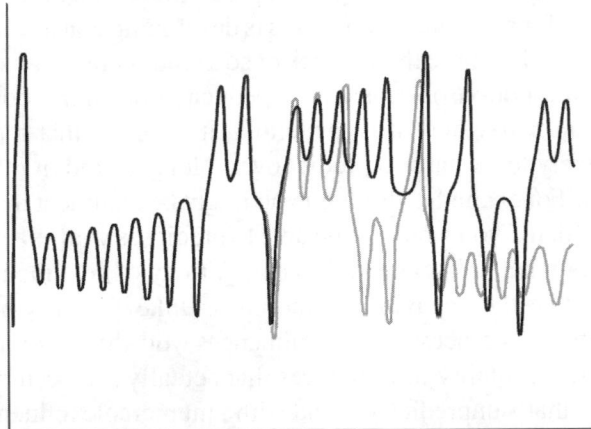

Figure 14.3. Lorenz (1963) was plotting results of a set of equations when he decided to rerun a portion of his output. Rather than start again from the beginning, he entered an intermediate value that (due to rounding) was close, but not identical, to the value that had existed at that stage of the initial run. The second run (plotted here in gray) tracked the first run closely for a while, then began to deviate slightly from it, then deviated more and more. Within a short period the deviations had become so extreme as to be totally unrelated to the outcome of the initial run. This discovery provides a stark illustration of the concept of sensitive dependence on initial differences.

sensitive dependence on initial conditions (e.g., Ruelle, 1991). That is, a very small difference between two conditions of a system can lead to divergence, and ultimately the absence of any correlation between the paths the system takes later on. The idea is (partly) that the small initial difference causes a difference in what's encountered just down the road, which yields slightly different influences, producing slightly different outcomes (Lorenz, 1963). Through repeated iterations of small differences, the paths diverge, eventually leading them to form very different trajectories. The paths do not endlessly *diverge* (Mandel, 1995), but after a surprisingly brief period they no longer have any noticeable relation to one another (see Figure 14.3).

A phrase identified with this phenomenon is the *butterfly effect*. This phrase stems from the idea that the flapping of a butterfly's wings changes local air conditions slightly, setting into motion a series of small, then potentially larger, changes that ultimately might result in a storm in another part of the world (Lorenz, 1963). The idea is apocryphal, but many embrace the metaphor as a way of thinking about sensitivity to small differences. It's the sensitivity of nonlinear systems to small differences at any given moment that makes the long-term prediction of them next to impossible. Thus, for example, a consensus is developing that accurate prediction of the weather more than a week or so ahead is not a realistic goal.

How does the notion of sensitive dependence on initial conditions relate to human behavior? Most generally, it suggests that a person's behavior is likely to be hard to predict over a long period in other than general terms. For example, although you might be confident that someone eats lunch daily, you wouldn't be able to predict as well exactly what time, where, or what he'll eat on the second Friday of next month. This doesn't mean that the behavior is random or unlawful. It just means that small differences between the influences you think are affecting the person and the totality of influences that actually *are* occurring will yield behavior that's unpredicted. And with innumerable influences acting constantly on people's behavior, it's easy to be slightly off in your perceptions.

This principle also holds true with respect to prediction of your own behavior. As we noted in Chapter 6, there's evidence that people don't plan very far into the future. People seem to have goals in which the general form is sketched out, but only a few program-level steps toward it have been planned. The notion of sensitive dependence on initial conditions provides a very reasonable explanation for this. It's pointless (and may even be counterproductive) to plan too far ahead too fully (cf. Kirschenbaum, 1985), partly because chaotic forces in play (forces that are hard to predict because of nonlinearities and sensitive dependence) can render much of the planning irrelevant. Thus, it makes sense to plan in general terms, chart a few steps, get there, reassess, and plan the next bits. This seems a perfect illustration of how people take chaos into account in their own lives.

Phase Space, Attractors, and Repellers

Another set of concepts important in dynamic systems thinking are variations on the terms *phase space* and *attractor* (Brown, 1995; Vallacher & Nowak, 1997). A *phase diagram* is a depiction of the behavior of a system over time. You plot the system's states along two (sometimes three) axes, with time displayed as the progression of the line of the plot, rather than on an axis of its own. A phase space is the array of states that a system occupies across a period of time. As the system changes states over time, it traces a *trajectory* within its phase space – a path of the successive states it occupies across that period.

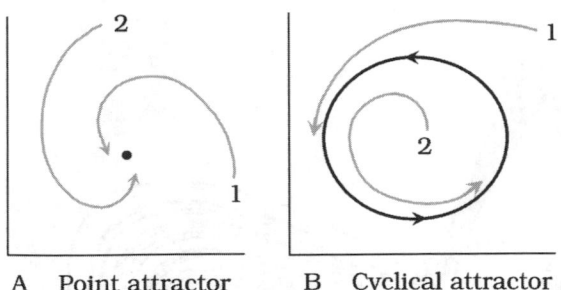

A   Point attractor   B   Cyclical attractor

Figure 14.4.   (A) A point attractor, in which all trajectories converge on a particular *point* in phase space. (B) A cyclical attractor, in which all trajectories converge on a particular *orbit* in phase space, whether they begin outside the orbit (1) or inside the orbit (2).

Phase spaces often contain one or more regions called attractors. Attractors are areas the system approaches, occupies, or tends toward more frequently than other areas. Attractors exert a kind of metaphorical gravitational pull on the system, bringing the system into proximity to them. Each attractor has what's called a *basin*, the attractor's region of attraction. All trajectories that enter the basin move toward that attractor (Brown, 1995).

There are several kinds of attractors, some simple, others complex. In a *point attractor*, all trajectories converge onto a particular point in phase space (Figure 14.4), no matter where they begin (e.g., normal body temperature). In a *cyclical attractor* (also called a periodic, or limit-cycle, attractor), regardless of the starting point, the system settles into a cycle around a particular zone in phase space (e.g., the circadian rhythm). In both cases, no matter where the system begins, the end result is equilibrium, stability. In the one case it's a stable point; in the other it's a stable orbit.

Of more interest are *chaotic attractors* (or *strange* attractors). The most widely known example is the Lorenz attractor, named for the meteorologist who first plotted it (Lorenz, 1963). The Lorenz attractor has two "ears," or basins of attraction (Figure 14.5). The trajectory periodically approaches each basin but is never finally "captured" by either one. Plotting the behavior of this system over time yields a tendency to loop around both ears, but unpredictably. The shifts from one to the other seem random. This irregularity and unpredictability in the system's movement gives rise to the label chaotic.

The behavior of this system displays sensitivity to initial conditions. A small change in starting point changes the specific path of motion

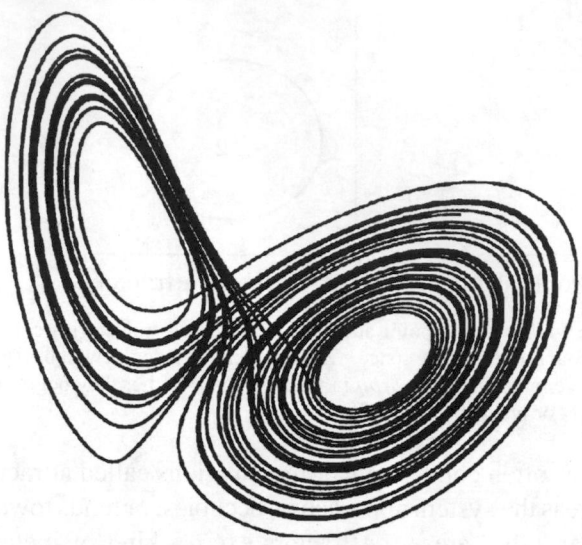

Figure 14.5.   The Lorenz attractor, an example of a system of what's known as chaotic or strange attractors.

entirely. The general tendencies remain the same – that is, the revolving around both attractors. But details, such as the number of revolutions around one ear before deflection to the other, form an entirely different pattern. Indeed, over time the trajectory displays this same sensitivity to small differences. As the system continues, it often nearly repeats itself but never quite does, and what appear to be nearly identical paths can diverge abruptly, with one path leading to one ear and the adjacent path leading to the other.

A phase space also contains regions called *repellers*, regions that are hardly ever occupied. Indeed, these regions seem to be actively avoided. That is, placement of the system near the focal point of a repeller leads to a rapid escape from that region of phase space. In a plot of attractors such as that shown in Figure 14.5, regions outside the areas of attraction are repellers.

Another Way of Picturing Attractors

The phase-space diagrams give a particularly vivid visual sense of what an attractor "looks like" and how it acts, but there's also another way to portray attractors visually. In this view (Figure 14.6), attractor basins are shown as wells, or basins, or valleys in a surface. A more technical label

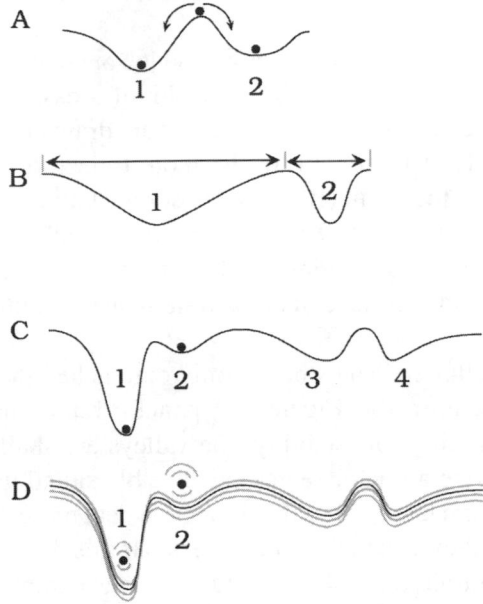

Figure 14.6.   Another way to portray attractors. (A) Attractor basins as valleys (local minima) in a surface. Behavior of the system is represented as a
ball. If the ball is in a valley (1 or 2), it's in an attractor basin and will tend
to stay there unless disturbed. If the ball is on a hill (between 1 and 2), it
will tend to escape its current location and move to an attractor. (B) A wider
basin (attractor 1) attracts more trajectories than a narrower basin (attractor
2). A steep basin (attractor 2) attracts more *abruptly* a trajectory that enters
the basin than does a more gradually sloping basin (attractor 1). (C) A system
in which attractor 1 is very stable, the others are less stable. It will take more
energy to free the ball from attractor 1 than from the others. (D) The system's
behavior is energized, much as the shaking of a metaphoric tambourine surface, keeping the system's behavior in flux and less than completely captured
by any particular attractor. Still, more shaking will be required to escape from
attractor 1 than attractor 2.

for a basin is a *local minimum*. Repellers, or regions of instability, are
ridges or hills. This portrayal assumes a metaphoric "gravitational" drift
downward in the diagram. (For simplicity, this usually is done as a two-
dimensional drawing, but keep in mind that the diagram often assumes
the merging of a large number of dimensions into the horizontal axis.)

The behavior of the system at a given moment is represented as a ball
on the surface. If the ball is in a valley (points 1 and 2 in Figure 14.6A),
it's in an attractor basin and will tend to stay there unless disturbed. If
it's on a hill (between 1 and 2), any slight movement in either direction

will cause it to escape its current location and move to an adjacent attractor.

A strength of this portrayal is that it does a good job of creating a sense of how attractors vary in robustness. The breadth of a basin indicates the diversity of the trajectories in phase space that are drawn into it. The broader the basin (B-1, in Figure 14.6), the more trajectories will be drawn in. The narrower the basin (B-2), the closer the ball has to come to its focal point to be drawn to it. The steepness of the valley indicates how *abruptly* a trajectory is drawn into it. The steeper the slope of the wall (B-2), the more sudden is the entry of a system that encounters that basin.

The depth of the valley indicates how firmly entrenched the system is, once drawn into the attractor. Figure 14.6 panel B represents a system of attractors with fairly low stability (the valleys are shallow). In Figure 14.6 panel C, one attractor represents a stable situation (valley 1), whereas the others are less so. It will take a great deal more "energy" to free the ball from valley 1 than from the others. (If this diagram were redrawn as a phase portrait, this valley would resemble a point attractor more than would the others.)

Breadth and depth both suggest importance, but in different senses. Breadth implies importance because the system is drawn to the attractor from widely divergent trajectories. Depth implies importance because the system that's been drawn into the well tends to stay there.

A weakness of this picture, compared to a phase-space portrait, is that it doesn't provide a sense of the erratic motion from one attractor to another in a multiple-attractor system. You can regain some of that sense of erratic shifting, however, if you think of the surface in Figure 14.6 as a tambourine, with a certain amount of shaking going on all the time (Figure 14.6 panel D). Even a little shaking causes the ball to bounce around in its well, and may jostle it from one well to another, particularly if the attractors aren't highly stable. An alternative would be to think of the ball as a jumping bean, hopping and bouncing. These two characterizations are analogous to the jostling that comes from situational influences and from internal dynamics, respectively.

Variability and Phase Changes

Another aspect of dynamic systems thinking that appears with some regularity in applications to psychology concerns the role of variability in phase changes. It's been suggested that increases in variability herald, and may even promote, phase changes (Davies, 1988; Kelso, 1995; Siegler, 1994; Thelen, 1995; Thelen & Smith, 1994). For example, Siegler (1994) noted that cognitive variability typically precedes important steps in cognitive development. In his studies of children's discovery of new strategies, the trials immediately before the discovery and the trial when the discovery is made often involve "especially variable behavior – disfluencies, unclear references, long pauses, and unusual gestures" (p. 3). Thelen (1995) refers to this function of variability as "exploration and selection."

Goldin-Meadow and Alibali (1995) made related points about children's transitions in understanding conservation problems and math problems. In their discussion, however, the variability reflects the fact that the child is starting to consider two approaches to the problem simultaneously. The variability in their studies isn't an erratic jumping from one solution to another, but rather an internal discordance reflecting the use of two strategies. Ultimately the two are reconciled in an emergent new strategy, and the variability disappears.

It's now being said increasingly that new patterns in behavior emerge when changes either in the environment or in the organism (e.g., via maturation) cause increased variability in behavior (Freedland & Bertenthal, 1994; Siegler & Jenkins, 1989; Thelen & Smith, 1994). How variability relates to emergence of new patterns is characterized differently by different people. Sometimes it's said that variability or instability *motivates a search* for new patterns to satisfy the demands of the situations better than the existing patterns (Freedland & Bertenthal, 1994, p. 31). Others talk as though the variability *stems from* the lack of fit between current behavior and the demands of the situation. Others argue that variability *causes* the shift to a new attractor (Kelso, 1995). Yet others regard variability as a condition that fosters the emergence of new behavior patterns simply by loosening the grip of preexisting patterns. It's unclear which picture is most accurate, but all share the assumption that variability is a harbinger of change (see also Brazelton, 1992).

How is the link between variability and phase change viewed in dynamic systems terms? Consider two sources of variability of the ball's behavior on the attractor landscape. Think of the energy imparted by the shaking of the system as the impact of outside events on the system (recall Figure 14.6D). Think of shifts in the contour of the landscape (something we haven't considered yet) as changes within the system over time. If there's an extra hard jostle, variability goes up. If the landscape shifts in certain ways, variability also goes up (given a constant level of shaking).

How is the variability manifest? Kelso (1995) pointed to two reflections of variability. *Critical fluctuation* refers to how far the bouncing ball is displaced laterally from the center of the basin. If you think about variability caused by a particularly hard jolt to the tambourine, the jolt has the potential of bouncing the ball farther laterally from the basin's center. *Critical slowing down* is the time required for the system to return to its attractor after a perturbation. Other things being equal, the farther the ball is bounced from the basin's center, the longer it will take to return. If the ball bounces around enough (producing increases in both of these indicators), the chance of a shift to a new basin – a phase change – becomes greater.

If you think about the variability caused by changes in the surface configuration (rather than changes in the amount of jostling), you get a picture that's a little different. Think of the basin the ball's in as flattening out. The flatter it gets, the easier it is for the ball to roll away from the center (critical fluctuations), and the slower is the ball to return to the center (critical slowing down), because the basin's attraction is now weaker (Figure 14.7). The flatter the basin gets (given even minimal shaking of the surface), the more likely is a phase change. The sense conveyed by this portrayal is that of one attractor fading out of existence, leading the ball to shift to another attractor.

SIMPLE APPLICATIONS
OF DYNAMIC SYSTEMS THINKING

The themes of dynamic systems thinking we've outlined here have had a number of applications in personality–social psychology.[1] Here are a few of them.

---

[1] Another theme in many discussions of dynamic systems is "self-similarity," the idea that comparable patterns occur at multiple levels of abstraction in a dynamic system (Gleick, 1987). This theme is also deeply embedded in general systems theory, one of the early statements about feedback in behavior (von Bertalanffy, 1968), in more recent derivations from general systems theory (Miller, 1978; Miller & Miller, 1992), and in the hierarchical model of control described in Chapter 5. However, because we have relatively little to say about this idea in this context, we simply note it in passing.

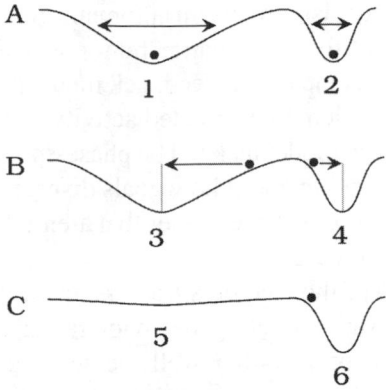

Figure 14.7. (A) Given a little random bouncing (energy from outside or within the system), there's more potential for lateral movement in an attractor with a broad, flat basin (1) than in one with a narrower, steeper basin (2). This is one marker of variability near a phase change. (B) Given a perturbation away from the center of the basin (but not removal from the basin), it will take longer for the system to return to the attractor with a broad, flat basin (3) than to an attractor with a narrower, steeper basin (4). This is a second marker of variability near a phase change. (C) If the effective basin of one attractor becomes more shallow (5), so that it no longer attracts (*thus greatly increasing both markers of variability*), the system at some point shifts to an alternate attractor (6). Thus, variability precedes a phase change.

Goals as Attractors

As Vallacher and Nowak (1997) pointed out, an easy and intuitive application of the attractor concept to human behavior is to the goal concept. Goals are points around which behavior is regulated. Thus, people spend much of their time doing things that keep their behavior in close proximity to their goals. It seems reasonable to suggest, then, that goals are attractors for behavior. Further, if goals can be seen as attractors, it seems reasonable that anti-goals (used by discrepancy-enlarging loops) can be viewed as repellers.

The idea of trajectories within phase space provides an interesting complement and supplement to the idea that behavior is guided by feedback processes with respect to goals and anti-goals. However, the ideas about phase space don't seem to *replace* the ideas about feedback and goals. Rather, the ideas mesh with each other. Each provides something the other lacks.

That is, movement toward a goal isn't really an automatic gravitational drift once the goal's been identified (no matter how convenient that image is).[2] Movement has to be created. The feedback model provides a particular mechanism through which goal-directed activity is managed, a mechanism that the phase-space model lacks. The phase-space model, in contrast, suggests ways of thinking about how goals diverge and how people shift among multiple goals over time, issues that aren't dealt with as easily in terms of feedback processes. [3]

That is, think of the diagram of the chaotic attractors, but think about there being *many* different basins attracting behavior rather than just two or three. This seems to capture rather well the sense of human behavior. Since no attractor basin in this system ever becomes a point attractor or a cyclical attractor, behavior tends toward one goal and then another, never completely captured by any one goal. The person does one thing for a while, then something else. The goals are all predictable – in the sense that they exist and have an influence on the person over time – an influence that's highly predictable when aggregated across

[2] On the other hand, the gravitational metaphor does have interesting further implications regarding feedback processes in behavior. A gravitational pull is mutual and reciprocal. Although the body that is smaller in mass moves more than does the larger one, each moves toward the other. There's some basis for seeing a parallel between this idea and the behavior of at least some feedback systems. A person who holds a goal that's out of reach responds first by trying harder to attain it. In the absence of progress, though, the goal eventually may be scaled back (Chapter 11). This latter process is much slower than is the former one, making it appear as though the goal has greater inertia than does present behavior. In some ways this pattern resembles the greater inertia of a planet compared to its moon. The planet is pulled toward the moon, but far less than the moon is pulled toward the planet. Perhaps the principle of reciprocal influence holds in the present context as well. That is, perhaps the focal point of an attractor fluctuates, minimally, as a function of what points in phase space are occupied over time by the system's actual state. We are unaware of any discussion of attractors in phase space that addresses this question.

[3] People who favor dynamic systems models sometimes imply (or assert directly) that these models are explanatory, in contrast to other models, which are only descriptive. But is this really true? These models place great emphasis on the idea that attractors form and that the behavior of the system can be described in terms of movement from one attractor to another. But only occasionally is there any discussion of what the attractor really *is*, why the system spends so much of its time in its vicinity, or why the movement from one to another occurs (other than to say that increasing variability makes it more likely to fall out of one basin into the next). Occasionally proponents of these ideas write as though a self-organization tendency by itself were reason enough for these things to happen, but that isn't very satisfying (see also commentary by Aslin, 1993, especially p. 394).

A   Trajectory in phase space

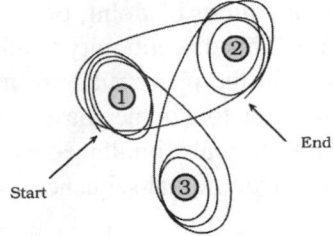

B   Topography of behavior across time

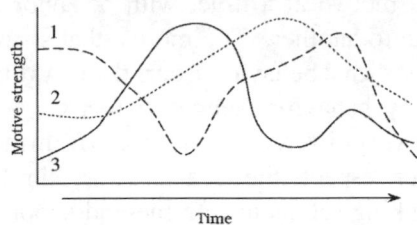

C   Variations in motive strengths

Figure 14.8.   Three views of changing behavior. (A) The trajectory of a system in phase space with three attractors, each shift representing a phase transition. (B) The trajectory plotted across time. (C) Variations in the relative strengths of the three motives that underlie and contribute to the behavior observed.

time (cf. Epstein, 1979). But the shifts from one activity to another occur unpredictably (thus being chaotic).[4]

Shifts among Attractors and Motivational Dynamics

As a system moves through its phase space (Figure 14.8A), imagine plotting a single-dimensional time line of its movement, changing labels on the time line every time a shift occurs from the basin of one attractor to

---

[4] Here's a more concrete example that may already have come to the minds of more cynical readers: You might think of a multibasin phase space as reflecting the behavior of a commitment-shy male with respect to several females: He never comes close enough to any one of them to be captured but rather orbits erratically among however many attractor basins are in his phase space.

another. This time line (Figure 14.8B) would describe a shifting series of discrete events. It would show a pattern of doing one thing, then something else, then something else. This discontinuity would exist on the time line, even though the flow in the phase diagram reflects the simultaneous involvement of *all* the attractors in the phase space. Thus, the idea that people usually hold multiple goals simultaneously, but often make efforts toward attaining them in an ordinal sequence, is nicely in line with the phase-space picture.

This extraction of linear sequencing from dynamic processes closely resembles a point we brought up in Chapter 11: The surface topography of behavior reflects an underlying dynamic of continually shifting levels of motive strength (Atkinson & Birch, 1970; Murray, 1938). Although the motives all rise and fall in intensity continuously (Figure 14.8C), action tends to reflect one motive at a time, with behavior changing qualitatively from one time to another. The motive that's strongest at any given moment determines what behavior occurs then. As the motives shift in comparative intensity, behavior changes its focus.

This conceptualization is very different in some ways from the concept of phase space. Yet in other respects the ideas are very similar. Once again, the new way of thinking seems to reframe and supplement the old, rather than replace it.[5]

Variability in the Construing of Social Behavior

Another application of dynamic systems to social behavior stems from the idea that variability precedes reorganization. We noted a bit earlier that this idea's been applied to developmental change. Vallacher and Kaufman (1996) have also applied it to what happens when people identify their behavior at low levels of abstraction and are about to drift to a higher level. They argue that people construing their actions in low-level terms are, in effect, in a condition of relative dis-order. They're understanding their behavior in terms of, and guiding it by, goals that are restricted in scope and brief and transitory in use.

Recall that people seem to have a natural tendency to gravitate to high identifications. In trying to arrive at a higher-order understanding of their actions, they use the unstable low-level information as raw

---

[5] Indeed, there is evidence that when Murray was working in physiology, before developing an interest in psychology, he studied processes that today would be viewed as dynamic systems, perhaps preparing him for the view of motives he would later espouse (see Robinson, 1992, pp. 69–70).

material. This raw material can be packaged in many ways (using bits of what's available in different mixes), each of which would give a higher-order identification. Vallacher and Kaufman (1996) argued that before adopting a higher-order identification, many possible higher identifications come and go in brief bursts, until one emerges and takes hold in the person's mind. They also described a study that yielded results consistent with this reasoning.

Vallacher and Kaufman's argument – that when people move to a higher identification from a lower one there's a burst of chaotic switching among images, with one emerging as the adopted construal – raises a number of questions. For example, what happens when you shift from one high-level action identification to another? Such a lateral shift can happen either when you reconstrue an ongoing activity in a new light ("I'm not really in a policy discussion with my boss, I'm being told to spy on my coworkers"), or when you stop one activity to take up another ("That letter's done, now let me clear up some of these other chores"). It's tempting to infer that a similar burst of mental turbulence should arise between the one construal and the other.

This inference seems particularly apt for cases in which an ongoing activity is reconceptualized while it's taking place. After all, a reconstrual presumably takes place precisely because information at a low level doesn't fit the current construal. Perhaps an accumulation of inconsistent low-level information causes the person to drop briefly to the lower level, mentally re-shake the package of elements (now a package somewhat different from the one previously considered), and let the multiple possible higher-level identities flash chaotically past until one identity fits well enough to emerge and lock in.

Fitting this line of thought to the case of ending one activity and starting another one is less intuitive but not entirely implausible. At the point where one action ends and another hasn't yet begun, a person probably is more readily distracted by cues signifying another action than at any other point in the behavioral stream. (All other things being equal, if your plan is to finish writing a letter then go to the supermarket, you're more easily thrown off track at the moment you finish the letter than during either the letter writing or the trip to the store.) This relative distractibility may imply a return to the lower level to reshake the package of lower-level behavioral elements.

In this portrayal of shifting construals of behavior, periods of clear identification of goals are punctuated by brief bursts of what amounts to mental static. These bursts of static must in many cases be quite brief, since people do sometimes shift abruptly from one activity to another. In other cases, the static may not be brief at all. Referring to them as "static," "turbulence," or "chaos" may be misleading. These periods may not feel like turbulence at all, since their occurrence is quite familiar. The chaos may feel instead like "implicit decision making" – which after all it is, even though the form Vallacher and Kaufman assume for the process isn't much like traditional views of decision making (see also Townsend & Busemeyer, 1995).

Variability and Consciousness

Viewing the identification of ongoing action as a process that jumps repeatedly from one construal to another suggests an interesting possibility regarding consciousness per se. This possibility, in turn, provides us an unexpected angle on a question that arose earlier in the book. In Chapter 6 we described how self-regulation at the program level has a sequential or digital feel, whereas it has more of a continuous or analog feel at both higher and lower levels. We've often wondered why that is so.

Conceiving of consciousness as shifting abruptly from one construal to another and even from level to level provides a different angle on the question. Perhaps the sequential property characterizes *consciousness* rather than program-level behavior. Because consciousness so often resides at the program level (due to the many decisions that have to be made there), the two tend to be conflated. Perhaps our question about the nature of control at the program level arose because we've been focusing on the wrong part of what we were looking at. Perhaps consciousness provides a sequential readout of whatever is in its lens at that moment (which may itself be analog at all levels of abstraction).

Of some interest, in this regard, is Bargh's (1997) argument that consciousness serves the function of "fitting a parallel mind to a serial world" (p. 53). That is, many kinds of self-regulation are taking place simultaneously within the person, but the time line of reality is linear. Only one thing can be focal at any given moment. This characterization of the nature and role of consciousness seems quite consistent with the line of speculation we just advanced.

Consciousness, Attractors, and Importance in Day-to-Day Life

Dynamic systems thinking also suggests a possible insight for another issue pertaining to consciousness. For this discussion, we return to

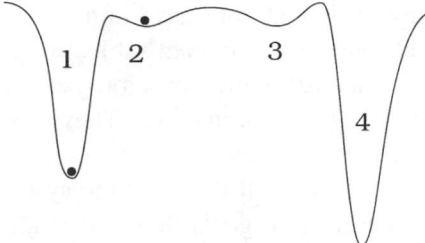

Figure 14.9. A deeper basin (1 and 4) holds a system more securely once it's entered than does a shallower basin (2 and 3). This *might* be taken as indicating that the behavior so represented is more automatic, requiring less attention.

the picture of attractor basins as valleys in a landscape (Figure 14.9). Throughout this discussion we'll treat the basins as behavioral goals to which the person is drawn.

Recall that the depth of a basin can be seen as indicating how firmly entrenched the system is, once drawn in. Another way to characterize this is to suggest that the more habitual, better learned, and firmly established is a pattern of action or thought, the deeper is the attractor well that represents it (Figure 14.9, wells 1 and 4). Once behavior starts toward that goal, it's likely to follow through. Behaviors that aren't well established are shallow wells (2 and 3). Their attraction is brief and ephemeral, easy to jostle out of, easy to be distracted from.

Now step away from this picture for the moment and consider the function of consciousness. Common wisdom is that attentional resources are required when decisions have to be made, when no default response is available (see Bargh, 1997; Norman & Shallice, 1986; Shallice, 1978). The more automatized a process has become, the less attention it gets. When experience has established a response as a default, little or no attention is needed to trigger it (Bargh, 1997). In situations where no automatic, habitual response is available, the person must attend – must consider – in order to make any response at all (Carver, 1997a).

Now put these two views together. We just characterized deep wells as corresponding to highly automatized activities or processes. The shallower the well, the less clearly specified is the attractor, and the less routine, automatic, or predictable is the attraction to it. We also said acts that aren't automatic require attention. These considerations suggest that consciousness should be most implicated in behavior surrounding *shallow* wells. The deeper the well, the less the need for attention.

Which have more impact on our lives, shallow wells or deep ones? (Which have more impact on our lives, behaviors that require attention or those that don't?) The answer is that both have impact, but in two different senses. Shallow wells have more impact subjectively most of the time, because they're the ones receiving conscious, effortful processing. They require evaluating, decision making. They're salient in the phenomenology of our daily lives.

The deep wells, in contrast, are automatic. When the system enters them, the tendencies they represent (the goals they serve) are readily manifest in behavior. They're impactful in the sense of being very predictable once engaged. They've become so routine that we may be unaware when we slip into them. We may even be unaware that they *exist*. These deep wells might be regarded in that sense as more fundamental to the person's nature.[6] The goals they represent are bedrock, taken for granted, forgotten.

It's of some interest that this line of thought recapitulates an assertion of psychoanalytic theory: that the big influences on behavior are those occurring outside consciousness. We're all aware of certain influences in our lives; we think we know our motives and goals. These conscious goals feel as though they matter as determinants of our behavior, and they certainly do. They matter in part because we have no default responses for them, and we therefore must consider our responses closely. In a different sense, however, these goals are more superficial influences. The things we're attending to are "newly" or "currently" important. They're important now partly because more fundamental questions were dealt with earlier, and default responses were developed for them.

Why did the defaults develop? A plausible answer is that the problems they bear on mattered enough (and were encountered often enough) earlier in life to make the responses well learned. Goal-seeking for issues that are critically important – important enough to have demanded close attention during infancy and childhood – is now automated, deeply embedded in the fabric of the self, perhaps out of awareness.

The point here isn't specific to early childhood. The same principle applies to issues that emerge as important later in life. As people grow and deal with activities that are more elaborate and abstract, new issues continually arise, requiring attention. Devoting that attention causes responses to the issues to become more automatic (when possible). These newly deepening wells may also drop out of awareness when they reach

---

[6] We thank Melinda Collins for this observation.

the point where they no longer require monitoring, and the person turns to yet other issues.[7]

In this view, fundamental wells and valleys are carved out early in life, and people spend their later lives sculpting embellishments around them, sometimes taking their existence into account and sometimes being almost oblivious to their existence. There's an irresistible parallel to this view in the idea that the natural history of air and water created the broad topography of the earth's surface, and people have gone on to carve suburban housing developments into the sides of mountains, sometimes taking the existing topography into account and sometimes acting as though they're oblivious to it.

Yet the tambourine rattles continuously and even jolts in a major way from time to time. People do sometimes escape, or shake out of, even deeply cut wells. Earthquakes and mudslides, as well as the changing courses of rivers, sometimes reconfigure low-lying areas or make the valleys disappear altogether. We return to this idea later.

Chaotic Variation as Frequency Distributions

Let's return now to the notion of chaotic variability and its applications in social psychology. Vallacher and Nowak (1977) noted that social psychologists tend to treat attitudes as points on bipolar dimensions of "like versus dislike," despite the fact that they know this is an oversimplification. As Cacioppo and Berntson (1994) pointed out, most attitudes are a mix of positive and negative feelings. It's misleading to average the positives and the negatives to create a summary score, despite the fact that people often do so. Vallacher and Nowak go a step further, arguing that the variation is even more complex. They hold that there's also a temporal variation in a subjective opinion. This variation occurs as a function of the relative activation in memory of the affect-relevant information nodes that constitute the attitude's basis in memory. (This view closely resembles a position articulated earlier, for different reasons, by Wyer, 1973.)

As seen from this view, an attitude might be viewed not as a point on a dimension (Figure 14.10A) but as a frequency distribution (Figure 14.10B). The distribution's mean (or mode or median) would correspond to the single-point attitude that might be marked on an opinion

---

[7] This discussion is speculative. As sometimes happens with speculation, we differ from one another in the degree to which we regard it as plausible.

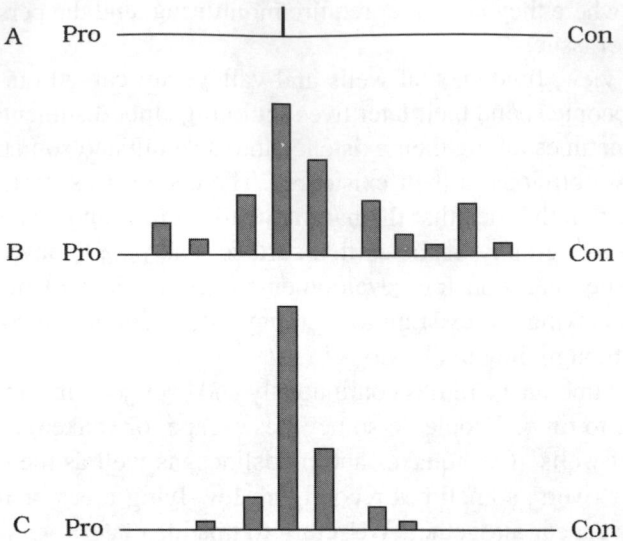

Figure 14.10.   (A) Attitudes are often measured as points on a dimension ranging from strong approval of the object to strong disapproval. (B) They may, however, actually constitute accumulations of elements distributed along the dimension, with the elements forming a frequency distribution. An interesting aspect of this view is that people who report the same single-measure attitude may have frequency distributions that are very different from one another. Thus the persons portrayed in panels (B) and (C) may behave quite differently over time, though they both report the attitude portrayed in (A). (From Carver, 1997b.)

scale ("How do you feel about professional basketball?"). The distribution around that value would reflect the extent of the diversity of the underlying contributing elements, together with the relative frequency with which each is brought to mind when considering the attitude object (how often you feel extremely positive about professional basketball; how often you feel moderately positive about it; how often you feel totally neutral about it; how often you feel moderately negative about it; how often you feel extremely negative about it). As Vallacher and Nowak (1997) suggest, how you feel at any given moment may be a product of the chaotic dance among the elements in the frequency distribution.

The notion that attitudes represent frequency distributions of elements relates to an idea we discussed briefly in Chapter 6: Traits represent not simple dimensions along which people differ, but a set of "if/then" contingencies, which are individualized to the person whose trait is being represented (Mischel & Shoda, 1995). Each of these contingencies may represent a frequency distribution of alternative actions, given a particular context. The resulting picture of traits (see also Buss & Craik, 1983) is similar in some respects to the Vallacher and Nowak picture of attitudes.

Thus, it seems reasonable to imagine a person who acts in an extraverted manner much of the time but is introverted during another fairly large portion of time, either because of variations in context (Mischel & Shoda, 1995) or because of temporal cycles (cf. Vallacher & Nowak's, 1997, discussion of periodic attractors). A person can deeply enjoy the process of being engaged with groups of others and just as deeply enjoy being immersed – alone – in a book. This view seems at odds with traditional trait theories, but it's in good accord with a view in which qualities of persons are not strictly dimensional but instead reflect chaotic variability.

Variability of Behavior in Iterative Systems

A point that's received little attention thus far in our discussion is that human behavior occurs as a continuing stream over an extended period of time. The pattern of influences changes and evolves continuously (Miller, Bettencourt, DeBro, & Hoffman, 1993; Newtson, 1994). It's arguable that a portrayal of behavior as a snapshot in time is not just imperfect, but indeed quite misleading. Such portrayals tend to make people think in terms of causal influences that are constant. They then think of the influences as either large – and therefore worth their interest – or small – and therefore not important. In reality, however, a particular variable's influence can be either large or small, depending on the matrix of other influences present at the moment (Miller et al., 1993). This implies the need to examine processes over time.

Discussions of this matter have been written both at a micro level and at a more macro level. At a micro level, Beer (1995) discussed the repetitive movement pattern of a leg in an artificial system. One variation on the movement of this system that he described involves a continuously deforming cyclical attractor (Beer, 1995, p. 200). That is, the leg moves toward the attractor's orbit; as it does, the orbit deforms, attracting the leg's motion toward the far end of the leg's available range of motion. As the leg's motion carries into that region, the attractor cycle continues to deform, drawing the leg now toward the alternate end of its range of motion. This cyclical deformation of the attractor's orbit then repeats. The result is that the behavior of the limb follows a constantly moving target.

This principle is very similar to something we argued earlier in the book about goals in human behavior. That is, many goals represent paths of activity, rather than simply end states. Conformity to those goals entails a continuous dynamic process, rather than a simple return to a steady state. As Beer (1995) put it, "If either the environment or the agent [has] dynamics on time scales that are long relative to the life of the agent, then the entire trajectory of interaction between them will take place on an extended transient" (p. 207). That is, the transaction will never arrive at its attractor point.

Miller et al. (1993) provide an excellent treatment of this issue at a macro level. They point out that even the meaning of one person's behavior (as viewed by another) is dynamic, shifting with the flux of other influences on the observer's mindset, including the observer's own actions. Specific motives become more salient and less salient as the interaction proceeds. As an example, Miller et al. analyzed the flow of a sexual encounter. As one person attempts to initiate condom use and the other responds adversely, the response isn't only condom-relevant. It may also create a sense of rejection in the first person and thereby increase the salience of her insecurity, potentially causing this motive to assume greater influence than her desire for self-protection. Thus actions have multiple influences, which inform subsequent perceptions and subsequent actions, in an ongoing cycle.

Miller et al. also discussed how computer simulations can reveal the effects of iterations of influences over time. Such simulations can be set up to incorporate a variety of assumptions about how particular variables influence other ones. By examining the impact of these influences over extended periods, the simulation permits dynamic influences to emerge, revealing interesting and sometimes unanticipated patterns. For example, sometimes oscillations develop, in which a person's behavior or psychological state varies between two attractors over time. It seems likely that such simulations will increasingly be seen as useful tools to examine the dynamics of social interaction.

15

Catastrophe Theory

Catastrophe theory is a topological model focusing on creation of discontinuities, bifurcations, or splittings (Brown, 1995; Saunders, 1980; Stewart & Peregoy, 1983; Thom, 1975; van der Maas & Molenaar, 1992; Woodcock & Davis, 1978; Zeeman, 1976, 1977). A catastrophe occurs when a small change in one variable produces an abrupt (and usually large) change in another variable. The fact that the change is abrupt implies nonlinearity or discontinuity.

Despite having quite different origins and purposes, catastrophe theory shares several themes with dynamic systems theory. This focus on nonlinearity is one. You can easily think of the discontinuity that's the focus of catastrophe theory as reflecting two attractors. Phrased in the terms of attractors, a catastrophe in a surface represents "the sudden disappearance of one attractor and its basin, combined with the dominant emergence of another attractor" (Brown, 1995, p. 51). This isn't the only link between these sets of ideas. Indeed, a secondary theme of this chapter is the several parallels between dynamic systems theory and catastrophe theory (though some view the two as quite different – see Kelso, 1995, chap. 2).

THE CUSP CATASTROPHE

Several types of catastrophe exist (Brown, 1995; Saunders, 1980; Woodcock & Davis, 1978), each resulting from the operation of a specific number of control parameters. As we noted in Chapter 14, control parameters are variables that change the dynamics of a system's behavior. A figure portraying a catastrophe has one dimension corresponding to each control parameter, and another showing the "behavior" of the system in response to changes in control parameters. The simplest catastrophe (i.e., with one control parameter) thus can be shown in a two-dimensional figure. A catastrophe with two interacting predictors

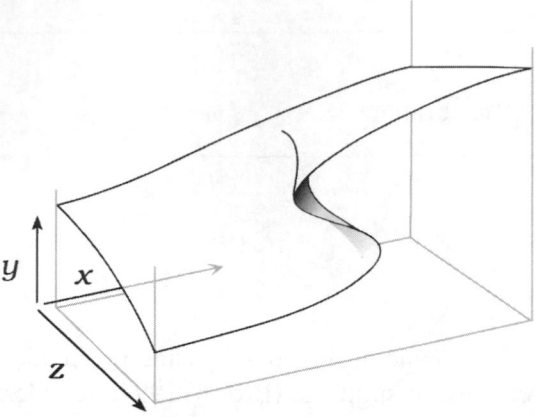

Figure 15.1.   Three-dimensional depiction of a cusp catastrophe. Variables *x* and *z* are control parameters; *y* is the system's "behavior," the dependent variable.

requires a three-dimensional figure. Beyond that, visualization becomes difficult.

The catastrophe that's been considered most frequently regarding human behavior is the *cusp catastrophe*, in which two control parameters influence an outcome. Figure 15.1 portrays its three-dimensional surface. The control parameters are *x* and *z*, the outcome is *y*. Figure 15.2 displays three cross sections of this surface, slices at three different values of variable *z* (moving from back to front of the surface in Figure 15.1). At lower values of *z*, the surface of the catastrophe expresses a roughly linear relationship between *x* and *y*. As *x* increases, so does *y*. As *z* (the second control parameter) increases, the relationship between *x* and *y* gradually becomes less linear. It first shifts toward something like a step function. With further increase in *z*, the *x*–*y* relationship becomes even more discontinuous, with the upper and lower surfaces now overlapping. Thus, changes in *z* cause a change in the way that *x* relates to *y*.

Sensitive Dependence on Initial Conditions

Earlier we said that the theme of nonlinearity is one notion that links catastrophe theory to dynamic systems. Another is the idea of sensitive dependence on initial conditions. The cusp catastrophe displays this characteristic quite clearly (Figure 15.3). Consider the portion of Figure 15.3 where *z* has low values and *x* has a continuous relation to *y*, the

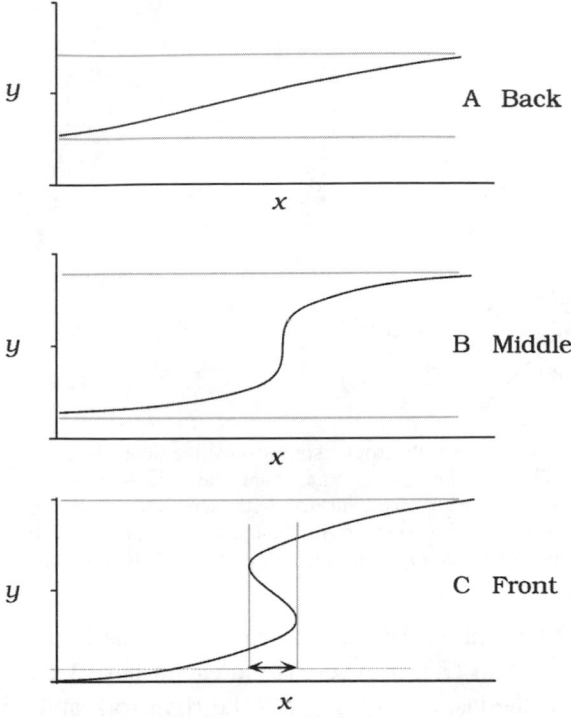

Figure 15.2. Three cross sections through a cusp catastrophe, illustrating relations between x and y from Figure 15.1. (A) Toward the back wall of the surface (where values of z are relatively low), the relation between x and y is relatively linear, with a low slope. (B) Toward the middle of the surface (where values of z are moderate), the function spreads on the verical axis and a nonlinear relation has begun to emerge between x and y, resembling a step function. (C) Toward the front of the surface (where values of z are larger), the function spreads even farther on the vertical axis, and a region of overlap develops between upper and lower surfaces of the figure.

system's behavior. Points 1 and 2 on x are nearly identical, but not quite. As z increases and we follow the movement of these points forward on the surface, for a while they track each other closely until suddenly they begin to be separated by the emerging fold. At even higher levels of z, one track ultimately projects to the upper region of the surface, the other to the lower region. Thus, a very slight initial difference results in a substantial difference farther along.

The effect here is very much the same as that of two people driving in lanes 2 and 3 of a 4-lane expressway, headed west from southwest Texas. They drive side by side through curves, hills, and valleys for 25 miles,

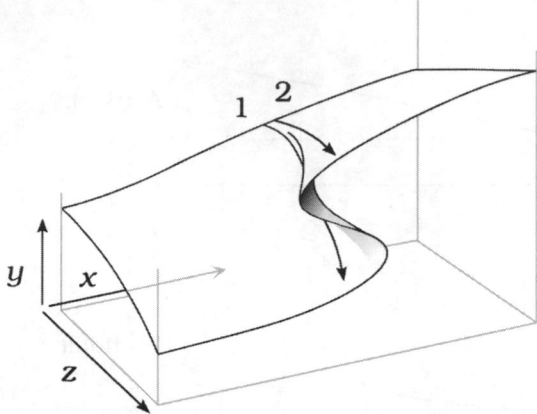

Figure 15.3. The catastrophe shows sensitive dependence on initial conditions. Where z is low, points 1 and 2 are nearly the same on x. If these points are projected forward on the surface (with increases in z), they move in parallel until the cusp begins to emerge. The lines are separated by the formation of the cusp, and eventually project to completely different regions of the surface.

when the highway splits. The car in lane 3 takes the flyover to the left and winds up in San Diego, whereas the car in lane 2 (no more than 4 feet away for the last 25 miles) takes the right fork and winds up in Las Vegas. A very slight initial difference (4 feet) leads to a very large difference farther along.

Hysteresis

Another interesting and important feature of a catastrophe is a phenomenon called *hysteresis*. There are several ways to get a handle on what this term means. A simple characterization is that at some levels of z, there's a "foldover" in the middle of the x–y relationship. A region of x exists in which there's more than one value of y. Another way to characterize the hysteresis is that two regions of the surface are attractors and one is a repeller (Brown, 1995). This unstable area is illustrated in Figure 15.4, which shows the same cross section as was shown earlier in Figure 15.2C. The dashed-line portion of Figure 15.4 that lies between values a and b on the x axis – the region where the fold is going backward – repels trajectories (Brown, 1995), whereas the areas near values c and d attract trajectories. To put it more simply, you can't *be* on the dashed part of this surface.

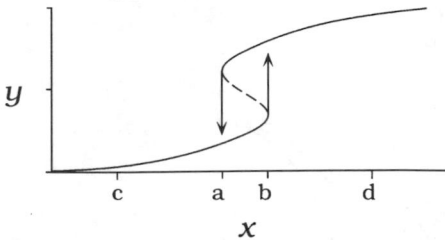

Figure 15.4. A cusp catastrophe exhibits a region of hysteresis (between values a and b on the *x* axis), in which *x* has two stable values of *y* (the solid lines) and one unstable value (the dotted line that reverses in the middle of the figure). The region on the dotted line repels trajectories, whereas the stable regions (those surrounding values c and d on the *x* axis) attract trajectories. Traversing the zone of hysteresis from the left of this figure results in an abrupt shift (at value b on the *x* axis) from the lower to the upper portion of the surface (right arrow). Traversing the zone of hysteresis from the right of this figure results in an abrupt shift (at value a on the *x* axis) from the upper to the lower portion of the surface (left arrow). Thus, the disjunction between portions of the surface occurs at two different values of *x*, depending on the starting point.

Yet another way of characterizing hysteresis is captured by the statement that the system's behavior depends on its recent history (Brown, 1995; Nowak & Lewenstein, 1994). For example, as you move into the zone of variable *x* that lies between points a and b in Figure 15.4, it matters which side of the figure you're coming from. If the system is moving from point c into the zone of hysteresis, it stays on the bottom surface until it reaches point b, where it jumps to the top surface. If the system is moving from d into the zone of hysteresis, it stays on the top surface until it reaches point a, where it jumps down to the bottom surface.

Catastrophes in Physical Reality

You might feel more comfortable with the idea of hysteresis if you knew it had some relation to reality, rather than being a mathematician's exotic fantasy. If hysteresis could actually be seen in the physical world, you might even be willing to consider the possibility that it's a property of nature. If it's a property of nature, it might feel more reasonable to think about its meaning in human experience.

In fact, hysteresis *is* displayed in physical reality. For example, thermal hysteresis occurs in supercooling: cooling a liquid carefully to a temperature below its normal freezing point. If the liquid is supercooled until it

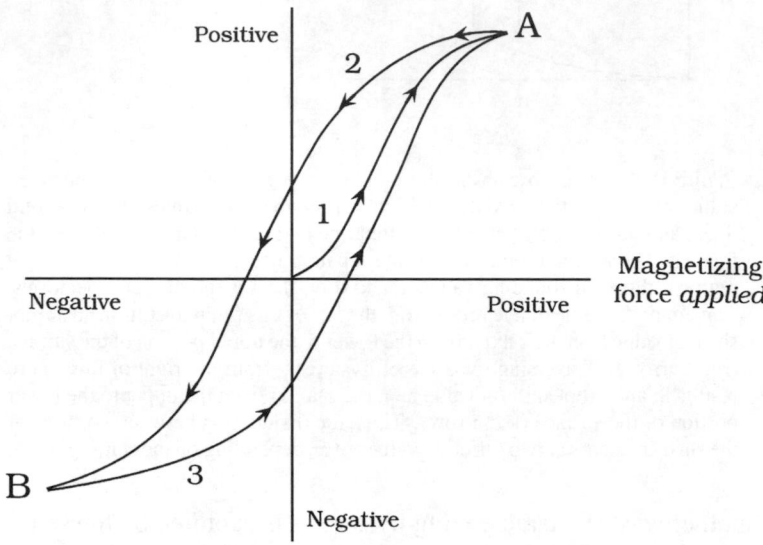

Figure 15.5. Magnetic hysteresis: If a nonmagnetic iron sample is subjected to a magnetizing force (horizontal axis), it acquires a magnetic charge (vertical axis). The induction of a positive charge is shown as movement on path 1 from the origin to point A. If the magnetizing force is reduced to zero (path 2 to the vertical axis), the iron retains a positive charge, even though the induction has been shut off. If the magnetizing force is reversed (continuing path 2 to point B), a negative magnetic charge is induced. If the force is returned again to zero (path 3 to the vertical axis), the iron retains a negative charge. Thus, at the point of zero induction, the sample can have positive or negative magnetism, depending on its history.

freezes, then is heated to melting, the freezing and melting temperatures differ slightly, displaying hysteresis (Huntington & MacCrone, 1993). Thus, the idea that water freezes and melts at the same temperature is true most of the time, but not under all conditions.

A similar effect appears in the induction of magnetism. If a nonmagnetic piece of iron is subjected to a magnetizing force, it acquires a magnetic charge. This is shown in Figure 15.5, as movement from the origin on path 1 to point A. If the magnetizing force is then reduced, the iron loses its charge (path 2), but does so more slowly than the decrease of the magnetizing force. Thus, when the magnetizing force returns to zero, the iron hasn't returned yet to a total lack of magnetism (which would be the origin in Figure 15.5). Rather, it retains a positive charge (where path 2 hits the vertical axis of Figure 15.5, it's above the origin).

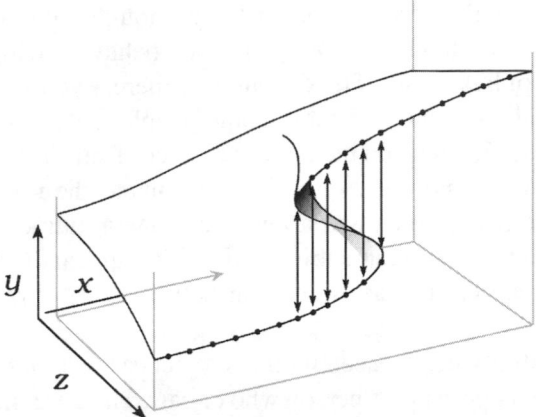

Figure 15.6.   High between-subjects variability can suggest the presence of a region of hysteresis. Disregarding measurement error, variability in *y* will be higher in that region than elsewhere, because some subjects will be providing data points on the upper surface and others will be providing data points on the lower surface.

If the induction is reversed (inducing toward a negative charge), the iron loses its positive magnetism and then acquires a negative magnetism (following path 2 to point B). If the induction is then reduced again back to zero (path 3), the iron will reach the vertical axis with a *negative* magnetic charge, and retain that charge as positive induction is resumed. Thus at the point of zero induction, the sample can have either positive or negative magnetism, depending on its history (Manning, 1993).

Variability

A third link between the ideas of dynamic systems and catastrophe theory concerns the notion of variability surrounding phase transitions (though see Kelso, 1995, for a different view). The zone of hysteresis in the cusp catastrophe is a region where two different states occur with equal frequency. Image you're studying a behavior that embodies a cusp catastrophe. You're studying many subjects, and each subject contributes only one instance of the behavior (so you aren't getting information about the behavior's history). Imagine that your subjects vary nicely along whatever variable is the *x* axis of Figure 15.6. Just to make it simple, assume you have perfect assessment of the behavior of interest, and assume the behavior is perfectly related to your predictor variables, so there's no random variability.

If the situation you're studying has a large enough value on the z variable, there will be huge variability in your behavioral (outcome) data in the region of hysteresis. There – but only there – you'll find both large and small values of the behavior. Some people will be on the top surface of Figure 15.6, others on the bottom surface. Both surfaces exist in that region of x, but nowhere else. The regions to the right and to the left of the hysteresis, which we earlier referred to as attractors, have little variability. Thus, between-subject variability appears to be large at points of bifurcation or phase transition between one attractor and another.

The same variability can be seen within subjects as well, though this gets a little trickier to portray. A person who engaged in the same behavior repeatedly, while varying along the x axis in and around the region of hysteresis, could replicate the behavior of the group just discussed, being sometimes on the top surface and sometimes on the bottom. There could be greater variability even in the course of a single act, if the act occurred at the *edge* of the hysteresis and the person shifted from one surface to the other. What does *not* appear to be implied by catastrophe theory is a basis for moment-to-moment variability within a person in a single act occurring entirely *within* the region of hysteresis (though it's been argued that this is implied by dynamic systems theory – Kelso, 1995).

APPLICATIONS OF CATASTROPHE THEORY

How does catastrophe theory apply to human behaviors of interest to personality and social psychologists? Several applications of the ideas have been made in the past decade or so, and several others seem obvious candidates. When looking at a phenomenon that might be viewed in terms of catastrophe, it's useful to keep in mind cues that suggest the existence of a catastrophe (van der Maas & Molenaar, 1992; Zeeman, 1977). These include sudden jumps, hysteresis, divergence, bimodality, and anomalous variance. The first three of these will be readily apparent in the examples discussed here.

Perception

We start with examples that are clear, if a bit removed from our main focus of interest. Perhaps the best-known illustration of the catastrophe is a perceptual phenomenon (Figure 15.7) in which ambiguous images are perceived in different ways in different contexts (Stewart & Peregoy,

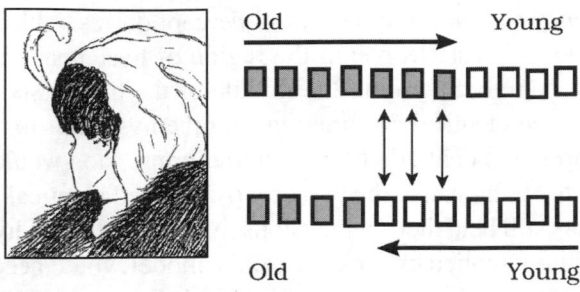

Figure 15.7.   A perceptual catastrophe (after Stewart & Peregoy, 1983). Images are created that vary gradually from a clear depiction of one figure (a young woman), through a highly ambiguous image (the image shown here), to a clear depiction of another figure (an old woman). Subjects view the series starting at one extreme or the other (where the image is clear and unambiguous). At some point in the series, the initial percept gives way and reorganizes abruptly into the other, illustrating the nonlinearity of some changes in perception. The most ambiguous of the images (those in the middle of the series) are perceived in terms of the initial percept. This creates a region of hysteresis. (Adapted from Boring, 1930.)

1983). Subjects see a series of drawings in which a relatively clear depiction of one figure gradually becomes more ambiguous, then transforms to a different figure. The initial perception is retained as the stimulus shifts toward the alternate image, until suddenly the perception reorganizes.

The reorganization illustrates the nonlinearity of the transition, because there's no in-between. You see either one image or the other. This example also illustrates hysteresis, because the most ambiguous stimuli are perceived differently, depending on which image was seen first (i.e., depending on the person's history). This example can also be used to illustrate the thematic similarity between catastrophe theory and the ideas of dynamic systems. One could easily characterize the reorganization as a phase change from one attractor to another.

A related effect is the primacy effect in social perception. Information about a stranger presented first has more impact on the impression than information presented later. Some subjects receive five positive descriptors about a target followed by one negative descriptor; other subjects receive the negative descriptor followed by the five positive ones. The first subjects will form a more positive impression of the target person than will the second group. This happens if the information comes in terms of trait labels (Asch, 1946) or if it comes in terms of behaviors (Luchins, 1957).

This tendency to hold onto the initial perception resembles the two surfaces of the cusp catastrophe in the region of hysteresis. However, these studies seem to go only to the middle of the hysteresis. That is, everyone received identical information. For the hysteresis to be unambiguous, information contradicting the initial impression would have to be given past the point where the two groups received identical information. If subjects still held their impressions, it would establish hysteresis. To show the jump implied by the catastrophe model, you'd need to keep giving information until the impression shifted. Presumably this would eventually happen, though whether it would jump as the catastrophe model implies is less clear.

Dating and Mating

What appears to have been the first serious treatment of catastrophe processes by a social psychologist was in an article published in 1980 by Tesser (1980b). He focused on two potential influences on a romantic relationship: attraction toward the partner and social pressures against the partner (e.g., due to race, social class, or religion). When social pressures are low, dating-related behavior is at the back plane of the catastrophe figure. Extent of dating activity shows a linear increase with attraction.

When social pressures against the relationship are high, however, dating-related behavior is at the forward plane of the figure. When attraction is low to moderate, the social pressure keeps dating activity low. When attraction is high, the social pressure is resisted and dating activity is high. In the middle range of attraction, the behavior that emerges depends on prior history. When attraction that once was high fades, the model predicts that dating-related behavior will continue until (and unless) attraction slips too far. When attraction that once was low increases, the model predicts that dating-related behavior will remain low unless attraction increases beyond the region of hysteresis.

Tesser (1980b; Tesser & Achee, 1994) expanded on this analysis of dating to suggest a more general model of the interaction between dispositions (broadly conceived) and social pressures. In essence, he suggested that social pressures intensify the bifurcation tendencies that are embedded in dispositions. For example, some people have stronger tendencies to conform than do others, and those differences are exaggerated under increased social pressure.

Relationship Formation and Dissolution

This analysis of dating-related behaviors resembles other analyses of processes involved in forming and ending close relationships (see also Baron, Amazeen, & Beek, 1994; Brickman, 1987). On first exposure to a person, you may have little thought of a close relationship. A sense of separateness may exist for some time even as the relationship grows closer. At some point, however, a sense of commitment to the relationship emerges – and may do so quite suddenly (thus people speak of "falling" in love with someone they've known for some time). Given a sense of commitment, the people view things differently – tending, for example, to put a positive interpretation on subsequent events between them (Murray & Holmes, 1993, 1997; Murray, Holmes, & Griffin, 1996). The view that's now held is that of a relationship.

Perhaps an even clearer abrupt transformation is the ending of a relationship. De-commitment is a critical event. As long as the perception is one of a committed relationship, the person keeps viewing events in those terms. Once the line is crossed and the commitment is gone, however, everything changes (cf. Gottman, 1993; Rusbult, 1980, 1983; Rusbult & Martz, 1995).

It seems likely that commitment and de-commitment occur at different points on the continuum of satisfaction (cf. Rusbult, 1983). A relationship can feel pretty satisfying before a sense of commitment to it arises (Figure 15.8, line 1). Once committed, people often will endure relationships that are quite dissatisfying – with lack of communication, infidelity, even emotional and physical abuse – before breaking off (Figure 15.8, line 2), particularly if the person sees the relationship as important (Rusbult & Martz, 1995). This illustrates the tendency to hold onto a given perceptual organization as long as possible, until it can no longer be sustained.

Gottman (1993) has developed a model of marital dissolution that has a good deal of resemblance to this depiction, and indeed makes explicit use of the catastrophe concept. He argues that when the balance of negativity to positivity in a couple's interaction gets too high, a cascade of processes occurs, in which the individuals create implicit barriers to communication, recast their understanding of the relationship, and ultimately move to separation. But more negativity is needed to begin this cascade than would have been tolerated in forming the relationship initially.

On the other hand, there's another way to look at dissolution of relationships, still amenable to the catastrophe model but differing in what

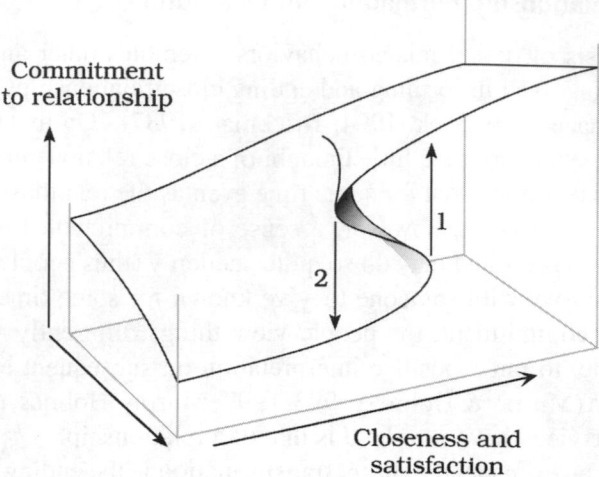

Figure 15.8.   Forming and dissolving relationships may display characteristics of a catastrophe. As you become closer to a person you hadn't thought of in terms of a close relationship, sometimes the sense of commitment comes abruptly (line 1). When closeness and satisfaction in a committed relationship are diminishing, sometimes there is an abrupt break in commitment (line 2). These two events don't happen at the same level of closeness and satisfaction. Rather, there's an overshoot, such that in the middle range the state of the relationship depends on recent history.

issue is focal. We've been assuming that the goal is having this relationship. From this angle, the person who's in a problematic relationship is on the top portion of the catastrophe surface, about to fall off the edge. Sometimes, though, people remain in unsatisfying relationships because of their position regarding a different goal: the goal of finding *another* relationship. This person is on the *bottom* part of a catastrophe surface, unable to make the effort to try finding someone else. The goal in this case is to seek a new partner, whereas the goal in the former case is to maintain the existing relationship.

Groups

Dyadic relationships aren't the only relationships people have, and the same tendencies may emerge in broader relationships. For example, consider membership in groups, and the contrast between initial acceptance into a group and dismissal from a group. It can be hard to get into a cohesive group. Once a person is in, there's a pull toward the group's values (manifest by the group as conformity pressure and by the individual as conformity).

Sometimes, however, the group can't get the person to conform to its norms, or the person can't seem to fit in properly. Friction between individual and group builds until a parting of the ways is imminent. At that point the group ejects the person or the person leaves the group. Can a person who has left (or been ejected from) a group return? Perhaps. But it seems likely that just as with individual relationships, doing so is difficult. The person trying to fit back into the group probably has a catastrophe to overcome. Indeed, the group may even be more demanding of this person than of someone who has no history with the group.

Persuasion and Belief Perseverance

Other candidates for examination in terms of catastrophes are easy to find. One is latitudes of acceptance and rejection in persuasion (for broader views on how these ideas might relate to attitudes and attitude change, see Kaplowitz & Fink, 1992; Latané & Nowak, 1994). When a persuasive message differs from the recipient's opinion but remains within the opinion range the recipient is willing to consider (the latitude of acceptance), it has persuasive influence. If the message is too deviant from the recipient's opinion (the latitude of rejection), it will be rejected out of hand, and no persuasion will occur. The fact that there's a break between these two latitudes suggests a discontinuity. But is there also a region of hysteresis?

What would happen if a persuasive message began within the latitude of acceptance and then wandered beyond it? What would happen if a persuasion attempt began in the latitude of rejection and then eased back toward the latitude of acceptance? Would there be hysteresis, in which the initially acceptable message continued to be seen as such (even when it actually had gone outside that range), and the initially rejected message continued to be taken as such (even when it was now within the acceptable range)?

Yet another application of these ideas concerns perseveration of beliefs. Once a person forms a belief, it's hard to change it. Once people make up their minds, information that would have had an influence as the belief was forming tends to be disregarded (e.g., Anderson, Lepper, & Ross, 1980). To change the belief to an opposing one now takes more contradictory information than would have been needed to form an opposing belief in the first place. We'd guess there's a region of hysteresis in this phenomenon. Try a thought experiment: Form one initial belief in one sample and an opposing belief in another. Then present each sample with information contradicting their initial belief. Would the preponderance of total information have to be on the side of the new belief before people – in each sample – changed their minds? We suspect the answer is yes.

Rumination versus Action

In Chapter 12 we discussed the idea that rumination is implicit problem solving, which occurs in service to discrepancy reduction in behavior (Martin & Tesser, 1996). We suggested there that there's a tradeoff between action and rumination. That is, both have the same ultimate function, but they tend to occur in different circumstances. Action dominates when obstacles aren't encountered, or when obstacles are minimal or manageable. Rumination dominates when the action is fully thwarted. There's a gray area in the middle where some of each probably happens.

Does this gray area display the hysteresis that marks a catastrophe? Is a person who's stuck in rumination more likely to remain there when the situation changes to a point where action is more effective? Is a person who's struggling behaviorally to overcome obstacles likely to keep struggling past the point where it would make more sense to step back and think things over?

A similar set of questions might be asked about the "Rubicon" model of decision making and action suggested by Heckhausen and Gollwitzer (1987; Gollwitzer, 1990, 1996). This theory holds that people have one mindset when deciding whether to adopt a goal and a different mindset once the decision's been made (thus crossing a psychological Rubicon). The first mindset, called *deliberative*, is characterized by careful consideration of competing goals and by objective weighing of each potential goal's pros and cons. It's oriented to open-minded and thorough weighing of evidence prior to making a judgment.

The *implemental* mindset is taken up after the decision has been made to commit oneself to attaining some goal. This mindset is aimed at creating movement toward the goal, at moving quickly and expeditiously to the desired outcome. It has a closed-minded, self-serving focus, biased toward thinking about success. This one isn't very thoughtful, but instead is action-oriented.

The model was given the name Rubicon because, in a sense, once the person is committed to action there's no looking back. The action takes place with little or no reevaluation of the decision. This isn't absolute, of course: Some implementations are unsuccessful and are reevaluated. An interesting question is how long people stay in the implemental mindset when movement to the desired goal is thwarted. If there were some way to measure the point at which deliberation first gives way to implementation, would it differ from the point at which there was a return to deliberation? Would there be a region of hysteresis? (Another interesting but unexplored question is how many points of contact exist between this model and the 1996 model of rumination presented by Martin and Tesser, in which rumination occurs when no effective action is apparent.)

Expectancies

Another important phenomenon that appears to display some of the characteristics of a catastrophe is people's expectancies for success. Evidence exists (though not a lot) that when people develop expectations about the future, they tend to hold onto them even when confronted with evidence to the contrary.

The study that bears most directly on this was conducted by Langer and Roth (1975). It actually focused on a different issue: whether success on a chance task would induce perceptions of skill. Subjects received (or observed someone else receiving) false feedback of success or failure on each of 30 trials guessing (rigged) coin tosses. There were always 15 successes and 15 failures, but with different patterns. In one condition, the early part of the series was mostly failures, with a gradual shift to successes. In another condition, the early part of the series was mostly successes, with a gradual shift to failures (there was also a random condition that we'll disregard). After 30 trials, subjects completed a questionnaire.

Of greatest relevance to this discussion are responses to items asking subjects how often they (or the person they observed) had been correct on the 30 trials, and how many successes they would have had if they went for 100 more trials. Subjects who'd started off with mostly successes reported more success than those who'd started off with mostly failures. A similar pattern, though weaker, emerged in expectations for the next 100 trials. Those who'd experienced early success expected more success; those who'd experienced early failure expected more failure. This pattern indicates, once more, that people tend to hold onto a perception, even in the face of contradictory information, as long as they can.

As was true in the impression formation studies described earlier, these findings show the beginning of hysteresis. As was also true earlier, support for that effect is limited. That is, the groups had experienced identical proportions of successes when the dependent measures were collected. What if the feedback had continued a little longer, so that those who'd started with successes had finished with *fewer* successes than those who'd started out with failures? If subjects retained their initial perceptions under those conditions, the overshoot of the hysteresis would have been clearly demonstrated.

Several further studies show that it's possible to anchor people's expectancies artificially, by having them consider outcome possibilities in either an ascending or descending order before starting an unfamiliar task. Cervone and Palmer (1990) found not only that was it possible to create such an anchor, but also that the anchoring effect was retained across a block of 10 task items. That is, the subject groups didn't perform at different levels on the items (which had been arranged to produce mostly failures), but the initial expectancy difference between groups remained.

EFFORT VERSUS DISENGAGEMENT

Expectancies matter because they influence behavior. We now reconsider the bifurcation discussed earlier between effort and engagement versus giving up. In Chapter 11, we described several theories that postulated such a disjunction (Brehm & Self, 1989; Kukla, 1972; Wortman & Brehm, 1975). In all of them, there's a point at which effort seems fruitless and the person stops trying. In Chapter 11 we simply emphasized that these models all assumed such a discontinuity. Now we'll take the reasoning one step further, and suggest that the phenomena in question may display more than a discontinuity: They may display a catastrophe.

Figure 15.9 shows a cross section of a cusp catastrophe seen earlier in Figure 15.2C. This figure displays a region of hysteresis in the engagement versus disengagement function. In that region, where task demands are close to people's perceived performance limits, there should be greater variability in effort or engagement, as some people are on the top surface of the catastrophe, and others are on the bottom surface. Some people would be continuing to exert efforts at the same point where others would be giving up.

Recall that the catastrophe figure also conveys the sense that the history of the behavior matters. A person who enters the region of hysteresis from the direction of high confidence (who starts out confident but confronts many cues indicating otherwise) will continue to display efforts and engagement, even as the situational cues imply less and less basis

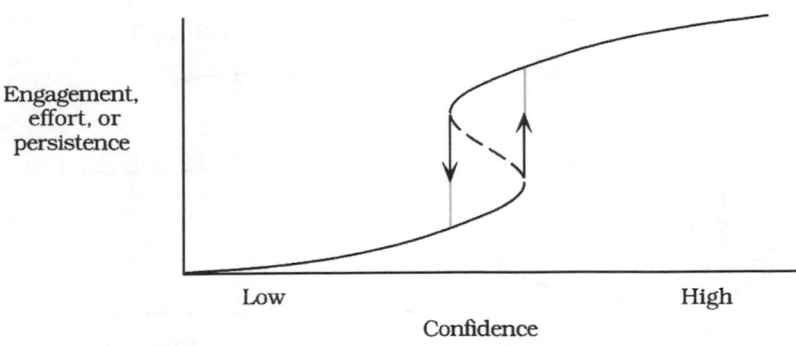

Figure 15.9.   A catastrophe model of effort versus disengagement.

for confidence. A person who enters that region from the direction of low confidence (who starts out doubtful but confronts cues indicating otherwise) will continue to display little effort, even as the situational cues imply more and more basis for confidence.

This model helps indicate why it can be so difficult to get someone with strong and chronic doubts about success in some domain to exert real effort and engagement in that domain. This model also provides a clearer sense of why a confident person is so rarely put off by encountering difficulties in the domain where the confidence lies. In terms of life in general, it helps show why optimists tend to stay optimistic and pessimists tend to stay pessimistic, even when their current circumstances are identical (i.e., are in the region of hysteresis; see also Aldwin, 1994, regarding divergent responses to stress).[1]

Figure 15.10 shows a slightly simplified version of the Wortman and Brehm (1975) model (flipped horizontally to be on a scale that's directionally similar to that of Figure 15.9), and the Brehm and Self (1989) model (which, for this discussion, is the same as Kukla's 1972 model).[2] These functions both show bifurcations between two classes of response. As proposed by the theories' authors, neither has a region of

---

[1] Indeed, personality qualities may display a similar anchoring function more generally. That is, dispositions influence how people view the world in many respects, and people tend to hold onto their perceptions as long as they can. This may result in anchoring different people in different places in their views of the world.

[2] The x axes of these various models do not represent quite the same variables, though the variables are related. Perceived task difficulty influences confidence (Brehm & Self, 1989), as does perceived facility at the task (Kukla, 1972) and extent of threat to control (Wortman & Brehm, 1975). Although none of these variables is a *complete* determinant of confidence, all are related to confidence closely enough to warrant our treating them as equivalent for purposes of this exercise.

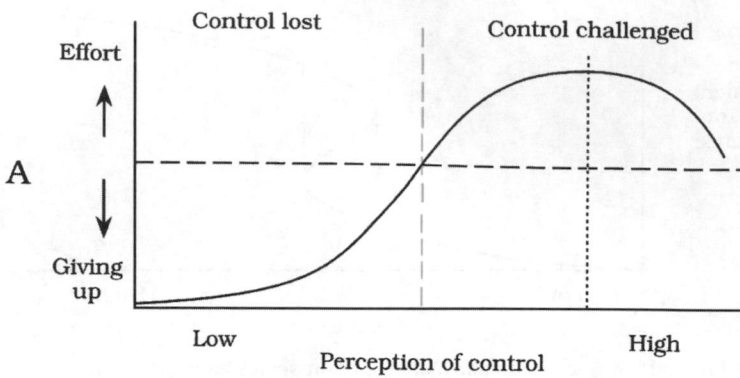

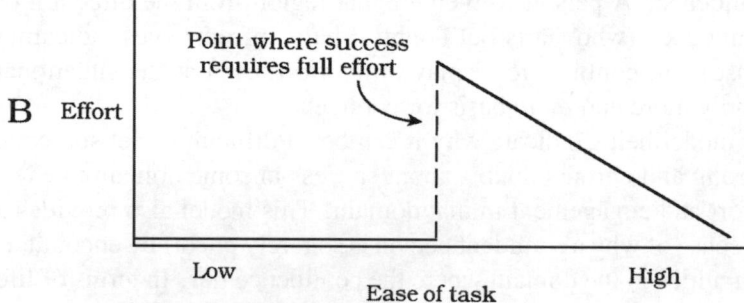

Figure 15.10.   Slightly modified depictions of (A) Wortman and Brehm's (1975) model of helplessness and reactance, and (B) Brehm and Self's (1989) model of effort (which for this purpose is essentially the same as Kukla's 1972 model).

hysteresis. Is this feature – missing from the diagrams – present in the phenomena addressed by the theories? We think a case can be made that it is.

The Wortman and Brehm model (Figure 15.10A) is reminiscent of the middle stage of the developing of the catastrophe surface, where something resembling a step function has begun to emerge but the region of hysteresis hasn't yet come to exist (recall Figure 15.2B). If you clipped off the part of the graph in Figure 15.10A that's to the right of the dashed vertical line, the resemblance would be even more striking. Should there be a region of hysteresis? We suspect that a person who enters the situation with the strong belief of no control will continue to show little effort even when control begins to emerge. We also suspect that a person struggling with a threat to control will continue to struggle even when control disappears. Such effects of the person's behavioral history would yield hysteresis.

The Brehm and Self model (15.10B) differs in a number of ways from Figure 15.10A and from Figure 15.9, but we think a case can be made that a region of hysteresis may exist here as well. The critical issue may be the ambiguity of the situation the person faces. The figure assumes that the person knows the point where maximum effort is required, but this won't always be true. A person who begins with a task that's far too hard to perform won't try. But if the task changes gradually so that success is now possible, how will the person know, if only minimal effort is being exerted? Not knowing, why would the person try harder? A person who begins with a task that's challenging but attainable will exert strong effort. But how will this person know if the task demands increase to exceed his maximum potential effort, unless he continues to try? In short, it appears there's good potential here for a region of hysteresis.

One remaining difference between both models in Figure 15.10 and the catastrophe in Figure 15.9 is that the models in Figure 15.10 both show a downturn at the right of the figures and the catastrophe does not. There are several possible reasons for this difference, and we aren't sure what interpretation is best. One way to think about it is to postulate that the catastrophe applies only when the person confronts adversity. If the person is confident about overcoming the obstacle, engagement is high. This view was implicit in our discussion two paragraphs ago, regarding the Wortman and Brehm figure. That is, in that figure effort is high only when there's threat to control. If it were the case that the catastrophe surface depicts responses to adversity, rather than behavior in general, the far right portion of Figure 15.10A would be irrelevant to the discussion because there's no adversity there.

Two further points should be emphasized about comparisons among these figures. First, no one has really studied the processes of effort and disengagement in a truly parametric manner that would allow plotting the full range represented by the figures. Most work on the Wortman–Brehm (1975) model focused on two points in the range of threat to control. Brehm, Wright, and co-workers have typically chosen three points on the range of task difficulty: easy, demanding but possible, and too hard to bother with. The exact shape of the function represented by these figures still isn't well known.

Second, it should be kept in mind that the catastrophe cross section in Figure 15.9 is the picture that emerges under catastrophe theory *only once a clear region of hysteresis has begun to develop* (Carver, 1997b). Farther back in the surface, the catastrophe model looks more like a step function (recall Figure 15.2). An important implication is that it's critical to engage the control variable that's responsible for bringing out the bifurcation in the catastrophe surface. It may be that in research bearing on this set of issues, this variable is at only a low to moderate level. If so, the hysteresis would be less observable, even if the research procedures were otherwise suitable to observe it.

Importance or Investment
as a Critical Control Parameter

What *is* the control variable that induces the bifurcation? We think that in the models under discussion – and perhaps much more broadly – the control parameter is *importance*. Tesser (1980b) pointed to social pressure as a critical control variable. Social pressure is one force that can make a behavior or a decision important, but it's only one instance of a broader set of pressures. Importance arises from several sources, but there's a common thread among important events. They demand mental resources. We suspect that almost any strong pressure that demands resources (time pressure, self-imposed pressure) will induce similar bifurcating effects.

In Chapter 13 we briefly addressed the influence of a goal's importance on people's persistence in trying to attain it. We argued there that people would continue in task efforts longer in the face of developing doubt when the goal was important than when it was not (lines A and B in Figure 15.11, which were displayed separately in Figure 13.2). Our argument was based on the idea that it's hard to disengage from a value that's central to the self. Thus, persistence should be greater for important than unimportant goals.

It's of considerable interest that the catastrophe principle makes the same point, and adds to it. Our previous discussion assumed a behavioral history in which the person began with the belief that the goal was attainable. This assumption remains in effect for lines A and B in Figure 15.11. However, the catastrophe model adds the prediction that a person who begins with the belief that the goal is *not* attainable (dashed line C) will stay in disengagement mode longer (as doubt fades) when the goal is important than when it is not. Thus lines A and C re-create the familiar zone of hysteresis.

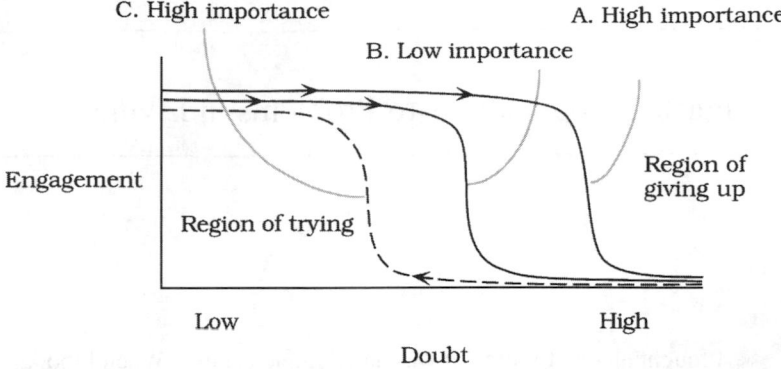

Figure 15.11. The point was made in Chapter 13 that people will be more persistent in the face of rising doubt when a goal is important than when it's not (lines A and B, respectively). However, that discussion assumed a progression in experience from low doubt to high doubt (illustrated here by arrows). The catastrophe model adds the following prediction: When importance is high and the behavior begins with high doubt, moving to lower doubt, greater confidence is required before the giving-up posture will be abandoned (dashed line C). This creates the familiar zone of hysteresis (between lines A and C).

In considering the circumstances that seem to create bifurcations, many terms might easily be applied to the control parameter. We've used the term *importance*. Latané and Nowak (1994) used the term *involvement*. Other labels such as *commitment, investment, ego involvement*, and so on convey the same general sense. In all these cases, the person preparing to act has something on the line. When things are important, when there's a lot at stake, there seems to be a tendency toward polarization and bifurcation (see also Baron, Vandello, & Brunsman, 1996). This principle has a number of implications. Among them are implications about the nature of psychological problems, to which we turn next.

16

Further Applications to Problems in Living

> I fought all day to forget it was an Olympic Games. When I thought
> about the Olympics and trying to win the gold, it was just
> overwhelming. I tried to convince myself, "This is just another
> decathlon. Just get through it and you'll be fine."
> (Dan O'Brien, 1996 Olympic gold medalist in the decathlon)

> Perhaps that is why desire causes men calamity. By identifying with
> our desires and taking them too seriously ... we actually create a
> climate inhospitable to the free and easy fulfillment of those desires.
> (Tom Robbins, *Jitterbug Perfume*)

> I've failed over, and over, and over again in my life.
> And that is why I succeed.
> (Michael Jordan, for Nike)

The preceding pair of chapters introduced some concepts that haven't
been widely discussed by personality and social psychologists until recently. Our goal there was to indicate how these ideas complement and
supplement those presented earlier in the book. We continue to examine them in this chapter, but now in relation to behavioral problems.
Just as the earlier ideas had implications for understanding problems
(Chapters 12 and 13), so do the newer ones. In this chapter we explore
implications of dynamic systems and catastrophe theories for problems
and their alleviation.

CATASTROPHES AND PSYCHOLOGICAL PROBLEMS

In Chapter 15 we described the cusp catastrophe as a construct that's
applicable to several aspects of human experience. It also appears to
be helpful in conceptualizing certain kinds of problems. Several such

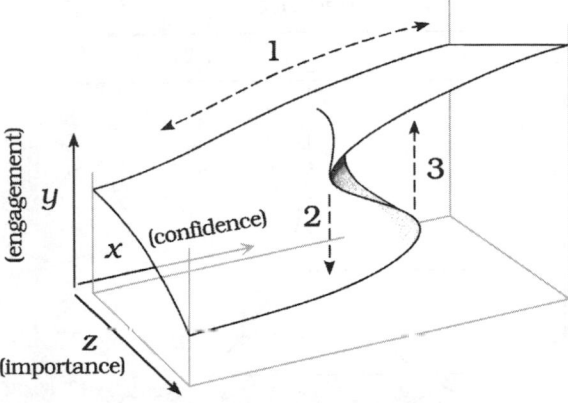

Figure 16.1. Hypothesized divergence between engagement and disengagement under increasing pressure. When pressure is low (z is small), there's a relatively linear relation between confidence (x) and engagement (y), such that trying gradually shades into withdrawing as x decreases (arrow 1). When pressure is high (when z is large), the relationship is no longer continuous. Engagement (top surface) yields abruptly to quitting (arrow 2); quitting (bottom surface) yields abruptly (if at all) to engagement (arrow 3).

applications are worth noting briefly. In one way or another, most of them concern the relevance of the catastrophe to motivational phenomena.

At the end of Chapter 15 we suggested that the divergence between engagement and disengagement under psychological pressure can be viewed as a cusp catastrophe surface (Figure 16.1). According to this view, an increase in pressure causes a shift from a linear to a nonlinear relation between confidence and engagement. When pressure is low (when z is small in Figure 16.1), there's a continuous and fairly linear relation between confidence (x) and engagement (arrow 1), such that trying and withdrawing shade gradually into one another as x varies. When pressure's high, when the behavior is important (when z is larger), the relationship is no longer continuous. There's an abrupt discontinuity. Engagement (on the top surface) yields abruptly to quitting (arrow 2), and quitting (on the bottom surface) yields abruptly (if at all) to engagement (arrow 3).

For the person on the top, there's a cliff face, rather than a smooth slope – a cliff to fall from, with a long drop. For the person on the bottom, effort is still possible, but *for it to happen now requires a higher degree of confidence* (Figure 16.2). That is, as importance increases, the region of hysteresis spreads wider and wider, moving its edge (where the shift

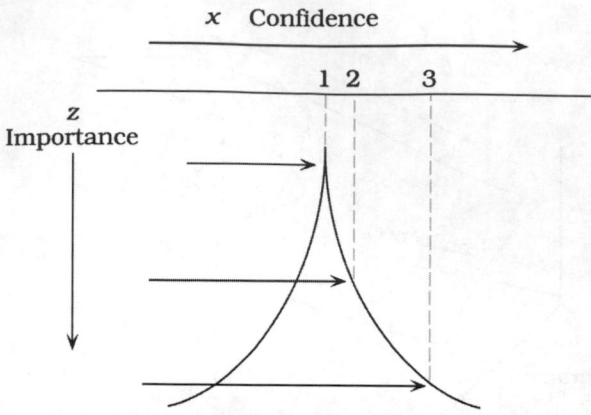

Figure 16.2.   The *bifurcation set* of the cusp catastrophe in Figure 16.1. This is essentially a "downward" projection of the two edges of the cusp onto a flat plane. It shows that as importance increases and the degree of hysteresis correspondingly increases, a person on the lower surface must move farther toward high confidence in order to be displaced to the top surface. When a goal has relatively low importance, the person must reach only point 1, but as importance increases, the confidence needed continues to increase (points 2 and 3).

upward to effort occurs) to a point farther toward the positive end of the confidence dimension.

Many problems in life seem to fit this picture, including all-or-none, black-and-white thinking. The easiest example is that people crippled by doubts in some important domain of life appear to live out that domain on the lower part of the front edge of Figure 16.1. Given their doubt, it's hard for them to try to perform adequately in the domain of the doubt *precisely because that domain matters so much.* They're facing an enormous challenge. To get to the point of exerting real effort, they need to be *very* confident. Since they're not, the effort doesn't come. They've lost the sense that they can make their lives better, and they feel stranded miles away from the possibility of reengagement.

People who are anxious or depressed have difficulty letting themselves act naturally. They aren't very good at taking chances, at letting themselves be vulnerable to making mistakes. Their behavior doesn't show much "flow." Instead, their doubts and worries cause them to repeatedly evaluate the likely outcome of the behavior they're engaged in. Even if things are going well at the moment, they tend to have the sense that the smooth sailing can't last. Being already on the bottom, they hardly ever attain the level of confidence that's needed to jump to the top.

The catastrophe model suggests that perceived importance of the outcome or behavioral domain is a key factor in keeping people with this outlook from taking chances. When something seems important, unless the person becomes very confident the effort never happens.

A Remedy: Care Less

The catastrophe model suggests that a partial remedy for problems such as these is to move the person somehow from the front plane of the surface toward the back. Near the back, the relation between confidence and engagement is more gradual and linear. A slight increase in confidence adds something in engagement (unlike the front, where you have to be very, very confident before a real gain occurs). For the moderately confident person at the back, the cost of an emerging doubt is gradual rather than sudden. The gradual nature of the changes keeps the person engaged in the process of goal pursuit, and staying engaged is a critical determinant of success.

People commonly talk of needing to "take the pressure off," to "get psychological distance." What do these phrases mean? "High-pressured" means "important" and "emotion-generating." We think it also means being toward the front of this surface. "Creating greater distance" and "taking the pressure off" mean moving toward the back of the surface. By devaluing the goal to which the feelings pertain, you diminish the event's distress-evoking potential (cf. Marsh, 1986; Pelham & Swann, 1989). Although this assertion doesn't require the catastrophe model, it's consistent with it.

This depiction follows from a purely descriptive examination of the topography of the catastrophe's surface, assuming no insight whatever on the part of the behaving person. It's just a statement of what happens according to that model. However, it seems likely that people often are aware of the situation they're experiencing. Someone on the bottom front part of the surface may feel a strong sense of hopelessness, corresponding to the large increase in confidence that needs to occur before serious effort will be made. If you move this person to the back where things don't matter so much, on the other hand, he can experiment. When it's a gentle hillside instead of a cliff, he can afford to take a chance and make a mistake, because the cost of failing isn't so great.

Although catastrophe theory does not directly imply it, being toward the back wall where the pressure is lower would seem to do other things, as well. It makes it easier for you to time-share your current, immediate perceptions of what's happening with other potential views on the experience. Considering this diversity of views, in turn, can result in greater objectivity.

This line of thought is particularly appealing if you're someone who's on the bottom front of the surface. This is where negative feelings are greatest (important event plus strong negative expectations). The virtue of devaluing the goal is less obvious for someone at the top front. As long as you're up there, why wouldn't it be just fine for the pressure to be on? The answer is partly that it *is* fine, as long as you're *way* up there. If you're in the region of hysteresis, though, the potential for disaster isn't too far away. If your confidence slips, a sudden shift to disengagement and distress awaits. Having the cliff too close can cause you to be overly concerned about the possibility of slipping, which can disrupt your concentration.

This argument converges nicely with ideas from other sources. The idea that removing pressure benefits even skilled performers is implied by a principle of Taoist thought, expressed as follows: "An archer who is shooting for a prize no more important than an earthenware dish will nonchalantly display his best skill. Offer him a brass buckle if he hits the mark, and he will shoot cautiously and less well. Offer a prize of gold, and he will become tense, and his skill will desert him entirely" (Creel, 1953, p. 90). The same point is also made, more prosaically, in the first quotation at the opening of this chapter, in which Olympic gold medalist Dan O'Brien described how he took pains to view the Olympic finals as no more than an ordinary meet, thereby preventing himself from becoming overly pressured.

Thinking about diminishing the importance of an event as a way to help people stay engaged in the event casts a slightly different light on techniques already used in therapy. An example is systematic exposure to cues that prompt fear while trying to reframe the cue or your response to it in concrete and nonthreatening terms (Foa & Kozak, 1986). Doing this (framing the cues as nonthreatening) may cause the event to become more distant or removed from the self, thus diminishing the event's importance. As another example, the "mindfulness" skills taught in Linehan's (1993) dialectical behavior therapy include the ability to step back from events being experienced. Stepping back implies a reduction in the subjective importance of the events.

This view also suggests an interpretation for the value of humor as a coping tactic. Making light of a stressful situation tends to deflate it, reduce its subjective importance. When you're laughing at something

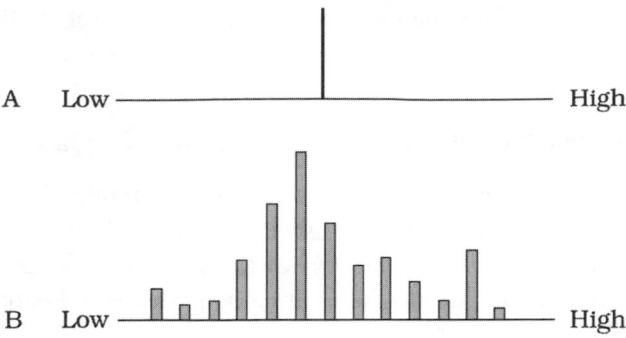

Figure 16.3. (A) The importance of a goal is often viewed as a point on a dimension ranging from very low to very high. (B) However, subjective importance may actually constitute a frequency distribution of positions, along the dimension. Thus, a person who views the importance of a goal as moderate overall (panel A) may actually view it as very important at some moments, and very unimportant at others.

that's bothering you, it doesn't matter as much. Consistent with this view, use of humor has been shown to predict less distress when people are experiencing negative events (e.g. Carver et al., 1993; Newman & Stone, 1996).

Chaotically Caring

This line of thought has one disquieting implication, however. If the key to being able to deal with problems is to become less invested, the logical conclusion is that it's better not to care about things in your life. Many would find this conclusion rather disconcerting. What's the point of life if you don't care about anything? Is it best to care a little, but only a little?

One way of resolving this quandary joins the idea of catastrophe to the idea of chaotic processes. Maybe investment shouldn't be viewed as a constant (Figure 16.3). Reducing the importance of the behavior needn't mean reducing it once and for all. Perhaps importance, or investment, shifts erratically forward and backward instead of being constant. This would render the behavior intensely important at some moments and unimportant at others. Such fluctuation would provide a way of being invested but not overwhelmed. If always being at the forward part of the catastrophe is dysfunctional, always being at the back may *also* be dysfunctional. A person who's always at the back edge is never really engaged in anything. Maybe what's best is a frequency distribution of moment-to-moment fluctuations among many places (cf. Vallacher & Nowak, 1997).

Further Possible Manifestations of the Cusp Catastrophe

Cases that pit confidence against doubt may best exemplify the pattern of the catastrophe, as indicated in the previous section. Another reflection of that is the well-known tendency toward black-and-white thinking about the self, the world, and the future among depressed people (e.g., Beck, 1972).

Black-and-white thinking isn't limited to issues of confidence versus doubt, though. It also shows up in other problems. Another example comes from literature on borderline personality disorder. This disorder has been described as reflecting extreme vacillation between two cognitive, emotional, and behavior patterns. One pattern is close, clingy, and dependent; the other is angry, confrontational, and rejecting (Linehan, 1993). There's little or no middle ground between patterns, and the shift between them rests on a hair trigger. The borderline individual may view a relationship in overidealized positive terms during one span, then suddenly become upset with something and shift abruptly to viewing the relationship with suspicion, mistrust, and a sense of betrayal and outrage. This person gives the appearance of having two wholly different understandings of the relationship, which can shift in and out of consciousness quite suddenly.

Do the shifts between these patterns display the properties of the catastrophe? There are at least some indications that they do. One indication is the fact that the change in orientation can occur abruptly and be relatively complete when it does occur. Another indication is that it can be hard to restore a sense of trust and positivity in the relationship, once the rage and sense of betrayal erupt (a reason the disorder is so hard to treat). To put it differently, there appears to be a zone of hysteresis. If this characterization were accurate, it would suggest that treatment for this behavior pattern might profit from incorporating procedures that have the effect of dampening or defusing the person's investment in relationships. If the relationship isn't as pressured, doesn't matter as much, presumably the vacillation will be less likely.

Another well-known fluctuation between divergent states is that between mania and depression in bipolar disorder. Bipolar disorder differs in important ways from other problems we've discussed here. For one thing, it appears to be fundamentally biological in origin. Nonetheless, some have begun to wonder whether the mood shifts in this disorder represent an example of a chaotic, rather than cyclical, process (Gottschalk, Bauer, & Whybrow, 1995). An interesting question that might be raised about this pattern of shifts in behavior and affect is whether the phases of mania and depression display characteristics such as hysteresis.

Other disorders may also display properties of a catastrophe. Berecz (1992) has argued that Tourette syndrome is driven by parameters of anger and shame, with tics emerging when shame and anger co-occur. He also suggested that the "starve or stuff" behavior of eating disorders and the sober–drunk cycles of alcoholism reflect similar bifurcations in behavior. This view casts a rather different light on the self-regulatory failures we discussed in Chapter 13. An interesting question is whether such phenomena exhibit regions of hysteresis (Carver & Scheier, 1996b). If this were shown, it would extend substantially the applicability of catastrophe theory into important areas of human behavior.

DYNAMIC SYSTEMS
AND THE CHANGE PROCESS

We turn now to an application of dynamic systems thinking. Several theorists have begun to apply these ideas to help understand the processes by which people change in response to therapeutic intervention (or even in response to disruptive life circumstances).

Attractors, Minima, Stability, and Optimality

Recall that in dynamic systems models an attractor is a region of conceptual space to which a system is drawn. This concept can be used at several levels of abstraction. In Chapter 14 we used it at the level of goals, saying that a person shifting goals could be viewed as moving from one attractor basin to another. In this discussion we're going to apply it in a broader way. Now we're going to think of an attractor as reflecting a summary, or aggregation, of a person's overall adaptation to the world on all the dimensions of the person's life.

As we noted in Chapter 14, the stability of an attractor basin can be portrayed graphically as the depth of a well in a surface (Figure 16.4). A basin that's shallow compared to the ridges around it is unstable (if there

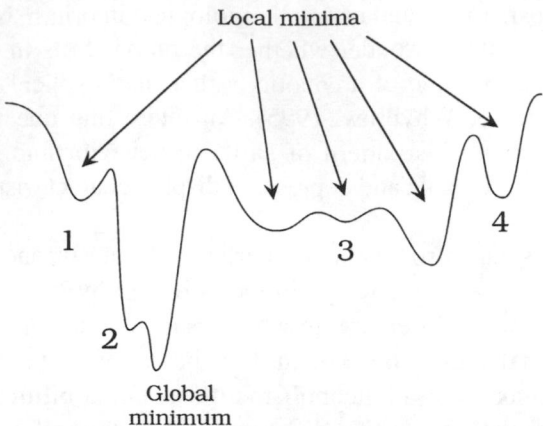

Figure 16.4.   A landscape portraying a surface in conceptual space may have several local minima: attractor basins less deep than the global minimum of the surface. Basins vary in depth, both overall and with respect to their immediately surrounding space. Overall depth implies optimality of functioning; depth with respect to immediate bounds space implies stability. Basin 3 is more shallow in terms of immediate surroundings than either basin 1 or basin 4, but it's deeper overall. Therefore, it's less stable but nearer the optimal. Basin 2 is even nearer the optimal, but the low ridge on one side implies that it's relatively unstable.

are other basins to shift to). One that's deeper is more stable, although it may still be a local minimum rather than the global minimum. Basin 3 in Figure 16.4 is shallower than basins 1 and 4, and thus less stable than they are. This is true despite the fact that basin 3 is at a lower level overall than is either 1 or 4. The *local* stability of an attractor thus is indicated by its depth relative to the ridges on either side.

There's also a way to think about the *overall* depth of a basin, which derives from thinking of these diagrams with a metaphor different from the one we used in Chapter 14. There we treated it as an energy landscape, but it's sometimes viewed as an *error* landscape (see Chapter 9 of Anderson, 1995). The latter view is particularly useful when thinking about adaptation, because the idea that low error implies better adaptation is intuitively appealing. Thinking in terms of an error landscape implies that it's desirable to be at a lower level. Thus, one might think of the *overall* depth of a basin (compared to the global minimum) as an index of the relative optimality of the pattern it represents.

Local stability and overall depth are at least partly independent. Thus, it's possible to be in a basin that's quite stable but far from optimal (basin 4). It's also possible to be in a basin that's nearly optimal but not very stable (basin 2).

Stability, Adaptation, and Optimality

The term stability as applied to an attractor landscape refers to the likelihood of shifting from one basin to another. When applied to psychological experience, it's the likelihood of shifting from one overall *life pattern* to another. Stability is something like the proportion of your thoughts and actions that are "adaptive and functional" with respect to your life space or constellation of goals. If the proportion is high, the pattern is stable and there's no tendency to change. If the proportion is lower (more actions fail to fit the constraints of the life space), the pattern is less stable. The worse the fit, the greater the potential for change.

Note that "adaptive and functional" is a relative characterization. This phrase takes its meaning by reference to the context in which the behavior occurs (as is true of adaptiveness in evolutionary theory). Behavior is in this sense adaptive if it fits with the person's life space and with the values that make up the person's self. Someone who steals to get money, dominates his relationships by physical force, and believes that the only meaningful values are power and strength may well be in a stable pattern – if the behaviors are well adapted to the life space he inhabits.

However, the niche to which he is adapted is narrow. His behaviors aren't well suited to the broader society outside this life space. He's adapted as long as he remains in this niche, but he may not stay there forever. If he steps outside it, he'll discover his behaviors don't fit as well. Taking the broad view (the view that takes into account the normative values of society), he's in a local minimum such as basin 4 – deep in comparison to its immediate surround, but not very deep overall (not optimal). Nonetheless, as long as his personal organization functions more or less adequately in its niche, it's maintained in roughly its current form. Even if a person's self is in a local minimum of functioning rather than its global minimum, it will tend to stay there (cf. Greenwald, 1980).

Only if the adaptive value of this pattern is eroded or challenged by force of events or personal growth (i.e., if the form of the landscape changes), will the pattern lose its stability. If the person we've been describing somehow comes to value honesty, he'll have trouble stealing; if he comes to value another's openness and trust, he'll have trouble abusing that person. An attempt to move farther into the larger society (or a need to deal more with it) will also cause problems to emerge. In any of these cases, the person's "error" will increase (more behavior will clash with the context). The basin will lose its relative depth and become less stable.

This example depicts a life that's well adapted to a niche but far from admirable. It's a life that's destructive and problematic for others. In contrast are lives that are less destructive societally but perhaps more poorly adapted to their niche. People are anxious or depressed at least partly because their actions (and their mental orientations to their experiences) don't fit well into their life space. The local minima in which these people are living may be quite shallow.

People in this situation may try to arrange their experiences to minimize error. A man who becomes anxious whenever he's in a group, but who's able to avoid groups, is keeping his pattern stable. The stability is threatened only if something requires him to be with a group (e.g., his work requires him to attend a convention) or if a desire to feel a sense of belonging arises and causes a conflict with the desire to avoid the anxiety that comes from being in groups. Often enough, such conflicts do arise.

It's arguable that most people are living in one or another local minimum, rather than in their global minimum. Their day-to-day functioning is adequate, but not optimal. Many people know very well that they're in a less than ideal pattern. But even though they yearn for change, they haven't sought out a better pattern. Their lives aren't fully stable, but they haven't yet bounced from the basin they're in to another one.

Many people are caught between the desire to hold onto a way of being that's moderately functional and a pressure to reorganize their lives to foster better adaptation. The idea of change is threatening, partly because it means entering the unknown. So, for the most part, people cling to the existing pattern, trying to tune it a little so it works more smoothly, rather than seeking fundamental change. To put it differently, they stay in their current basin and try to dig it a little deeper, by changing their behaviors in small ways to fit their niche better, or by narrowing their life space to avoid situations that produce feelings of poor fit.

Minima in Specific Problems

This view of stability and optimality can be applied to a life as a whole, as we just did, or to a particular problem. That is, problem solving can be characterized as seeking the global minimum on the landscape of possible ways to deal with the problem. Many problems are such that their topography has several local minima (Figure 16.5), where parts of the problem are dealt with adequately but the problem isn't dealt with optimally. In such cases, several solutions can be developed, varying in quality.

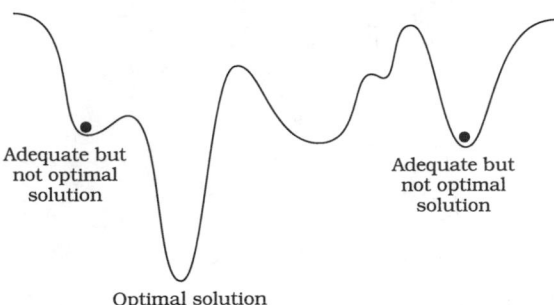

Adequate but
not optimal
solution

Adequate but
not optimal
solution

Optimal solution

Figure 16.5.   A problem-solving phase space may have several local minima,
representing partial solutions that aren't optimal. Systems may become caught
in these local minima and thereby fail to reach the global minimum, arriving
at an adequate but not great solution and failing to reach a better solution.

In Chapter 12 we pointed out that rumination causes depressed people
to generate poorer problem solutions (Lyubomirsky & Nolen-Hoeksema,
1995). Another way to characterize this is to say that depressed people
are vulnerable to being caught in local minima, rather than being able to
bounce and tumble their way to the global minimum. They find themselves stuck in solutions that "sort of" work, but not really, and they may
have trouble freeing themselves from those partial solutions.

To get out of a local minimum, you have to get up and over a ridge.
If you think of the landscape as an error surface, moving upward means
increasing error. Thus, to get out of a basin, you need to increase error.
In terms of problem solving, sometimes to reach the best solution you
have to consider elements that seem wrong at first, and see where they
lead. More generally, to solve problems in life you have to be willing
to tolerate making mistakes – being wrong, appearing foolish to others.
It may be that depressed people are reluctant to do this, that they can't
tolerate increasing error, even temporarily. As a result, they don't try
out unusual problem-solving options, and they fail to escape from the
local minima in which they're caught.

Therapy

How can situations such as these be changed? The goal of therapy,
broadly speaking, might be viewed as moving the person to a minimum
that's closer to the optimal – a new attractor, one in which the problem is
more fully resolved or in which global adaptation is more broadly positive than it now is. Doing this requires some reorganization of what now

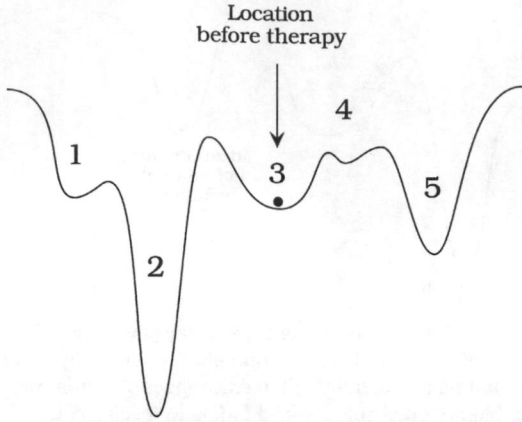

Figure 16.6. The goal of therapy: to move the person closer to the global minimum, a new attractor in which adaptation is better. Doing this requires a shakeup of the system. It requires destabilizing of the person's functioning, extricating the person from the current minimum. This permits (though doesn't ensure) the possibility of arriving at a more optimal attractor (2). Sometimes the result, though a change, is not appreciably better (5). Potentially the result can even be worse than the starting status (4).

exists. It may require some extra heavy shaking, maybe even jostling, of the "tambourine" of the person's life space (Figure 16.6).

It's recently been suggested that successful therapy has exactly this character (Hayes & Strauss, in press; Mahoney, 1991). Certain kinds of experiences in therapy (or outside it, for that matter) can jostle or destabilize the system (cf. Heatherton & Nichols, 1994; Miller & C'deBaca, 1994). If the system (the person) is sufficiently destabilized, it may bounce into a reorganization. The reorganization won't happen, though, unless the system is destabilized enough to shake it free of the current attractor. Without enough variability within the basin, the person won't get over the borders of the local minimum he's in now (well 3 in Figure 16.6).

This view argues that a new organization is potentially more stable, more adaptive and functional, than the preexisting one (Heatherton & Nichols, 1994; Miller & C'deBaca, 1994). That, at least, is the goal. It should be acknowledged that destabilizing the system doesn't itself ensure that the reorganization will be better than the prior organization. A person could jump from a dysfunctional organization to a worse one (the person in Figure 16.6 could hop up to well 4). An important issue may be how close in phase space the more adaptive reorganization is, compared to other local minima.

Obviously, there are forces in operation in therapy other than desta-bilization per se. Of particular importance is social influence from the therapist. A skilled therapist might induce movement in the direction of well 2, when the client might otherwise be in danger of bounding toward well 5. Well 5 – though different from well 3 – isn't appreciably deeper than well 3, and therefore isn't an especially desirable change.

Hayes and Strauss (in press) have recently applied the general line of reasoning sketched out here to an analysis of the process and out-come of cognitive therapy for depression. They examined transcripts of therapy sessions of 30 people in treatment for depression, looking for evidence of destabilization. Destabilization was assessed as variability in cognitive, affective, behavioral, and somatic aspects of participants' depressive patterns during sessions. Hayes and Strauss found that peri-ods of destabilization predicted later reduction in depression, consistent with the model.

Destabilization and the Metaphors of Dynamic Systems

If destabilization is an important precursor to therapeutic gain, it's im-portant to know what destabilization consists of. After all, you have to know what it is to be able to foster it. Hayes and Strauss operationalized it with an index formed from variability in different aspects of behavior, affect, and cognition (cf. Lang, 1979). But how should the process be viewed conceptually?

We've been discussing stability from the perspective of an attractor landscape. However, the metaphoric nature of the landscape differs from one discussion to another. How you think of the landscape can greatly influence how you conceptualize the creating of instability.

We've used several metaphors in our discussions of the landscape. In Chapter 14 we treated it as having a metaphoric gravitation, and we used the image of a shaking tambourine to reflect the temporary escaping of this pull. Many discussions treat it as an energy landscape or a temperature landscape (these discussions also include an implicit gravitational pull). Minima are conditions of lower energy or heat; ridges imply higher energy or heat. To move from one minimum to another requires a temporary increase in energy or heat (think hot-air balloon). Earlier in this chapter we added the image of an error surface, with higher levels implying larger amounts of aggregated error.

These various characterizations of the landscape have different psy-chological "feels." They also lead to different inferences about what it means to create psychological instability in a person whose life is in a local minimum. The gravity-and-tambourine view suggests you have to "shake" the system. The energy- or heat-landscape view suggests you "heat up" the system. To many psychologists, "heating the system" will translate to creating emotional arousal (cf. Hayes & Strauss, in press). The more emotional the client in therapy becomes, the more heated is the system, and the greater is the potential for change.

The error-landscape view suggests something a little different. In this view, what's needed is a temporary increase in overall error. The person must experience adaptational failures, errors in predicting the outcomes of transactions. (Of course, adaptational failure is one way to characterize the events that lead people to therapy in the first place.) If aggregated error becomes great enough, the person has the potential of escaping from one attractor basin into another, where the level of error is lower than in the previous local minimum.[1]

Thinking in terms of an error landscape raises two further associations. First, this view leads back to the theme of emotionality, albeit from a different direction. That is, it's consistent with the model presented earlier in this book to assume that negative affect is created by "error" (failure to move toward goals). It follows that more error leads to greater affect. This inference comes not from a metaphorical link, but from theory. It's worth noting that both landscape metaphors ultimately suggest greater affect as an indicant of greater instability. It's also worth noting, though, that the error-landscape view treats it simply as an *indicant* of instability, rather than as a precipitator of change.

The second association is a historical resonance to this discussion. Conceptualizing life space as an error landscape has strong overtones of the personal construct psychology of George Kelly (1955). Kelly argued that people use construct systems to predict their experiences. As long as they predict events fairly accurately, constructs retain their form. If predictive error gets too high, the construct (or something about how it's used) has to change. Kelly held that even very important aspects of

---

[1] There's something of a paradox here regarding the principle of investment or importance. Earlier in the chapter we argued that it may be necessary to decrease investment in a problem area of life – to move the person back from the hysteresis in the catastrophe surface – to get the person to try in the face of strong doubts. However, it's also obvious that people won't try to change their lives unless the problem (whatever it is) is experienced as important. Once again, the answer may be that a varying sense of importance is best. Too much investment and the person becomes paralyzed. Too little and there's no reason to change.

a construct system can be challenged by the failure to predict, yielding the experience of threat. Threat, according to Kelly, is the awareness of an imminent comprehensive change in one's construct system. To frame his view slightly differently, when accumulated error is getting larger, negative affect rises, and the person's way of dealing with reality may reorganize. This picture is remarkably consonant with the dynamic systems model described here.

EXTENSIONS

The application of dynamic systems ideas to the process of behavior change is relatively new. There appear, however, to be a couple of additional ways in which they can be applied. One of them concerns the idea that traumatic events can lead to a change process that may have a great deal in common with the principles described in the preceding section. The second concerns how to conceptualize the experience of psychological growth.

Destabilization, Reorganization, and Beneficial Effects of Trauma

A line of thought very similar to that underlying the Hayes and Strauss research emerges from Tedeschi and Calhoun's (1995) work on the idea that many people (though not all) experience positive consequences – even growth – after trauma. Tedeschi and Calhoun argue that the traumatic event initiates the potential for growth. They emphasize that for this to occur the event must be "of seismic proportions," shaking and partly destroying the person's world view (cf. Janoff-Bulman, 1992; Kelly, 1955). The choice of metaphor here is striking, when taken in combination with the metaphor depicted in Figure 16.6. Tedeschi and Calhoun weren't writing from a dynamic systems point of view, but their conceptualization shares much with it.

In their view, besides tremendous emotional distress (or perhaps because of it), trauma creates what in effect is a naturally occurring instance of the destabilization produced by therapy. Tedeschi and Calhoun suggest that growth begins with posttraumatic rumination, aimed at making sense of the world as it's just been experienced (cf. Martin & Tesser, 1996). Growth is reflected in the construction of a new, more meaningful world view or self-view. This reconstructed viewpoint permits the person to interact with the world in a more effective and fulfilling way than had been the case before the traumatic event. The result is a better adaptation (an attractor well that's closer to the global minimum) than existed before.

We should note that no one claims this experience is universal. The aftereffects of trauma vary greatly. Trauma victims experience tendencies toward both rumination about the event and avoidance of cues that remind them of the event (Foa & Kozak, 1986; Foa, Rothbaum, Riggs, & Murdock, 1991). If rumination has the potential of starting the person on the road to growth, that road is an uncertain one. Avoidance, on the other hand, might be seen as an effort to avoid further change – as holding tightly to one's present minimum no matter how distant it may be from optimal. Still, if some people do sometimes grow from trauma, it's important to understand that growth process.

Obviously there are great differences between experiencing a trauma and entering a potentially unsettling therapy experience. However, it's remarkable how similar these theoretical models are to one another. The shaking of the system that promotes change can come from an event that the world delivers to you, from a series of self-explorations, or potentially from other sources. Wherever it comes from, the argument is that the shaking opens the potential for a more adaptive reorganization of the self.

Psychological Growth

The preceding discussions concerned cases in which a person stuck in a local minimum is trying to move to the global minimum, and cases in which a traumatic event shakes the person from the local minimum. What happens, however, when the person *reaches* that global minimum? Is that the end? Is there no room for further development, further growth?

One answer to this question is that the landscape doesn't necessarily remain stable over time. It shifts and transforms, both through changes in external circumstances and through internal changes. There are sudden upheavals and erosions, as well as more gradual transitions, changing the shape of the surface. Thus far we've only occasionally touched on the idea that the landscape can change form (though it was implicit in some of what we said earlier in this chapter). Change in form is a distinct possibility, though, and it's a possibility that bears on the question of growth.

Keep in mind that the two-dimensional picture is an oversimplification, aggregating the error (or energy) in a multidimensional space. It

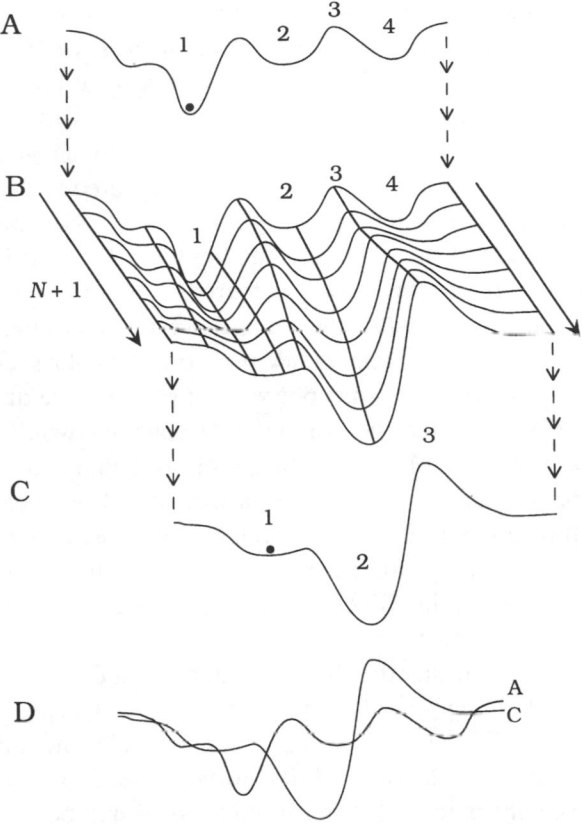

Figure 16.7.   (A) An error landscape in which N dimensions have been aggregated into the horizontal axis. (B) Taking another variable $(N + 1)$ into consideration by making the representation three-dimensional. This three-dimensional figure steps through seven shifts "forward" on $N + 1$ (for clarity in viewing, the "forward" dimension has been canted to the right). (C) The configuration of the error landscape of N dimensions, at the seventh level of $N + 1$ (the "front" face of panel B). (D) Juxtaposition of the starting landscape (at the first level of $N + 1$), in gray, and the final landscape (at the seventh level of $N + 1$). The form of the landscape has changed substantially.

uses the vertical axis to indicate the extent of energy or error (or whatever) in the aggregate and it condenses N dimensions to the horizontal dimension of the display (Figure 16.7A). Because this horizontal dimension is an aggregate, it's often hard to label it meaningfully.

Additional variables always exist that haven't been taken into account. Their values have been (or have been presumed to be) stable. Now it's time to think about one of them (call it $N + 1$). Think again of the portrayal of N dimensions in two-dimensional space. This is actually a display of those N dimensions *at some particular level* of $N + 1$.

But $N + 1$ can have other values. If it were to take on a different value, there could be major reverberations elsewhere. All the relationships among variables that were previously taken into account are potentially influenced by changes in this newly considered variable. That is, if $N + 1$ changed, the relations among the N variables previously taken into account could also change. (Another way of saying this is that variable $N + 1$ can *interact* with one or more of variables 1 to N.)

Here's a trivial illustration of the importance of this issue. All the known principles of behavior apply under the condition of a life-sustaining atmosphere. Remove the atmosphere (change the value of this particular variable $N + 1$), and the principles of behavior won't apply in quite the same way. As a less stark but more psychological example, consider the pattern of ways a man and a woman relate to each other during courtship and early years of marriage. These patterns are predicated on other constant conditions. Add a baby to the family (or a live-in mother-in-law or a crippling illness) and previously developed patterns may be subject to change.

Let's follow a little further the changing situation at different levels of $N + 1$. As $N + 1$ changes across several levels, you'd have something similar to Figure 16.7B. The "back" slice of that panel is the same as the line in panel A, and there are seven shifts "forward" on dimension $N + 1$. Across the seven shifts in $N + 1$, minimum 1 rises and becomes more shallow (and flatter, thus less stable). Minimum 2 deepens and shifts slightly to the left. Ridge 3 rises. Minimum 4 fades out and disappears.

The error landscape taking into account N dimensions at seven steps forward on dimension $N + 1$ is shown in Figure 16.7C (C is identical to the front face of B). It's obvious that it's very different from what's in panel A (see also D, which juxtaposes A with C). The person in panel A (the ball) was at the global minimum. However, as the situation changed (with increases in $N + 1$), *that basin is no longer the global minimum*. At this point on variable $N + 1$, the person would be better off in basin 2.

Let's go back to human terms again. If you've reached what appears to be your global minimum in your life space, you may feel as though you're done. Unless your life space is frozen, though, the sense of completion will be temporary. New forces constantly enter your life. Every time a new force enters from outside (a life event that changes the nature of your life space), or you develop a new dimension of your life from within, the landscape reconfigures. When it does, you may find you aren't in the global minimum anymore. It was the global minimum where you stood earlier, but now it may be only a local minimum.

As a more concrete example, consider a single person who hasn't been in a relationship in some time, and who's been depressed. Let's assume for the moment he's begun to see a therapist who is adept at fostering positive change. He succeeds in moving from the local minimum to a place that feels comfortable. He reorganizes the way he lives his life and the depression eases. His adaptation is far better, given his life situation. But now he considers an elaboration of his life space – tackling a new relationship. This changes things. As he tries to branch out, his adaptation to the changing circumstance isn't necessarily as good as it was to the previous niche, and his evolution must continue if he is to continue to approximate his global minimum.[2]

Viewed from this perspective, continued growth depends on the continued introduction of new dimensions of influence, new experiences that make possible erosion and reconfiguration of the landscape. Growth occurs when the person takes on new kinds of tasks, considers new possibilities, branches out in new directions – whether those changes are induced by decisions made by the self or by occurrences to which the self is exposed. The person who lives a sheltered life, who seeks constancy and sameness, who gravitates strongly to the predictable, may be extremely well adapted *to that niche*. However, he isn't growing.

---

[2] Remember that the flat landscape is an abstraction, reflecting an aggregation of the N variables taken into account thus far. Adding the new variable $N + 1$ increases the dimensionality of the system. Although this newly constituted system can be represented in three dimensions, as in Figure 16.7, it could also be represented in a flat landscape. Now, however, the horizontal axis would condense across a reality incorporating the many levels of $N + 1$ as well as variables 1 through N. If this were done, the shape of the two-dimensional line would be different from the original line, but it would also differ from any particular slice across Figure 16.7B. Rather, it would aggregate over those slices. Thus *either* moving to a new level of $N + 1$ *or* taking the full range of $N + 1$ into account would reshape the preexisting landscape, but in different ways.

What would be the psychological meaning of taking the full dimension of $N + 1$ into account? In the concrete example we used, the person's new adaptation wouldn't be to the new condition of having a relationship. Rather, the adaptation would be to the multiple possible levels of a relationship–no relationship continuum. It's arguable that such an adaptation wouldn't be optimal, that the person would be better off seeking a global minimum on whatever landscape he's presently inhabiting (whatever combination of levels on the $N + 1$ variables currently exists), rather than seeking a "universal" adaptation. In either case, though, the fact that new variables can always be recognized and responded to means that the person's evolution is never entirely complete.

This conclusion may not seem especially profound. It's more or less what common wisdom would dictate. However, there are multiple ways to react to that humbling realization. We derived the conclusion from considering a particular meta-theoretical conception of reality. The commonsensical nature of the conclusion may seem deflating. But it can also be comforting when an abstract conceptual analysis leads to a conclusion that converges with intuition and common sense.

17

Is Behavior *Controlled* or Does It *Emerge*?

Thus far in the book we've tried to build a conceptual edifice that portrays a self-regulating person, including problems. In this chapter we do something different. We raise the question of whether we've been leading you down a primrose path.

In our earlier discussions we evaded some questions. In this chapter we confront one of them, from several different angles (evading others successfully for the rest of the book). In particular, we've assumed that self-regulation at the level of our interest tends to involve something resembling an executive process. People form intentions to do things, then they go and do them. But is this assumption necessary? Is it a mistake?

Conceptual bases for raising this question occur in several literatures. The literatures are intriguing, and the points they make are very different from those made elsewhere in this book. We address three of them here: the literature of coordinations (which leads us back into the domain of dynamic systems), the literature of connectionism, and the literature of robotics (see Montefiore & Noble, 1989, for other views on these questions).

COORDINATION AND COMPLEXITY EMERGENT FROM SIMPLE SOURCES

The literature of coordinations focuses largely on coordination of physical movement. This literature is substantial, dealing with many interesting questions (e.g., Kugler & Turvey, 1987; Turvey, 1990), but our present interest is confined to a few of its themes.

Theorizing on movement control and coordination has been guided partly by the recognition that the number of muscle groups and joints in the body yields a huge number of potential combinations of instructions for movement, a number so large as to be computationally intractable (the "degrees of freedom" problem – Bernstein, 1967). This led quickly to the idea that a general command from an executive is carried out by loosely coupled subordinate systems, with the executive being ignorant of the details of the subsystem's functioning, despite having called it into action. This view appears compatible with the model presented earlier in the book.

Some Apparent Complexity Need Not Be Created

An idea emerging more recently is that complexity in the appearance of behavior can emerge from very simple processes. The complexity need not be either represented or controlled centrally. A related theme is that a lot less has to be managed by active controllers than may seem to be the case. That is, movement isn't all about controlling. Movement takes advantage of physical properties of the body and its relation to the environment. For example, the force of gravity causes downward movement. There's no need to take an action to make a limb go down. If upward effort relaxes, the limb goes down on its own. Part of understanding movement, then, is realizing when control is necessary and when the laws of physics are actually doing most of the work (Greene, 1982).

Recent work on coordination also emphasizes the study of rhythmicities, oscillatory movements (cf. Gallistel, 1980). Such movements, viewed as dynamic systems, evolve over time. After initial variation, they settle into a regular pattern, which can be viewed as an attractor. There's evidence that the patterns that come to exist in coordinative movement have a describable phase space and that they undergo phase transitions.

A simple example is what happens if you coordinate your index fingers in a table-tapping task with the fingers out of phase: one up, the other down. Now do it faster and faster. At some point, your coordination jumps – abruptly and involuntarily – to an in-phase coordination: both up, both down (Kelso, Scholz, & Schöner, 1986). Apparently no higher mental controller requests this change in the organization of your behavior. It emerges from the nature of the task and your management of its simple elements.

Another example of a phase transition in movement coordination is the shift from walking to running (in humans), or from walking to trotting to cantering (in quadrupeds). These shifts in gait seem to follow a rule, but they're not thought out and planned by a set of executive processes. The rule reflects the laws of physics: Gravity returns a limb to its equilibrium position according to a formula involving limb mass, limb length, and gravity. To stay in stride (moving through the air), the animal must become a biological spring to counter this force.

Different gaits require the creation of springs with different amounts of torque. While a horse is walking, the spring's torque is equal to gravity's torque. It's six times larger while the horse is trotting, and nine times larger while it's cantering. The same ratios seem to hold for other four-legged creatures. For this reason, it's been suggested that these ratios of torque are universals in the gaitedness of quadrupeds, that they reflect a natural exploitation of the laws of physics in the process of locomotion (Turvey, 1990, p. 947).

What's important at the moment, though, is this: These torque ratios aren't "programmed in" or requested by an executive. Rather they "fall out" as self-organized tendencies deriving from properties of the environment in conjunction with properties of the organism.

One apparent determinant of attractor regions in the phase space of gaitedness is efficiency. Each gait of a quadruped has an energetic efficiency curve running from low to high back to low. As a horse moves from the lowest speed that it can sustain in a given gait to the highest, it starts inefficiently, becomes efficient, then becomes inefficient again (Hoyt & Taylor, 1981; Kelso, 1995, pp. 71–72). Horses tend to locomote in the most efficient part of the range. Thus, if a trotting horse is slowed too much, it will tend to speed up again. If it gets going too fast, it will tend to slow down.

If a horse that's trotting efficiently wants to go faster, it won't shift to just a *little* faster. To keep trotting faster would cost efficiency. If it shifted to a canter at the slightly faster pace, it would be an inefficient canter. Instead, the horse would pick up the pace a *couple* of notches, shifting into efficient-canter zone. The efficient range of each gait is an attractor, and the horse makes phase transitions from one attractor to another as its rate of forward movement changes.

Thus, for the most part, horses tend to move in three fairly restricted speed zones, rather than employing the entire available range (Figure 17.1). This isn't because they like those speeds as *speeds*. It's because those speeds are less work, given the structure of their bodies. Those ranges are attractors, but that fact appears not to derive from executive decisions. It derives from the nature of physical reality and the tendency to maximize efficiency. (On the other hand, there remains a question about whether the tendency to maximize efficiency is intrinsic or simply a matter of preference in the absence of a compelling reason to do otherwise).

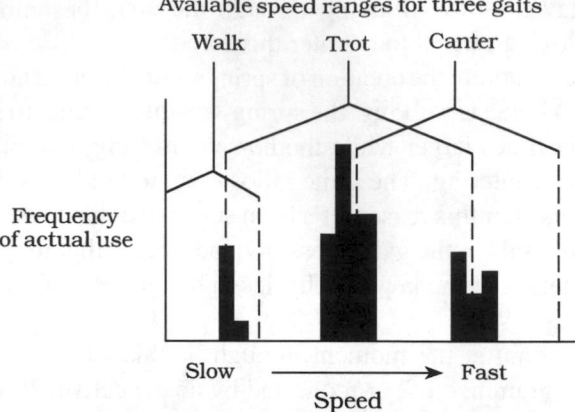

Available speed ranges for three gaits

Figure 17.1.   Speeds of movement of horses allowed to locomote freely. Although the gaits overlap substantially in the range of speeds at which they can occur, the horses strongly prefer the portion of each range that's energetically efficient for them. Thus they tend to travel at certain speeds (which act as attractors) and almost never travel at other speeds unless forced. (After Hoyt & Taylor, 1981.)

Properties Emergent from Social Interaction

The idea that patterns of coordination fall out of the structure of the body and the environment, and the idea that complexity emerges from simple actions, have been taken up by people interested in social behavior. For instance, Newtson (1993, 1994) has argued that the organization seen in dyadic interaction also has emergent properties, qualities that aren't represented in the goals of either interactant.

Newtson's metaphor for interaction is a wave. Waves can be portrayed by the simple parameters of intensity, frequency, and phase. In interacting, each person generates a wave of behavior. The wave generated by each person influences the other's wave, so that they acquire a relationship to one another. Newtson says that people don't have wave-generating mechanisms inside; rather, the wave pattern is emergent and self-organizing from the flow of interaction. He's studied the interactions of a number of dyads and found evidence of regular waves of body-position change in all of them. The wave in a conversation consists of periods of little position change punctuated by brief bursts of high-magnitude change.

It seems that the periodicity of an interaction arises from the process of interacting, rather than simply being brought to the conversation by either person. Perhaps the best evidence of this comes from Jaffe and Feldstein (1970), who had each person in a sample interact with each other person. They found that dyads had regular patterns of turn length, which were generally stable across an interval of several weeks. The patterns were unique to the dyad, though, and were not easily derived from only the characteristics of the individual interactants.

Aspects of the pattern of social interaction, then, may be emergent from the process of interacting. This line of thought raises the possibility that large amounts of what appears to be executive-driven complexity in behavior is actually emergent from the intersection and interweaving of simpler processes.

Does Emergence of Some Imply Emergence of All?

The idea that coordinations are a surface complexity that's emergent from the action of simple systems is an interesting one that's worth examination. It's not clear, however, that this is an all-or-none question. Kelso, a leading proponent of concepts of self-organization and emergent coordinations, devoted a chapter of his 1995 book to intentions. We should acknowledge that he did this primarily to show that intentions aren't as important as most people think. He noted, for example, that a body's preexisting coordinations place constraints on intentions (it's hard to form the intention to do something for which your body doesn't have the action coordinations). He also pointed out the ironic fact that carrying out an intention to perform a behavior can take longer than it takes to do the same behavior as a *reaction* (which makes it seems as though intentions are more detrimental than helpful).

Nonetheless, it's clear from his discussion that in Kelso's dynamic systems view of action, intentions *can* influence action. He stops well short of treating intentions as involving an executive. "Rather than playing the role of a program sending instructions, intentionality is viewed as an integral part of the overall orchestration of the organism. Formally, an intention is conceived as specific information acting on the dynamics, attracting the system toward the intended pattern" (Kelso, 1995, p. 141). Thus, intentions act to nudge the system toward a given attractor basin. Kelso didn't characterize the nature of this nudging, though, other than to say what it's *not*.

Despite this hesitancy, Kelso seems to accept that two different kinds of influence on behavior can happen at once. In describing an experiment in which subjects tried to resist the self-organizing tendency to tap in-phase at higher speeds, he wrote that "all subjects were able to intentionally maintain the anti-phase pattern . . . even at frequencies well beyond each subject's *spontaneous* transition frequency. Thus, [the person] is able to intentionally sustain a pattern that is intrinsically unstable. This is because, in our theory, an intention, as a crucial part of the dynamics, is able to change the stability of the attractors.... *Yet the presence of the intrinsic pattern dynamics – preferred coordination tendencies – is always felt*" (1995, pp. 151–152, original emphasis).

From this account it appears that Kelso's conceptualization of emergent coordinations is not intended to supplant models in which executive control plays a role (see also Aslin, 1993, p. 393). Rather, he wants to emphasize that other forces are at work, interweaving with, and constraining, the intentional processes. His language implies that he believes both exist.

Two Modes of Functioning?

Surely there is good reason to suspect there are rhythmicities and cycles in human behavior that haven't yet come to light, which may have important influences on human experience that haven't been well appreciated. There's also reason to suspect that there's merit to the idea that patterns in behavior self-organize in the initial stages of their emergence (Smith & Thelen, 1993). Yet it also seems reasonable to suggest that emergent patterns eventually stabilize, that information about their nature is coded into memory in a form in which the patterns can then be invoked for re-creation by an intentional process. To put it differently, the bottom-up processes of self-organized pattern development may consolidate in a way that leaves an entry point for top-down processes.

Does such consolidation occur? Clearly something like this happens. One result is a reduction in, and possibly even disappearance of, the variability that Kelso (1995) sees as the hallmark of phase transitions: "It is surely not surprising that it is difficult to observe critical fluctuations when a horse changes gait. Any self-respecting horse would want to change gears smoothly without subjecting itself to erratic fluctuations" (p. 71); "... any complex motor skill looks natural and smooth when performed by pros" (p. 74). Something changes, as behaviors – even self-organized coordinations – are repeated over and over.

Does this consolidation leave an entry point for intentional triggering of the behavior? The evidence is less explicit here, but Kelso's characterization of the self-respecting horse suggests that it does. "Want[ing] to change gears smoothly" sounds suspiciously like the preference of an executive process.

We do not mean to imply that one mode of functioning is important and the other not. They seem complementary. Executive use of compiled capabilities can't happen without emergence and consolidation of lower-order coordinations. Yet it seems very unlikely that people behave entirely on the basis of situationally emergent coordinations, with no top-down direction at all. As Aslin (1993, p. 393) noted, the dynamic systems perspective addresses how the specific implementation of a goal-directed behavior can be "assembled" during the act itself, but it doesn't really address where the goal comes from to which the act is directed. Thinking about that overall goal seems more consonant with a view that assumes the existence of some sort of executive process.

CONNECTIONISM

The previous section dealt with the idea that complexity in the surface appearance of behavior can result from the activity of very simple processes, without the complexity being represented or controlled centrally. This idea is also contained in another literature in psychology.

This body of theory has generated a good deal of interest in cognitive psychology and is doing so in other areas as well. It's known by several names. Today it is most frequently called *connectionism*. Other labels include parallel distributed processing (PDP) (McClelland, Rumelhart, & PDP Research Group, 1986; Rumelhart, McClelland, & PDP Research Group, 1986) and neural networks (Anderson, 1995; Caudill, 1992; Levine & Leven, 1992). The label *PDP* derives in part from the idea that the human nervous system doesn't process the world sequentially, but rather has many different flows that occur in parallel. Further, it reflects the idea that a given representation isn't centralized in one place but is distributed across a network of nodes. The label *neural networks* derives from the use of neuronal organization as a metaphor for thinking about cognitive processes. Thus the neural network is a neuron-*like* system. It should be kept in mind, however, that the link between these conceptual systems and the nervous system is tenuous and metaphorical.

Connectionists seek to model thought processes in networks of simple neuron-like units, in which "processing" consists of passing activation among units in parallel. As in neurons, the signal from one unit to another can be an activation (excitatory) or a deactivation (inhibitory). Energy passes in only one direction (though some networks incorporate

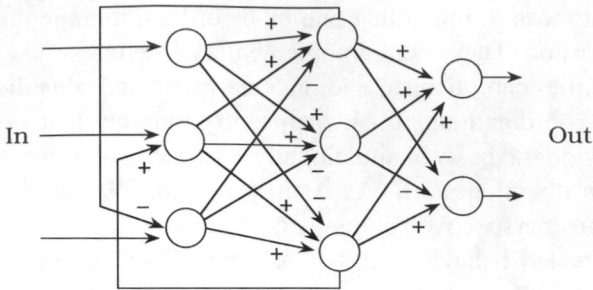

Figure 17.2.   A connectionist network consists of a set of units linked by unidirectional paths of activation, and (sometimes) feedback circuits in which a unit farther into the network activates a unit earlier in the network. The activation can be excitatory (+) or inhibitory (−). The input enters the network as activation to one layer of units and eventually leaves the network as activation from another layer.

feedback links). The network reacts to an input stimulus by generating a pattern of activity. This activity is transmitted through the layers of the network from the input side to the output side (Figure 17.2). The pattern that emerges on the output side is the response to the input stimulus.

Processing in a network proceeds entirely by the spread of activation. There's no higher-order executive to direct traffic or control the processing. Further, in a distributed connectionist network, knowledge is not represented in a central way, or as nodes of information. Rather, knowledge is represented in terms of the *pattern* of activation taken by the network as a whole. Thus knowledge is distributed.

Perhaps the most interesting aspect of these networks is that the activation passed from one unit to another isn't fixed; rather, a learning rule specifies how the activation weight changes in response to experience. This feature of the network reflects the assumption of neuroscientists that the physical basis of memory is changes in the strengths of connections between neurons. Thus, a learning function that changes the weights of inputs mimics what's believed to occur during learning in the nervous system.

Some connectionist networks have only unidirectional connections, with no feedback relations among nodes. Messages (activation levels) are sent forward from input to output in a single sweep. The weights in such a network are updated only once in a given "event," though the network can experience a large number of events.

Although this type of network can do some interesting things, of greater interest are networks with connections that yield feedback relations.[1] Describing the elements of the feedback here is a little tricky. In effect, in a network with feedback, "error" occurs when the input to a unit that makes a feedback projection causes the unit to pass its threshold for sending a message onward along its projections. Since the sending doesn't distinguish among the various projections, this message is fed backward as well as passed forward.

The pattern of weights and activations is updated repeatedly – thus modifications are made iteratively throughout the network, clarifying the pattern. In such a network, processing occurs dynamically across a large number of cycles. The activation of each node is updated repeatedly, as are the weighting functions involved in summing the activation. Gradually these values asymptote, as error signals are minimized, and the system "settles" into a configuration. This settling reflects the least amount of overall error the system has been able to create, given its input and the weights with which it began.

One way to think about this process is that the system simultaneously satisfies multiple constraints that the elements create on each other (Thagard, 1989). For example, two mutually inhibitory nodes can't both be highly active at the same time. These constraints among the nodes are settled out during the iterative updating of activation levels.

Networks incorporating feedback are dynamic systems, in that they are subject to multiple influences and are often sensitive to small initial influences. Not surprisingly, then, there are a number of links between connectionist thinking and dynamic systems thinking. One of these links is that the phase-space landscape used to discuss dynamic systems also appears here, as an error landscape (Anderson, 1995, chap. 9). Neural nets attempt to minimize overall error, working their way to one of the minima on the error landscape, which act as attractors. As usual, there are both local minima and a global minimum. If the system settles into a local minimum, it retains more aggregated error than would be the case if it had attained the global minimum.

How does a network wind up in a local rather than a global minimum? The answer depends partly on the learning algorithm that adjusts the

---

[1] A strategy called *backpropagation* is often used in networks with no feedback projections. Backpropagation is a way to create informational feedback without such projections, by sending information about error back through the same connections that sent the activations forward. This tactic produces interesting results, but as Anderson (1995, chaps. 9 and 10) pointed out, it has problems. Most important, it doesn't fit what's known about real neurons. There's no indication that weight adjustments go backward along axons. In contrast, there's a great deal of evidence of downward projections – actual feedback links – from a given part of the nervous system to a lower part.

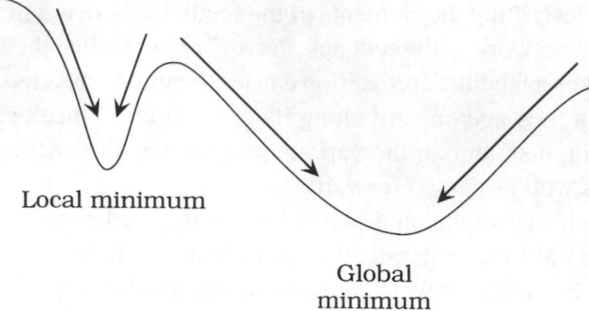

Local minimum

Global
minimum

Figure 17.3.   A learning algorithm that opts for the largest available reduction
in error is vulnerable to being captured by a local minimum that has a steep
slope (thus yielding fast reduction in error), preventing it from attaining the
global minimum if the latter has a more gradual slope.

weights.[2] If, for example, the learning algorithm opts for the largest
reduction in error in each next step, the system will tend toward a minimum that has a steep descent, regardless of whether its ultimate depth
is the global minimum (Figure 17.3). If the algorithm instead permits
temporary increases in the system's "energy," it will permit the system
to rise out of the local minimum, bounce over the ridge between this and
the global minimum, and make its way into the latter.

If you think of the landscape as an error landscape, this latter tactic
means temporarily increasing overall error. This literature thus suggests
the same conclusion as we suggested in Chapter 16: Being intolerant of
error in the short run can be counterproductive in the long run.

This idea also suggests a way of inducing a system into its global
minimum (Kirkpatrick, Gelatt, & Vecchi, 1983): Raise the "energy
level," creating easy movement, then gradually reduce it. Given high
initial energy, the system can bounce into the global minimum by the
time the energy becomes low enough to impede movement. As energy
drops, the system will be caught there. A critical question is how fast
the reduction should be. If it's too fast, the system may not have found
its way to the global minimum. If it's too slow, the process may take
too long to be acceptable. Another way to frame this question (returning
to the error metaphor) is how long should large amounts of error be

---

[2] Note that the learning algorithm of a connectionist network is usually specified by the
researcher. This begs the question of what defines the algorithm in a naturally occurring
system. Presumably, some are genetically specified and others are acquired. However,
the process of specifying one algorithm rather than another looks suspiciously like a
higher-order process influencing the nature of a lower-order process. Thus, although
connectionist models are portrayed as involving no executive function, some such
function may actually be implied in the specification of the model itself.

tolerated? If you try to eliminate error too fast, you risk being caught in a local minimum (cf. Schmidt & Bjork, 1992). Letting error go on too long, on the other hand, has other costs (cf. the well-known tradeoff between accuracy and speed).

Need Everything Be Distributed?

As indicated earlier, a distributed connectionist view holds that the nervous system represents reality as patterns of activation. The same network of units represents different events by different patterns. The representation isn't centralized, but is distributed across the network in the form of weights of various links and activations of various elements. Such a massively parallel and distributed manner of representation does not seem to comport well with the idea of an executive process.

Not all connectionists accept the assumption that representation must be distributed this way. This difference of opinion within connectionism has serious implications for the issues we're interested in here. One camp (the PDP group) holds the view on representation we just sketched out: Representation accrues to the pattern in the entire network, so that a concept or a hypothesis is a pattern of activation across multiple units (Figure 17.4A). There's no single place where the concept is represented.

Another camp (called localists) permits nodes in a network to have meaning, so a single unit can represent a proposition or hypothesis (e.g., Feldman & Ballard, 1982; Thagard, 1989).[3] Thus (Figure 17.4B), one node might have information about ethnic identity, another node might contain a hypothesis about a personal characteristic (hostility). The nodes are linked either by excitatory connections (implying positive association in memory) or inhibitory connections (implying that the two nodes hold incompatible information).

These localist models are parallel in functioning, but their representation is not distributed in the sense emphasized by PDP. In effect, the localist models take the spreading-activation models of nonconnectionist cognitive psychology, embed the feature of inhibitory connections, and add the connectionist idea that the network makes multiple parallel

---

[3] Additional confusion stems from the fact that the term connectionism has multiple referents. Many now use it to refer collectively to a wide range of theories that differ substantially in their assumptions. However, it first was identified with the more specific view now known as localist. Indeed, Smolensky (1988) says the label parallel distributed processing was chosen to differentiate between the distributed models and the localist models. In some discussions, however, localist models are treated as poor representatives of connectionist thinking (e.g., Smith, 1996), thereby reversing the association between label and camp.

A Distributed: Nodes contain no meaning

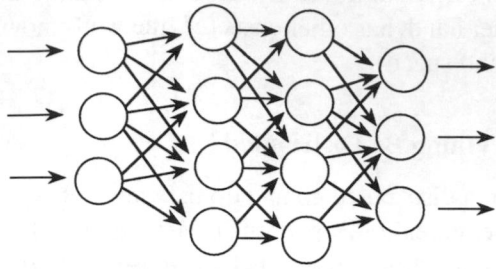

B Localist: Nodes contain meaning

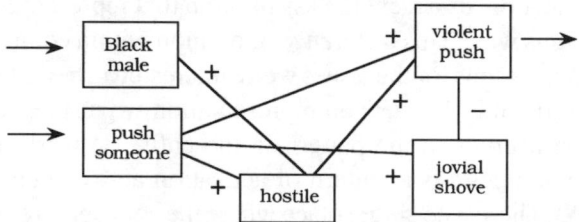

Figure 17.4.   Two kinds of networks. (A) In a network with distributed representation, meaning is inherent in the overall pattern of activation but not in
individual elements. (B) In a localist network, individual elements have meaning. This illustrates a hypothetical network of hypotheses acting as mutual
constraints in the mind of a White college student interpreting an event in which
a Black student elbowed someone else (Duncan, 1976). The presumption illustrated here is that the observer has a positive mental association between
Black males and the concept of hostility, and between the concept of hostility
and the inference of violence. (Panel B after Kunda & Thagard, 1996.)

iterations in order to come to mutual constraint satisfaction. Some argue
that models such as this poorly represent connectionist thinking, because
they model structure (in the form of parallelism and iterative cycling)
but not process (see Smith, 1996; Smolensky, 1988).

Whatever the ultimate resolution of this disagreement, it's clear that
the localist version of connectionism has had far more impact on personality–social psychology than has the distributed version (see Smith,
1996, for a different view). Read, Vanman, and Miller (1997) used this
model to discuss a variety of issues in social psychology, including a
fresh look at gestalt processes; Kunda and Thagard (1996) used it to
discuss impression formation; Schultz and Lepper (1996) used it to
analyze dissonance phenomena. In short, the idea of parallel constraint

satisfaction has had much appeal in social psychology, though the notion of distributed representation has not.

Let's examine multiple constraint satisfaction more closely. Think of each node as a hypothesis about the presence or absence of a feature in the input (Read et al., 1997). The precise meaning of nodes and links depends on the theoretical assumptions of a given model. Weights of links between nodes represent the extent to which the hypotheses support each other or contradict each other. The links thus represent constraints among hypotheses. Pairs of elements with positive connections are mutually supportive. If one is active, it will try to activate the other. Pairs of elements with negative connections are contradictory or competing. If one is active, it will try to deactivate the other. The size of the weight is an index of the magnitude of the constraint.

The final activation pattern represents the solution of a settling-out process. The parallel constraint satisfaction process is an implicit attempt to create the greatest degree of organization across the network, consistent with the mutual constraints imposed by the relations among nodes. Thus, in the hypothetical network shown in Figure 17.4B, a constraint prevents the observed shove from being seen simultaneously as a violent push and as a jovial shove. Given a series of other presumed excitatory constraints (a positive link between Black males and the stereotype of hostility, and a positive link between the ideas of hostility and violent push), the result is an inference that the observed event was a violent push.

Planning and Goal-Relevant Decisions

The literature of connectionism is large and growing rapidly (e.g., Anderson, 1995; Arbib, 1995; Bechtel & Abrahamsen, 1991; Churchland & Sejnowski, 1992; Smolensky, 1988; Smolensky, Mozer, & Rumelhart, 1996; Murre, 1992). There have also been several recent attempts to indicate why these ideas are useful for the fields of social, personality, and clinical psychology (Caspar, Rothenfluh, & Segal, 1992; Kunda & Thagard, 1996; Read & Miller, 1998; Read et al., 1997; Schultz & Lepper, 1996; Smith, 1996).

Of particular relevance here is the discussion by Read et al. (1997) of two theories of goal-related decision making, based on constraint satisfaction models. These theories address ways to mediate among the influences of many goals (sometimes in conflict with one another) that are operative at any given time. The task is to produce behavior that's responsive both to the person's desires and to the constraints of the situation. These models also suggest new angles on planning, which is known to be less thorough than a perfectly rationalist account would have it.

One of these theories (Mannes & Kintsch, 1991) sees planning as starting with a set of imprecise production rules that activate a wide range of potentially relevant information. This vague picture of the situation is then integrated and refined, as a parallel constraint satisfaction process. Actions that fit together activate each other and inhibit or deactivate contradictory actions. In this theory, activation of an action also increases to the extent that its preconditions are satisfied. The result of iterations in this system is the induction of a plan that has a good deal of the necessary structure in place to move the person toward the goal.

The second theory (Thagard & Millgram, 1995) focuses on situations where alternative plans are already available, asking how a person chooses the best plan. It focuses on situations where the person has multiple goals, some of which are incompatible, and considers how these goals are balanced or traded off in selecting a plan. Thagard and Millgram hold that there's a coherence principle at work: The plans and goals that cohere best are the ones that are selected for implementation.

This model presumes the continuing evaluation of goals as well as of the plans or actions that serve as means to attain the goals. It also has a place for the idea that goals differ in priority or importance. This is handled by linking important goals to a special unit that recurrently sends them activation. (This has overtones of a model in which a close link to the superordinate sense of self renders a goal more important, as we argued earlier.)

It's important to reiterate that parallel constraint satisfaction models don't assume an overriding executive function that makes decisions. The decision regarding what plan to use is made from within the network. The decision *emerges* or settles out from the repeated updating of elements within the decision-making space. Even though localist models involve symbolic processing, they represent a very different view from one in which an executive process weighs evidence and renders a judgment.

We undertook this account of connectionism in order to address the same question about self-regulation as we considered in the context of coordinations. Specifically, is the model presented earlier in this book fundamentally challenged by the idea that representation is distributed, and that decisions are made without the need for an executive? We think not, partly because even some people who find a good deal of value in connectionist thinking assume the potential influence of an executive process, a point to which we now turn.

Dual-Process Models

Cognitive psychologists have tried hard to deal with issues raised by differences between the symbolic approach (which tends to assume an executive function) and the connectionist approach. In so doing, several have turned to the idea that thinking involves two processes rather than one. Smolensky (1988) argued that a top-level *conscious processor* is used for effortful reasoning and following of programs of instructions. An *intuitive processor*, which manages intuitive problem solving, heuristic strategies, and skilled or automatic activities, relies on connectionist processes. In this view influence can come from the top downward and also from the bottom upward.

This general idea recurs in several other theories (see Holyoak & Spellman, 1993; Sloman, 1996). Although theories differ, they characterize the two modes of processing similarly (see also Buck, 1985). What Smolensky called a conscious processor, Sloman (1996) called *rule-based* and Shastri and Ajjanagadde (1993) called *reflective*, implying deliberative and effortful. What Smolensky called an intuitive processor, Sloman called *associative* and Shastri and Ajjanagadde called *reflexive*, implying quick and spontaneous (see also Norman, 1986). Indeed, the general idea of two modes of functioning has been around for a long time, in discussions of the idea that the two hemispheres of the brain are specialized to engage in analytic versus holistic processing (e.g., Bradshaw & Nettleton, 1983; Gazzaniga, 1972).[4]

---

[4] An issue that goes beyond the scope of what we're discussing here concerns the relation between these ideas about hemispheric dominance and more recent ideas about frontal lobe function. As we noted in Chapter 9, some now argue that the right frontal area is involved in regulating avoidance behavior and in the experience of affects such as fear, and that the left frontal area is involved in appetitive behavior and in affects such as pleasure (Davidson, 1992a, 1992b). How do these ideas map onto older ideas about hemispheric dominance?

Might it be that regulation of aversive motivation is intuitively based, responsive to novelty, bound up with "information that does not readily lend itself to verbalization" (Lezak, 1995, p. 61)? Is the regulation of appetitive motivation intrinsically more linear and sequential, more rule-based and elaborated? This would fit the idea that avoidance of danger is an evolutionarily more pressing need than is approach. That is, the cost of being killed once is much greater than the cost of having many false alarms (Nesse & Williams, 1995), and it's also greater than the cost of repeatedly failing to secure desired ends. Maybe people are wired such that the mechanisms managing avoidance are faster, more global, and more intuitive than the mechanisms that manage approach.

How do the subjective experiences of the two modes differ? When engaged in controlled processing, the mind in effect says, "Find a rule, apply it to the situation, carry out its logical steps of inference and action, and make decisions as needed. If no rule is available, come up with whatever's closest." This mode follows a process of deductive reasoning. When the mind is in connectionist mode, the settling process goes on until the elements shake out and a pattern emerges. This mode seems inductive (cf. Bechara et al., 1997). This characterization of connectionist processing is consistent with the notion that inductive thinking is especially creative, and the idea that creativity reflects the emergence of unexpected patterns. This mode fits the experience of insight – a pattern appears suddenly where none did before. It also provides a descriptive context for the experience of putting a problem out of mind (to let it incubate) and having a solution pop into mind later.[5]

How do the two processing modes relate to one another? The connectionist, multiple constraint satisfaction mode reflects something akin to what Kelso calls pattern emergence. Patterns emerge because there are constraints – physical and environmental – that mutually settle into a pattern that takes them into account. The other mode reflects intentions, a purposeful seeking out of regularities in memory to apply to the case at hand.

It might be useful to return briefly to a metaphor used earlier in the book – the administration of a university. Connectionist processing is roughly equivalent to a department's deciding that it wants to implement a new program of graduate training and taking this vision of its future to the dean for help in enlisting the support of the upper administration for the new program. The other mode of processing might be equivalent to a provost's deciding that some department isn't managing its affairs well and instructing it to behave in specific ways, trying to force it into appropriate action.

TWO-MODE MODELS IN PERSONALITY–SOCIAL PSYCHOLOGY

The idea that people experience the world through two different modes of processing, which emerged from this discussion of connectionism, also appears in the literature of personality and social psychology. Indeed,

---

[5] An interesting question is whether certain circumstances favor one or the other processing mode. Does meditation foster intuitive processing? Does cognitive load – performing some attention-absorbing activity – foster it, by limiting the intrusion of controlled processing?

two models from that literature show similarities to what we described in the previous section that are striking enough to warrant discussion (for treatment of a broader range of two-mode models, see Chaiken & Trope, in press).

Cognitive–Experiential Self-Theory

The depictions of two modes of processing by Smolensky (1988), Sloman (1996), and others bear a very strong resemblance to an argument in personality psychology made by Epstein (1985, 1990, 1994). Epstein's cognitive–experiential self-theory assumes the existence of two systems for processing information. The *rational* system operates primarily consciously, functions according to logical rules of inference, and operates relatively slowly. Epstein holds that this system is less important in day-to-day activity than most people assume.

In contrast, the *experiential* system is intuitive, is crudely differentiated, and operates by generalization, providing a "quick and dirty" way of assessing and responding to reality. As such, it relies on heuristics and information that's readily available. It functions automatically and in an experientially determined manner. Epstein argues that the more emotionally charged a situation is, the more a person's thinking is dominated by the experiential system.

Although Epstein's ideas don't explicitly rest on psychoanalytic thinking, there are resemblances. The experiential system has overtones of primary process thinking, whereas the rational system has overtones of secondary process thinking (Freud, 1962/1923). Similarly, Jung (1971/ 1931) postulated rational and irrational functions that influence behavior in varying degrees.

Epstein holds that both systems are always at work in normal humans, and that they jointly determine behavior. Each can be evoked to a greater or lesser degree under the right circumstances. For example, asking people to give strictly logical responses to hypothetical events tends to place them in the rational mode, whereas asking them how they would respond if the events happened to them tends to place them in the experiential mode (Epstein, Lipson, Holstein, & Huh, 1992). Being in the rational mode reduces (though it does not entirely eliminate) the tendency to use a well-known heuristic in responding to unexpected adverse events.

In another study that attempted to pit the two processing modes against each other (Denes-Raj & Epstein, 1994), subjects had a chance to win money by choosing jelly beans from one of two bowls on a series of trials.

Subjects viewed the two bowls before starting, but drew blindly from one or the other on each trial. The bowls differed in absolute number of winners, and they differed *in the opposite direction* in percentage of winners (e.g., 1 out of 10 versus 5 out of 100). Subjects often drew from the bowl with the larger number (but lower percentage) of winners. At the same time they admitted knowing that this put the odds against them. This result was taken as indicating that the experiential mode, seeing salient evidence of more winners, overrode the rational mode (which knew that odds are odds, no matter how many salient winners there are).

In Epstein's view, the experiential system is the default response resulting from eons of evolution. It's invoked whenever speed is needed. You can't be thorough when you need to act fast (e.g., when the situation is emotionally charged). Maybe you can't even wait to form an intention. Recall from an earlier section that it seems to take longer to form and execute an intention to act than to perform the same act in reaction to a stimulus (Kelso, 1995, p.141). This observation is very much in the spirit of Epstein's distinction between processing modes.

Deliberative and Implemental Mindsets

Another conceptualization that assumes two processing modes was suggested by Heckhausen and Gollwitzer (1987; Gollwitzer, 1990, 1996). This theory holds that there are important differences between the mindset that people have when deciding whether to adopt a goal and the mindset that they have once that decision's been made. The *deliberative* mindset is characterized by careful examination of competing goals, objective weighing of pros and cons of each. It's assumed to foster accurate and open-minded appraisal of evidence and thorough judgment processes.

The *implemental* mindset, taken up only once the decision has been made to commit oneself to attaining some goal, is aimed at serving movement toward the goal. It's oriented toward moving quickly and expeditiously to a positive outcome. It's assumed to have a determined, closed-minded, self-serving focus, biased toward thinking about success (Beckmann & Gollwitzer, 1987). There's evidence that people in implemental mindsets exhibit a variety of heuristic biases: They're more likely to perceive themselves as in control of their outcomes (Gollwitzer & Kinney, 1989) and to experience various positive illusions (Taylor & Gollwitzer, 1995) than people in deliberative mindsets.

Comparisons among Theories

The Epstein (1985, 1990) and Heckhausen–Gollwitzer (1987; Goll-witzer, 1996) theories developed from very different perspectives. Epstein wanted to understand how spontaneous and irrational aspects of human behavior coexist with more rational aspects of behavior. Heckhausen and Gollwitzer began with an interest in how achievement behavior takes place. Yet there are similarities.[6]

Both emphasize the idea that one mode of functioning is less careful than the other – more likely to show positive illusions and more likely to rely on heuristics than to examine the data thoroughly and dispassion-ately. Both models imply that this mode of functioning is less careful because it functions more quickly, more automatically than the other. The other mode – rational, or deliberative – is engaged less often but is capable of overriding the other system when decisions must be made (or reevaluated).

There are also important differences between the models. Heckhausen and Gollwitzer appear to have assumed that the implemental mindset

[6] A distinction between two modes of processing is also indicated in the writings of Mc-Clelland and his colleagues on motives and their assessment (McClelland, Koestner, & Weinberger, 1989; Weinberger & McClelland, 1990). Implicit motives, believed to be biologically based and automatic, are assessed through projective devices. Self-attributed motives, believed to depend on abstract cognition, are assessed by self-report. McClelland et al. suggest that implicit motives derive from early experiences with natural incentives, that they're more primitive and don't involve conscious me-diation. Self-attributed motives develop later, based on development of language and concepts of self, others, and values. The two assessment approaches aren't strongly correlated with each other, and although they both predict meaningful behavioral out-comes, they tend to predict different *kinds* of outcomes (for detail, see McClelland et al., 1989).

Several other topics in personality psychology also incorporate perplexing disjunc-tions between self-reports of psychological characteristics and less direct assessments of what are believed to be the same characteristics. Although this is speculation, we wonder whether these topics might also embody a distinction between an intentional, conscious processing mode and an automatic, intuitive processing mode. For exam-ple, one literature of optimism is based on self-reports of generalized expectancies (Scheier & Carver, 1992), another is based on the more diffuse quality of how people explain events (Peterson & Seligman, 1984). Although both measurements predict relevant outcomes, they don't correlate well. There's also a literature of adult attach-ment based on self-reports of attachment styles (Hazan & Shaver 1994), another based on an interview assessing recollections of childhood experiences (Berman, Marcus, & Berman, 1994; Cohn, Silver, Cowan, Cowan, & Pearson, 1992; Main & Goldwyn, 1991). Again, although both measurement strategies predict relevant outcomes, they don't correlate strongly. An interesting question is whether (in either case) there's a dichotomy among the behaviors predicted by the two sorts of measures that might resemble that found between the two ways of assessing achievement motives.

occurs only to attain the goal planned for by the deliberative mindset. There's little consideration in their writing of the possibility that the implemental mindset might roam around on its own, undertaking and carrying out actions. The latter possibility is clearly inherent in the Epstein model. Epstein says that people can engage their deliberative, rational system when they make the effort to do so, but he believes that *all* behavior is affected by the experiential system. For him, the issue is the extent of influence of that system.

Another important difference is that, according to Epstein, these two ways of thinking are at work simultaneously. One may dominate, but both are active. In the Heckhausen–Gollwitzer model, these two mindsets emerge at different times.

Two Automaticities

These theories – as the connectionist two-mode theories – tend to view the functioning of one system as involving greater automaticity than the other (though this is less true of Heckhausen and Gollwitzer's model than of the others). Further, they all appear to allow for *two distinguishable sources of automaticity*. In some cases, automaticity is inherent. A process is wired in, or it's newly self-organizing (see also Bechara et al., 1997). Epstein sees the experiential system as employing primitive, built-in tendencies, tendencies also present in infrahuman species. Implicit in connectionist thinking is the idea that patterns emerge on their own, arising from the (automatic) constraint satisfaction process.

The other source of automaticity is repetition (see Bargh, 1997). Given enough repetition, an activity may drop out of consciousness altogether. Having reached that point, the activity is now under the management of the experiential system or the implemental mindset. Smolensky (1988) argued similarly that when a behavior becomes automatic, responsibility for its management is being transferred from the conscious processor to the intuitive processor.

There are some loose ends to this depiction, which we'll try to tidy up with some speculation, drawing on an idea mentioned in the section on coordinations. Perhaps dynamic (connectionist) processes at a low level automatically (without intent) produce emergent patterns. After repeated emergence of a pattern, it becomes an attractor. After yet further recurrences it's easier to get into without excess variability or noise (cf. Kelso's 1995 discussion of the loss of variability in professionals).

This acquired ease of getting into the pattern implies that something is coalescing or consolidating in memory. The consolidated pattern – the emergent quality at the higher level – is now becoming recognizable to a rational or conscious mode of processing. At some point it can be invoked by the conscious processor as a guide to behavior, even if the ability to execute it from the top down is poorly consolidated. (Think of someone trying to learn to dance, who can be induced into reasonably coordinated movements – as *movements* – as long as he doesn't try to "dance," at which point everything falls apart.) With enough practice, the patterned information can be used top-down effectively, as well as reemerge bottom-up from another recurrence of the connectionist (or emergent coordination) experience.

With further top-down use, the application of the rule (whatever the emergent quality is) becomes more accurate (matches more closely the patterns that were initially induced bottom-up). Having become more accurate, it then begins to become more automatic. Gradually the awareness of using it fades, as there's less and less need to invoke it explicitly. The more it fades, the more its use may become a matter of management by the intuitive (connectionist) mode (Smolensky, 1988).

Presumably, there are differences between a pattern that's self-organizing in the early stages of consolidation (and thus emerges intuitively, if it exists at all) and a pattern that has been consolidated, made available to the conscious processor, and then rendered automatic by frequent use. Just what those differences might be is an interesting question.

AUTONOMOUS ARTIFICIAL AGENTS

Before concluding this discussion, we'd like to consider one more source of ideas regarding the organization of self-regulation. This final source is the literature of robotics. Robots are artificial agents. The fact that an agent can be designed and built to function in a particular way provides no assurance that a human being functions in remotely the same way. Nonetheless, work on artificial agents provides interesting hints about the plausibility of various kinds of organizations (Maes, 1994, presents a lucid review; see also Beer, 1995). Interestingly enough, there are parallels between recent developments in robotics and aspects of the issues we've been discussing.

One of the more interesting bodies of work in that area comes from the laboratory of Brooks and his collaborators (Brooks, 1986, 1991a, 1991b; Brooks & Stein, 1994; Maes, 1990a; Maes & Brooks, 1990). Brooks has taken the position that traditional work in artificial intelligence approached the problem of modeling intelligence backward. The goal was to implement in an artificial device some human function (e.g., vision, planning, etc.). The presumption was that when specific functions could be done artificially, they could be strung together as a coherent agent.

Brooks argues that a better starting point is creation of simple behaviors. From simple behaviors, complexity would emerge. Instead of creating *function*-specific modules (perception, planning, acting), he created *task*-achieving modules, each involving both perception and action qualities. Complexity is created by adding layers of modules. In this layering, the actions of newer (higher) layers may depend on the successful operation of lower layers, but they don't call on the lower layers as explicit subroutines. Brooks argues that this strategy represents a crude analogy of the process of evolution, in which basic capabilities remain in place but newer ones may be added.

One characteristic of his agents is that there's no executive (see also Rosenschein, 1985). Nor is there a central representation of the overall goal of the agent, or of the world in which it's functioning. Rather, each layer simply does what it does, and continues to act with its implicit goal in place. The goals of layers often are fully compatible (e.g., locomote, avoid hitting things, explore), but in some situations conflicts arise (e.g., locomotion would lead to a collision, which is to be avoided). Such cases are handled by a prearranged arbitration scheme – giving the layers different priorities so that a "higher" one can override a "lower" one. Because the arbitration scheme permits one layer to override another, it implies a kind of hierarchicality.

Complexity and Coordination

Another striking characteristic of the more elaborate agents Brooks has created is the emergence of surface behavioral complexity from the simultaneous (but generally independent) operation of very simple processes. One agent travels down the halls of the laboratory, enters rooms, and locates, picks up, and retrieves empty soda cans. That goal, however, is not part of the machine's design, nor is it represented anywhere. This robot has only specific action modules involving such action qualities as staying away from walls, approaching cylindrical objects, closing grips when an object is between its grippers, ungripping if an object is too heavy, retracing a path when the grippers are full. The agent comprising these modules goes down the hall, enters offices, notices cans, reaches for them, closes on them, lifts them if they are light (empty), and returns with them. It retrieves empty cans. But it has no intention of doing so, and no knowledge that it's doing so.

Most of the mobile robots in this research program locomote by means of wheels and electric motors. Thus, the researchers did not have to deal with the question of how to coordinate movement, except at higher levels of abstraction (e.g., coordinating moving forward with avoiding collisions). However, one robot – called Genghis – confronts the problem of coordination directly (Maes & Brooks, 1990; see also Beer, 1995).

Genghis has six legs, each separately controlled. Its programming has no provision for coordination. Every time Genghis is powered, it must reacquire the ability to walk. It learns, but there's no central repository of learning. Instead, each leg learns things on its own. Each leg starts with a random precondition list for its behavior (the behavior occurs only when the list is satisfied). The learning algorithm for each leg involves maximizing a success signal (delivered to the robot as a whole) and minimizing a failure signal (delivered to the robot as a whole), and correlating the leg's actions to the feedback signals. Gradually, the list of preconditions is altered. The behavior of the leg becomes active only under the conditions in which the behavior has been strongly and positively correlated with success and uncorrelated with failure.

When powered up, Genghis begins with random flailing and falling. Across a surprisingly short set of cycles, it learns to walk, with a characteristic "tripod" gait that re-emerges every time it learns. In this gait, three legs hold it up (two on one side, one on the other) and the other three move forward together (Figure 17.5). The learning is distributed. In this respect, the gait is also distributed. It isn't represented anywhere *as a gait*, but parts of it are represented in each leg. Interestingly enough, this gait appears to be universal among fast-walking insects (Graham, 1985).

These demonstrations raise questions about human behavior, questions that echo those addressed earlier in the chapter from the viewpoint of human movement control. How much of the apparent complexity of human behavior actually reflects the simultaneous operation of simple behavior qualities? How elaborate can behavior become without an executive? How wise is it to assume that goals underlie complexity and coordination?

Another View of Goals in Autonomous Agents

The agents Brooks created have stimulated a good deal of interest. However, not all of his assumptions have been adopted, even by those with whom he's worked closely. Maes (1990b, 1994) agrees with Brooks

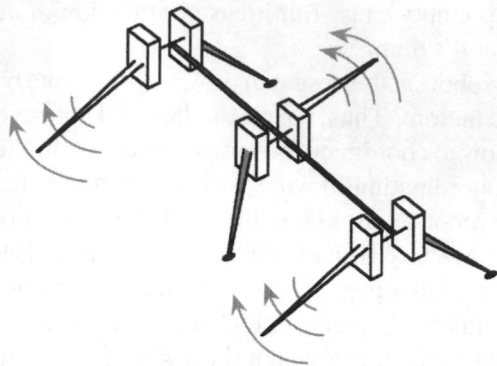

Figure 17.5. An artificial agent called Genghis has six legs, each of which controls its own behavior and does its own learning. When powered up, Genghis must learn to walk, using feedback delivered as a success signal and a failure signal. Surprisingly quickly, a "tripod" gait emerges (illustrated here), in which two legs on one side and one on the other stand still while the other three legs move forward. The gait looks complex, but it has no central representation. It is acquired anew from the learning algorithm every time Genghis is reawakened. (After Maes & Brooks, 1990.)

on many points, but disagrees on others. She believes that autonomous agents responsive to the situations in which they're acting can and should have goals.

Her approach retains the coupling of perception to action, and the decentralization and "distributedness" of action. It shares the idea of decomposing along tasks rather than in terms of input versus output systems. However, her approach explicitly acknowledges that it can be useful for an agent to have superordinate purposes with subgoals. Maes notes several advantages to the agent's having goals. Having a goal makes selection of action easier, because it biases the range of possible choices. Having a goal also permits the agent to take a next action that serves an overall desired result, even if that action doesn't seem advantageous from a narrow immediate perspective.

The action selection mechanism described by Maes (1990b) is an attempt to model action choice as an emergent property of a set of activation and inhibition processes, taking place with reference to the various actions the agent can take. There's no "decision making" as such, and again no executive. Rather, decisions emerge in a continuous way from the flow of changing activation levels of specific modules.

In effect, Maes has taken a production-systems approach in which a given act is triggered when its preconditions are satisfied, and welded it to a localist-connectionist network that iterates repeatedly to update current conditions. Unlike connectionist networks that yield categorizations as their output, the "categorization" reached by this network is the triggering of an action. Thus, in this system action is virtually the embodiment of perception (cf. Weimer, 1977).

In this approach the agent is a set of modules, each with a particular competence. Each module is executed (the action is carried out) when a list of preconditions is satisfied. The list of preconditions is modifiable through experience, both by addition and by deletion. Modules are connected through three kinds of links, which activate and inhibit one another. Both the current situation and the current global goals of the agent influence the network's pattern of activation.

At a given moment in time, activation levels of given modules represent their readiness to act. One might think of the total pattern as a current picture of the "best" actions to take, given the present situation, even if no action is currently called for (i.e., if the full list of preconditions for no action is presently satisfied). The algorithm that specifies the relations between modules and the values for various parameters is repeated indefinitely. At each iteration the system updates the activation levels of its elements and the satisfaction status of the elements' preconditions.

This network plans, but the planning doesn't involve a complete central representation of the steps of the plan. It's much more like the opportunistic planning notion discussed in Chapter 6. A general plan is in place, in the sense that certain goals are identified as important, but what the network actually does at any point depends on many situational variables. As Maes (1990b) put it, the network "does not construct an explicit representation of a single plan, but instead expresses its 'intention' or 'urge' to take certain actions . . ." (pp. 57–58).

Given its weighting and update scheme, this system has functional characteristics that resemble those of adaptive human behavior. The system favors actions that are goal-directed. It especially favors actions that contribute to several goals at once. It favors actions that are relevant to the current situation, thus exploiting opportunities and dealing with unforeseen circumstances. It favors actions that contribute to ongoing goal seeking, thus persistently sticking to what it's started unless there's an obvious advantage to shifting. It "looks ahead" to avoid hazards and conflicts.

Maes also took pains to ensure that the system could deal with a world about which it didn't know much. The system was devised to operate with incomplete – even incorrect – knowledge of the situation, and was constrained to operate quickly and with limited computational resources. Thus, the action-selection system wasn't designed to be optimal. It satisfices.

This model explicitly confronts the inherent tradeoffs between desirable tendencies in an agent's operation. The algorithm includes specifications for several parameters, including the threshold for an element to become active, the amount of activation that a true proposition injects into the network, the amount of activation a goal injects into a network, and the activation extracted from the network by a "protected" goal (one that's already been attained and is trying not to be undone). The values of these parameters can be used to "tune" the dynamics of the spreading activation of the system as a whole, thereby influencing the action selection that occurs (cf. Gallistel, 1980).

This tuning has systematic influences on action selection. For example, it can determine how single-minded versus opportunistic the agent is. A strongly goal-driven system is less reactive to the environment, takes less notice of alternative opportunities, and is less biased by what it sees in the situation and anticipates for the immediate future. In effect, there's a tradeoff here between goal focus and situation relevance. How this tradeoff should be balanced for an artificial agent (or for a person) depends on the nature of the problem space it needs to deal with.

There's also a tradeoff between following a plan in operation and being distracted by an emergent opportunity. If the system is too flexible, responding too readily to opportunities, nothing ever gets finished. The system is constantly distracted to new things. If it's too goal-focused, on the other hand, changing conditions are ignored, and the system fails to recognize both emergent opportunities and emergent problems. This is a critical issue in the functioning of people, as well – the balance of persistence versus distractability.

A common bind for artificial agents (and for human beings) is that sometimes an action that moves toward a goal in the short term creates a problem later on. The agent can get stuck in a local minimum. Maes addressed this issue, and again there's a tradeoff. In this case the tradeoff is between being overly concerned about a potential future goal conflict (so that too much evaluation occurs before any action is taken) and being too rigid about following a current action plan (so the system won't let go of an achieved subgoal to back out of a blind alley and try a different path).

There's also a tradeoff concerning thoughtfulness. If the threshold for activation is high, the spreading activation process goes on for a long time before a specific action is selected. If you set the threshold high enough, you tend to get an "optimal" solution, but there are two shortcomings: First, the agent may get bogged down in considering the effects of a broad array of actions that might be taken in the future, including actions that are so unlikely as to be not worth considering. Second, the process may take too long to be functional in a real-time world.

Comparison with Two-Mode Models of Thinking

Maes addressed these tradeoffs for very practical reasons. Her action-selection scheme was intended to provide a basis by which an agent could deal with situations it might confront in an unpredictable, and potentially hostile, environment. The tuning parameters she discussed create predictable problems for the agent if adjusted too far in one direction or the other. Simulations with this artificial system permit easy testing of the consequences of these adjustments, giving valuable guidance for planning real implementations of the algorithm in environments where performance has real-world consequences (as opposed to research consequences). However, the simulations also give some interesting clues about the nature of human behavior.

In particular, some of these tradeoffs could be characterized as pitting a comparatively rational way of dealing with the world against a more experiential and intuitive way (see also Arkin, 1990; Malcolm & Smithers, 1990). When tuning of the arbitration scheme yields a goal focus, avoidance of goal conflict, and thoughtfulness, the agent is displaying the pattern that Epstein terms rational. When the tuning produces a situational orientation, distractability, and impulsiveness, the agent is displaying influences that Epstein terms experiential. Because the action-selection scheme in the Maes model is a single processing entity, these two ways of dealing with the world don't coexist in her agent, as they do in Epstein's model. Nonetheless, the two patterns of tuning seem to fit the characterizations quite well.[7]

---

[7] This raises an interesting side question about two-mode models of thinking. Smolensky, Sloman, and Epstein all presume two sets of processes operating simultaneously. In contrast, Heckhausen and Gollwitzer wrote as though one mindset gives way to the other. The latter is more in line with the Maes algorithm, in which the (single) system is tuned to be biased in one way or another by shifts of certain parameter values. An interesting question is whether the two modes of Smolensky, Sloman, and Epstein are really separate systems, or whether instead they represent two ends of a continuum of tuning in processing style. We know of no evidence that addresses this question.

In considering this similarity, though, it's also important to note a difference. When we considered two-mode models earlier, we did so by way of suggesting a rapprochement between connectionist models without an executive and more top-down models that assume an executive. However, the behavior selection algorithm created by Maes has no executive, regardless of its tuning. It yields a flow of actions that's emergent from a network, even when its tuning is set to be "rational." This raises questions about the extent to which the presence of an executive needs to be assumed in human functioning, even when it involves apparently rational decision making and pursuit of goals.

CONCLUSIONS

The areas of work we've addressed in this chapter raise interesting questions and challenges about the nature of self-regulation. Many questions remain to be answered (and more questions doubtlessly will arise). Nevertheless, a few tentative conclusions can be drawn.

First, it seems clear that not all behavior is actively controlled. Sometimes apparent complexity and patterning occur for reasons that don't require explanation via internal mechanisms. An interesting set of problems will be to identify patterns arising from self-organizing tendencies, and to assess how large a role this pattern emergence plays in human behavior.

Second, the idea that people think in more than one way is worth further exploration. Maybe the differences between these ways of thinking will ultimately reduce to variations along a continuum, as the mind is cognitively "tuned" in different patterns at different times. Maybe there are substantive differences between two modes of functioning that are at work all the time. This is another interesting set of questions for the future.

Third, despite the challenges raised in this chapter, it doesn't seem to be time to dispense with the idea of a set of executive functions. Its role may prove to be less important in many human behaviors than initially thought. Ultimately, the notion may even prove to be wrong (cf. McFarland, 1989; McFarland & Bösser, 1993). But we haven't reached that conclusion yet.

Fourth, the idea of multiple constraint satisfaction, which emerges from the connectionist model, is useful in several areas of personality–social psychology. Aside from specific examples noted earlier in this chapter, this idea is also broadly consistent with the control-process approach to self-regulation (see also Narenda & Li, 1996). The attempt to attain multiple goals in your life space is a continual process of trying to reach one goal while handling the constraints imposed by the other goals. These constraints sometimes yield conflicts, but one way or another the conflicts are dealt with and behavior continues. Characterizing behavior as viewed in connectionist models, Caspar et al. (1992) wrote, "It is quite normal to deviate from how we actually want to behave ... and then to adapt and compensate" (p. 747). This characterization could be applied just as well to feedback models of behavior.

18

Goal Engagement, Life, and Death

Hope makes us live.
(Haitian proverb)

It is wonderful to have a plan. A plan can make the whole future
rosy.... To have a plan is like having a little canoe and even the
fiercest rapids can be negotiated.
(Stephen Dobyns, *The Wrestler's Cruel Study*)

He is not busy being born is busy dying.
(Bob Dylan, *It's Alright Ma [I'm Only Bleeding]*)

This book has focused on a particular way of thinking about how people
live their lives. Although a few complexities came up along the way, the
underlying idea is pretty simple: People live life by identifying goals
and moving toward them, and by identifying anti-goals and staying
away from them. Some goals reflect biological programming; others
stem from conscious weighing of alternatives; others arise from dreams
and fantasies and even from a self-organizing process of bootstrapping.
Whatever their origins, these values are the constellations people use to
guide their journey through life.

In this closing chapter we extend this way of thinking a step further,
with the assertion that goal engagement is a *necessity* of life. There
must be goals, striving toward one end or another, for life to continue.
Without goal engagement, life ceases. As has been true more than once
in this book, this assertion follows a path blazed by Miller, Galanter,
and Pribram (1960). They wrote, "Plans are executed because people
are alive. This is not a facetious statement, for so long as people are
behaving, some Plan or other must be executed" (p. 62). They also
wrote, "*complete* planlessness must be equivalent to death" (p. 112).

Miller et al. emphasized that in making those statements they weren't
focusing on concrete "attainment" goals for which striving has a specific
final end point. They envisioned the human being as an entity in which

many of the goals they called Plans are more dynamic and even ethereal. "It is not necessary ... to organize one's Plans in terms of frozen and brittle terminal states. Unlike good problems in science or mathematics, successful living is not a 'well-defined problem,' and attempts to convert it into a well-defined problem by selecting explicit goals and subgoals can be an empty deception.... It is better to plan toward a kind of continual 'becoming' than toward a final goal" (1960, p. 114).

That statement is very much in the same spirit as the conceptual model portrayed in this book. The view we described includes not only concrete goals but also goals toward which people strive recurrently or continuously, goals that are diffuse and ill-defined and have a long temporal course, and goals that are not met finally and forever. All of them play a role in the quality of goal engagement we're now discussing.

CONCEPTUALIZATION

There are several facets to the notion that goal engagement is critical to life. One concerns initial adoption and pursuit of a goal. Without initial engagement there's no movement, no action, no life. Another concerns the *continuance* of engagement. A beginning with no follow-through is hardly better than no engagement at all. Adopting a goal and continuing its pursuit are two sides of a coin. People need to have goals to adopt, and they need to be able to stay engaged with them.

Adopting a goal and staying engaged both depend on two variables. One is the goal's value. We don't take up goals that don't matter to us, and if we did we wouldn't persist at pursuing them when things got difficult. The other variable is sensed attainability. If the goal seems unattainable before we start, we don't try at all. If we continually fail to progress toward goals we've committed ourselves to, our lives lose meaning and the unattainable goals become like dust in our mouth. In contrast, hope is the holding onto valued goals, the remaining engaged in the feedback process, the attempt to move forward (see also Snyder et al., 1991).

These assertions, of course, resonate with generations of expectancy–value models of motivation (Atkinson, 1964; Feather, 1982; Shah & Higgins, 1997; Vroom, 1964; see also Lewin, 1948). In such models, if engagement of effort is to occur, there must be a goal that matters enough to try to reach it (value), and one must have sufficient confidence about its eventual attainment (expectancy). Neither value nor confidence has meaning without the other.

In much of the work that bears on this chapter's themes, hope or confidence has been used as a proxy for goal engagement. Less attention was paid to value. It shouldn't be concluded from this that value is irrelevant to these issues. But more evidence is available on the role of confidence and doubt. Therefore our discussion is necessarily somewhat unbalanced. In trying to focus on the need for commitment to pursuit of goals, we often emphasize the need to feel a sense of hope or confidence about the possibility of their attainment.

One more important part of the picture must also be considered. The loss of engagement in a goal is not necessarily followed by a vacuum of goal-lessness. Indeed, in Chapters 10 and 11 we discussed the ebb and flow of engagement and disengagement in terms of competition among goals. We suggested there that disengagement from one goal may simply reflect a weakening of attraction to it. Because people are commonly attracted to other goals, this weakening permits another one to become prepotent and behavior to shift toward *its* pursuit. The shift to the new goal is concurrent with (maybe even isomorphic to) the disengagement from the prior goal. Thus, often the loss of one goal is followed directly by pursuit of another one.

By taking up an attainable alternative, the person remains engaged in forward movement (Figure 18.1). This is particularly important when the blocked path concerns a central value of the self. People need multiple paths to these core values (cf. Linville, 1985, 1987; Showers & Ryff, 1996; Wicklund & Gollwitzer, 1982). If one path is barricaded, people need to be able to jump to another one. If someone who deeply values athletics is rendered paraplegic by an auto accident, he or she can participate in athletic events other than the ones previously preferred. If the person who has valued a sense of connectedness in a close marriage relationship loses his or her spouse, the sense of connection can be experienced in different ways. A couple trying to have children who discover they are infertile can have fulfilled and happy family experiences in other ways (Clark, Henry, & Taylor, 1991).

It seems likely that substituting a new path for an obstructed one is made easier by having clearly specified goals at the more abstract level. Someone who understands that the core desire is to *experience closeness* can more readily recognize that there are many ways to do this than can someone who's less clear about the nature of the higher-level goal. Whatever the mechanism, it seems apparent that the ability to shift to a new goal, or a new path to a continuing goal, is a very important part of remaining goal-engaged.

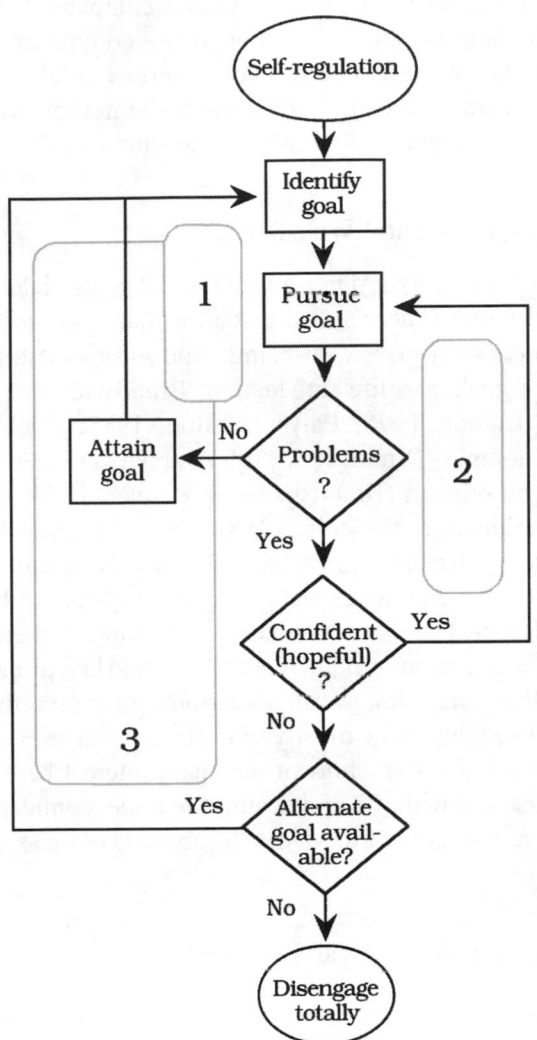

Figure 18.1.   Successful self-regulation is a continuing process of identifying goals, pursuing them, attaining them, and identifying further ones (cycle 1). Given adversity, a step of evaluating chances of success may be added (cycle 2), but sufficient confidence returns the person to the first cycle. If confidence is low enough, the person may seek an alternative goal (cycle 3); if available, it returns the person to goal pursuit and attainment. If, however, the original goal is seen as unattainable and no alternative is available, the person may disengage completely.

If there's no alternative goal, if nothing else attracts the person to act, disengagement from an unattainable goal is not accompanied by a shift, because there's nothing to shift to. Although the commitment to the unattainable goal may subside, nothing else emerges to take its place. This is the worst situation, where there seems to be nothing to pursue, no alternative to take the place of what's seen as unattainable.

Goal Engagement and Well-Being

In Chapter 8 we said that forward *movement* toward goals yields a sense of subjective well-being. There's also evidence that goal *engagement* per se relates to better subjective well-being. Studies show relationships between pursuit of goals and life satisfaction (Brandstadter & Renner, 1990; Harlow & Cantor, 1996; Palys & Little, 1983; Ruehlman & Wolchik, 1988), happiness (Smith et al., 1993), and less negative affect, depression, and neuroticism (Brandstadter & Renner, 1990; Emmons & King, 1988; Ruehlman & Wolchik, 1988). Having a strong sense of purpose and a strong investment in those purposes are related to both self-reported health and emotional well-being throughout the life span (Holahan, 1988; Reker, Peacock, & Wong, 1987). Indeed, there's even evidence that people in prisons remain more "sane" and less prone to violence if they're able to pursue long-term educational goals (Worth, 1995).

These effects of engagement mostly concern subjective sensations of well-being. They fall a step short of our main interest here. In this chapter we're concerned with life and death. Are hope, confidence, and goal engagement necessary for life? Does the absence of these qualities *threaten* life?

DISENGAGEMENT AND DEATH

Much of the evidence on this question concerns the giving-up tendency and how it's expressed. Most obviously, giving up is expressed in actions – in the stopping of effort and sometimes in the attempt to obliterate the awareness of the situation. Some of these expressions of giving up can be self-damaging, even if that's not the person's intent.

Doubt, Disengagement, and Self-Destructive Behavior

Sometimes people respond to the lack of hope, the loss of engagement, with strategic numbing of their awareness through such mechanisms as alcohol (Hull, 1981) and drugs. Pessimistic people – people who doubt that good things will befall them in their lives – are more likely to turn to alcohol to dull their sense of despair than those who hold out more hope for their future (Strack, Carver, & Blaney, 1987). By doing this, they're able to disengage themselves temporarily from the goals that elude them, and thereby free themselves temporarily from the pain of confronting the circumstances of their lives.

These are people who haven't yet truly disengaged from their goals (as we suggested in Chapters 12 and 13). They're trying to disengage, but are doing so only temporarily. This strategy is problematic in several ways. It appears to interfere with disengaging fully (and adaptively) from goals that are truly unattainable. It diverts people from engaging themselves with alternate goals that *are* attainable. It also can cause health problems and interpersonal problems.

Staying intoxicated is a kind of self-destructive behavior, but its self-destructiveness is indirect, a side effect. Sometimes the behavioral response to doubt is more literally self-destructive. If the doubt is deep enough and if an acceptable substitute goal is lacking, people sometimes take steps to disengage more quickly and more completely. This may be the essence of the impulse to commit suicide (cf. Baumeister, 1990).

In support of this line of thought is a 10-year followup of people who'd been hospitalized with suicidal ideation (Beck, Steer, Kovacs, & Garrison, 1985). While hospitalized, all completed a measure of hopelessness and a measure of depression. Ten years later, those who'd reported more hopelessness were more likely to have killed themselves than those reporting less hopelessness. The measure of depression didn't reliably predict suicide, but a single item on that measure dealing explicitly with pessimism about the future did. Conceptually similar results have been reported by others (Beck, Steer, Beck, & Newman, 1993; Fawcett, Scheftner, Clark, Hedeker, Gibbons, & Coryell, 1987; Petrie & Chamberlain, 1983). Thus, suicide may be the ultimate disengagement in response to a general hopelessness about life, reflecting a complete inability to shift to alternative goals.

Further support for this line of thought, albeit less direct, comes from the work of Chandler and his colleagues (Ball & Chandler, 1989; Chandler & Lalonde, 1995) on suicidal behavior among adolescents. This work stems from the argument that normal development requires adolescents to forge an understanding of how they (and others) can change in important ways over time yet remain themselves. In effect, such an understanding provides the basis for a self-goal that incorporates a sense of continuity far into the future. Without this sense of continuity, the adolescent loses an important reason for self-protection (i.e., in order to protect the future self).

Without this reason for self-protection, the adolescent may become more susceptible to self-destructive impulses because those impulses won't conflict as immediately or as sharply with self-protection goals. The result is the increase in suicide that occurs during the adolescent years. Consistent with this reasoning, Ball and Chandler (1989) found that adolescents at risk for suicide were less able than comparison groups to generate interpretations of how they (and other people) could change over time and still remain themselves. Without having this sense of continuity, adolescents apparently are more likely to lose their bearings and respond behaviorally to impulses leading to self-destruction.

Chandler and Lalonde (1995) also reported intriguing findings concerning suicide among members of various Canadian First Nations tribes. The tribes vary enormously (by a factor of 250) in suicide rates. In an effort to discern why, Chandler and Lalonde examined the degree to which specific tribes were trying to retain or recover their aboriginal rights. The tribes with the lowest suicide rates all had recently gone to court to reassert rights to cultural self-determination. Among tribes with high suicide rates, none had done so. This pattern suggests that engagement in the struggle to attain and hold onto a cultural identity serves to engage people in the struggle of life itself, thereby diminishing the likelihood of self-destruction. This finding is consistent with terror management theory (Greenberg et al., 1986), which maintains that people hold the fear of death at bay by affirming the values of their culture. In the case studied by Chandler and Lalonde, however, it's not just fear of death that's held at bay by cultural affirmation, but impulses to hasten death.

Disengagement and Passive Death

The preceding section dealt with two overtly behavioral manifestations of the giving-up response. Other data suggest that the giving-up tendency also can be expressed physiologically. Evidence on this point is sketchy but provocative. Apparently not all hopelessness-induced death involves overt self-destructive actions. Popular wisdom has long held that human beings (and other animals) can die from a loss of the "will to live." The folklore of many cultures also contains the idea that people can die from hexes or curses. Such deaths have been documented often enough to confirm the reality of this phenomenon (see Cannon, 1942).

What causes it? Apparently it's not a matter of making up one's mind to die, an active choice of self-destruction by exerting control over one's body. Rather, it seems to be a matter of developing the conviction that one is *bound* to die (cf. Cannon, 1942), that survival is impossible, hopeless, beyond reach. Dying in these cases is the result of failing to keep living.

Seligman (1975, chap. 8) has argued that these cases represent a profound and complete giving-up response. The person under a hex believes his death is inevitable, and so succumbs (see also Phillips, Todd, & Wagner, 1993, regarding "ill-fated" persons). The same reasoning has been applied to people who died in Nazi concentration camps without clear physical causes, apparently from profound hopelessness (Bettelheim, 1960). Apart from such extreme cases, it's been argued that people who experience a deep loss may be at risk for death from the broad sense of despair and loss of hope for the future stemming from that loss (Engel, 1971; Lefcourt, 1973). Researchers have observed that wild rats forced to confront hopelessness of escape have died by failing to continue the struggle to live (Richter, 1957) – death coming from a slowing and stopping of the heart (though see Kamarck & Jennings, 1991, regarding the many complexities underlying sudden cardiac death).

DISENGAGEMENT, DISEASE, AND DEATH

Cases of sudden and unexplained death are dramatic suggestions that a pervasive giving up (the experiencing of a broad disengagement from efforts at continuing life) can cause death. They don't establish the case unequivocally, of course, and they're rare enough to be hard to study. However, the same logic can be applied more broadly, to the idea that the psychological experience of doubt and disengagement may render people more vulnerable to disease onset, poor response to treatment, disease progression, or death from disease.

Disengagement and Disease Vulnerability

Several studies suggest that engagement is related to disease vulnerability, though much of the evidence bears on fairly minor illness. One project suggests that engagement in relatively high-level goals (the things Miller et al., 1960, seemed to have had in mind regarding the importance of Plans) is inversely related to vulnerability to a variety of minor illnesses (Emmons, 1992; see also Holahan, 1988). Another recent study (Cohen, Doyle, Skoner, Rabin, & Gwaltney, 1997) suggests that engagement in diverse social relationships can protect people against the common cold.

Susceptibility to health-care visits and vulnerability to the common cold are interesting, but they don't have much of a life-or-death flavor. At least one study, however, suggests that people's orientation to the experiences of life can play a role in whether they develop a specific, potentially life-threatening disease: cervical cancer. This study (Antoni & Goodkin, 1988) examined women who were undergoing testing after an abnormal PAP smear. Some of the women later proved to have cancer, some had a precancerous condition that might develop into cancer, others showed little or no abnormality. Before the testing, they completed measures of tendencies toward helplessness–hopelessness and despair about the future. These tendencies related to disease promotion: Women whose abnormality was more severe were those reporting more hopelessness and despair.

Doubt, Disengagement, and
Adverse Responses to Disease

There's also evidence that doubt and disengagement have adverse physical consequences for people who are attempting to manage a disease they've already contracted. These effects aren't as extreme as cases of unexplained sudden death, nor are they as striking as vulnerability to disease onset. However, their longer-term consequences are potentially very serious.

One study that begins to make this case (Scheier et al., 1989) examined the experiences of men undergoing coronary artery bypass surgery. Before surgery, the men completed a variety of measures, including one on dispositional optimism (Scheier & Carver, 1985, 1987), the generalized sense of confidence versus doubt about future outcomes. Several kinds of evidence indicated that pessimists fared more poorly than optimists. Pessimists were more likely to display two markers during surgery that are widely taken as indicants of myocardial infarction. Pessimists were also slower to reach behavioral milestones of recovery while hospitalized (sitting up in bed, walking around the room), slower to normalize their lives after leaving the hospital, and less likely to be working full-time five years after treatment. In considering these findings, it's noteworthy that when interviewed during the period surrounding surgery, pessimists were more likely than optimists to characterize themselves as trying to avoid thinking about their plans for the future. It's almost as though they were already showing a tendency to disengage from their future lives.

Scheier and colleagues (1998) have very recently collected data on a second sample of bypass patients. Initial analyses of data from that sample focused on a problem that often arises after major surgery: the need for rehospitalization, due either to infection from the surgery or to complications from the disease underlying the surgery. Scheier et al. (1998) found that optimistic persons were significantly less likely to be rehospitalized either for problems related to postsurgical infection or for problems related to the coronary artery disease, even after controlling for medical variables and other personality measures.

Another research group (Leedham, Meyerowitz, Muirhead, & Frist, 1995) has explored how positive expectations before heart transplant surgery related to later adjustment, medical adherence, and health. Patients (and their nurses) completed questionnaires prior to surgery, at discharge, and at three and six months postsurgery. Initial questionnaires assessed patients' confidence about the efficacy of treatment, their expectations about their future health and survival, and broader expectations for the future. Positive expectations related to higher quality of life later on, even among patients who had health setbacks. Importantly, confidence predicted better adherence to the postoperative medical regimen, and strongly predicted nurses' ratings of the patients' physical health at six months after surgery. There was also a tendency for positive expectations to predict longer delays before development of infection (which is a near-universal side effect of heart transplantation).

Two other studies relevant to disease management examined the development of symptoms in men who were HIV-positive but symptom-free. Would psychological variables predict who developed symptoms first? In one study (Reed, Kemeny, Taylor, & Visscher, in press), a measure of coping strategies the men completed yielded a factor of particular interest. It was an index of stoic acceptance, involving mental preparation for the worst and acceptance of the inevitable. This index, which has been characterized as reflecting adverse disease-specific expectancies (Reed, Kemeny, Taylor, Wang, & Visscher, 1994), predicted earlier symptom onset in this sample (Reed et al., in press).

Another study (Ironson et al., 1994) followed asymptomatic participants for two years after informing them of their positive serostatus. Measures of coping reactions were collected both before diagnosis and again five weeks after diagnosis. Participants who at postdiagnosis reported greater denial (the tendency to try to push the reality of the positive disagnosis away and treat it as though it wasn't real) and greater disengagement (a measure of the giving-up response) were more likely to have developed AIDS symptoms two years later.

Yet another study examined progression of cancer across the period of a year (Epping-Jordan, Compas, & Howell, 1994). Subjects were cancer patients who varied in terms of disease site and prognosis. They completed a variety of measures at the study's initiation. At one-year follow-up, after controlling for initial prognosis, patients who'd earlier reported trying to avoid thinking or talking about the cancer exhibited greater disease progression than those who'd been less avoidant.

Disengagement, Recurrence, Disease Progression, and Death

Another body of work moves the discussion from management of disease and progression of disease to recurrence of disease and even mortality. Greer and his colleagues have studied individual differences among breast cancer patients. Some patients react to their diagnosis and surgery with what's termed "fighting spirit" – a focused engagement with the struggle of living and regaining strength. Others react with stoic acceptance (fatalism) or feelings of hopelessness and helplessness. Patients who reacted with fighting spirit were more likely to have recurrence-free survival at 5-year follow-up than women who reacted with hopelessness and helplessness (Greer, Morris, & Pettingale, 1979). This pattern held up at both 10-year follow-up (Pettingale, Morris, Greer, & Haybittle, 1985) and 15-year follow-up (Greer, Morris, Pettingale, & Haybittle, 1990).

Another project bearing on survival (Fawzy et al., 1993) tested a six-week group intervention in a sample of malignant melanoma patients. Among measures collected was a measure of active-behavioral coping with the illness. Active-behavioral coping was defined as trying to alter the course of the disease by engaging in activities such as exercise, relaxation, and frequent consultations with physicians. We'd argue that people with this coping pattern were staying engaged with the struggle to stay alive. Fawzy et al. found that higher initial levels of this pattern predicted lower rates of recurrence and death.

In the previous section we described a study in which stoic acceptance of bad outcomes had adverse effects on symptom development in HIV patients. Further evidence of the ill effects of this attitude comes from research on survival time among patients whose disease has progressed to AIDS (Reed et al., 1994). This study followed a sample of men with

AIDS. By the end of the study, 82% had died from complications related to the disease. Higher scores on the index of stoic acceptance (reflecting negative disease-specific expectancies) related to shorter survival times. It was as though individuals with this attitude were preparing to die, and death then came to them more quickly.

Another project bearing on the role of doubt and disengagement in disease progression examined a sample of recurrent cancer patients (Schulz et al., 1996). Patients were followed for eight months, by which time approximately one-third had died. All had earlier completed a measure of pessimism about the future. Controlling for levels of symptoms at baseline, greater pessimism predicted shorter survival time. Further, the findings were specific to pessimism. Depression didn't predict mortality. The pessimism finding held only among relatively younger patients in this study (those under age 60), leading the researchers to suggest that the role of psychological factors in disease progression may diminish with age as biological pressures become stronger and more weighty.

Another project, conducted in Finland (Everson et al., 1996), studied the relationship between a sense of hopelessness about the future and mortality. The sample consisted of 2,428 middle-aged Finnish men who'd been treated for cancer or heart attacks. Hopelessness was assessed by two items: "I feel that it is impossible to reach the goals I would like to strive for" and "The future seems for me to be hopeless, and I can't believe things are changing for the better." These men were followed for six years. Those who reported relatively high degrees of hopelessness had greater disease-specific mortality (and all-cause mortality) than men with less hopelessness.

Conclusions

Substantial evidence exists that an attitude of hopelessness, pessimism, and disengagement from the struggle to continue life predict adverse medical outcomes. People who orient to life this way are more likely to experience certain disease processes than are people whose approach to life embodies greater engagement. They're more likely to deal poorly with surgery and its aftermath. And they seem more vulnerable to rapid disease progression and death. We would be remiss if we failed to note that these studies are open to alternative interpretations. They show associations, but as correlational studies they cannot demonstrate cause and effect. Nonetheless, the accumulation of evidence creates a compelling picture.

The mechanisms underlying these effects are far from well understood (see also Antonovsky, 1987). There are questions both at the psychological level and at the biological level. For example, are the people who fared well in these studies struggling primarily to hold onto the goals that form their lives, or struggling primarily to distance themselves from the anti-goals of disability and death? Whichever of these dominates, it's clear that when a person struggles with life-threatening illness, doubts about winning the battle are important. The illness threatens *all* the activities that make up your life. If you can't overcome the obstacles to this goal, there's no other goal to jump to.

Despite the many questions remaining, the pattern seems consistent with a picture in which continued engagement with life goals promotes better health outcomes, and in which the loss of such engagement – giving up – promotes poorer outcomes. It will not surprise us if future research reveals further cases in which an engagement with life is associated with better medical outcomes.

DYNAMICS AND ENGAGEMENT

We close with a final speculation about engagement and life. It follows in part from the observation that older people seem to be less emotionally reactive than younger people, an observation made mostly with respect to adverse events (though not entirely, see Kaye, Lawton, Gitlin, Kleban, Windsor, & Kaye, 1988). Several studies of patient populations have found that equating for medical and disease variables, older patients report less distress or disruption than do younger patients (e.g., Ganz, Schag, & Heinrich, 1985; Mor, Allen, & Malin, 1994; Vinokur, Threatt, Vinokur-Kaplan, & Satariano, 1990).

A variety of interpretations have been offered for this finding. A common one is that older people are less bothered because they feel as though they've experienced most of the important events of their lives. Another is that having physical illness is more normative, and thus expected, for older than for younger persons. Another interpretation (not incompatible with either of these) is that the experience of having a disease doesn't seem as *important* to older people as to younger ones. Less importance (less value, in the terms of our discussion earlier in the chapter) results in less emotional response.

The idea of attaching less importance to (for example) the development of an illness brings to mind the cusp catastrophe. In Chapters 15 and 16 we suggested that in many applications of the catastrophe to behavior (and emotional experience), importance is one variable forming

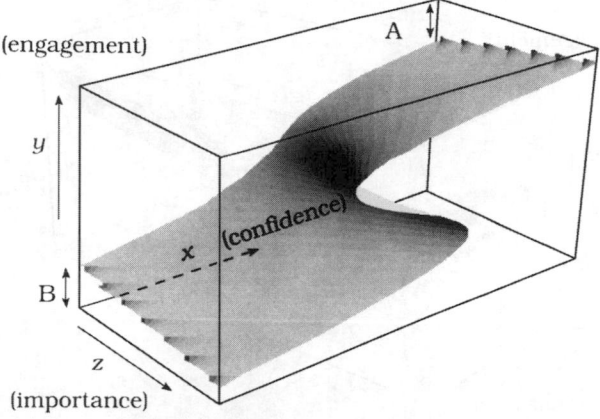

Figure 18.2. Catastrophe model of engagement and disengagement (after Figure 16.1). This figure was plotted with an equation-graphing program using only partial resolution, to illustrate more clearly (left-side face) the increase in y with decreasing z at low levels of x, and (right-side face) the decrease in y with decreasing z at high levels of x. Thus, on the back face of this figure (compared to the front), the high side of the surface is less high (line A) and the low side is less low (line B). This implies less range in engagement, and emotion, when importance is lower than when it is high.

the surface. More specifically, we suggested that importance may often be the dimension that's displayed as the z axis in Figure 18.2. Toward the back wall of the surface, things aren't terribly important subjectively. Toward the front, importance is greater.

Being toward the back of this figure does several things. It removes the nonlinear quality of the x–y relation – the hysteresis abates and even the step function smooths out. Being toward the back also does something else: It makes the high side less high (line A) and the low side less low (line B). This implies that there's less variation in engagement and less emotion when importance is low than when it's high. In Chapter 16 we emphasized the potential benefit of being toward the back of this figure, away from the region of hysteresis. When the nonlinearity dampens, behavior is more gradually responsive in small increments to incremental variations in confidence.

But there's a twist that we didn't consider in our previous discussion: Previously we moved *part* of the way back on axis z, but not all the way to zero. If you go back far enough, y becomes uniform and unchanging along the x axis (Figure 18.3). In that region, the "high" and "low" part of the surface don't differ. To put it in terms of the psychological variables we're discussing, when things are *really* unimportant, whatever x is

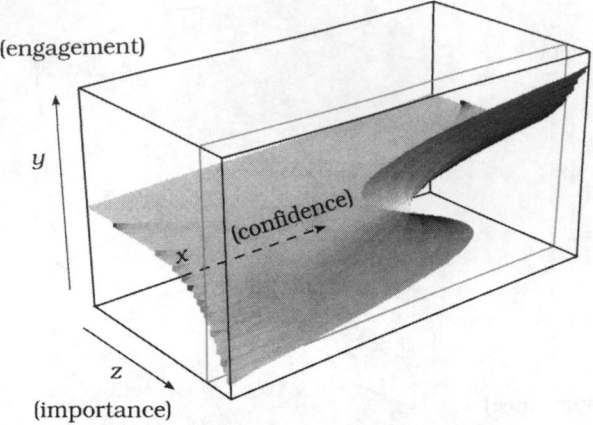

(engagement)

y

(confidence)

x

z

(importance)

Figure 18.3.   Catastrophe model of engagement and disengagement plotted over a range of *z* extending closer to zero. The front "slice" of this figure (the narrow box marked by gray lines) contains the values that were in Figure 18.2, condensed to permit a broader range of *z* to be captured within the same-sized grid overall as in Figure 18.2. It is apparent that as values of *z* *continue* to decrease, the *x–y* relationship begins to approximate a flat line. Though less obvious, a second point is made here. As *z* decreases from the region of hysteresis, the changes in *y* (at both high and low levels of *x*) are relatively abrupt at first, but then they asymptote more gradually to the middle value of *y*.

(e.g., confidence) doesn't matter. There's no uplift from being more confident (though there's also no decrement from being more doubtful).

Is there anything momentous about this? The picture, taken as a whole, appears to suggest that a reduction in importance dampens emotion and attenuates the jump between engagement and disengagement. But it appears to suggest as well that *eliminating* importance eliminates emotion and the very process of engagement. When an action doesn't matter, there's no reason to attempt it. Similarly, it may be that when life doesn't matter, there's no reason to make efforts to engage in it.[1] Surely, then, there's a need for some degree of importance (hardly a counterintuitive assertion).

Is there a need for nonlinearity as well? Writers who discuss dynamic systems often argue that nonlinearity is more common in life than people have realized until recently. Nonlinearities (whether you choose to think

---

[1] Maybe these effects extend beyond action and emotion, even to issues of life and death. This principle might account for the finding by Schulz et al. (1996), cited earlier, that optimism played a smaller role in survival among older patients than among younger patients. Perhaps that finding reflects a loss of the sense of importance of life among older patients.

of them in terms of catastrophes or dynamic systems) are necessary to make hearts beat (abruptly shifting from one phase to another). Nonlinearities underlie the process of walking. Nonlinearities jump people from one topic to another, in their minds and in their actions.

Maybe the functions that yield these nonlinearities are somehow critical to life. Maybe when the z variable is reduced far enough that the nonlinearity disappears, a problem is looming. Maybe the removal of nonlinearity is a bad thing, moving people eventually toward a flat line of no responsiveness (Figure 18.3). No importance, no variation in engagement, no life.

Aging and the Reduction of Importance

Why might the subjective sense of importance diminish through aging? Here's a *highly* speculative account, suggested by the idea (which we brought up in Chapter 14) that the sense of importance is aligned in part with attention-demandingness and thus with uncertainty. That is, attention is drawn to points in behavior where decisions have to be made, where uncertainty is high. Those aspects of behavior are important in the sense of requiring effortful processing and therefore attention. When clear default values accumulate, on the other hand, whatever issue was formerly attended to is no longer as important as it was. Uncertainty has diminished, and attention is removed from this issue and deployed elsewhere. What's most important (in the sense of being most in need of an effortful decision) is what gets the attention.

Given this orienting premise, it seems plausible that the more experience a person has had, the more evidence the person has accumulated about what decisions are appropriate for a wide range of experiences. Thus, the stronger and more established are the person's default responses. Put differently, as people get older, they become more set in their ways (and even the fact of being set in their ways is taken for granted). If they remain in circumstances that change little, defaults take over more and more of their action patterns, more and more of their lives. With more and more default responses, less and less is important – in the sense of being attention-demanding (decision-demanding).

What would happen if a person reached the point where *nothing* needs a decision, where there's a default response for everything? This situation would in some respects be analogous to having no alternate goal to shift to when disengaging from a current goal. That is, attention is withdrawn from the previously attention-demanding decision, but there's no alternate decision to shift to. With nothing to attend to, what happens? Perhaps the resources of attention diffuse. As attention diffuses, maybe the forces holding the person together begin to unbind.

Bob Dylan's lyric "he not busy being born is busy dying" is familiar to many children of the 1960s and '70s. To be "busy being born" is to continue to find absorption in life, to keep learning new things about the world, to feel that life is important. To be "busy dying" is to have no psychological investment in the events of one's life.

The catastrophe model and the extrapolations we've just made from it provide an interesting lens through which to examine this lyric. The nonlinearity doesn't emerge unless what you're engaged in is important. Passions, strong feelings, can't occur unless the goal matters. Investment of importance thus confers a sense of life, along with the creation of nonlinearity.

If the aggregation of experiences in your life begin to produce the sense of unimportance (through the familiarity of strong default responses), you are dying, even if you don't realize it. The engagement and the passion are slipping away. "Being born" is the attention-demanding (absorbing) sorting through of the unfamiliar to determine the appropriate responses and begin to turn those responses into defaults. "Dying" is the clogging up of the mind with established defaults, no longer questioned, no longer examined.

In Chapter 16, we suggested that personal growth occurs when people confront situations they hadn't experienced before. In these new situations they have to take something different into account than they'd done before (some new value on a previously ignored dimension of variability). That newly noticed difference doesn't simply add a new bit of information to be integrated. It has the potential to rearrange relations among *old* variables that were nicely understood until then, because the new variable may interact with variables previously taken into account.[2]

---

[2] People who have extramarital affairs sometimes claim the new love has made them feel "alive," which they hadn't felt for some time. Married couples who are attentive to maintenance of their relationships often take explicit steps from time to time to make the relationship feel fresh and different, to keep the relationship feeling "alive." In either of these cases, one might speculate that the event precipitating the "alive" feeling has caused the person to experience a shift in his or her view of the world. The shift (the addition of variable $N + 1$) is great enough to force accommodation, growth, change, reconsideration of default responses. The new experience demands attention.

Sometimes, of course, the impact of such experiences is short-lived. In such cases, it may be that the person has failed to reconsider his or her default responses to any great degree or has immediately lapsed back to the default patterns. Thus, what might at first have seemed to be a meaningful change in understanding ultimately was experienced as just a temporary perturbation, with no new dimension to take into account after all.

That picture fits the point we're making here, as well. To be busy being born is to continue to take up new experiences, explore aspects of life that are unfamiliar, where it's not clear what the defaults are. To be busy being born is also to reexamine old defaults in light of insights from new experiences, because the new picture (with the new dimension now taken into account) may yield new understandings of old realities that people thought they understood, but did only partly, because of the lack of the new variable. Thus we can continue to "arrive where we started and know the place for the first time" – not once, but over and over again.

This is the path of growth, the path of continuing development. By recurrently rendering some issue or other newly important, newly engaging and demanding, it may also be literally the path of life.

References

Abrams, D. (1994). Social self-regulation. *Personality and Social Psychology Bulletin, 20*, 473–483.

Abrams, D., & Hogg, M. A. (Eds.) (1990). *Social identity theory: Constructive and critical advances*. New York: Springer-Verlag.

Abramson, L. Y., Metalsky, G. I., & Alloy, L. B. (1989). Hopelessness depression: A theory-based subtype of depression. *Psychological Review, 96*, 358–372.

Abramson, L. Y., Seligman, M. E. P., & Teasdale, J. D. (1978). Learned helplessness in humans: Critique and reformulation. *Journal of Abnormal Psychology, 87*, 49–74.

Affleck, G., Tennen, H., Pfeiffer, C., & Fifield, J. (1987). Appraisals of control and predictability in adapting to a chronic disease. *Journal of Personality and Social Psychology, 53*, 273–279.

Affleck, G., Tennen, H., Urrows, S., Higgins, P., Abeles, M., Hall, C., Karoly, P, & Newton, C. (1998). Fibromyalgia and women's pursuit of personal goals: A daily process analysis. *Health Psychology, 17*, 40–47.

Ager, D. (1995). *The new catastrophism: The importance of the rare event in geological history*. New York: Cambridge University Press.

Ahrens, A. H., & Haaga, A. F. (1993). The specificity of attributional style and expectations to positive and negative affectivity, depression, and anxiety. *Cognitive Therapy and Research, 17*, 83–98.

Ajzen, I. (1985). From intentions to actions: A theory of planned behavior. In J. Kuhl & J. Beckmann (Eds.), *Action control: From cognition to behavior* (pp. 11–39). Heidelberg & New York: Springer-Verlag.

(1988). *Attitudes, personality, and behavior*. Chicago: Dorsey Press.

Ajzen, I., & Fishbein, M. (1980). *Understanding attitudes and predicting social behavior*. Englewood Cliffs, NJ: Prentice-Hall.

Aldwin, C. M. (1994). *Stress, coping, and development: An integrative perspective*. New York: Guilford.

Aldwin, C. M., & Stokols, D. (1988). The effects of environmental change on individuals and groups: Some neglected issues in stress research. *Journal of Environmental Psychology, 8*, 57–75.

Allen, J. J., Iacono, W. G., Depue, R. A., & Arbisi, X. (1993). Regional EEG asymmetries in bipolar affective disorder before and after phototherapy. *Biological Psychiatry, 33*, 642–646.

Alligood, K. T., Sauer, T. D., & Yorke, J. A. (1997). *Chaos: An introduction to dynamical systems.* New York: Springer-Verlag.

Ames, C., & Archer, J. (1988). Achievement goals in the classroom: Student learning strategies and motivation process. *Journal of Educational Psychology, 80*, 260–267.

Anderson, C. A., Lepper, M. R., & Ross, L. (1980). Perseverance of social theories: The role of explanation in the persistence of discredited information. *Journal of Personality and Social Psychology, 39*, 1037–1049.

Anderson, J. A. (1995). *An introduction to neural networks.* Cambridge, MA: MIT Press.

Anderson, J. R. (1990). *The adaptive character of thought.* Hillsdale, NJ: Erlbaum.

Antoni, M. H., & Goodkin, K. (1988). Host moderator variables in the promotion of cervical cancer: I. Personality facets. *Journal of Psychosomatic Research, 32*, 327–338.

Antonovsky, A. (1987). *Unraveling the mystery of health: How people manage stress and stay well.* San Francisco: Jossey-Bass.

Arbib, J. A. (Ed.) (1995). *Handbook of brain theory and neural networks.* Cambridge, MA: MIT Press.

Arkin, R. C. (1990). Integrating behavioral, perceptual, and world knowledge in reactive navigation. In P. Maes (Ed.), *Designing autonomous agents: Theory and practice from biology to engineering and back* (pp. 105–122). Cambridge, MA: MIT Press.

Arkin, R., & Duval, S. (1975). Focus of attention and causal attributions of actors and observers. *Journal of Experimental Social Psychology, 11*, 427–438.

Armor, D. A., & Taylor, S. E. (1998). Situated optimism: Specific outcome expectancies and self-regulation. In M. Zanna (Ed.), *Advances in experimental social psychology* (Vol. 30, pp. 309–379). San Diego: Academic Press.

Asch, S. E. (1946). Forming impressions of personality. *Journal of Abnormal and Social Psychology, 41*, 258–290.

—— (1951). Effects of group pressure upon the modification and distortion of judgments. In H. Guetzkow (Ed.), *Groups, leadership, and men* (pp. 177–190). Pittsburgh: Carnegie Press.

—— (1956). Studies of independence and conformity: I. A minority of one against a unanimous majority. *Psychological Monographs, 70*, 9 (whole No. 416).

Ashby, W. R. (1961). *An introduction to cybernetics.* London: Chapman.

Aslin, R. N. (1993). Commentary: The strange attractiveness of dynamic systems to development. In L. D. Smith & E. Thelen (Eds.), *A dynamic systems approach to development: Applications* (pp. 385–399). Cambridge, MA: MIT Press.

Aspinwall, L. G., & Taylor, S. E. (1993). Effects of social comparison direction, threat, and self-esteem on affect, self-evaluation, and expected success. *Journal of Personality and Social Psychology, 64*, 708–722.

Atkinson, J. W. (1964). *An introduction to motivation.* Princeton, NJ: Van Nostrand.

Atkinson, J. W., & Birch, D. (1970). *The dynamics of action.* New York: Wiley.

Austin, J. T., & Vancouver, J. B. (1996). Goal constructs in psychology: Structure, process, and content. *Psychological Bulletin, 120*, 338–375.

Averill, J. R. (1973). Personal control over aversive stimuli and its relationship to stress. *Psychological Bulletin, 80*, 286–303.

Baggett, H. L., Saab, P. G., & Carver, C. S. (1996). Appraisal, coping, task performance, and cardiovascular responses during the evaluated speaking task. *Personality and Social Psychology Bulletin, 22*, 483–494.

Ball, L., & Chandler, M. J. (1989). Identity formation in suicidal and nonsuicidal youth: The role of self-continuity. *Development and Psychopathology, 1*, 257–275.

Baltes, M. M., & Baltes, P. B. (Eds.) (1986). *Aging and the psychology of control.* Hillsdale, NJ: Erlbaum.

Bandura, A. (1969). *Aggression: A social learning analysis.* Englewood Cliffs, NJ: Prentice-Hall.

(1977). Self-efficacy: Toward a unifying theory of behavior change. *Psychological Review, 84*, 191–215.

(1982). Self-efficacy mechanism in human agency. *American Psychologist, 37*, 122–147.

(1986). *Social foundations of thought and action: A social cognitive theory.* Englewood Cliffs, NJ: Prentice-Hall.

(1989). Self-regulation of motivation and action through internal standards and goal systems. In L. A. Pervin (Ed.), *Goal concepts in personality and social psychology* (pp. 19–85). Hillsdale, NJ: Erlbaum.

(1994). *Self-efficacy: The exercise of control.* New York: Freeman.

Bargh, J. A. (1997). The automaticity of everyday life. In R. S. Wyer, Jr. (Ed.), *Advances in social cognition* (Vol. 10, pp. 1–61). Mahwah, NJ: Erlbaum.

Baron, R. J. (1987). *The cerebral computer: An introduction to the computational structure of the human brain.* Hillsdale, NJ: Erlbaum.

Baron, R. M., Amazeen, P. G., & Beek, P. J. (1994). Local and global dynamics of social relations. In R. R. Vallacher & A. Nowak (Eds.), *Dynamical systems in social psychology* (pp. 111–138). San Diego: Academic Press.

Baron, R. S., Vandello, J. A., & Brunsman, B. (1996). The forgotten variable in conformity research: Impact of task importance on social influence. *Journal of Personality and Social Psychology, 71*, 915–927.

Barsalou, L. W. (1985). Ideals, central tendency, and frequency of instantiation as determinants of graded structure in categories. *Journal of Experimental Psychology: Learning, Memory, and Cognition, 11*, 629–654.

Bartholomew, K., & Perlman, D. (Eds.). (1994). *Attachment processes in adult-hood.* London: Jessica Kingsley Publishers.

Barton, S. (1994). Chaos, self-organization, and psychology. *American Psychologist, 49*, 5–14.

Baumann, L. J., & Leventhal, H. (1985). "I can tell when my blood pressure is up, can't I?" *Health Psychology, 4*, 203–218.

Baumeister, R. F. (1982). A self-presentational view of social phenomena. *Psychological Bulletin, 91*, 3–26.

(Ed.) (1986). *Public self and private self.* New York: Springer-Verlag.

(1988). Masochism as escape from self. *Journal of Sex Research, 25*, 28–59.

(1989). The problem of life's meaning. In D. M. Buss & N. Cantor (Eds.), *Personality psychology: Recent trends and emerging directions* (pp. 138–148). New York: Springer-Verlag.

(1990). Suicide as escape from the self. *Psychological Review, 97*, 90–113.

(1991). *Escaping the self.* New York: Basic Books.

Baumeister, R. F., & Heatherton, T. F. (1996). Self-regulation failure: An overview. *Psychological Inquiry, 7*, 1–15.

Baumeister, R. F., Heatherton, T. F., & Tice, D. M. (1994). *Losing control: Why people fail at self-regulation.* San Diego: Academic Press.

Baumeister, R. F., & Scher, S. J. (1988). Self-defeating behavior patterns among normal individuals: Review and analysis of common self-destructive tendencies. *Psychological Bulletin, 104*, 3–22.

Baumeister, R. F., Shapiro, J. P., & Tice, D. M. (1985). Two kinds of identity crisis. *Journal of Personality, 53*, 407–424.

Baumeister, R. F., Stillwell, A. M., & Heatherton, T. F. (1994). Guilt: An interpersonal approach. *Psychological Bulletin, 115*, 243–267.

Baumeister, R. F., & Wotman, S. R. (1992). *Breaking hearts: The two sides of unrequited love.* New York: Guilford.

Baumgardner, A. H. (1990). To know oneself is to like oneself: Self-certainty and self-affect. *Journal of Personality and Social Psychology, 58*, 1062–1072.

Beach, L. R. (1993). Broadening the definition of decision making: The role of prechoice screening of options. *Psychological Science, 4*, 215–220.

Beaman, A. L., Klentz, B., Diener, E., & Svanum, S. (1979). Self-awareness and transgression in children: Two field studies. *Journal of Personality and Social Psychology, 37*, 1835–1846.

Bechara, A., Damasio, H., Tranel, D., & Damasio, A. R. (1997). Deciding advantageously before knowing the advantageous strategy. *Science, 275*, 1293–1295.

Bechtel, W., & Abrahamsen, A. (1991). *Connectionism and the mind: An introduction to parallel processing in networks.* Cambridge: Basil Blackwell.

Beck, A. T. (1967). *Depression: Clinical, experimental, and theoretical aspects.* New York: Harper & Row.

(1972). *Depression: Causes and treatment*. Philadelphia: University of Pennsylvania Press.

Beck, A. T., Steer, R. A., Beck, J. S., & Newman, C. F. (1993). Hopelessness, depression, suicidal ideation, and clinical diagnosis of depression. *Suicide & Life-Threatening Behavior, 23*, 139–145.

Beck, A. T., Steer, R. A., Kovacs, M., & Garrison, B. (1985). Hopelessness and eventual suicide: A 10-year prospective study of patients hospitalized with suicidal ideation. *American Journal of Psychiatry, 142*, 559–563.

Beckmann, J., & Gollwitzer, P. M. (1987). Deliberative versus implemental states of mind: The issue of impartiality in pre- and postdecisional information processing. *Social Cognition, 5*, 259–279.

Beer, R. D. (1995). A dynamical systems perspective on agent-environment interaction. *Artificial Intelligence, 72*, 173–215.

Berecz, J. M. (1992). *Understanding Tourette syndrome, obsessive compulsive disorder, and related problems: A developmental and catastrophe theory perspective*. New York: Springer.

Berman, W. H., Marcus, L., & Berman, E. R. (1994). Attachment in marital relations. In M. B. Sperling & W. H. Berman (Eds.), *Attachment in adults* (pp. 204–231). New York: Guilford.

Bernstein, N. (1967). *The coordination and regulation of movements*. London: Pergamon.

Bertenthal, B. I., Campos, J. J., & Kermoian, R. (1994). An epigenetic perspective on the development of self-produced locomotion and its consequences. *Current Directions in Psychological Science, 3*, 140–145.

Berzonsky, M. D. (1994). Self-identity: The relationship between process and content. *Journal of Research in Personality, 28*, 453–460.

Bettelheim, B. (1960). *The informed heart – Autonomy in a mass age*. New York: Free Press.

Billings, A. G., & Moos, R. H. (1984). Coping, stress, and social resources among adults with unipolar depression. *Journal of Personality and Social Psychology, 46*, 877–891.

Blaney, P. H. (1986). Affect and memory: A review. *Psychological Bulletin, 99*, 229–246.

Block, J. (1996). Some jangly remarks on Baumeister and Heatherton. *Psychological Inquiry, 7*, 28–32.

Bolger, N. (1990). Coping as a personality process: A prospective study. *Journal of Personality and Social Psychology, 59*, 525–537.

Bolles, R. C. (1972). Reinforcement, expectancy, and learning. *Psychological Review, 79*, 394–409.

Bond, C. F. (1982). Social facilitation: A self-presentational view. *Journal of Personality and Social Psychology, 42*, 1042–1050.

Bond, R., & Smith, P. B. (1996). Culture and conformity: A meta-analysis of studies using Asch's (1952b, 1956) line judgment task. *Psychological Bulletin, 119*, 111–137.

Boring, E. G. (1930). A new ambiguous figure. *American Journal of Psychology, 42*, 444–445.

Bouton, M. E. (1993). Context, time, and memory retrieval in the interference paradigms of Pavlovian learning. *Psychological Bulletin, 114*, 80–99.

(1994). Context, ambiguity, and classical conditioning. *Current Directions in Psychological Science, 3*, 49–53.

Bowen, M. (1978). *Family therapy in clinical practice.* New York: Jason Aronson.

Bower, G. H. (1978). Contacts of cognitive psychology with social learning theory. *Cognitive Therapy and Research, 2*, 123–146.

(1981). Mood and memory. *American Psychologist, 36*, 129–148.

(1991). Mood congruity of social judgments. In J. P. Forgas (Ed.), *Emotion and social judgments* (pp. 31–53). Oxford: Pergamon.

Bowlby, J. (1969). *Attachment and loss: Vol. 1. Attachment.* New York: Basic Books.

(1988). *A secure base: Parent–child attachment and healthy human development.* New York: Basic Books.

Bradshaw, J. (1988). *Bradshaw on: The family.* Deerfield Beach, FL: Health Communications, Inc.

Bradshaw, J. L., & Nettleton, N. (1983). *Human cerebral asymmetry.* Englewood Cliffs, NJ: Prentice-Hall.

Braitenberg, V. (1984). *Vehicles: Experiments in synthetic psychology.* Cambridge, MA: MIT Press.

Brandstadter, J., & Renner, G. (1990) Tenacious goal pursuit and flexible goal adjustments: Explication and age-related analysis of assimilative and accommodative strategies of coping. *Psychology and Aging, 5*, 58–67.

Brazelton, T. B. (1992). *Touchpoints: Your child's emotional and behavioral development.* Reading, MA: Addison-Wesley.

Brehm, J. W. (1966). *A theory of psychological reactance.* New York: Academic Press.

Brehm, J. W., & Self, E. A. (1989). The intensity of motivation. *Annual Review of Psychology, 40*, 109–131.

Brennan, K. A., & Morris, K. A. (1997). Attachment styles, self-esteem, and patterns of seeking feedback from romantic partners. *Personality and Social Psychology Bulletin, 23*, 23–31.

Brewer, M. B. (1979). In-group bias in the minimal intergroup situation: A cognitive-motivational analysis. *Psychological Bulletin, 86*, 307–324.

(1991). The social self: On being the same and different at the same time. *Personality and Social Psychology Bulletin, 17*, 475–482.

Brickman, P. (1987). *Commitment, conflict, and caring.* Englewood Cliffs, NJ: Prentice-Hall.

Broadbent, D. E. (1977). Levels, hierarchies, and the locus of control. *Quarterly Journal of Experimental Psychology, 29*, 181–201.

Brockner, J., Shaw, M. C., & Rubin, J. Z. (1979). Factors affecting withdrawal from an escalating conflict: Quitting before it's too late. *Journal of Experimental Social Psychology, 15*, 492–503.

Brooks, R. A. (1986). A robust layered control system for a mobile robot. *IEEE Journal of Robotics and Automation, RA-2*, 14–23.

(1991a). Intelligence without representation. *Artificial Intelligence, 47*, 139–159.

(1991b). New approaches to robotics. *Science, 253*, 1227–1232.

Brooks, R. A., & Stein, L. A. (1994). Building brains for bodies. *Autonomous Robots, 1*, 7–25.

Brown, C. (1995). *Chaos and catastrophe theories* (Quantitative applications in the social sciences, No. 107). Thousand Oaks, CA: Sage.

Brunstein, J. C. (1993). Personal goals and subjective well-being: A longitudinal study. *Journal of Personality and Social Psychology, 65*, 1061–1070.

Brunstein, J. C., Dangelmayer, G., & Schultheiss, O. C. (1996). Personal goals and social support in close relationships: Effects on relationship mood and marital satisfaction. *Journal of Personality and Social Psychology, 71*, 1006–1019.

Buchsbaum, M. S., Wu, J., Haier, R., Hazlett, E., Ball, R., Katz, M., Sokolski, M. L-S., & Langer, D. (1987). Positron emission tomography assessment of effects of benzodiazepines on regional glucose metabolic rate in patients with anxiety disorder. *Life Sciences, 40*, 2393–2400.

Buck, R. (1985). Prime theory: An integrated view of motivation and emotion. *Psychological Review, 92*, 389–413.

Burger, J. M. (1989). Negative reactions to increases in perceived personal control. *Journal of Personality and Social Psychology, 56*, 246–256.

Burger, J. M., McWard, J., & LaTorre, D. (1989). Boundaries of self-control: Relinquishing control over aversive events. *Journal of Social and Clinical Psychology, 8*, 209–221.

Burgess, C., Morris, T., & Pettingale, K. W. (1988). Psychological response to cancer diagnosis: II. Evidence for coping styles (coping styles and cancer diagnosis). *Journal of Psychosomatic Research, 32*, 263–272.

Burgio, K. L., Merluzzi, T. V., & Pryor, J. B. (1986). Effects of performance expectancy and self-focused attention on social interaction. *Journal of Personality and Social Psychology, 50*, 1216–1221.

Burke, P. J. (1991). Identity processes and social stress. *American Sociological Review, 56*, 836–849.

Buss, A. H., & Plomin, R. (1984). *Temperament: Early developing personality traits*. Hillsdale, NJ: Erlbaum.

Buss, D. M. (1991). Evolutionary personality psychology. *Annual Review of Psychology, 42*, 459–491.

(1994). *The evolution of desire: Strategies of human mating*. New York: Basic Books.

Buss, D. M., & Craik, K. H. (1983). The act frequency approach to personality. *Psychological Review, 90*, 105–126.

Butler, R. (1992). What young people want to know when: Effects of mastery and ability goals on interest in different kinds of social comparisons. *Journal of Personality and Social Psychology, 62*, 934–943.

(1993). Effects of task- and ego-achievement goals in information seeking during task engagement. *Journal of Personality and Social Psychology, 65*, 18–31.

Buunk, B. P., & Gibbons, F. X. (Eds.) (1997). *Health, coping, and well-being: Perspectives from social comparison theory*. Mahwah, NJ: Erlbaum.

Cacioppo, J. T., & Berntson, G. G. (1994). Relationship between attitudes and evaluative space: A critical review, with emphasis on the separability of positive and negative substrates. *Psychological Bulletin, 115*, 401–423.

Cacioppo, J. T., & Petty, R. E. (1980). The effects of orienting task on differential hemispheric EEG activation. *Neuropsychologia, 18*, 675–683.

Cannon, W. B. (1942). "Voodoo" death. *American Anthropologist, 44*, 169–181.

Cantor, N., & Fleeson, W. (1991). Life tasks and self-regulatory processes. In M. Maehr & P. Pintrich (Eds.), *Advances in motivation and achievement* (Vol. 7, pp. 327–369). Greenwich, CT: JAI Press.

Cantor, N., & Kihlstrom, J. F. (1987). *Personality and social intelligence*. Englewood Cliffs, NJ: Prentice-Hall.

Carlston, D. E., & Skowronski, J. J. (1986). Trait memory and behavior memory: The effects of alternative pathways on impression judgment response times. *Journal of Personality and Social Psychology, 50*, 5–13.

(1994). Savings in the relearning of trait information as evidence of spontaneous trait inference generation. *Journal of Personality and Social Psychology, 66*, 840–856.

Carr, S. J., Teasdale, J. D., & Broadbent, D. (1991). Effects of induced elated and depressed mood on self-focused attention. *British Journal of Clinical Psychology, 31*, 273–275.

Carver, C. S. (1974). Facilitation of physical aggression through objective self-awareness. *Journal of Experimental Social Psychology, 10*, 365–370.

(1975). Physical aggression as a function of objective self awareness and attitudes toward punishment. *Journal of Experimental Social Psychology, 11*, 510–519.

(1977). Self-awareness, perception of threat, and the expression of reactance through attitude change. *Journal of Personality, 45*, 501–512.

(1979). A cybernetic model of self-attention processes. *Journal of Personality and Social Psychology, 37*, 1251–1281.

(1996a). Cognitive interference and the structure of behavior. In I. G. Sarason, G. R. Pierce, & B. R. Sarason (Eds.), *Cognitive interference: Theories, methods, and findings* (pp. 25–45). Hillsdale, NJ: Erlbaum.

(1996b). Emergent integration in contemporary personality psychology. *Journal of Research in Personality, 30*, 319–334.

(1996c). Goal engagement and the human experience. In R. S. Wyer, Jr. (Ed.), *Advances in social cognition* (Vol. 9, pp. 49–61). Mahwah, NJ: Erlbaum.

(1996d). Some ways in which goals differ and some implications of those differences. In P. M. Gollwitzer & J. A. Bargh (Eds.), *The psychology of action: Linking cognition and motivation to behavior* (pp. 645–672). New York: Guilford.

(1997a). Associations to automaticity. In R. S. Wyer, Jr. (Ed.), *Advances in social cognition* (Vol. 10, pp. 95–103). Mahwah, NJ: Erlbaum.

(1997b). Dynamical social psychology: Chaos and catastrophe for all. *Psychological Inquiry, 8*, 110–119.

(1997c). The IE scale confounds internal locus of control with expectancies of positive outcomes. *Personality and Social Psychology Bulletin, 23*, 580–585.

(1998). Generalization, adverse events, and development of depressive symptoms. *Journal of Personality, 66*, 609–620.

Carver, C. S., Antoni, M., & Scheier, M. F. (1985). Self-consciousness and self-assessment. *Journal of Personality and Social Psychology, 48*, 117–124.

Carver, C. S., Blaney, P. H., & Scheier, M. F. (1979a). Focus of attention, chronic expectancy, and responses to a feared stimulus. *Journal of Personality and Social Psychology, 37*, 1186–1195.

(1979b). Reassertion and giving up: The interactive role of self-directed attention and outcome expectancy. *Journal of Personality and Social Psychology, 37*, 1859–1870.

Carver, C. S., & Ganellen, R. J. (1983). Depression and components of self-punitiveness: High standards, self-criticism, and overgeneralization. *Journal of Abnormal Psychology, 92*, 330–337.

Carver, C. S., & Humphries, C. (1981). Havana daydreaming: A study of self-consciousness and the negative reference group among Cuban Americans. *Journal of Personality and Social Psychology, 40*, 545–552.

Carver, C. S., La Voie, L., Kuhl, J., & Ganellen, R. J. (1988). Cognitive concomitants of depression: A further examination of the roles of generalization, high standards, and self-criticism. *Journal of Social and Clinical Psychology, 7*, 350–365.

Carver, C. S., Lawrence, J. W., & Scheier, M. F. (in press). Self-discrepancies and affect: Incorporating the role of the feared self. *Personality and Social Psychology Bulletin*.

Carver, C. S., Peterson, L. M., Follansbee, D. J., & Scheier, M. F. (1983). Effects of self-directed attention on performance and persistence among persons high and low in test anxiety. *Cognitive Therapy and Research, 7*, 333–354.

Carver, C. S., Pozo, C., Harris, S. D., Noriega, V., Scheier, M. F., Robinson, D. S., Ketcham, A. S., Moffat, F. L., Jr., & Clark, K. C. (1993). How coping mediates the effect of optimism on distress: A study of women with early stage breast cancer. *Journal of Personality and Social Psychology, 65*, 375–390.

Carver, C. S., & Scheier, M. F. (1978). Self-focusing effects of dispositional self-consciousness, mirror presence, and audience presence. *Journal of Personality and Social Psychology, 36*, 324–332.

(1981a). *Attention and self-regulation: A control-theory approach to human behavior*. New York: Springer-Verlag.

(1981b). The self-attention-induced feedback loop and social facilitation. *Journal of Experimental Social Psychology, 17*, 545–568.

(1981c). Self-consciousness and reactance. *Journal of Research in Personality, 15*, 16–29.

(1982). Outcome expectancy, locus of attributions for expectancy, and self-directed attention as determinants of evaluations and performance. *Journal of Experimental Social Psychology, 18*, 184–200.

(1983). A control-theory model of normal behavior, and implications for problems in self-management. In P. C. Kendall (Ed.), *Advances in cognitive-behavioral research and therapy* (Vol. 2, pp. 127–194). New York: Academic Press.

(1984). Self-focused attention in test anxiety: A general theory applied to a specific phenomenon. In H. van der Ploeg, R. Schwarzer, & C. D. Spielberger (Eds.), *Advances in test anxiety research* (Vol. 3, pp. 3–20). Hillsdale, NJ: Erlbaum.

(1985). Aspects of self, and the control of behavior. In B. R. Schlenker (Ed.), *The self and social life* (pp. 146–174). New York: McGraw-Hill.

(1986a). Analyzing shyness: A specific application of broader self-regulatory principles. In W. H. Jones, J. M. Cheek, & S. R. Briggs (Eds.), *Shyness: Perspectives on research and treatment* (pp. 173–185). New York: Plenum.

(1986b). Self and the control of behavior. In L. M. Hartman & K. R. Blankstein (Eds.), *Perception of self in emotional disorder and psychotherapy* (pp. 5–35). New York: Plenum.

(1987). The blind men and the elephant: Selective examination of the public-private literature gives rise to a faulty perception. *Journal of Personality, 55*, 525–541.

(1989). Social intelligence and personality: Some unanswered questions and unresolved issues. In R. S. Wyer, Jr., & T. K. Srull (Eds.), *Advances in social cognition* (Vol. 2, pp. 93–109). Hillsdale, NJ: Erlbaum.

(1990a). Origins and functions of positive and negative affect: A control-process view. *Psychological Review, 97*, 19–35.

(1990b). Principles of self-regulation: Action and emotion. In E. T. Higgins & R. M. Sorrentino (Eds.), *Handbook of motivation and cognition: Foundations of social behavior* (Vol. 2, pp. 3–52). New York: Guilford.

(1994). Situational coping and coping dispositions in a stressful transaction. *Journal of Personality and Social Psychology, 66*, 184–195.

(1996a). *Perspectives on personality* (3rd ed.). Needham Heights, MA: Allyn & Bacon.

(1996b). Self-regulation and its failures. *Psychological Inquiry, 7*, 32–40.

Carver, C. S., Scheier, M. F., & Klahr, D. (1987). Further explorations of a control-process model of test anxiety. In R. Schwarzer, H. M. van der Ploeg, & C. D. Spielberger (Eds.), *Advances in test anxiety research* (Vol. 5, pp. 15–22). Lisse, Netherlands: Swets & Zeitlinger.

Carver, C. S., Scheier, M. F., & Pozo, C. (1992). Conceptualizing the process of coping with health problems. In H. S. Friedman (Ed.), *Hostility, coping, & health* (pp. 167–199). Washington, DC: American Psychological Association.

Carver, C. S., Scheier, M. F., & Weintraub, J. K. (1989). Assessing coping strategies: A theoretically based approach. *Journal of Personality and Social Psychology, 56*, 267–283.

Carver, C. S., & White, T. L. (1994). Behavioral inhibition, behavioral activation, and affective responses to impending reward and punishment: The BIS/BAS scales. *Journal of Personality and Social Psychology, 67*, 319–333.

Caspar, F., Rothenfluh, T., & Segal, Z. (1992). The appeal of connectionism to clinical psychology. *Clinical Psychology Review, 12*, 719–762.

Caudill, M. (1992). *In our own image: Building an artificial person.* New York: Oxford University Press.

Cervone, D., Kopp, D. A., Schaumann, L., & Scott, W. D. (1994). Mood, self-efficacy, and performance standards: Lower moods induce higher standards for performance. *Journal of Personality and Social Psychology, 67*, 499–512.

Cervone, D., & Palmer, B. W. (1990). Anchoring biases and the perseverance of self-efficacy beliefs. *Cognitive Therapy and Research, 14*, 401–416.

Chaiken, S. L., & Trope, Y. (Eds.) (in press). *Dual-process theories in social psychology.* New York: Guilford.

Chandler, M. J., & Lalonde, C. E. (1995). The problem of self-continuity in the context of rapid personal and cultural change. In A. Oosterwegel & R. A. Wicklund (Eds.), *The self in European and North American culture: Development and processes* (pp. 45–63). Dordrecht, Holland: Kluwer.

Cheek, J. M. (1989). Identity orientations and self interpretations. In D. M. Buss & N. Cantor (Eds.), *Personality psychology: Recent trends and emerging directions* (pp. 275–285). New York: Springer-Verlag.

Cheek, J. M., & Briggs, S. R. (1982). Self-consciousness and aspects of identity. *Journal of Research in Personality, 16*, 401–408.

Churchland, P. S., & Sejnowski, T. J. (1992). *The computational brain.* Cambridge, MA: MIT Press.

Cialdini, R. B., Levy, A., Herman, C. P., Kozlowski, L. T., & Petty, R. E. (1976). Elastic shifts of opinion: Determinants of direction and durability. *Journal of Personality and Social Psychology, 34*, 663–672.

Clark, D. A., Beck, A. T., & Brown, G. (1989). Cognitive mediation in general psychiatric outpatients: A test of the content-specificity hypothesis. *Journal of Personality and Social Psychology, 56*, 958–964.

Clark, L. A., Watson, D., & Mineka, S. (1994). Temperament, personality, and the mood and anxiety disorders. *Journal of Abnormal Psychology, 103*, 103–116.

Clark, L. F., Henry, S. M., & Taylor, D. M. (1991). Cognitive examination of motivation for childbearing as a factor in adjustment to infertility. In A. L. Stanton & C. Dunkel-Schetter (Eds.), *Infertility: Perspectives from stress and coping research* (pp. 157–180). New York: Plenum.

Clark, M. S., Milberg, S., & Ross, J. (1983). Arousal cues arousal-related material in memory: Implications for understanding effects of mood on memory. *Journal of Verbal Learning and Verbal Behavior, 22*, 633–649.

Clark, M. S., & Mills, J. (1979). Interpersonal attraction in exchange and communal relationships. *Journal of Personality and Social Psychology, 37*, 12–24.

(1993). The difference between communal and exchange relationships: What it is and is not. *Personality and Social Psychology Bulletin, 19*, 684–691.

Clark, R. N. (1996). *Control system dynamics*. New York: Cambridge University Press.

Cleiren, M. (1993). *Bereavement and adaptation: A comparative study of the aftermath of death*. Washington, DC: Hemisphere.

Cloninger, C. R. (1987). A systematic method for clinical description and classification of personality variants. *Archives of General Psychiatry, 44*, 573–588.

(1988). A unified biosocial theory of personality and its role in the development of anxiety states: A reply to commentaries. *Psychiatric Developments, 2*, 83–120.

Clore, G. L., Schwarz, N., & Conway, M. (1994). Affective causes and consequences of social information processing. In R. S. Wyer, Jr., & T. K. Srull (Eds.), *Handbook of social cognition* (2nd ed., pp. 323–417). Hillsdale, NJ: Erlbaum.

Coats, E. K., Janoff-Bulman, R., & Alpert, N. (1996). Approach versus avoidance goals: Differences in self-evaluation and well-being. *Personality and Social Psychology Bulletin, 22*, 1057–1067.

Cohen, J. D., Romero, R. D., Servan-Schreiber, D., & Farah, M. J. (1994). Mechanisms of spatial attention: The relation of macrostructure to microstructure in parietal neglect. *Journal of Cognitive Neuroscience, 6*, 377–387.

Cohen, S. (1980). After effects of stress on human performance and social behavior: A review of research and theory. *Psychological Bulletin, 88*, 82–108.

Cohen, S., Doyle, W. J., Skoner, D. P., Rabin, B. S., & Gwaltney, J. M., Jr. (1997). Social ties and susceptibility to the common cold. *Journal of the American Medical Association, 277*, 1940–1944.

Cohn, D. A., Silver, D. H., Cowan, C. P., Cowan, P. A., & Pearson, J. (1992).

Working models of childhood attachment and couple relationships. *Journal of Family Issues, 13,* 432–449.

Collins, R. L. (1996). For better or worse: The impact of upward social comparison on self-evaluation. *Psychological Bulletin, 119,* 51–69.

Colwill, R. M. (1993). An associative analysis of instrumental learning. *Current Directions in Psychological Science, 2,* 111–116.

Conolley, E. S., Gerard, H. B., & Kline, T. (1978). Competitive behavior: A manifestation of motivation for ability comparison. *Journal of Experimental Social Psychology, 14,* 123–131.

Cooley, C. H. (1902). *Human nature and the social order.* New York: Scribner's.

Costa, P. T., Jr., & McCrae, R. R. (1988). From catalog to classification: Murray's needs and the five-factor model. *Journal of Personality and Social Psychology, 55,* 258–265.

(1992). *Revised NEO Personality Inventory (NEO PI-R) and NEO Five-Factor Inventory (NEO-FFI): Professional manual.* Odessa, FL: Psychological Assessment Resources.

Creel, H. G. (1953). *Chinese thought: From Confucius to Mao to Tsê-Tung.* New York: New American Library.

Crocker, J., Luhtanen, R., Blaine, B., & Broadnax, S. (1994). Collective self-esteem and psychological well-being among White, Black, and Asian college students. *Personality and Social Psychology Bulletin, 20,* 503–513.

Crocker, J., & Major, B. (1989). Social stigma and self-esteem: The self-protective properties of stigma. *Psychological Review, 96,* 608–630.

Cronkite, R. C., & Moos, R. H. (1984). The role of predisposing and moderating factors in the stress-illness relationship. *Journal of Health and Social Behavior, 25,* 372–393.

Cross, S. E., & Madson, L. (1997). Models of the self: Self-construals and gender. *Psychological Bulletin, 122,* 5–37.

Crutchfield, R. A. (1955). Conformity and character. *American Psychologist, 10,* 191–198.

Csikszentmihalyi, M. (1990). *Flow: The psychology of optimal experience.* New York: Harper & Row.

Curtis, R. C., & Miller, K. (1986). Believing another likes or dislikes you: Behavior making the beliefs come true. *Journal of Personality and Social Psychology, 51,* 284–290.

Dalgleish, T., & Watts, F. N. (1990). Biases of attention and memory in disorders of anxiety and depression. *Clinical Psychology Review, 10,* 589–604.

Darley, J. M., & Fazio, R. H. (1980). Expectancy confirmation processes arising in the social interaction sequence. *American Psychologist, 35,* 867–881.

Davidson, R. J. (1992a). Anterior cerebral asymmetry and the nature of emotion. *Brain and Cognition, 20,* 125–151.

(1992b). Prolegomenon to the structure of emotion: Gleanings from neuropsychology. *Cognition and Emotion, 6,* 245–268.

(1995). Cerebral asymmetry, emotion, and affective style. In R. J. Davidson & K. Hugdahl (Eds.), *Brain asymmetry* (pp. 361–387). Cambridge, MA: MIT Press.

Davidson, R. J., Ekman, P., Saron, C. D., Senulis, J. A., & Friesen, W. V. (1990). Approach–withdrawal and cerebral asymmetry: Emotional expression and brain physiology: I. *Journal of Personality and Social Psychology, 58*, 330–341.

Davidson, R. J., & Sutton, S. K. (1995). Affective neuroscience: The emergence of a discipline. *Current Opinion in Neurobiology, 5*, 217–224.

Davies, P. (1988). *The cosmic blueprint: New discoveries in nature's creative ability to order the universe.* New York: Simon & Schuster.

Dawkins, R. (1976). Hierarchical organization: A candidate principle for ethology. In P. P. G. Bateson & R. A. Hinde (Eds.), *Growing points in ethology* (pp. 7–54). Cambridge: Cambridge University Press.

DeAngelis, D. L., Post, W. M., & Travis, C. C. (1986). *Positive feedback in natural systems (Biomathematics, Vol. 15).* Berlin and New York: Springer-Verlag.

Deci, E. L. (1992). On the nature and functions of motivation theories. *Psychological Science, 3*, 167–171.

Deci, E. L., & Ryan, R. M. (1985). *Intrinsic motivation and self-determination in human behavior.* New York: Plenum.

(1991). A motivational approach to self: Integration in personality. In R. Dienstbier (Ed.), *Nebraska symposium on motivation: Vol. 38. Perspectives on motivation* (pp. 237–288). Lincoln: University of Nebraska Press.

Denes-Raj, V., & Epstein, S. (1994). Conflict between intuitive and rational processing: When people behave against their better judgments. *Journal of Personality and Social Psychology, 66*, 819–829.

Denning, P. J. (1992). Work is a closed-loop process. *American Scientist, 80*, 314–317.

Depue, R. A., & Iacono, W. G. (1989). Neurobehavioral aspects of affective disorders. *Annual Review of Psychology, 40*, 457–492.

Depue, R. A., Krauss, S. P., & Spoont, M. R. (1987). A two-dimensional threshold model of seasonal bipolar affective disorder. In D. Magnusson & A. Öhman (Eds.), *Psychopathology: An interactional perspective* (pp. 95–123). Orlando, FL: Academic Press.

Dewan, E. M. (1976). Consciousness as an emergent causal agent in the context of control system theory. In G. G. Globus, G. Maxwell, & I. Savodnik (Eds.), *Consciousness and the brain: A scientific and philosophical inquiry* (pp. 181–198). New York: Plenum.

Dewberry, C., & Richardson, S. (1990). Effect of anxiety on optimism. *Journal of Social Psychology, 130*, 731–738.

Diener, C. I., & Dweck, C. S. (1978). An analysis of learned helplessness: Continuous changes in performance strategy and achievement cognitions following failure. *Journal of Personality and Social Psychology, 36*, 451–462.

Diener, E. (1979). Deindividuation, self-awareness, and disinhibition. *Journal of Personality and Social Psychology, 37*, 1160–1171.

Diener, E., & Emmons, R. A. (1984). The independence of positive and negative affect. *Journal of Personality and Social Psychology, 47*, 1105–1117.

Diener, E., & Iran-Nejad, A. (1986). The relationship in experience between various types of affect. *Journal of Personality and Social Psychology, 50*, 1031–1038.

Diener, E., Larsen, R. J., Levine, S., & Emmons, R. A. (1985). Intensity and frequency: Dimensions underlying positive and negative affect. *Journal of Personality and Social Psychology, 48*, 1253–1265.

Digman, J. M. (1990). Personality structure: Emergence of the five-factor model. *Annual Review of Psychology, 41*, 417–440.

Dodge, K. A. (1986). A social information processing model of social competence in children. In M. Perlmutter (Ed.), *Minnesota symposium on child psychology* (Vol. 18). Hillsdale, NJ: Erlbaum.

Dodge, K. A., Asher, S. R., & Parkhurst, J. T. (1989). Social life as a goal-coordination task. In C. Ames & R. Ames (Eds.), *Research on motivation in education: Goals and cognitions* (Vol. 3, pp. 107–135). San Diego: Academic Press.

Dodge, K. A., & Crick, N. R. (1990). Social information-processing bases of aggressive behavior in children. *Personality and Social Psychology Bulletin, 16*, 8–22.

Drake, R. A. (1984). Lateral asymmetry of personal optimism. *Journal of Research in Personality, 18*, 497–507.

(1985). Lateral asymmetry of risky recommendations. *Personality and Social Psychology Bulletin, 11*, 409–417.

(1987). Conceptions of own versus others' outcomes: Manipulation by monoaural attentional orientation. *European Journal of Social Psychology, 17*, 373–375.

Duck, S. W. (Ed.) (1982). *Personal relationships 4: Dissolving personal relationships*. London: Academic Press.

Duncan, B. L. (1976). Differential social perception and attribution of intergroup violence: Testing the lower limits of stereotyping of Blacks. *Journal of Personality and Social Psychology, 34*, 590–598.

Dutton, K. A., & Brown, J. D. (1997). Global self-esteem and specific self-views as determinants of people's reactions to success and failure. *Journal of Personality and Social Psychology, 73*, 139–148.

Duval, S., & Wicklund, R. A. (1972). *A theory of objective self-awareness*. New York: Academic Press.

(1973). Effects of objective self-awareness on attribution of causality. *Journal of Experimental Social Psychology, 9*, 17–31.

Duval, T. S., Duval, V. H., & Mulilis, J.-P. (1992). Effects of self-focus, discrepancy between self and standard, and outcome expectancy favorability on the tendency to match self to standard or to withdraw. *Journal of Personality and Social Psychology, 62*, 340–348.

Dweck, C. S. (1996). Implicit theories as organizers of goals and behavior. In P. M. Gollwitzer & J. A. Bargh (Eds.), *The psychology of action: Linking cognition and motivation to behavior* (pp. 69–90). New York: Guilford.

Dweck, C. S., & Elliott, E. S. (1983). Achievement motivation. In P. H. Mussen (Ed.), *Handbook of child psychology, 4th ed.* (pp. 643–691). New York: Wiley.

Dweck, C. S., Hong, Y., & Chiu, C. (1993). Implicit theories: Individual differences in the likelihood and meaning of dispositional inferences. *Personality and Social Psychology Bulletin, 19*, 644–656.

Dweck, C. S., & Leggett, E. L. (1988). A social-cognitive approach to motivation and personality. *Psychological Review, 95*, 256–273.

Eitel, P., Hatchett, L., Friend, R., Griffin, K. W., & Wadhwa, N. K. (1995). Burden of self-care in seriously ill patients: Impact on adjustment. *Health Psychology, 14*, 457–463.

Ekman, P., & Davidson, R. J. (1993). Voluntary smiling changes regional brain activity. *Psychological Science, 4*, 342–345.

Ekman, P., Levenson, R. W., & Friesen, W. V. (1983). Autonomic nervous system activity distinguishes between emotions, *Science, 221*, 1208–1210.

Elliot, A. J., & Church, M. A. (1997). A hierarchical model of approach and avoidance achievement motivation. *Journal of Personality and Social Psychology, 72*, 218–232.

Elliot, A. J., & Sheldon, K. M. (1997). Avoidance achievement motivation: A personal goals analysis. *Journal of Personality and Social Psychology, 73*, 171–185.

Elliot, A. J., Sheldon, K. M., & Church, M. A. (1997). Avoidance personal goals and subjective well-being. *Personality and Social Psychology Bulletin, 23*, 915–927.

Elliott, E. S., & Dweck, C. S. (1988). Goals: An approach to motivation and achievement. *Journal of Personality and Social Psychology, 54*, 5–12.

Ellsworth, P. C., & Smith, C. A. (1988). From appraisal to emotion: Differences among unpleasant feelings. *Motivation and Emotion, 12*, 271–302.

Emmons, R. A. (1986). Personal strivings: An approach to personality and subjective well being. *Journal of Personality and Social Psychology, 51*, 1058–1068.

   (1992). Abstract versus concrete goals: Personal striving level, physical illness, and psychological well being. *Journal of Personality and Social Psychology, 62*, 292–300.

   (1996). Striving and feeling: Personal goals and subjective well-being. In

P. M. Gollwitzer & J. A. Bargh (Eds.), *The psychology of action: Linking cognition and motivation to behavior* (pp. 313–337). New York: Guilford.

Emmons, R. A., & King, L. A. (1988). Conflict among personal strivings: Immediate and long-term implications for psychological and physical well-being. *Journal of Personality and Social Psychology, 54*, 1040–1048.

Endler, N. S., Cox, B. J., Parker, J. D. A., & Bagby, R. M. (1992). Self-reports of depression and state–trait anxiety: Evidence for differential assessment. *Journal of Personality and Social Psychology, 63*, 832–838.

Engel, G. L. (1971). Sudden and rapid death during psychological stress, folklore or folkwisdom? *Annals of Internal Medicine, 74*, 771–782.

Enzle, M. E., & Anderson, S. C. (1993). Surveillant intentions and intrinsic motivation. *Journal of Personality and Social Psychology, 64*, 257–266.

Epping-Jordan, J. E., Compas, B. E., & Howell, D. C. (1994). Predictors of cancer progression in young adult men and women: Avoidance, intrusive thoughts, and psychological symptoms. *Health Psychology, 13*, 539–547.

Epstein, S. (1973). The self-concept revisited: Or a theory of a theory. *American Psychologist, 28*, 404–416.

(1979). The stability of behavior: I. On predicting most of the people much of the time. *Journal of Personality and Social Psychology, 37*, 1097–1126.

(1985). The implications of cognitive–experiential self theory for research in social psychology and personality. *Journal for the Theory of Social Behavior, 15*, 283–310.

(1990). Cognitive–experiential self-theory. In L. Pervin (Ed.), *Handbook of personality: Theory and research* (pp. 165–192). New York: Guilford.

(1992). Coping ability, negative self-evaluation, and overgeneralization: Experiment and theory. *Journal of Personality and Social Psychology, 62*, 826–836.

(1994). Integration of the cognitive and the psychodynamic unconscious. *American Psychologist, 49*, 709–724.

Epstein, S., Lipson, A., Holstein, C., & Huh, E. (1992). Irrational reactions to negative outcomes: Evidence for two conceptual systems. *Journal of Personality and Social Psychology, 62*, 328–339.

Erber, R. (1991). Affective and semantic priming: Effects of mood on category accessibility and inference. *Journal of Experimental Social Psychology, 27*, 480–498.

Erber, R., & Tesser, A. (1992). Task effort and the regulation of mood: The absorption hypothesis. *Journal of Experimental Social Psychology, 28*, 339–359.

Evarts, E. V. (1973). Motor cortex reflexes associated with learned movement. *Science, 179*, 501–503.

Everson, S. A., Goldberg, D. E., Kaplan, G. A., Cohen, R. D., Pukkala, E., Tuomilehto, J., & Salonen, J. T. (1996). Hopelessness and risk of mortality and incidence of myocardial infarction and cancer. *Psychosomatic Medicine, 58*, 113–121.

Eysenck, H. J. (1967). *The biological basis of personality*. Springfield, IL: Charles C Thomas.

Fairbairn, W. R. D. (1954). *An object-relations theory of the personality*. New York: Basic Books.

Fawcett, J., Scheftner, W., Clark, D., Hedeker, D., Gibbons, R., & Coryell, W. (1987). Clinical predictors of suicide in patients with major affective disorders: A controlled prospective study. *American Journal of Psychiatry, 144*, 35–40.

Fawzy, F. I., Fawzy, N. W., Hyun, C. S., Elashoff, R., Guthrie, D., Fahey, J., & Morton, D. (1993). Malignant melanoma: Effects of an early structured psychiatric intervention, coping, and affective state on recurrence and survival 6 years later. *Archives of General Psychiatry, 50*, 681–689.

Feather, N. T. (1961). The relationship of persistence at a task to expectations of success and achievement-related motives. *Journal of Abnormal and Social Psychology, 63*, 552–561.

(Ed.) (1982). *Expectations and actions: Expectancy-value models in psychology*. Hillsdale, NJ: Erlbaum.

(1989). Trying and giving up: Persistence and lack of persistence in failure situations. In R. C. Curtis (Ed.), *Self-defeating behaviors: Experimental research, clinical impressions, and practical implications* (pp. 67–95). New York: Plenum.

Fehr, B., & Russell, J. A. (1984). Concept of emotion viewed from a prototype perspective. *Journal of Experimental Psychology: General, 113*, 464–486.

Feldman, J. A., & Ballard, D. H. (1982). Connectionist models and their properties. *Cognitive Science, 6*, 205–254.

Felton, B. J., Revenson, T. A., & Hinrichsen, G. A. (1984). Stress and coping in the explanation of psychological adjustment among chronically ill adults. *Social Science & Medicine, 18*, 889–898.

Fenigstein, A. (1979). Self-consciousness, self-attention, and social interaction. *Journal of Personality and Social Psychology, 37*, 75–86.

Fenigstein, A., & Levine, M. P. (1984). Self-attention, concept activation, and the causal self. *Journal of Experimental Social Psychology, 20*, 231–245.

Fenigstein, A., Scheier, M. F., & Buss, A. H. (1975). Public and private self-consciousness: Assessment and theory. *Journal of Consulting and Clinical Psychology, 43*, 522–527.

Festinger, L. (1950). Informal social communication. *Psychological Review, 57*, 271–282.

(1954). A theory of social comparison processes. *Human Relations, 7*, 117–140.

Festinger, L., Pepitone, A., & Newcomb, T. (1952). Some consequences of deindividuation in a group. *Journal of Abnormal and Social Psychology,* *47*, 382–389.

Festinger, L., Torrey, J., & Willerman, B. (1954) Self-evaluation as a function of attraction to the group. *Human Relations, 7,* 161–174.

Field, M., & Golubitsky, M. (1992). *Symmetry in chaos: A search for pattern in mathematics, art, and nature.* Oxford: Oxford University Press.

Finlay-Jones, R., & Brown, G. W. (1981). Types of stressful life event and the onset of anxiety and depressive disorders. *Psychological Medicine, 11,* 803–815.

Fischer, K. W., & Rose, S. P. (1994). Dynamic development of coordination of components in brain and behavior: A framework for theory and research. In G. Dawson & K. W. Fischer (Eds.), *Human behavior and the developing brain* (pp. 3–66). New York: Guilford.

Fiske, A. P. (1992). The four elementary forms of sociality: Framework for a unified theory of social relations. *Psychological Review, 99,* 689–723.

Foa, E. B., & Kozak, M. J. (1986). Emotional processing of fear: Exposure to corrective information. *Psychological Bulletin, 99,* 20–35.

Foa, E. B., Rothbaum, B. O., Riggs, D. S., & Murdock, R. S. (1991). Treatment of post-traumatic stress disorder in rape victims: A comparison between cognitive-behavioral procedures and counseling. *Journal of Consulting and Clinical Psychology, 59,* 715–723.

Folkman, S. (1984). Personal control and stress and coping processes: A theoretical analysis. *Journal of Personality and Social Psychology, 46,* 839 852.

Folkman, S., & Lazarus, R. S. (1985). If it changes it must be a process: A study of emotion and coping during three stages of a college examination. *Journal of Personality and Social Psychology, 48,* 150–170.

Ford, D. H. (1987). *Humans as self-constructing living systems: A developmental perspective on behavior and personality.* Hillsdale, NJ: Erlbaum.

Forgas, J. P. (1994). Sad and guilty? Affective influences on the explanation of conflict in close relationships. *Journal of Personality and Social Psychology, 66,* 56–68.

Forgas, J. P., & Moylan, S. (1987). After the movies: Transient mood and social judgments. *Personality and Social Psychology Bulletin, 13,* 467–477.

Fowles, D. C. (1980). The three arousal model: Implications of Gray's two-factor learning theory for heart rate, electrodermal activity, and psychopathy. *Psychophysiology, 17,* 87–104.

Fox, N. A., & Davidson, R. J. (1988). Patterns of brain electrical activity during facial signs of emotion in 10-month-old infants. *Developmental Psychology, 24,* 230–236.

Frankel, C. B., & Froming, W. J. (1992). *Adaptation and self-regulation.* Unpublished manuscript.

Freedland, R. L., & Bertenthal, B. I. (1994). Developmental changes in inter-limb coordination: Transition to hands-and-knees crawling. *Psychological Science, 5*, 26–32.

Frese, M., & Sabini, J. (1985). *Goal-directed behavior: The concept of action in psychology*. Hillsdale, NJ: Erlbaum.

Freud, S. (1949). *An outline of psychoanalysis*. New York: Norton.

(1962). *The ego and the id*. New York: Norton. (Original work published 1923.)

Friedrich, J. (1993). Primary error detection and minimization (PEDMIN) strategies in social cognition: A reinterpretation of confirmation bias phenomena. *Psychological Review, 100*, 298–319.

Frijda, N. H. (1986). *The emotions*. Cambridge: Cambridge University Press.

(1988). The laws of emotion. *American Psychologist, 43*, 349–358.

Froming, W. J., & Carver, C. S. (1981). Divergent influences of private and public self-consciousness in a compliance paradigm. *Journal of Research in Personality, 15*, 159–171.

Froming, W. J., Moser, R. P., Mychack, P., & Nasby, W. (1995). A control-theory approach to social development. In N. Eisenberg (Ed.), *Review of personality and social psychology* (Vol. 15, pp. 261–288). Newbury Park, CA: Sage.

Froming, W. J., Walker, G. R., & Lopyan, K. J. (1982). Public and private self-awareness: When personal attitudes conflict with societal expectations. *Journal of Experimental Social Psychology, 18*, 476–487.

Galassi, J. P., Frierson, H. T., Jr., & Sharer, R. (1981). Behavior of high, moderate, and low test anxious students during an actual test situation. *Journal of Consulting and Clinical Psychology, 49*, 51–62.

Gallistel, C. R. (1980). *The organization of action: A new synthesis*. Hillsdale, NJ: Erlbaum.

Ganz, P. A., Schag, C. C., & Heinrich, R. L. (1985). The psychosocial impact of cancer on the elderly: A comparison with younger patients. *Journal of the American Geriatric Society, 33*, 429–435.

Gazzaniga, M. S. (1972). One brain – two minds? *American Scientist, 60*, 311–317.

Gehring, W. J., Goss, B., Coles, M. G. H., Meyer, D. E., & Donchin, E. (1993). A neural system for error detection and compensation. *Psychological Science, 4*, 385–390.

Gerard, H. B. (1963). Emotional uncertainty and social comparison. *Journal of Abnormal and Social Psychology, 66*, 568–573.

Gibbons, F. X. (1978). Sexual standards and reactions to pornography: Enhancing behavioral consistency through self-focusesd attention. *Journal of Personality and Social Psychology, 36*, 976–987.

Gibbons, F. X., Carver, C. S., Scheier, M. F., & Hormuth, S. E. (1979). Self-focused attention and the placebo effect: Fooling some of the people some of the time. *Journal of Experimental Social Psychology, 15*, 263–274.

Gleick, J. (1987). *Chaos: Making a new science*. New York: Viking Penguin.

Gobet, F., & Simon, H. A. (1996). The roles of recognition processes and look-ahead search in time-constrained expert problem solving: Evidence from grand-master-level chess. *Psychological Science, 7*, 52–55.

Goethals, G. R., & Nelson, R. E. (1973). Similarity in the influence process: The belief-value distinction. *Journal of Personality and Social Psychology, 25*, 117–122.

Goldin-Meadow, S., & Alibali, M. W. (1995). Mechanisms of transition: Learning with a helping hand. In D. Medin (Ed.), *The psychology of learning and motivation* (Vol. 33, pp. 115–157). San Diego, CA: Academic Press.

Gollwitzer, P. M. (1990). Action phases and mind sets. In E. T. Higgins & R. M. Sorrentino (Eds.), *Handbook of motivation and cognition: Foundations of social behavior* (Vol. 2, pp. 53–92). New York: Guilford.

(1996). The volitional benefits of planning. In P. M. Gollwitzer & J. A. Bargh (Eds.), *The psychology of action: Linking cognition and motivation to behavior* (pp. 287–312). New York: Guilford.

Gollwitzer, P. M., & Brandstätter, V. (1997). Implementational intentions and effective goal pursuit. *Journal of Personality and Social Psychology, 73*, 186–199.

Gollwitzer, P. M., & Kinney, R. F. (1989). Effects of deliberative and implemental mindsets on illusion of control. *Journal of Personality and Social Psychology, 56*, 531–542.

Gottman, J. M. (1993). A theory of marital dissolution and stability. *Journal of Family Psychology, 7*, 57–75.

Gottschalk, A., Bauer, M. S., & Whybrow, P. C. (1995). Evidence of chaotic mood variation in bipolar disorder. *Archives of General Psychiatry, 52*, 947–959.

Graham, D. (1985). Pattern and control of walking in insects. *Advances in Insect Physiology, 18*, 31–140.

Gray, J. A. (1972). The psychophysiological basis of introversion-extraversion: A modification of Eysenck's theory. In V. D. Nebylitsyn & J. A. Gray (Eds.), *The biological bases of individual behaviour* (pp. 182–205). New York: Academic Press.

(1977). Drug effects on fear and frustration: Possible limbic site of action of minor tranquilizers. In L. L. Iversen, S. D. Iversen, & S. H. Snyder (Eds.), *Handbook of psychopharmacology* (Vol. 8, pp. 433–529). New York: Plenum.

(1978). The 1977 Myers lecture: The neuropsychology of anxiety. *British Journal of Psychology, 69*, 417–434.

(1981). A critique of Eysenck's theory of personality. In H. J. Eysenck (Ed.), *A model for personality* (pp. 246–276). Berlin: Springer-Verlag.

(1982). *The neuropsychology of anxiety: An enquiry into the functions of the septo-hippocampal system*. New York: Oxford University Press.

(1987a). Perspectives on anxiety and impulsivity: A commentary. *Journal of Research in Personality, 21*, 493–509.

(1987b). *The psychology of fear and stress*. Cambridge: Cambridge University Press.

(1990). Brain systems that mediate both emotion and cognition. *Cognition and Emotion, 4*, 269–288.

(1994). Personality dimensions and emotion systems. In P. Ekman & R. J. Davidson (Eds.), *The nature of emotion: Fundamental questions* (pp. 329–331). New York: Oxford University Press.

Greenberg, J. (1980). Attentional focus and locus of performance causality as determinants of equity behavior. *Journal of Personality and Social Psychology, 38*, 579–585.

(1982). Self-image versus impression management in adherence to distributive justice standards: The influence of self-awareness and self-consciousness. *Journal of Personality and Social Psychology, 44*, 5–19.

Greenberg, J., Pyszczynski, T., & Solomon, S. (1986). The causes and consequences of the need for self-esteem: A terror management theory. In R. F. Baumeister (Ed.), *Public self and private self* (pp. 189–212). New York: Springer-Verlag.

Greenberg, M. S., & Alloy, L. B. (1989). Depression versus anxiety: Processing of self- and other-referent information. *Cognition & Emotion, 3*, 207–223.

Greenberg, M. S., & Beck, A. T. (1989). Depression versus anxiety: A test of the content-specificity hypothesis. *Journal of Abnormal Psychology, 98*, 9–13.

Greene, P. H. (1972). Problems of organization of motor systems. In R. Rosen & F. M. Snell (Eds.), *Progress in theoretical biology* (Vol. 2, pp. 303–338). New York: Academic Press.

(1982). Why is it easy to control your arms? *Journal of Motor Behavior, 14*, 260–286.

Greenwald, A. G. (1980). The totalitarian ego: Fabrication and revision of personal history. *American Psychologist, 35*, 603–618.

(1982). Ego task analysis: An integration of research on ego-involvement and self-awareness. In A. H. Hastorf & A. M. Isen (Eds.), *Cognitive social psychology* (pp. 109–147). New York: Elsevier North-Holland.

Greenwald, A. G., & Breckler, S. J. (1985). To whom is the self presented? In B. R. Schlenker (Ed.), *The self and social life* (pp. 126–145). New York: McGraw-Hill.

Greer, S., Morris, T., & Pettingale, K. W. (1979). Psychological response to breast cancer: Effect on outcome. *Lancet, ii*, 785–787.

Greer, S., Morris, T., Pettingale, K. W., & Haybittle, J. L. (1990). Psychological response to breast cancer and 15-year outcome. *Lancet, i*, 49–50.

Gruenberg, A. M., & Goldstein, R. D. (1997). Depressive disorders. In A. Tasman, J. Kay, & J. A. Lieberman (Eds.), *Psychiatry* (Vol. 2, pp. 990–1019). Philadelphia: W. B. Saunders.

Guisinger, S., & Blatt, S. J. (1994). Individuality and relatedness: Evolution of a fundamental dialectic. *American Psychologist, 49*, 104–111.

Hamilton, J. C., Greenberg, J., Pyszczynski, T., & Cather, C. (1993). A self-regulatory perspective on psychopathology and psychotherapy. *Journal of Psychotherapy Integration, 3*, 205–248.

Han, S., & Shavitt, S. (1994). Persuasion and culture: Advertising appeals in individualistic and collectivistic societies. *Journal of Experimental Social Psychology, 30*, 326–350.

Hansen, C. H., & Hansen, R. D. (1988). Finding the face in the crowd: An anger superiority effect. *Journal of Personality and Social Psychology, 54*, 917–924.

Harlow, R. E., & Cantor, N. (1996). Still participating after all these years: A study of life task participation in later life. *Journal of Personality and Social Psychology, 71*, 1235–1249.

Harmon-Jones, E., & Allen, J. J. (1997). Behavioral activation sensitivity and resting frontal EEG asymmetry: Covariation of putative indicators related to risk for mood disorders. *Journal of Abnormal Psychology, 106*, 159–163.

Harver, A. (1994). Effects of feedback on the ability of asthmatic subjects to detect increases in the flow-resistive component to breathing. *Health Psychology, 13*, 52–62.

Hatfield, E., Cacioppo, J. T., & Rapson, R. L. (1993). *Emotional contagion*. Cambridge: Cambridge University Press.

Hayes, A. M., & Strauss, J. L. (in press). Dynamic systems theory as a paradigm for the study of change in psychotherapy: An application to cognitive therapy for depression. *Journal of Consulting and Clinical Psychology*.

Hayes-Roth, B., & Hayes-Roth, F. (1979). A cognitive model of planning. *Cognitive Science, 3*, 275–310.

Hazan, C., & Shaver, P. (1994). Attachment as an organizational framework for research on close relationships. *Psychological Inquiry, 5*, 1–22.

Heatherton, T. F., & Baumeister, R. F. (1991). Binge eating as escape from self-awareness. *Psychological Bulletin, 110*, 86–108.

Heatherton, T. F., & Nichols, P. A. (1994). Personal accounts of successful versus failed attempts at life change. *Personality and Social Psychology Bulletin, 20*, 664–675.

Heberlein, T. A., & Black, J. S. (1976). Attitudinal specificity and the prediction of behavior in a field setting. *Journal of Personality and Social Psychology, 33*, 474–479.

Heckhausen, H., & Gollwitzer, P. M. (1987). Thought contents and cognitive functioning in motivational versus volitional states of mind. *Motivation and Emotion, 11*, 101–120.

Heckhausen, J., & Schulz, R. (1995). A life-span theory of control. *Psychological Review, 102*, 284–304.

Helgeson, V. S. (1994). The relation of agency and communion to well-being: Evidence and potential explanations. *Psychological Bulletin, 116*, 412–428.

Helgeson, V. S., & Taylor, S. E. (1993). Social comparisons and adjustment among cardiac patients. *Journal of Applied Social Psychology, 23*, 1171–1195.

Henriques, J. B., & Davidson, R. J. (1991). Left frontal hypoactivation in depression. *Journal of Abnormal Psychology, 100*, 535–545.

Henriques, J. B., Glowacki, J. M., & Davidson, R. J. (1994). Reward fails to alter response bias in depression. *Journal of Abnormal Psychology, 103*, 460–466.

Higgins, E. T. (1987). Self-discrepancy: A theory relating self and affect. *Psychological Review, 94*, 319–340.

(1989). Knowledge accessibility and activation: Subjectivity and suffering from unconscious sources. In J. S. Uleman & J. A. Bargh (Eds.), *Unintended thought: The limits of awareness, intention, and control* (pp. 75–123). New York: Guilford.

(1996). Ideals, oughts, and regulatory focus: Affect and motivation from distinct pains and pleasures. In P. M. Gollwitzer & J. A. Bargh (Eds.), *The psychology of action: Linking cognition and motivation to behavior* (pp. 91–114). New York: Guilford.

(1997). Beyond pleasure and pain. *American Psychologist, 52*, 1280–1300.

Higgins, E. T., Bond, R., Klein, R., & Strauman, T. J. (1986). Self-discrepancies and emotional vulnerability: How magnitude, accessibility and type of discrepancy influence affect. *Journal of Personality and Social Psychology, 41*, 1–15.

Higgins, E. T., Roney, C. J. R., Crowe, E., & Hymes, C. (1994). Ideal versus ought predilections for approach and avoidance: Distinct self-regulatory systems. *Journal of Personality and Social Psychology, 66*, 276–286.

Higgins, E. T., Shah, J., & Friedman, R. (1997). Emotional responses to goal attainment: Strength of regulatory focus as moderator. *Journal of Personality and Social Psychology, 72*, 515–525.

Higgins, E. T., & Tykocinski, O. (1992). Self-discrepancies and biographical memory: Personality and cognition at the level of psychological situation. *Personality and Social Psychology Bulletin, 18*, 527–535.

Hiroto, D. S., & Seligman, M. E. P. (1975). Generality of learned helplessness in man. *Journal of Personality and Social Psychology, 31*, 311–327.

Hirt, E. R., Melton, R. J., McDonald, H. E., & Harackiewicz, J. M. (1996). Processing goals, task interest, and the mood–performance relationship: A mediational analysis. *Journal of Personality and Social Psychology, 71*, 245–261.

Hjelle, L. A., & Bernard, M. (1994). Private self-consciousness and the retest reliability of self-reports. *Journal of Research in Personality, 28*, 52–67.

Hobfoll, S. E. (1989). Conservation of resources: A new attempt at conceptualizing stress. *American Psychologist, 44*, 513–524.

Hoffman, C., Mischel, W., & Mazze, K. (1981). The role of purpose in the organization of information about behavior: Trait-based versus goalbased categories in person cognition. *Journal of Personality and Social Psychology, 40*, 211–225.

Hoffman, M. L. (1986). Affect, cognition, and motivation. In R. M. Sorrentino & E. T. Higgins (Eds.), *Handbook of motivation and cognition* (pp. 244–280). New York: Guilford.

Holahan, C. K. (1988). Relation of life goals at age 70 to activity participation and health and psychological well-being among Terman's gifted men and women. *Psychology and Aging, 3*, 286–291.

Hollenbeck, J. R., & Williams, C. R. (1987). Goal importance, self-focus, and the goal setting process. *Journal of Applied Psychology, 72*, 204–211.

Holyoak, K. J., & Spellman, B. A. (1993). Thinking. *Annual Review of Psychology, 44*, 265–315.

Hope, D. A., Heimberg, R. G., & Klein, J. F. (1990). Social anxiety and the recall of interpersonal information. *Journal of Cognitive Psychotherapy: An International Quarterly, 4*, 185–195.

Hoyt, D. F., & Taylor, C. R. (1981). Gait and energetics of locomotion in horses. *Nature, 292*, 239–240.

Hsee, C. K., & Abelson, R. P. (1991). Velocity relation: Satisfaction as a function of the first derivative of outcome over time. *Journal of Personality and Social Psychology, 60*, 341–347.

Hsee, C. K., Salovey, P., & Abelson, R. P. (1994). The quasi-acceleration relation: Satisfaction as a function of the change of velocity of outcome over time. *Journal of Experimental Social Psychology, 30*, 96–111.

Hull, C. L. (1943). *Principles of behavior*. New York: Appleton-Century-Crofts.

Hull, J. G. (1981). A self-awareness model of the causes and effects of alcohol consumption. *Journal of Abnormal Psychology, 90*, 586–600.

Hull, J. G., & Rielly, N. P. (1986). An information processing approach to alcohol use and its consequences. In R. E. Ingram (Ed.), *Information processing approaches to clinical psychology* (pp. 151–167). New York: Academic Press.

Hunt, J. McV. (1965). Intrinsic motivation and its role in psychological development. In D. Levine (Ed.), *Nebraska symposium on motivation* (Vol. 13, pp. 189–282). Lincoln: University of Nebraska Press.

Huntington, H. B., & MacCrone, R. K. (1993). Thermal hysteresis. In S. P. Parker (Ed.), *McGraw-Hill encyclopedia of physics* (2nd ed., p. 1426). New York: McGraw-Hill.

Hyland, M. (1987). Control theory interpretation of psychological mechanisms of depression: Comparison and integration of several theories. *Psychological Bulletin, 102*, 109–121.

Ingram, R. E. (1990). Self-focused attention in clinical disorder: Review and a conceptual model. *Psychological Bulletin, 107*, 156–176.

Ingvar, D. H. (1985). "Memory of the future": An essay on the temporal organization of conscious awareness. *Human Neurobiology, 4*, 127–136.

Ironson, G., Friedman, A., Klimas, N., Antoni, M., Fletcher, M. A., LaPerriere, A., Simoneau, J., & Schneiderman, N. (1994). Distress, denial, and low adherence to behavioral interventions predict faster disease progression in gay men infected with human immunodeficiency virus. *International Journal of Behavioral Medicine, 1*, 90–105.

Ito, T. A., Miller, N., & Pollock, V. E. (1996). Alcohol and aggression: A meta-analysis on the moderating effects of inhibitory cues, triggering events, and self-focused attention. *Psychological Bulletin, 120*, 60–82.

Izard, C. E. (1977). *Human emotions*. New York: Plenum.

Jaffe, J., & Feldstein, S. (1970). *Rhythms of dialogue*. New York: Academic Press.

James, W. (1890). *The principles of psychology*. New York: Holt, Rinehart, & Winston.

Janoff-Bulman, R. (1992). *Shattered assumptions: Towards a new psychology of trauma*. New York: Free Press.

Janoff-Bulman, R., & Brickman, P. (1982). Expectations and what people learn from failure. In N. T. Feather (Ed.), *Expectations and actions: Expectancy-value models in psychology* (pp. 207–237). Hillsdale, NJ: Erlbaum.

Johnson, E. J., & Tversky, A. (1983). Affect, generalization, and the perception of risk. *Journal of Personality and Social Psychology, 45*, 20–31.

Joiner, T. E., Jr., & Metalsky, G. I. (1995). A prospective test of an integrative interpersonal theory of depression: A naturalistic study of college roommates. *Journal of Personality and Social Psychology, 69*, 778–788.

Jones, S. C., & Regan, D. T. (1974). Ability evaluation through social comparison. *Journal of Experimental Social Psychology, 10*, 133–146.

Jung, C. G. (1971). A psychological theory of types. In C. G. Jung, *Collected Works* (Vol. 6). Princeton, NJ: Princeton University Press. (Original work published 1931.)

Kagan, J. (1981). *The second year: The emergence of self-awareness*. Cambridge, MA: Harvard University Press.

Kahneman, D., Fredrickson, B. L., Schreiber, C. A., & Redelmeier, D. A. (1993). When more pain is preferred to less: Adding a better end. *Psychological Science, 4*, 401–405.

Kahneman, D., & Tversky, A. (1984). Choices, values, and frames. *American Psychologist, 39*, 341–350.

Kamarck, T., & Jennings, J. R. (1991). Biobehavioral factors in sudden cardiac death. *Psychological Bulletin, 109*, 42–75.

Kanfer, F. H., & Busemeyer, J. R. (1982). The use of problem-solving and decision-making in behavior therapy. *Clinical Psychology Review, 2*, 239–266.

Kaplowitz, S. A., & Fink, E. L. (1992). Dynamics of attitude change. In R. L. Levine & H. E. Fitzgerald (Eds.), *Analysis of dynamic psychological systems: Vol. 2. Methods and applications* (pp. 341–369). New York: Plenum.

Karoly, P. (1993). Mechanisms of self-regulation: A systems view. *Annual Review of Psychology, 44,* 23–52.

Kaye, J. M., Lawton, M. P., Gitlin, L. N., Kleban, M. H., Windsor, L. A., & Kaye, D. (1988). Older people's performance on the Profile of Mood States (POMS). *Clinical Gerontologist, 7,* 35–56.

Keele, S. W., Cohen, A., & Ivry, R. (1990). Motor programs: Concepts and issues. In M. Jeannerod (Ed.), *Attention and performance XIII: Motor representation and control* (pp. 77–110). Hillsdale, NJ: Erlbaum.

Kelly, G. A. (1955). *The psychology of personal constructs.* New York: Norton.

Kelso, J. A. S. (1995). *Dynamic patterns: The self-organization of brain and behavior.* Cambridge, MA: MIT Press.

Kelso, J. A. S., Scholz, J. P., & Schöner, G. (1986). Nonequilibrium phase transitions in coordinated biological motion: Critical fluctuations. *Physics Letters, 118,* 279–284.

Kernis, M. H., & Reis, H. T. (1984). Self-consciousness, self-awareness, and justice in reward allocation. *Journal of Personality, 52,* 58–70.

Kirmeyer, S. L. (1988). Coping with competing demands: Interruption and the Type A pattern. *Journal of Applied Psychology, 73,* 621–629.

Kirkpatrick, S., Gelatt, C. D., Jr., & Vecchi, M. P. (1983). Optimization by simulated annealing. *Science, 220,* 671–680.

Kirschenbaum, D. S. (1985). Proximity and specificity of planning: A position paper. *Cognitive Therapy and Research, 9,* 489–506.

 (1987). Self-regulatory failure: A review with clinical implications. *Clinical Psychology Review, 7,* 77–104.

Klein, J. (1987). *Our need for others and its roots in infancy.* London: Tavistock.

Klein, S. B., & Loftus, J. (1993). The mental representation of trait and autobiographical knowledge about the self. In T. K. Srull & R. S. Wyer, Jr. (Eds.), *The mental representation of trait and autobiographical knowledge about the self: Advances in social cognition* (Vol. 5, pp. 1–49). Hillsdale, NJ: Erlbaum.

Klein, S. B., Loftus, J., Trafton, J. G., & Fuhrman, R. W. (1992). The use of exemplars and abstractions in trait judgments: A model of trait knowledge about the self and others. *Journal of Personality and Social Psychology, 63,* 739–753.

Kling, K. C., Ryff, C. D., & Essex, M. J. (1997). Adaptive changes in the self-concept during a life transition. *Personality and Social Psychology Bulletin, 23,* 981–990.

Klinger, E. (1975). Consequences of commitment to and disengagement from incentives. *Psychological Review, 82,* 1–25.

(1977). *Meaning and void: Inner experience and the incentives in people's lives*. Minneapolis: University of Minnesota Press.

Klinger, E., Barta, S. G., & Maxeiner, M. E. (1980). Motivational correlates of thought content, frequency, and commitment. *Journal of Personality and Social Psychology, 39*, 1222–1237.

(1981). Current concerns: Assessing therapeutically relevant motivation. In P. C. Kendall & S. D. Hollon (Eds.), *Assessment strategies for cognitive behavioral interventions* (pp. 161–196). New York: Academic Press.

Kochanska, G. (1993). Toward a synthesis of parental socialization and child temperament in early development of conscience. *Child Development, 64*, 325–347.

Konorski, J. (1967). *Integrative activity of the brain: An interdisciplinary approach*. Chicago: University of Chicago Press.

Kopp, C. B. (1982). Antecedents of self-regulation: A developmental perspective. *Developmental Psychology, 18*, 199–214.

Kramer, P. D. (1993). *Listening to Prozac: A psychiatrist explores antidepressant drugs and the remaking of the self*. New York: Viking Penguin.

Kruglanski, A. W., Miller, N., & Geen, R. G. (1996). The self and social identity [Special issue]. *Journal of Personality and Social Psychology, 71*(6).

Kugler, P. N., & Turvey, M. T. (1987). *Information, natural law, and the self-assembly of rhythmic movement*. Hillsdale, NJ: Erlbaum.

Kuhl, J. (1981). Motivational and functional helplessness: The moderating effect of state versus action orientation. *Journal of Personality and Social Psychology, 40*, 155–170.

(1984). Volitional aspects of achievement motivation and learned helplessness: Toward a comprehensive theory of action control. In B. A. Maher (Ed.), *Progress in experimental personality research* (Vol. 13, pp. 99–170). New York: Academic Press.

(1985). Volitional mediators of cognition-behavior consistency: Self-regulatory processes and action versus state orientation. In J. Kuhl & J. Beckmann (Eds.), *Action control: From cognition to behavior* (pp. 101–128). New York: Springer-Verlag.

(1994a). Motivation and volition. In G. d'Ydewalle, P. Eelen, & P. Bertelson (Eds.), *International perspectives on psychological science* (Vol. 2, pp. 311–340). Howe, England: Erlbaum.

(1994b). A theory of action and state orientations. In J. Kuhl & J. Beckmann (Eds.), *Volition and personality: Action versus state orientation* (pp. 9–46). Göttingen, Germany: Hogrefe.

Kuhl, J., & Helle, P. (1986). Motivational and volitional determinants of depression: The degenerated-intention hypothesis. *Journal of Abnormal Psychology, 95*, 247–251.

Kukla, A. (1972). Foundations of an attributional theory of performance. *Psychological Review, 79*, 454–470.

Kunda, Z., & Thagard, P. (1996). Forming impressions from stereotypes, traits, and behaviors: A parallel-constraint-satisfaction theory. *Psychological Review, 103*, 284–308.

Lamphere, R. A., & Leary, M. R. (1990). Private and public self-processes: A return to James's constituents of the self. *Personality and Social Psychology Bulletin, 16*, 717–725.

Landrine, H. (1992). Clinical implications of cultural differences: The referential versus the indexical self. *Clinical Psychology Review, 12*, 401–415.

Lang, P. J. (1979). A bio-informational theory of emotional imagery. *Psychophysiology, 16*, 495–512.

Lang, P. J., Bradley, M. M., & Cuthbert, B. N. (1992). A motivational analysis of emotion: Reflex–cortex connections. *Psychological Science, 3*, 44–49.

Langer, E. J., & Roth, J. (1975). Heads I win, tails it's chance: The illusion of control as a function of the sequence of outcomes in a purely chance task. *Journal of Personality and Social Psychology, 32*, 951–955.

Langewiesche, W. (1993). The turn. *The Atlantic Monthly, 272*, 115–122.

Langston, C., & Cantor, N. (1989). Social anxiety and social constraint: When "making friends" is hard. *Journal of Personality and Social Psychology, 56*, 649–661.

Larsen, R. J. (1987). The stability of mood variability: A spectral analytic approach to daily mood assessments. *Journal of Personality and Social Psychology, 52*, 1195–1204.

Larsen, R. J., & Diener, E. (1992). Promises and problems with the circumplex model of emotion. In M. S. Clark (Ed.), *Review of personality and social psychology* (Vol. 13, pp. 25–59). Newbury Park, CA: Sage.

Latané, B., & Nowak, A. (1994). Attitudes as catastrophes: From dimensions to categories with increasing involvement. In R. R. Vallacher & A. Nowak (Eds.), *Dynamical systems in social psychology* (pp. 219–249). San Diego: Academic Press.

Law, A., Logan, H., & Baron, R. S. (1994). Desire for control, felt control, and stress inoculation training during dental treatment. *Journal of Personality and Social Psychology, 67*, 926–936.

Lawrence, J. W., Carver, C. S., & Scheier, M. F. (1997). *Velocity and affect in immediate personal experience*. Unpublished manuscript.

Lazarus, R. S. (1966). *Psychological stress and the coping process*. New York: McGraw-Hill.

   (1991). *Emotion and adaptation*. New York: Oxford University Press.

Lazarus, R. S., & Folkman, S. (1984). *Stress, appraisal, and coping*. New York: Springer.

Leary, M. R. (1993). The interplay of private self-processes and interpersonal factors in self-presentation. In J. Suls (Ed.), *Psychological perspectives on the self: Vol. 4. The self in social perspective* (pp. 127–155). Hillsdale, NJ: Erlbaum.

Lecci, L., Okun, M. A., & Karoly, P. (1994). Life regrets and current goals as predictors of psychological adjustment. *Journal of Personality and Social Psychology, 66*, 731–741.

Leedham, B., Meyerowitz, B. E., Muirhead, J., & Frist, W. H. (1995). Positive expectations predict health after heart transplantation. *Health Psychology, 14*, 74–79.

Lefcourt, H. M. (1973). The function of the illusions of control and freedom. *American Psychologist, 28*, 417–425.

    (1976). *Locus of control: Current trends in theory and research.* Hillsdale, NJ: Erlbaum.

Levenson, R. W., Ekman, P., & Friesen, W. V. (1990). Voluntary facial action generates emotion-specific autonomic nervous-system activity. *Psychophysiology, 27*, 363–384.

Levine, D. S., & Leven, S. J. (Eds.) (1992). *Motivation, emotion, and goal direction in neural networks.* Hillsdale, NJ: Erlbaum.

Levine, R. L. (1992). An introduction to qualitative dynamics. In R. L. Levine & H. E. Fitzgerald (Eds.), *Analysis of dynamic psychological systems: Vol. 1. Basic approaches to general systems, dynamic systems, and cybernetics* (pp. 267–330). New York: Plenum.

Levine, R. L. & Fitzgerald, H. E. (Eds.) (1992a). *Analysis of dynamic psychological systems: Vol. 1. Basic approaches to general systems, dynamic systems, and cybernetics.* New York: Plenum.

    (1992b). Systems and systems analysis: Methods and applications. In R. L. Levine & H. E. Fitzgerald (Eds.), *Analysis of dynamic psychological systems: Vol. 2. Methods and applications* (pp. 1–16). New York: Plenum.

Lewin, K. (1935). *A dynamic theory of personality.* New York: McGraw-Hill.

    (1948). Time perspective and morale. In G. W. Lewin (Ed.), *Resolving social conflicts: Selected papers on group dynamics* (pp. 103–124). New York: Harper.

Lewinsohn, P. M., Larson, D. W., & Muñoz, R. F. (1982). The measurement of expectancies and other cognitions in depressed individuals. *Cognitive Therapy and Research, 6*, 437–446.

Lezak, M. D. (1995). *Neuropsychological assessment* (3rd ed.). New York: Oxford University Press.

Lichtenstein, E. H., & Brewer, W. F. (1980). Memory for goal-directed events. *Cognitive Psychology, 12*, 412–445.

Linehan, M. M. (1993). *Cognitive–behavioral treatment of borderline personality disorder.* New York: Guilford.

Linville, P. (1985). Self-complexity and affective extremity: Don't put all of your eggs in one cognitive basket. *Social Cognition, 3*, 94–120.

    (1987). Self-complexity as a cognitive buffer against stress-related illness and depression. *Journal of Personality and Social Psychology, 52*, 663–676.

Little, B. R. (1983). Personal projects: A rationale and methods for investigation. *Environment and Behavior, 15*, 273–309.

    (1989). Personal projects analysis: Trivial pursuits, magnificent obsessions, and the search for coherence. In D. M. Buss & N. Cantor (Eds.), *Personality psychology: Recent trends and emerging directions* (pp. 15–31). New York: Springer-Verlag.

Locke, E. A., & Latham, G. P. (1990a). *A theory of goal setting and task performance*. Englewood Cliffs, NJ: Prentice-Hall.

    (1990b). Work motivation and satisfaction: Light at the end of the tunnel. *Psychological Science, 1*, 240–246.

Lockwood, P., & Kunda, Z. (1997). Superstars and me: Predicting the impact of role models on the self. *Journal of Personality and Social Psychology, 73*, 91–103.

Loewenstein, G. (1994). The psychology of curiosity: A review and reinterpretation. *Psychological Bulletin, 116*, 75–98.

Lord, R. G., & Hanges, P. J. (1987). A control system model of organizational motivation: Theoretical development and applied implications. *Behavioral Science, 32*, 161–178.

Lord, R. G., & Levy, P. E. (1994). Moving from cognition to action: A control theory perspective. *Applied Psychology: An International Review, 43*, 335–398.

Lorenz, E. N. (1963). Deterministic nonperiodic flow. *Journal of Atmospheric Science, 20*, 130–141.

Luchins, A. S. (1957). Primacy–recency in impression formation. In C. I. Hovland (Ed.), *The order of presentation in persuasion* (pp. 33–61). New Haven: Yale University Press.

Lykken, D., & Tellegen, A. (1996). Happiness is a stochastic phenomenon. *Psychological Science, 7*, 186–189.

Lyubomirsky, S., & Nolen-Hoeksema, S. (1993). Self-perpetuating properties of depressive rumination. *Journal of Personality and Social Psychology, 65*, 339–349.

    (1995). Effects of self-focused rumination on negative thinking and interpersonal problem solving. *Journal of Personality and Social Psychology, 69*, 176–190.

MacKay, D. M. (1956). The epistemological problem for automata. In C. E. Shannon & J. McCarthy (Eds.), *Automata studies* (pp. 235–251). Princeton, NJ: Princeton University Press.

    (1963). Mindlike behavior in artefacts. In K. M. Sayre & F. J. Crosson (Eds.), *The modeling of mind: Computers and intelligence* (pp. 225–241). Notre Dame, IN: University of Notre Dame Press.

    (1966). Cerebral organization and the conscious control of action. In J. C. Eccles (Ed.), *Brain and conscious experience* (pp. 422–445). Berlin: Springer-Verlag.

MacLeod, C., & Campbell, L. (1992). Memory accessibility and probability judgments: An experimental evaluation of the availability heuristic. *Journal of Personality and Social Psychology, 63*, 890–902.

MacNair, R. R., & Elliott, T. R. (1992). Self-perceived problem-solving ability, stress appraisal, and coping over time. *Journal of Research in Personality, 26*, 150–164.

Macrae, C. N., Bodenhausen, G. V., & Milne, A. B. (1998). Saying no to unwanted thoughts: Self-focus and the regulation of mental life. *Journal of Personality and Social Psychology, 74*, 578–589.

Maes, P. (Ed.) (1990a). *Designing autonomous agents: Theory and practice from biology to engineering and back*. Cambridge, MA: MIT Press.

    (1990b). Situated agents can have goals. In P. Maes (Ed.), *Designing autonomous agents: Theory and practice from biology to engineering and back* (pp. 49–70). Cambridge, MA: MIT Press.

    (1994). Modeling adaptive autonomous agents. *Artificial Life, 1*, 135–162.

Maes, P., & Brooks, R. A. (1990). Learning to coordinate behaviors. *Proceedings of the American Association of Artificial Intelligence* (pp. 796–802). Los Alto, CA: Morgan Kaufmann.

Mahoney, M. J. (1991). *Human change processes: The scientific foundations of psychotherapy*. New York: Basic Books.

Main, M., & Goldwyn, R. (1991). *An adult attachment classification system*. Unpublished manuscript.

Malcolm, C., & Smithers, T. (1990). Symbol grounding via a hybrid architecture in an autonomous assembly system. In P. Maes (Ed.), *Designing autonomous agents: Theory and practice from biology to engineering and back* (pp. 123–144). Cambridge, MA: MIT Press.

Mandel, D. R. (1995). Chaos theory, sensitive dependence, and the logistic equation. *American Psychologist, 50*, 106–107.

Manne, S. L., & Zautra, A. J. (1989). Spouse criticism and support: Their association with coping and psychological adjustment among women with rheumatoid arthritis. *Journal of Personality and Social Psychology, 56*, 608–617.

Mannes, S. M., & Kintsch, W. (1991). Routine computing tasks: Planning as understanding. *Cognitive Science, 15*, 305–342.

Manning, K. V. (1993). Magnetic hysteresis. In S. P. Parker (Ed.), *McGraw-Hill encyclopedia of physics* (2nd ed., p. 733). New York: McGraw-Hill.

Marken, R. S. (1986). Perceptual organization of behavior: A hierarchical control model of coordinated action. *Journal of Experimental Psychology: Human Perception and Performance, 12*, 267–276.

Markus, H. R., & Kitayama, S. (1991). Culture and the self: Implications for cognition, emotion, and motivation. *Psychological Review, 98*, 224–253.

    (1994). A collective fear of the collective: Implications for selves and theories of selves. *Personality and Social Psychology Bulletin, 20*, 568–579.

Markus, H., & Nurius, P. (1986). Possible selves. *American Psychologist, 41*, 954–969.

(1987). Possible selves: The interface between motivation and the self-concept. In K. Yardley & T. Honess (Eds.), *Self and identity: Psychosocial perspectives* (pp. 157–172). Chichester, England: Wiley.

Markus, H., & Wurf, E. (1987). The dynamic self-concept: A social psychological perspective. *Annual Review of Psychology, 38*, 299–337.

Marsh, H. W. (1986). Global self-esteem: Its relation to specific facets of self-concept and their importance. *Journal of Personality and Social Psychology, 51*, 1224–1236.

(1993). Academic self-concept: Theory, measurement, and research. In J. Suls (Ed.), *Psychological perspectives on the self: Vol. 4. The self in social perspective* (pp. 59–98). Hillsdale, NJ: Erlbaum.

Marteniuk, R. G. (1992). Issues in goal directed motor learning: Feedforward control, motor equivalence, specificity, and artificial neural networks. In G. E. Stelmach & J. Requin (Eds.), *Tutorials in motor behavior II* (pp. 101–124). Amsterdam: Elsevier North-Holland.

Martin, L. L., & Stoner, P. (1996). Mood as input: What we think about how we feel determines how we think. In L. L. Martin & A. Tesser (Eds.), *Striving and feeling: Interactions among goals, affect, and self-regulation* (pp. 279–301). Mahwah, NJ: Erlbaum.

Martin, L. L., & Tesser, A. (1989). Toward a motivational and structural model of ruminative thought. In J. S. Uleman & J. A. Bargh (Eds.), *Unintended thought: The limits of awareness, intention, and control* (pp. 306–326). New York: Guilford.

(1996). Some ruminative thoughts. In R. S. Wyer, Jr. (Ed.), *Advances in social cognition* (Vol. 9, pp. 1–47). Mahwah, NJ: Erlbaum.

Martin, L. L., Ward, D. W, Achee, J. W., & Wyer, R. S., Jr. (1993). Mood as input: People have to interpret the motivational implications of their mood. *Journal of Personality and Social Psychology, 64*, 317–326.

Maruyama, M. (1963). The second cybernetics: Deviation-amplifying mutual causal processes. *American Scientist, 51*, 164–179.

(1986). Morphogenetic economics: Change-amplification by causal loops. *Technological Forecasting and Social Change, 21*, 205–213.

Mayer, J. D., & Gaschke, Y. (1988). The experience and meta-experience of mood. *Journal of Personality and Social Psychology, 55*, 102–111.

Mayer, J. D., Gaschke, Y. N., Braverman, D. L., & Evans, T. W. (1992). Mood-congruent judgment is a general effect. *Journal of Personality and Social Psychology, 63*, 119–132.

McClelland, D. C., Koestner, R., & Weinberger, J. (1989). How do self-attributed and implicit motives differ? *Psychological Review, 96*, 690–702.

McClelland, J. L., Rumelhart, D. E., & PDP Research Group. (Eds.). (1986). *Parallel distributed processing: Explorations in the microstructure of cognition: Vol. 2. Psychological and biological models.* Cambridge, MA: MIT Press.

McFarland, D. J. (1971). *Feedback mechanisms in animal behavior.* New York: Academic Press.

McFarland, D. (1989). Goals, no-goals, and own goals. In A. Montefiore & D. Noble (Eds.), *Goals, no-goals, and own goals: A debate on goal-directed and intentional behavior* (pp. 39–57). London: Unwin Hyman.

McFarland, D., & Bösser, T. (1993). *Intelligent behavior in animal and robots.* Cambridge, MA: MIT Press.

McGregor, I., & Little, B. R. (1998). Personal projects, happiness, and meaning: On doing well and being yourself. *Journal of Personality and Social Psychology, 74,* 494–512.

McIntosh, W. D., & Martin, L. L. (1992). The cybernetics of happiness: The relation of goal attainment, rumination, and affect. In M. S. Clark (Ed.), *Review of personality and social psychology: Vol. 14. Emotion and social behavior* (pp. 222–246). Newbury Park, CA: Sage.

McIntyre, J., & Bizzi, E. (1993). Servo hypotheses for the biological control of movement. *Journal of Motor Behavior, 25,* 193–202.

Mead, G. H. (1934). *Mind, self, and society.* Chicago: University of Chicago Press.

Melton, R. J. (1995). The role of positive affect in syllogism performance. *Personality and Social Psychology Bulletin, 21,* 788–794.

Meyer, D., Leventhal, H., & Gutmann, M. (1985). Common-sense models of illness: The example of hypertension. *Health Psychology, 4,* 115–135.

Millar, K. U., Tesser, A., & Millar, M. G. (1988). The effects of a threatening life event on behavior sequences and intrusive thought: A self-disruption explanation. *Cognitive Therapy and Research, 12,* 441–458.

Miller, D. T, & Prentice, D. A. (1994). The self and the collective [Special issue]. *Personality and Social Psychology Bulletin, 20*(5).

Miller, G. A., Galanter, E., & Pribram, K. H. (1960). *Plans and the structure of behavior.* New York: Holt, Rinehart, & Winston.

Miller, I. H., & Norman, W. H. (1979). Learned helplessness in humans: A review and attribution theory model. *Psychological Bulletin, 86,* 93–118.

Miller, J. G. (1978). *Living systems.* New York: McGraw-Hill.

Miller, J. G., & Miller, J. L. (1992). Cybernetics, general systems theory, and living systems theory. In R. L. Levine & H. E. Fitzgerald (Eds.), *Analysis of dynamical psychological systems: Vol. 1. Basic approaches to general systems, dynamic systems, and cybernetics* (pp. 9–34). New York: Plenum.

Miller, L. C., Bettencourt, B. A., DeBro, S. C., & Hoffman, V. (1993). Negotiating safer sex: Interpersonal dynamics. In J. B. Pryor & G. D. Reeder (Eds.), *The social psychology of HIV infection* (pp. 85–123). Hillsdale, NJ: Erlbaum.

Miller, L. C., & Cox, C. L. (1981). *Public self-consciousness and makeup use:*

Individual differences in preparational tactics. Paper presented at the annual meeting of the American Psychological Association, Los Angeles.

Miller, L. C., & Read, S. J. (1987). Why am I telling you this? Self-disclosure in a goal-based model of personality. In V. J. Derlega & J. Berg (Eds.), *Self-disclosure: Theory, research, and therapy* (pp. 35–58). New York: Plenum.

Miller, S. M. (1979). Controllability and human stress: Method, evidence, and theory. *Behavior Research and Therapy, 17*, 287–304.

Miller, W. R., & C'deBaca, J. (1994). Quantum change: Toward a psychology of transformation. In T. Heatherton & J. Weinberger (Eds.), *Can personality change?* (pp. 253–280). Washington, DC: American Psychological Association.

Mills, J., & Clark, M. S. (1982). Communal and exchange relationships. *Review of Personality and Social Psychology, 3*, 121–144.

Mineka, S., & Sutton, S. K. (1992). Cognitive biases and the emotional disorders. *Psychological Science, 3*, 65–69.

Minsky, M. (1985). *The society of mind*. New York: Simon & Schuster.

Minuchin, S. (1974). *Families and family therapy*. Cambridge, MA: Harvard University Press.

Mischel, W. (1973). Toward a cognitive social learning reconceptualization of personality. *Psychological Review, 80*, 252–283.

Mischel, W., & Shoda, Y. (1995). A cognitive-affective system theory of personality: Reconceptualizing the invariances in personality and the role of situations. *Psychological Review, 102*, 246–268.

Mizruchi, M. S. (1991). Urgency, motivation, and group performance: The effect of prior success on current success among professional basketball teams. *Social Psychology Quarterly, 54*, 181–189.

Moffitt, K. H., & Singer, J. A. (1994). Continuity in the life story: Self-defining memories, affect, and approach/avoidance personal strivings. *Journal of Personality, 62*, 21–43.

Montefiore, A., & Noble, D. (Eds.) (1989). *Goals, no-goals, and own goals: A debate on goal-directed and intentional behavior*. London: Unwin Hyman.

Mor, V., Allen, S., & Malin, M. (1994). The psychosocial impact of cancer on older versus younger patients and their families. *Cancer, 74*, 2118–2127.

Moskowitz, J. T., Folkman, S., Collette, L., & Vittinghoff, E. (1996). Coping and mood during AIDS-related caregiving and bereavement. *Annals of Behavioral Medicine, 18*, 49–57.

Mullen, B. (1986). Atrocity as a function of lynch mob composition: A self–attention perspective. *Personality and Social Psychology Bulletin, 12*, 187–197.

Murray, H. A. (1938). *Explorations in personality*. New York: Oxford University Press.

Murray, S. L., & Holmes, J. G. (1993). Seeing virtues in faults: Negativity and the transformation of interpersonal narratives in close relationships. *Journal of Personality and Social Psychology, 65*, 707–722.

(1997). A leap of faith? Positive illusions in romantic relationships. *Personality and Social Psychology Bulletin, 23*, 586–604.

Murray, S. L., Holmes, J. G., & Griffin, D. W. (1996). The benefits of positive illusions: Idealization and the construction of satisfaction in close relationships. *Journal of Personality and Social Psychology, 70*, 79–98.

Murre, J. M. J. (1992). *Learning and categorization in modular neural networks*. Hillsdale, NJ: Erlbaum.

Myers, D. G., & Diener, E. (1995). Who is happy? *Psychological Science, 6*, 10–19.

Narenda, K. S., & Li, S-M. (1996). Neural networks in control systems. In P. Smolensky, M. C. Mozer, & D. E. Rumelhart (Eds.), *Mathematical perspectives on neural networks* (pp. 347–393). Mahwah, NJ: Erlbaum.

Nasby, W. (1985). Private self-consciousness, articulation of the self-schema, and recognition memory of trait adjectives. *Journal of Personality and Social Psychology, 49*, 704–709.

(1989a). Private and public self-consciousness and articulation of the self-schema. *Journal of Personality and Social Psychology, 56*, 117–123.

(1989b). Private self-consciousness, self-awareness, and the reliability of self-reports. *Journal of Personality and Social Psychology, 56*, 950–957.

Neisser, U. (Ed.) (1993). *The perceived self: Ecological and interpersonal sources of self-knowledge*. New York: Cambridge University Press.

Nesse, R. M., & Williams, G. C. (1995). *Why we get sick: The new science of Darwinian medicine*. New York: Random House.

Newcomb, T. M. (1958). Attitude development as a function of reference groups: The Bennington study. In E. E. Maccoby, T. M. Newcomb, & E. L. Hartley (Eds.), *Readings in social psychology* (3rd ed., pp. 265–275). New York: Holt, Rinehart, & Winston.

Newell, A. (1973). Production systems: Models of control structures. In W. G. Chase (Ed.), *Visual information processing* (pp. 463–526). New York: Academic Press.

Newell, A., & Simon, H. A. (1972). *Human problem solving*. Englewood Cliffs, NJ: Prentice-Hall.

Newman, M. G. & Stone, A. A. (1996). Does humor moderate the effects of experimentally induced stress? *Annals of Behavioral Medicine, 18*, 101–119.

Newtson, D. (1993). The dynamics of action and interaction. In L. D. Smith & E. Thelen (Eds.), *A dynamic systems approach to development: Applications* (pp. 241–264). Cambridge, MA: MIT Press.

(1994). The perception and coupling of behavioral waves. In R. R. Vallacher & A. Nowak (Eds.), *Dynamical systems in social psychology* (pp. 139–167). San Diego: Academic Press.

Newtson, D., & Czerlinsky, T. (1974). Adjustments of attitude communications for contrasts by extreme audiences. *Journal of Personality and Social Psychology, 30,* 829–837.

Nicholls, J. G. (1984). Achievement motivation: Conceptions of ability, subjective experience, task choice, and performance. *Psychological Review, 91,* 328–346.

Niedenthal, P. M., Setterlund, M. B., & Wherry, M. B. (1992). Possible self-complexity and affective reactions to goal-relevant evaluation. *Journal of Personality and Social Psychology, 63,* 5–16.

Nolen-Hoeksema, S. (1991). Responses to depression and their effects on the duration of depressive episodes. *Journal of Abnormal Psychology, 100,* 569–582.

    (1996). Chewing the cud and other ruminations. In R. S. Wyer, Jr. (Ed.), *Advances in social cognition* (Vol. 9, pp. 135–144). Mahwah, NJ: Erlbaum.

Nolen-Hoeksema, S., & Morrow, J. (1993). The effects of rumination and distraction on naturally occurring depressed moods. *Cognition and Emotion, 7,* 561–570.

Nolen-Hoeksema, S., Parker, L. E., & Larson, J. (1994). Ruminative coping with depressed mood following loss. *Journal of Personality and Social Psychology, 67,* 92–104.

Norman, D. A. (1981). Categorization of action slips. *Psychological Review, 88,* 1–15.

    (1986). Reflections on cognition and parallel distributed processing. In J. L. McClelland, D. E. Rumelhart, & the PDP Research Group (Eds.), *Parallel distributed processing: Explorations in the microstructure of cognition. Vol. 2. Psychological and biological models* (pp. 531–546). Cambridge, MA: MIT Press.

Norman, D. A., & Shallice, T. (1986). Attention to action: Willed and automatic control of behavior. In R. J. Davidson, G. E. Schwartz, & D. Shapiro (Eds.), *Consciousness and self-regulation: Advances in research and theory* (Vol. 4, pp. 1–18). New York: Plenum.

Nottelman, E. D., & Hill, K. T. (1977). Test anxiety and off-task behavior in evaluative situations. *Child Development, 48,* 225–231.

Nowak, A., & Lewenstein, M. (1994). Dynamical systems: A tool for social psychology. In R. R. Vallacher & A. Nowak (Eds.), *Dynamical systems in social psychology* (pp. 17–53). San Diego: Academic Press.

Nowak, A., & Vallacher, R. R. (in press). *Dynamical social psychology.* New York: Guilford.

O'Brien, T. (1990). *The things they carried.* Boston: Houghton Mifflin.

Ogata, K. (1970). *Modern control engineering.* Englewood Cliffs, NJ: Prentice-Hall.

Ogilvie, D. M. (1987). The undesired self: A neglected variable in personality research. *Journal of Personality and Social Psychology, 52,* 379–385.

402   References

Orbuch, T. L. (Ed.). (1992). *Close relationship loss: Theoretical approaches*. New York: Springer-Verlag.

Ortony, A., Clore, G. L., & Collins, A. (1988). *The cognitive structure of emotions*. Cambridge: Cambridge University Press.

Overmier, J. B., & Seligman, M. E. P. (1967). Effects of inescapable shock upon subsequent escape and avoidance learning. *Journal of Comparative and Physiological Psychology, 63*, 28–33.

Oyserman, D. (1993). The lens of personhood: Viewing the self and others in a multicultural society. *Journal of Personality and Social Psychology, 65*, 993–1009.

Oyserman, D., & Markus, H. (1990). Possible selves and delinquency. *Journal of Personality and Social Psychology, 59*, 112–125.

Palys, T. S., & Little, B. R. (1983). Perceived life satisfaction and the organization of personal project systems. *Journal of Personality and Social Psychology, 44*, 1221–1230.

Papp, P. (1983). *The process of change*. New York: Guilford.

Park, B., DeKay, M. L., & Kraus, S. (1994). Aggregating social behavior into person models: Perceiver-induced consistency. *Journal of Personality and Social Psychology, 66*, 437–459.

Parkes, C. M., Stevenson-Hinde, J., & Marris, P. (Eds.) (1991). *Attachment across the life cycle*. London and New York: Tavistock/Routledge.

Payton, D. W. (1990). Internalized plans: A representation for action resources. In P. Maes (Ed.), *Designing autonomous agents: Theory and practice from biology to engineering and back* (pp. 89–103). Cambridge, MA: MIT Press.

Pelham, B. W. (1991). On the benefits of misery: Self-serving biases in the depressive self-concept. *Journal of Personality and Social Psychology, 61*, 670–681.

Pelham, B. W., & Swann, W. B., Jr. (1989). From self-conceptions to self-worth: On the sources and structure of global self-esteem. *Journal of Personality and Social Psychology, 57*, 672– 680.

(1994). The juncture of intrapersonal and interpersonal knowledge: Self-certainty and interpersonal congruence. *Personality and Social Psychology Bulletin, 20*, 349–357.

Penner, L. A., Shiffman, S., Paty, J. A., & Fritzsche, B. A. (1994). Individual differences in intrapersonal variability in mood. *Journal of Personality and Social Psychology, 66*, 712–721.

Penner, L. A., & Wymer, W. E. (1983). The moderator variable approach to behavioral predictability: Some of the variables some of the time. *Journal of Research in Personality, 17*, 339–353.

Pervin, L. A. (1982). The stasis and flow of behavior: Toward a theory of goals. In M. M. Page & R. Dienstbier (Eds.), *Nebraska symposium on motivation* (Vol. 30, pp. 1–53). Lincoln: University of Nebraska Press.

(Ed.) (1989). *Goal concepts in personality and social psychology.* Hillsdale, NJ: Erlbaum.

(1992). The rational mind and the problem of volition. *Psychological Science, 3,* 162–164.

Peterson, C., & Seligman, M. E. P. (1984). Causal explanations as a risk factor for depression: Theory and evidence. *Psychological Review, 91,* 347–374.

Peterson, J. B., Rothfleisch, J., Zelazo, P. D., & Pihl, R. O. (1990). Acute alcohol intoxication and cognitive functioning. *Journal of Studies on Alcohol, 51,* 114–122.

Petrie, K., & Chamberlain, K. (1983). Hopelessness and social desirability as moderator variables in predicting suicidal behavior. *Journal of Consulting and Clinical Psychology, 51,* 485–487.

Petroski, H. (1997). Designed to fail. *American Scientist, 85,* 412–416.

Pettingale, K. W., Morris, T., Greer, S., & Haybittle, J. L. (1985). Mental attitudes to cancer: An additional prognostic factor. *Lancet, i,* 750.

Phillips, D. P., Todd, E. R., & Wagner, L. M. (1993). Psychology and survival. *Lancet, 342,* 1142–1145.

Piaget, J. (1963). *The child's conception of the world.* Patterson, NJ: Littlefield, Adams.

(1964). *Judgment and reasoning in the child.* Patterson, NJ: Littlefield, Adams.

(1971). *Biology and knowledge.* Chicago: University of Chicago Press.

Pietromonaco, P. R., & Markus, H. (1985). The nature of negative thoughts in depression. *Journal of Personality and Social Psychology, 48,* 799–807.

Pietromonaco, P. R., & Rook, K. S. (1987). Decision style in depression: The contribution of perceived risks and benefits. *Journal of Personality and Social Psychology, 52,* 399–408.

Pinkerton, S. D. (1993). Optimization of hierarchical structures. *Journal of Information Processing and Cybernetics, 29,* 221–231.

Pittman, T. S., & Pittman, N. L. (1980). Deprivation of control and the attribution process. *Journal of Personality and Social Psychology, 39,* 377–389.

Port, R. F., & van Gelder, T. (Eds.) (1995). *Mind as motion: Explorations in the dynamics of cognition.* Cambridge, MA: MIT Press.

Posner, M. I., Walker, J. A., Friedrich, F. J., & Rafal, R. D. (1984). Effects of parietal lobe injury on covert orienting of visual attention. *Journal of Neuroscience, 4,* 1863–1874.

Powers, W. T. (1973a). *Behavior: The control of perception.* Chicago: Aldine.

(1973b). Feedback: Beyond behaviorism. *Science, 179,* 351–356.

Pozo, C., Carver, C. S., Wellens, A. R., & Scheier, M. F. (1991). Social anxiety and social perception: Construing others' reactions to the self. *Personality and Social Psychology Bulletin, 17,* 355–362.

Pratto, F., & John, O. P. (1991). Automatic vigilance: The attention-grabbing power of negative social information. *Journal of Personality and Social Psychology, 61*, 380–391.

Prentice-Dunn, S., & Rogers, R. W. (1980). Effects of deindividuating situational cues and aggressive models on subjective deindividuation and aggression. *Journal of Personality and Social Psychology, 39*, 104–113.

(1982). Effects of public and private self-awareness on deindividuation and aggression. *Journal of Personality and Social Psychology, 43*, 503–513.

(1989). Deindividuation and the self-regulation of behavior. In P. B. Paulus (Ed.), *Psychology of group influence* (2nd ed., pp. 87–109). Hillsdale, NJ: Erlbaum.

Pribram, K. H. (1990). From metaphors to models: The use of analogy in neuropsychology. In D. E. Leary (Ed.), *Metaphors in the history of psychology* (pp. 79–103). Cambridge: Cambridge University Press.

Pyszczynski, T., & Greenberg, J. (1985). Depression and preference for self-focusing stimuli after success and failure. *Journal of Personality and Social Psychology, 49*, 1066–1075.

(1987). Self-regulatory perseveration and the depressive self-focusing style: A self-awareness theory of reactive depression. *Psychological Bulletin, 102*, 122–138.

(1992a). *Hanging on and letting go: Understanding the onset, progression, and remission of depression*. New York: Springer-Verlag.

(1992b). Putting cognitive constructs in their place: Is depression really just a matter of interpretation? *Psychological Inquiry, 3*, 255–258.

Pyszczynski, T., Greenberg, J., Hamilton, J., & Nix, G. (1991). On the relationship between self-focused attention and psychological disorder: A critical reappraisal. *Psychological Bulletin, 110*, 538–543.

Radloff, R. (1961). Opinion evaluation and affiliation. *Journal of Abnormal and Social Psychology, 62*, 578–585.

Read, S. J., Druian, P. R., & Miller, L. C. (1989). The role of causal sequence in the meaning of action. *British Journal of Social Psychology, 28*, 341–351.

Read, S. J., Jones, D. K., & Miller, L. C. (1990). Traits as goal-based categories: The importance of goals in the coherence of dispositional categories. *Journal of Personality and Social Psychology, 58*, 1048–1061.

Read, S. J., & Miller, L. C. (1989). Inter-personalism: Toward a goal-based theory of persons in relationships. In L. Pervin (Ed.), *Goal concepts in personality and social psychology* (pp. 413–472). Hillsdale, NJ: Erlbaum.

(Eds.) (1998). *Connectionist models of social reasoning and social behavior*. Mahwah, NJ: Erlbaum.

Read, S. J., Vanman, E. J., & Miller, L. C. (1997). Connectionism, parallel constraint satisfaction processes, and Gestalt principles: (Re)introducing cognitive dynamics to social psychology. *Review of Personality and Social Psychology, 1*, 26–53.

Reed, G. M., Kemeny, M. E., Taylor, S. E., & Visscher, B. R. (in press). Negative HIV-specific expectancies and AIDS-related bereavement as predictors of symptom onset in asymptomatic HIV-positive gay men. *Health Psychology, 16.*

Reed, G. M., Kemeny, M. E., Taylor, S. E., Wang, H-Y. J., & Visscher, B. R. (1994). Realistic acceptance as a predictor of decreased survival time in gay men with AIDS. *Health Psychology, 13,* 299–307.

Reis, T. J., Gerrard, M., & Gibbons, F. X. (1993). Social comparison and the pill: Reactions to upward and downward comparison of contraceptive behavior. *Personality and Social Psychology Bulletin, 19,* 13–20.

Reker, G. T., Peacock, E. J., & Wong, P. T. P. (1987). Meaning and purpose in life and well-being: A life-span perspective. *Journal of Gerontology, 42,* 44–49.

Rescorla, R. A. (1987). A Pavlovian analysis of goal-directed behavior. *American Psychologist, 42,* 119–129.

Rhee, E., Uleman, J. S., & Lee, H. K. (1996). Variations in collectivism and individualism by ingroup and culture: Confirmatory factor analyses. *Journal of Personality and Social Psychology, 71,* 1037–1054.

Rhodewalt, F. (1994). Conceptions of ability, achievement goals, and individual differences in self-handicapping behavior: On the application of implicit theories. *Journal of Personality, 62,* 67–85.

Rhodewalt, F., & Agustsdottir, S. (1986). Effects of self-presentation on the phenomenal self. *Journal of Personality and Social Psychology, 50,* 47–55.

Rich, A. R., & Woolever, D. K. (1988). Expectancy and self-focused attention: Experimental support for the self-regulation model of test anxiety. *Journal of Social and Clinical Psychology, 7,* 246–259.

Richter, C. P. (1957). On the phenomenon of sudden death in animals and man. *Psychosomatic Medicine, 19,* 191–198.

Riskind, J. H., Kelley, K., Harman, W., Moore, R., & Gaines, H. S. (1992). The loomingness of danger: Does it discriminate focal phobia and general anxiety from depression? *Cognitive Therapy and Research, 16,* 603–622.

Robinson, F. G. (1992). *Love's story told: A life of Henry A. Murray.* Cambridge, MA: Harvard University Press.

Rodin, J. (1986). Aging and health: Effects of the sense of control. *Science, 233,* 1271–1276.

Rogers, C. R. (1961). *On becoming a person.* Boston: Houghton Mifflin.
    (1980). *A way of being.* Boston: Houghton Mifflin.

Rohde, P., Lewinsohn, P. M., Tilson, M., & Seeley, J. R. (1990). Dimensionality of coping and its relation to depression. *Journal of Personality and Social Psychology, 58,* 499–511.

Rook, K. S. (1984). The negative side of social interaction: Impact on psychological well-being. *Journal of Personality and Social Psychology, 46,* 1097–1108.

Roseman, I. J. (1984). Cognitive determinants of emotions: A structural theory. In P. Shaver (Ed.), *Review of personality and social psychology* (Vol. 5, pp. 11–36). Beverly Hills, CA: Sage.

Rosenbaum, D. A. (1987). Hierarchical organization of motor programs. In S. Wise (Ed.), *Neural and behavioral approaches to higher brain function* (pp. 45–66). New York: Wiley.

(1991a). *Human motor control*. San Diego: Academic Press.

(1991b). Programs for movement sequences. In D. J. Napoli & J. A. Kegl (Eds.), *Bridges between psychology and linguistics: A Swarthmore festschrift for Leila Gleitman*. Hillsdale, NJ: Erlbaum.

Rosenschein, S. J. (1985). Formal theories of knowledge in AI and robotics. *New Generation Computing, 3*, 345–357.

Ross, M., & Sicoly, F. (1979). Egocentric biases in availability and attribution. *Journal of Personality and Social Psychology, 37*, 322–336.

Roth, S., & Cohen, L. J. (1986). Approach, avoidance, and coping with stress. *American Psychologist, 41*, 813–819.

Rotter, J. B. (1954). *Social learning and clinical psychology*. New York: Prentice-Hall.

Ruble, D. N. (1994). A phase model of transitions: Cognitive and motivational consequences. In M. Zanna (Ed.), *Advances in experimental social psychology* (Vol. 26, pp. 163–214). San Diego: Academic Press.

Ruble, D. N., & Frey, K. S. (1991). Changing patterns of behavior as skills are acquired: A functional model of self-evaluation. In J. Suls & T. A. Wills (Eds.), *Social comparison: Contemporary theory and research* (pp. 79–113). Hillsdale, NJ: Erlbaum.

Ruehlman, L. S., & Wolchik, S. A. (1988). Personal goals and interpersonal support and hindrance as factors in psychological distress and well-being. *Journal of Personality and Social Psychology, 55*, 293–301.

Ruelle, D. (1991). *Chance and chaos*. Princeton, NJ: Princeton University Press.

Rumelhart, D. E., McClelland, J. L., & PDP Research Group. (Eds.) (1986). *Parallel distributed processing: Explorations in the microstructure of cognition: Vol. 1. Foundations*. Cambridge, MA: MIT Press.

Rusbult, C. E. (1980). Commitment and satisfaction in romantic associations: A test of the investment model. *Journal of Experimental Social Psychology, 16*, 172–186.

(1983). A longitudinal test of the investment model: The development (and deterioration) of satisfaction and commitment in heterosexual involvements. *Journal of Personality and Social Psychology, 45*, 101–117.

Rusbult, C. E., & Martz, J. M. (1995). Remaining in an abusive relationship: An investment model analysis of nonvoluntary dependence. *Personality and Social Psychology Bulletin, 21*, 558–571.

Rusbult, C. E., Verette, J., Whitney, G. A., Slovik, L. F., & Lipkus, I. (1991). Accommodation processes in close relationships: Theory and preliminary research evidence. *Journal of Personality and Social Psychology, 60*, 53–78.

Ryan, R. M. (1993). Agency and organization: Intrinsic motivation, autonomy, and the self in psychological development. In J. Jacobs (Ed.), *Nebraska symposium on motivation* (Vol. 40, pp. 237–288). Lincoln: University of Nebraska Press.

Ryan, R. M., & Connell, J. P. (1989). Perceived locus of causality and internalization: Examining reasons for acting in two domains. *Journal of Personality and Social Psychology, 57*, 749–761.

Ryan, R. M., Rigby, S., & King, K. (1993). Two types of religious internalization and their relations to religious orientations and mental health. *Journal of Personality and Social Psychology, 65*, 586–596.

Ryan, R. M., Sheldon, K. M., Kasser, T., & Deci, E. L. (1996). All goals are not created equal: An organismic perspective on the nature of goals and their regulation. In P. M. Gollwitzer & J. A. Bargh (Eds.), *The psychology of action: Linking cognition and motivation to behavior* (pp. 7–26). New York: Guilford.

Salovey, P. (1992). Mood-induced self-focused attention. *Journal of Personality and Social Psychology, 62*, 699–707.

Salovey, P., & Birnbaum, D. (1989). Influence of mood on health-relevant cognitions. *Journal of Personality and Social Psychology, 57*, 539–551.

Sanna, L. J. (1992). Self-efficacy theory: Implications for social facilitation and social loafing. *Journal of Personality and Social Psychology, 62*, 774–786.

Santee, R. T., & Maslach, C. (1982). To agree or not to agree: Personal dissent amid social pressure to conform. *Journal of Personality and Social Psychology, 42*, 690–700.

Sarason, I. G. (1975). Anxiety and self-preoccupation. In I. G. Sarason & C. D. Spielberger (Eds.), *Stress and anxiety* (Vol. 2, pp. 27–44). Washington, DC: Hemisphere.

Sarason, I. G., Pierce, G. R., & Sarason, B. R. (Eds.) (1996). *Cognitive interference: Theories, methods, and findings.* Hillsdale, NJ: Erlbaum.

Saunders, P. T. (1980). *An introduction to catastrophe theory.* Cambridge: Cambridge University Press.

Schachter, S. (1951). Deviation, rejection, and communication. *Journal of Abnormal and Social Psychology, 46*, 190–207.

(1959). *The psychology of affiliation.* Minneapolis: University of Minnesota Press.

Schank, R. C., & Abelson, R. P. (1977). *Scripts, plans, goals, and understanding.* Hillsdale, NJ: Erlbaum.

Scheier, M. F. (1976). Self-awareness, self-consciousness, and angry aggression. *Journal of Personality, 44*, 627–644.

(1980). Effects of public and private self-consciousness on the public expression of personal beliefs. *Journal of Personality and Social Psychology, 39*, 514–521.

Scheier, M. F., & Bridges, M. W. (1995). Person variables and health: Personality predispositions and acute psychological states as shared determinants for disease. *Psychosomatic Medicine, 57*, 255–268.

Scheier, M. F., & Carver, C. S. (1977). Self-focused attention and the experience of emotion: Attraction, repulsion, elation, and depression. *Journal of Personality and Social Psychology, 35*, 625–636.

(1982). Self-consciousness, outcome expectancy, and persistence. *Journal of Research in Personality, 16*, 409–418.

(1983). Self-directed attention and the comparison of self with standards. *Journal of Experimental Social Psychology, 19*, 205–222.

(1985). Optimism, coping, and health: Assessment and implications of generalized outcome expectancies. *Health Psychology, 4*, 219–247.

(1987). Dispositional optimism and physical well-being: The influence of generalized outcome expectancies on health. *Journal of Personality, 55*, 169–210.

(1988). A model of behavioral self-regulation: Translating intention into action. In L. Berkowitz (Ed.), *Advances in experimental social psychology*, Vol. 21 (pp. 303–346). New York: Academic Press.

(1992). Effects of optimism on psychological and physical well-being: Theoretical overview and empirical update. *Cognitive Therapy and Research, 16*, 201–228.

Scheier, M. F., Carver, C. S., & Bridges, M. W. (1994). Distinguishing optimism from neuroticism (and trait anxiety, self-mastery, and self-esteem): A re-evaluation of the Life Orientation Test. *Journal of Personality and Social Psychology, 67*, 1063–1078.

Scheier, M. F., Carver, C. S., & Gibbons, F. X. (1979). Self-directed attention, awareness of bodily states, and suggestibility. *Journal of Personality and Social Psychology, 37*, 1576–1588.

(1981). Self-focused attention and reactions to fear. *Journal of Research in Personality, 15*, 1–15.

Scheier, M. F., Fenigstein, A., & Buss, A. H. (1974). Self-awareness and physical aggression. *Journal of Experimental Social Psychology, 10*, 264–273.

Scheier, M. F., Matthews, K. A., Owens, J. F., Magovern, G. J., Sr., Lefebvre, R. C., Abbott, R. A., & Carver, C. S. (1989). Dispositional optimism and recovery from coronary artery bypass surgery: The beneficial effects on physical and psychological well being. *Journal of Personality and Social Psychology, 57*, 1024–1040.

Scheier, M. F., Matthews, K. A., Owens, J. F., Schulz, R., Bridges, M. W., Magovern, G. J., Sr., & Carver, C. S. (1998). *Optimism and rehospitalization following coronary artery bypass graft surgery*. Manuscript under review.

Schell, T. L., Klein, S. B., & Babey, S. H. (1996). Testing a hierarchical model of self-knowledge. *Psychological Science, 7*, 170–173.

Scherer, K. R., & Ekman, P. (Eds.) (1984). *Approaches to emotion.* Hillsdale, NJ: Erlbaum.

Schlenker, B. R. (1980). *Impression management: The self-concept, social identity, and interpersonal relations.* Monterey, CA: Brooks/Cole.

Schlenker, B. R., & Leary, M. R. (1982). Social anxiety and self-presentation: A conceptualization and model. *Psychological Bulletin, 92*, 641–669.

Schlenker, B. R., & Weigold, M. F. (1990). Self-consciousness and self-presentation: Being autonomous versus appearing autonomous. *Journal of Personality and Social Psychology, 59*, 820–828.

(1992). Interpersonal processes involving impression regulation and management. *Annual Review of Psychology, 43*, 133–168.

Schmidt, R. A. (1976). The schema as a solution to some persistent problems in motor learning theory. In G. E. Stelmach (Ed.), *Motor control: Issues and trends* (pp. 41–65). New York: Academic Press.

(1987). The acquisition of skill: Some modifications to the perception-action relationship through practice. In H. Heuer & A. F. Sanders (Eds.), *Perspectives on perception and action* (pp. 77–103). Hillsdale, NJ: Erlbaum.

(1988). *Motor control and learning: A behavioral emphasis* (2nd ed.). Champaign, IL: Human Kinetics Publishers.

Schmidt, R. A., & Bjork, R. A. (1992). New conceptualizations of practice: Common principles in three paradigms suggest new concepts for training. *Psychological Science, 3*, 207–217.

Schneirla, T. C. (1959). An evolutionary and developmental theory of biphasic processes underlying approach and withdrawal. In M. R. Jones (Ed.), *Nebraska symposium on motivation* (Vol. 7, pp. 1–42). Lincoln: University of Nebraska Press.

Schultz, T. R., & Lepper, M. R. (1996). Cognitive dissonance reduction as constraint satisfaction. *Psychological Review, 103*, 219–240.

Schulz, R., Bookwala, J., Knapp, J. E., Scheier, M. F., & Williamson, G. M. (1996). Pessimism, age, and cancer mortality. *Psychology and Aging, 11*, 304–309.

Schwarz, N. (1990). Feelings as information: Informational and motivational functions of affect. In E. T. Higgins & R. M. Sorrentino (Eds.), *Handbook of motivation and cognition: Foundations of social behavior* (Vol. 2, pp. 527–561). New York: Guilford.

Sedek, G., Kofta, M., & Tyszka, T. (1993). Effects of uncontrollability on subsequent decision making: Testing the cognitive exhaustion hypothesis. *Journal of Personality and Social Psychology, 65*, 1270–1281.

Seligman, M. E. P. (1975). *Helplessness: On depression, development, and death.* San Francisco: Freeman.

Seligman, M. E. P., & Maier, S. F. (1967). Failure to escape traumatic shock. *Journal of Experimental Psychology, 74*, 1–9.

Selvini Palazzoli, M., Boscolo, L., Cecchin, G., & Prata, G. (1978). *Paradox and counterparadox.* New York: Jason Aronson.

Shah, J., & Higgins, E. T. (1997). Expectancy X value effects: Regulatory focus as determinant of magnitude *and* direction. *Journal of Personality and Social Psychology, 73*, 447–458.

Shallice, T. (1978). The dominant action system: An information-processing approach to consciousness. In K. S. Pope & J. L. Singer (Eds.), *The stream of consciousness: Scientific investigations into the flow of human experience* (pp. 117–157). New York: Wiley.

Shastri, L., & Ajjanagadde, V. (1993). From simple associations to systematic reasoning: A connectionist representation of rules, variables, and dynamic bindings using temporal synchrony. *Behavioral and Brain Sciences, 16*, 417–494.

Shaver, P., Schwartz, J., Kirson, D., & O'Connor, C. (1987). Emotion knowledge: Further exploration of a prototype approach. *Journal of Personality and Social Psychology, 52*, 1061–1086.

Sherer, K. R., & Ekman, P. (Eds.) (1984). *Approaches to emotion.* Hillsdale, NJ: Erlbaum.

Shibutani, T. (1961). *Society and personality: An interactionist approach to social psychology.* Englewood Cliffs, NJ: Prentice-Hall.

Shoda, Y., Mischel, W., & Wright, J. C. (1989). Intuitive interactionism in person perception: Effects of situation–behavior relations on dispositional judgments. *Journal of Personality and Social Psychology, 56*, 41–53.

Showers, C. J., & Cantor, N. (1985). Social cognition: A look at motivated strategies. *Annual Review of Psychology, 36*, 275–305.

Showers, C. J., & Ryff, C. D. (1996). Self-differentiation and well being in a life transition. *Personality and Social Psychology Bulletin, 22*, 448–460.

Siegler, R. S. (1994). Cognitive variability: A key to understanding cognitive development. *Current Directions in Psychological Science, 3*, 1–5.

Siegler, R. S., & Jenkins, E. A. (1989). *How children discover new strategies.* Hillsdale, NJ: Erlbaum.

Simon, H. A. (1953). *Models of man.* New York: Wiley.

   (1955). A behavioral model of rational choice. *Quarterly Journal of Economics, 69*, 99–118.

   (1967). Motivational and emotional controls of cognition. *Psychology Review, 74*, 29–39.

Skinner, B. F. (1938). *The behavior of organisms.* New York: Appleton-Century-Crofts.

Skinner, E. A. (1996). A guide to constructs of control. *Journal of Personality and Social Psychology, 71*, 549–570.

Sloman, A. (1987). Motives, mechanisms, and emotions. *Cognition and Emotion, 1*, 217–233.

Sloman, S. A. (1996). The empirical case for two forms of reasoning. *Psychological Bulletin, 119*, 3–22.

Smith, C. A., & Ellsworth, P. C. (1987). Patterns of appraisal and emotion related to taking an exam. *Journal of Personality and Social Psychology, 52*, 475–488.

Smith, C. A., Haynes, K. N., Lazarus, R. S., & Pope, L. K. (1993). In search of the "hot" cognitions: Attributions, appraisals, and their relation to emotion. *Journal of Personality and Social Psychology, 65*, 916–929.

Smith, E. R. (1984). Model of social inference processes. *Psychological Review, 91*, 392–413.

(1996). What do connectionism and social psychology offer each other? *Journal of Personality and Social Psychology, 70*, 893–912.

Smith, L. B., & Thelen, E. (1993). *A dynamic systems approach to development: Applications.* Cambridge, MA: MIT Press.

Smith, R. E., & Sarason, I. G. (1975). Social anxiety and the evaluation of negative interpersonal feedback. *Journal of Consulting and Clinical Psychology, 43*, 429.

Smolensky, P. (1988). On the proper treatment of connectionism. *Behavioral and Brain Sciences, 11*, 1–23.

Smolensky, P., Mozer, M. C., & Rumelhart, D. E. (Eds.) (1996). *Mathematical perspectives on neural networks.* Mahwah, NJ: Erlbaum.

Snyder, C. R., Harris, C., Anderson, J. R., Holleran, S. A., Irving, L. M., Sigmon, S. T., Yoshinobu, L., Gibb, J., Langelle, C., & Harney, P. (1991). The will and the ways: Development and validation of an individual-differences measure of hope. *Journal of Personality and Social Psychology, 60*, 570–585.

Snyder, C. R., Higgins, R. L., & Stucky, R. J. (1983). *Excuses: Masquerades in search of grace.* New York: Wiley.

Snyder, M. L., & Frankel, A. (1989). Making things harder for yourself: Pride and joy. In R. C. Curtis (Ed.), *Self-defeating behaviors: Experimental research, clinical impressions, and practical implications* (pp. 131–157). New York: Plenum.

Snyder, M. L., & Wicklund, R. A. (1976). Prior exercise of freedom and reactance. *Journal of Experimental Social Psychology, 12*, 120–130.

Sobotka, S. S., Davidson, R. J., & Senulis, J. A. (1992). Anterior brain electrical asymmetries in response to reward and punishment. *Electroencephalography and Clinical Neurophysiology, 83*, 236–247.

Solomon, M. R., & Schopler, J. (1982). Self-consciousness and clothing. *Personality and Social Psychology Bulletin, 8*, 508–514.

Solomon, R. L. (1980). The opponent-process theory of acquired motivation:

412   References

The costs of pleasure and the benefits of pain. *American Psychologist, 35*, 691–712.

Solomon, R. L., & Corbit, J. D. (1974). An opponent-process theory of motivation: III. Temporal dynamics of affect. *Psychological Review, 81*, 119–145.

Solomon, S., Greenberg, J., & Pyszczynski, T. (1991). A terror management theory of social behavior: The psychological functions of self-esteem and cultural worldviews. In M. P. Zanna (Ed.), *Advances in experimental social psychology* (Vol. 24, pp. 93–159). New York: Academic Press.

Sperry, R. W. (1950). Neural basis of the spontaneous optokinetic response produced by visual inversion. *Journal of Comparative and Physiological Psychology, 43*, 482–489.

Srull, T. K., & Wyer, R. S., Jr. (1986). The role of chronic and temporary goals in social information processing. In R. M. Sorrentino & E. T. Higgins (Eds.), *Handbook of motivation and cognition: Foundations of social behavior* (pp. 503–549). New York: Guilford.

———. (1989). Person memory and judgment. *Psychological Review, 96*, 58–83.

Staddon, J. E. R., & Higa, J. J. (1996). Multiple time scales in simple habituation. *Psychological Review, 103*, 720–733.

Steele, C. M. (1988). The psychology of self-affirmation: Sustaining the integrity of the self. In L. Berkowitz (Ed.), *Advances in experimental social psychology* (Vol. 21, pp. 261–302). New York: Academic Press.

Steele, C. M., & Josephs, R. A. (1990). Alcohol myopia: Its prized and dangerous effects. *American Psychologist, 45*, 921–933.

Stepper, S., & Strack, F. (1993). Proprioceptive determinants of emotional and nonemotional feelings. *Journal of Personality and Social Psychology, 64*, 211–220.

Sternberg, S., Knoll, R. L., & Turock, D. L. (1990). Hierarchical control in the execution of action sequences: Tests of two invariance properties. In M. Jeannerod (Ed.), *Attention and performance XIII: Motor representation and control* (pp. 3–55). Hillsdale, NJ: Erlbaum.

Stewart, I. N. (1990). *Does God play dice?* London: Basil Blackwell.

Stewart, I. N., & Peregoy, P. L. (1983). Catastrophe theory modeling in psychology. *Psychological Bulletin, 94*, 336–362.

Stipek, D., Recchia, S., & McClintic, S. (1992). Self-evaluation in young children. *Monographs of the Society for Research in Child Development, 57* (serial no. 226).

Strack, S., Carver, C. S., & Blaney, P. H. (1987). Predicting successful completion of an aftercare program following treatment for alcoholism: The role of dispositional optimism. *Journal of Personality and Social Psychology, 53*, 579–584.

Strathman, A., Gleicher, F., Boninger, D. S., & Edwards, C. S. (1994). The consideration of future consequences: Weighing immediate and distant outcomes of behavior. *Journal of Personality and Social Psychology, 66,* 742–752.

Strauman, T. J. (1989). Self-discrepancies in clinical depression and social phobia: Cognitive structures that underlie emotional disorders? *Journal of Abnormal Psychology, 98,* 14–22.

Strauman, T. J., & Higgins, E. T. (1987). Automatic activation of self-discrepancies and emotional syndromes: When cognitive structures influence affect. *Journal of Personality and Social Psychology, 53,* 1004–1014.

Stroebe, M. S., Stroebe, W., & Hansson, R. O. (Eds.) (1993). *Handbook of bereavement: Theory, research, and intervention.* Cambridge: Cambridge University Press.

Stroebe, W., Stroebe, M. S., Gergen, K. J., & Gergen, M. (1982). The effects of bereavement on mortality: A social psychological analysis. In J. R. Eiser (Ed.), *Social psychology and behavioral medicine* (pp. 527–560). Chichester, England: Wiley.

Stuss, D. T. (1991). Self, awareness, and the frontal lobes: A neuropsychological perspective. In J. Strauss & G. R. Goethals (Eds.), *The self: Interdisciplinary approaches* (pp. 255–278). New York: Springer-Verlag.

Stuss, D. T., & Benson, D. F. (1986). *The frontal lobes.* New York: Raven Press.

Suls, J. (Ed.) (1993). *Psychological perspectives on the self: Vol. 4. The self in social perspective.* Hillsdale, NJ: Erlbaum.

Suls, J., Gastorf, J., & Lawhon, J. (1978). Social comparison choices for evaluating sex- and age-related ability. *Personality and Social Psychology Bulletin, 4,* 102–105.

Suls, J., & Wills, T. A. (Eds.) (1991). *Social comparison: Contemporary theory and research.* Hillsdale, NJ: Erlbaum.

Suomi, S. J. (1991). Primate separation models of affective disorder. In J. Madden IV (Ed.), *Neurobiology of learning, emotion, and affect* (pp. 195–214). New York: Raven Press.

Sutton, S. K., & Davidson, R. J. (1997). Prefrontal brain asymmetry: A biological substrate of the behavioral approach and inhibition systems. *Psychological Science, 8,* 204–210.

Swann, W. B., Jr. (1990). To be adored or to be known? The interplay of self-enhancement and self-verification. In E. T. Higgins & R. M. Sorrentino (Eds.), *Handbook of motivation and cognition: Foundations of social behavior* (Vol. 2, pp. 408–448). New York: Guilford.

(1996). *Self-traps: The elusive quest for higher self-esteem.* New York: Freeman.

Swann, W. B., Jr., De La Ronde, C., & Hixon, J. G. (1994). Authenticity and positivity strivings in marriage and courtship. *Journal of Personality and Social Psychology, 66*, 857–869.

Swann, W. B., Jr., & Ely, R. J. (1984). A battle of wills: Self-verification versus behavioral confirmation. *Journal of Personality and Social Psychology, 46*, 1287–1302.

Swann, W. B., Jr., Hixon, J. G., & De La Ronde, C. (1992). Embracing the bitter "truth": Negative self-conceptions and marital commitment. *Psychological Science, 3*, 118–121.

Swann, W. B., Jr., Pelham, B. W., & Krull, D. S. (1989). Agreeable fancy or disagreeable truth? Reconciling self-enhancement and self-verification. *Journal of Personality and Social Psychology, 57*, 782–791.

Swann, W. B., Jr., & Read, S. J. (1981). Acquiring self-knowledge: The search for feedback that fits. *Journal of Personality and Social Psychology, 41*, 1119–1128.

Swann, W. B., Jr., Stein-Seroussi, A., & McNulty, S. E. (1992). Outcasts in a white-lie society: The enigmatic worlds of people with negative self-conceptions. *Journal of Personality and Social Psychology, 62*, 618–624.

Swann, W. B., Jr., Wenzlaff, R. M., Krull, D. S., & Pelham, B. W. (1992). Allure of negative feedback: Self-verification strivings among depressed persons. *Journal of Abnormal Psychology, 101*, 293–306.

Tait, R., & Silver, R. C. (1989). Coming to terms with major negative life events. In J. S. Uleman & J. A. Bargh (Eds.), *Unintended thought: The limits of awareness, intention, and control* (pp. 351–381). New York: Guilford.

Tajfel, H. (1978). *Differentiation between social groups: Studies in the social psychology of intergroup relations*. London: Academic Press.

(1981). *Human groups and social categories: Studies in social psychology*. Cambridge: Cambridge University Press.

Tangney, J. P. (1990). Assessing individual differences in proneness to shame and guilt: Development of the Self-Conscious Affect and Attribution Inventory. *Journal of Personality and Social Psychology, 59*, 102–111.

Tangney, J. P., Wagner, P., Fletcher, C., & Gramzow, R. (1992). Shamed into anger? The relation of shame and guilt to anger and self-reported aggression. *Journal of Personality and Social Psychology, 56*, 958–964.

Taylor, S. E. (1983). Adjustment to threatening events: A theory of cognitive adaptation. *American Psychologist, 38*, 1161–1173.

(1989). *Positive illusions: Creative self-deception and the healthy mind*. New York: Basic Books.

(1990). Health psychology: The science and the field. *American Psychologist, 45*, 40–50.

(1991). Asymmetric effects of positive and negative events: The mobilization-minimization hypothesis. *Psychological Bulletin, 110*, 67–85.

Taylor, S. E., & Brown, J. D. (1988). Illusion and well-being: A social psychological perspective on mental health. *Psychological Bulletin, 103*, 193–210.

Taylor, S. E., & Gollwitzer, P. M. (1995). Effects of mindset on positive illusions. *Journal of Personality and Social Psychology, 69*, 213–226.

Taylor, S. E., & Lobel, M. (1989). Social comparison activity under threat: Downward evaluation and upward contacts. *Psychological Review, 96*, 569–575.

Taylor, S. E., & Pham, L. B. (1996). Mental stimulation, motivation, and action. In P. M. Gollwitzer & J. A. Bargh (Eds.), *The psychology of action: Linking cognition and motivation to behavior* (pp. 219–235). New York: Guilford.

Tedeschi, R. G., & Calhoun, L. G. (1995). *Trauma and transformation*. Thousand Oaks, CA: Sage.

Terry, D. J., & Hogg, M. A. (1996). Group norms and the attitude–behavior relationship: A role for group identification. *Personality and Social Psychology Bulletin, 22*, 776–793.

Tesser, A. (1980a). Self-esteem maintenance in family dynamics. *Journal of Personality and Social Psychology, 39*, 77–91.

(1980b). When individual dispositions and social pressure conflict: A catastrophe. *Human Relations, 33*, 393–407.

(1986). Some effects of self-evaluation maintenance on cognition and action. In R. M. Sorrentino & E. T. Higgins (Eds.), *Handbook of motivation and cognition: Foundations of social behavior* (pp. 435–464). New York: Guilford.

(1988). Toward a self-evaluation maintenance model of social behavior. In L. Berkowitz (Ed.), *Advances in experimental social psychology* (Vol. 21, pp. 181–227). New York: Academic Press.

(1990). Smith and Ellsworth's appraisal model of emotion: A replication, extension, and test. *Personality and Social Psychology Bulletin, 16*, 210–223.

Tesser, A., & Achee, J. (1994). Aggression, love, conformity, and other social psychological catastrophes. In R. R. Vallacher & A. Nowak (Eds.), *Dynamical systems in social psychology* (pp. 95–109). San Diego: Academic Press.

Tesser, A., & Campbell, J. (1983). Self-definition and self-evaluation maintenance. In J. Suls & A. G. Greenwald (Eds.), *Psychological perspectives on the self* (Vol. 2, pp. 1–31). Hillsdale, NJ: Erlbaum.

Tesser, A., & Cornell, D. P. (1991). On the confluence of self processes. *Journal of Experimental Social Psychology, 27*, 501–526.

Tesser, A., Martin, L. L., & Cornell, D. P. (1996). On the substitutability of self-protective mechanisms. In P. M. Gollwitzer & J. A. Bargh (Eds.), *The psychology of action: Linking cognition and motivation to behavior* (pp. 48–68). New York: Guilford.

Thagard, P. (1989). Explanatory coherence. *Behavioral and Brain Sciences, 12*, 435–467.

Thagard, P., & Millgram, E. (1995). Inference to the best plan: A coherence theory of decision. In A. Ram & D. B. Leake (Eds.), *Goal-driven learning* (pp. 439–454). Cambridge, MA: MIT Press.

Thayer, R. E. (1989). *The biopsychology of mood and arousal*. New York: Oxford.

Thelen, E. (1992). Development as a dynamic system. *Current Directions in Psychological Science, 1*, 189–193.

(1995). Motor development: A new synthesis. *American Psychologist, 50*, 79–95.

Thelen, E., & Smith, L. B. (1994). *A dynamic systems approach to the development of cognition and action*. Cambridge, MA: MIT Press.

Thoits, P. A. (1991). On merging identity theory and stress research. *Social Psychology Quarterly, 54*, 101–112.

Thom, R. (1975). *Structural stability and morphogenesis*. Reading, MA: Benjamin.

Thompson, S. C. (1981). Will it hurt less if I can control it? A complex answer to a simple question. *Psychological Bulletin, 90*, 89–101.

Thompson, S. C., Sobolew-Shubin, A., Galbraith, M. E., Schwankovsky, L., & Cruzen, D. (1993). Maintaining perceptions of control: Finding perceived control in low-control circumstances. *Journal of Personality and Social Psychology, 64*, 293–304.

Thompson, S. C., & Spacapan, S. (1991). Perceptions of control in vulnerable populations. *Journal of Social Issues, 47*, 1–21.

Timberlake, W. (1993). Behavior systems and reinforcement: An integrative approach. *Journal of the Experimental Analysis of Behavior, 60*, 105–128.

Toates, F. M. (1980). *Animal behavior – A systems approach*. Chichester, England: Wiley.

Tobey, E. L., & Tunnell, G. (1981). Predicting our impressions on others: Effects of public self-consciousness and acting, a self-monitoring subscale. *Personality and Social Psychology Bulletin, 7*, 661–669.

Tobin, L. D., Holroyd, K. A., Reynolds, R. V., & Wigal, J. K. (1989). The hierarchical factor structure of the Coping Strategies Inventory. *Cognitive Therapy and Research, 13*, 343–361.

Tolman, E. C. (1932). *Purposive behavior in animals and men*. New York: Appleton-Century-Crofts.

(1938). The determiners of behavior at a choice point. *Psychological Review, 45*, 1–41.

Tomarken, A. J., Davidson, R. J., Wheeler, R. E., & Doss, R. C. (1992). Individual differences in anterior brain asymmetry and fundamental dimensions of emotion. *Journal of Personality and Social Psychology, 62*, 676–687.

Tomkins, S. S. (1984). Affect theory. In K. R. Sherer & P. Ekman (Eds.), *Approaches to emotion* (pp. 163–195). Hillsdale, NJ: Erlbaum.

Townsend, J. T., & Busemeyer, J. (1995). Dynamic representation of decision-making. In R. F. Port & T. van Gelder (Eds.), *Mind as motion: Explorations in the dynamics of cognition* (pp. 101–120). Cambridge, MA: MIT Press.

Trafimow, D., & Finlay, K. A. (1996). The importance of subjective norms for a minority of people: Between-subjects and within-subjects analyses. *Personality and Social Psychology Bulletin, 22*, 820–828.

Triandis, H. C. (1989). The self and social behavior in differing cultural contexts. *Psychological Review, 96*, 506–520.

Triandis, H. C., McCusker, C., & Hui, C. H. (1990). Multimethod probes of individualism and collectivism. *Journal of Personality and Social Psychology, 59*, 1006–1020.

Triplett, N. (1897). The dynamogenic factors in pacemaking and competition. *American Journal of Psychology, 9*, 507–533.

Trope, Y., & Neter, E. (1994). Reconciling competing motives in self-evaluation: The role of self-control in feedback seeking. *Journal of Personality and Social Psychology, 66*, 646–657.

Tulving, E. (1989). Memory: Performance, knowledge, and experience. *European Journal of Cognitive Psychology, 1*, 3–26.

(1993). Self-knowledge of an amnesic individual is represented abstractly. In T. K. Srull & R. S. Wyer, Jr. (Eds.), *Advances in social cognition* (Vol. 5, pp. 157–169). Hillsdale, NJ: Erlbaum.

Turner, J. C., Hogg, M. A., Oakes, P. J., Reicher, S. D., & Wetherall, M. S. (1987). *Rediscovering the social group: A self-categorization theory.* Oxford: Basil Blackwell.

Turvey, M. T. (1977). Preliminaries to a theory of action with reference to vision. In R. Shaw & J. Bransford (Eds.), *Perceiving, acting, and knowing: Toward an ecological psychology* (pp. 211–265). Hillsdale, NJ: Erlbaum.

(1990). Coordination. *American Psychologist, 45*, 938–953.

Tykocinski, O., Higgins, E. T., & Chaiken, S. (1994). Message framing, self-discrepancies, and yielding to persuasive messages: The motivational significance of psychological situations. *Personality and Social Psychology Bulletin, 20*, 107–115.

Valentiner, D. P., Holahan, C. J., & Moos, R. H. (1994). Social support, appraisals of event controllability, and coping: An integrative model. *Journal of Personality and Social Psychology, 66*, 1094–1102.

Vallacher, R. R., & Kaufman, J. (1996). Dynamics of action identification: Volatility and structure in the mental representation of behavior. In P. M. Gollwitzer & J. A. Bargh (Eds.), *The psychology of action: Linking cognition and motivation to behavior* (pp. 260–282). New York: Guilford.

Vallacher, R. R., & Nowak, A. (Eds.) (1994). *Dynamical systems in social psychology.* San Diego: Academic Press.

(1997). The emergence of dynamical social psychology. *Psychological Inquiry, 8*, 73–99.

Vallacher, R. R., & Wegner, D. M. (1985). *A theory of action identification.* Hillsdale, NJ: Erlbaum.

(1987). What do people think they're doing? Action identification and human behavior. *Psychological Review, 94*, 3–15.

(1989). Levels of personal agency: Individual variation in action identification. *Journal of Personality and Social Psychology, 57*, 660–671.

Vallacher, R. R., Wegner, D. M., McMahan, S. C., Cotter, J., & Larsen, K. A. (1992). On winning friends and influencing people: Action identification and self-presentation success. *Social Cognition, 10*, 335–355.

Vallacher, R. R., Wegner, D. M., & Somoza, M. P. (1989). That's easy for you to say: Action identification and speech fluency. *Journal of Personality and Social Psychology, 56*, 199–208.

van der Maas, H. L. J., & Molenaar, P. C. M. (1992). Stagewise cognitive development: An application of catastrophe theory. *Psychological Review, 99*, 395–417.

van Geert, P. (1994). *Dynamic systems of development: Change between complexity and chaos.* London: Harvester Wheatsheaf.

Van Hook, E., & Higgins, E. T. (1988). Self-related problems beyond the self-concept: Motivational consequences of discrepant self-guides. *Journal of Personality and Social Psychology, 55*, 625–633.

Van Lange, P. A. M., Rusbult, C. E., Drigotas, S. M., Arriaga, X. B., Witcher, B. S., & Cox, C. L. (1997). Willingness to sacrifice in close relationships. *Journal of Personality and Social Psychology, 72*, 1373–1395.

Vaughan, D. (1986). *Uncoupling: Turning points in intimate relationships.* Oxford: Oxford University Press.

Vinokur, A. D., Threatt, B. A., Vinokur-Kaplan, D., & Satariano, W. A. (1990). The process of recovery from breast cancer for younger and older patients. *Cancer, 65*, 1242–1254.

von Bertalanffy, L. (1968). *General systems theory.* New York: Braziller.

Vroom, V. H. (1964). *Work and motivation.* New York: Wiley.

Waldrop, M. (1992). *Complexity: The emerging science at the edge of order and chaos.* New York: Simon & Schuster.

Warr, P., Barter, J., & Brownbridge, G. (1983). On the independence of positive and negative affect. *Journal of Personality and Social Psychology, 44*, 644–651.

Watson, D., Clark, L. A., & Tellegen, A. (1988). Development and validation of brief measures of positive and negative affect: The PANAS scales. *Journal of Personality and Social Psychology, 54*, 1063–1070.

Watson, D., & Tellegen, A. (1985). Toward a consensual structure of mood. *Psychological Bulletin, 98*, 219–235.

Weary, G. (1980). An examination of affect and egotism as mediators of bias in causal attributions. *Journal of Personality and Social Psychology, 38*, 348–357.

Wegener, D. T., & Petty, R. E. (1996). Effects of mood on persuasion processes: Enhancing, reducing, and biasing scrutiny of attitude-relevant information. In L. L. Martin & A. Tesser (Eds.), *Striving and feeling: Interactions among goals, affect, and self-regulation* (pp. 329–362). Mahwah, NJ: Erlbaum.

Wegener, D. T., Petty, R. E., & Klein, D. J. (1994). Effects of mood on high elaboration attitude change: The mediating role of likelihood judgments. *European Journal of Social Psychology, 23*, 25–44.

Wegner, D. M. (1994). Ironic processes of mental control. *Psychological Review, 101*, 34–52.

Wegner, D. M., & Bargh, J. A. (1998). Control and automaticity in social life. In D. Gilbert, S. T. Fiske, & G. Lindzey (Eds.), *Handbook of social psychology* (4th ed., pp. 446–496). Boston, MA: McGraw-Hill.

Wegner, D. M., & Giuliano, T. (1980). Arousal-induced attention to the self. *Journal of Personality and Social Psychology, 38*, 719–726.

Wegner, D. M., & Vallacher, R. R. (1986). Action identification. In R. M. Sorrentino & E. T. Higgins (Eds.), *Handbook of cognition and motivation* (Vol. 1, pp. 550–582). New York: Guilford.

Wegner, D. M., Vallacher, R. R., Kiersted, G., & Dizadji, D. (1986). Action identification in the emergence of social behavior. *Social Cognition, 4*, 18–38.

Weigel, R. H., & Newman, L. S. (1976). Increasing attitude–behavior correspondence by broadening the scope of the behavioral measure. *Journal of Personality and Social Psychology, 33*, 793–802.

Weigel, R. H., Vernon, D. T. A., & Tognacci, L. N. (1974). Specificity of the attitude as a determinant of attitude–behavior congruence. *Journal of Personality and Social Psychology, 30*, 724–728.

Weimer, W. B. (1977). A conceptual framework for cognitive psychology: Motor theories of the mind. In R. Shaw & J. Bransford (Eds.), *Perceiving, acting, and, knowing: Toward an ecological psychology* (pp. 267–311). Hillsdale, NJ: Erlbaum.

Weinberger, J., & McClelland, D. C. (1990). Cognitive versus traditional motivational models: Irreconcilable or complementary? In E. T. Higgins & R. M. Sorrentino (Eds.), *Handbook of motivation and cognition: Foundations of social behavior* (Vol. 2, pp. 562–597). New York: Guilford.

Weiner, B. (1982). The emotional consequences of casual ascriptions. In M. S. Clark & S. T. Fiske (Eds.), *Affect and cognition: The 17th annual Carnegie symposium on cognition* (pp. 185–209). Hillsdale, NJ: Erlbaum.

(1985). An attributional theory of achievement motivation and emotion. *Psychological Review, 92*, 548–573.

(1986a). *An attributional theory of motivation and emotion*. New York: Springer-Verlag.

(1986b). Attribution, emotion, and action. In R. M. Sorrentino & E. T.

Higgins (Eds.), *Handbook of motivation and cognition* (pp. 281–312). New York: Guilford.

Weiss, R. S. (1988). Loss and recovery. *Journal of Social Issues, 44*, 37–52.

Werner, P. D., & Pervin, L. A. (1986). The content of personality inventory items. *Journal of Personality and Social Psychology, 51*, 622–628.

Wessman, A. E., & Ricks, D. F. (1966). *Mood and personality*. New York: Holt.

Wheeler, L., & Kim, Y. (1997). What is beautiful is culturally good: The physical attractiveness stereotype has different content in collectivist cultures. *Personality and Social Psychology Bulletin, 23*, 795–800.

Wheeler, L., & Miyake, K. (1992). Social comparison in everyday life. *Journal of Personality and Social Psychology, 62*, 760–773.

Wheeler, R. E., Davidson, R. J., & Tomarken, A. J. (1993). Frontal brain asymmetry and emotional reactivity: A biological substrate of affective style. *Psychophysiology, 30*, 82–89.

Wickless, C., & Kirsch, I. (1988). Cognitive correlates of anger, anxiety, and sadness. *Cognitive Therapy and Research, 12*, 367–377.

Wicklund, R. A. (1974). *Freedom and reactance*. Hillsdale, NJ: Erlbaum.

(1975). Objective self-awareness. In L. Berkowitz (Ed.), *Advances in experimental social psychology* (Vol. 8, pp. 233–275). New York: Academic Press.

Wicklund, R. A., & Duval, S. (1971). Opinion change and performance facilitation as a result of objective self-awareness. *Journal of Experimental Social Psychology, 7*, 319–342.

Wicklund, R. A., & Gollwitzer, P. M. (1982). *Symbolic self-completion*. Hillsdale, NJ: Erlbaum.

Wiener, N. (1948). *Cybernetics: Control and communication in the animal and the machine*. Cambridge, MA: MIT Press.

Wills, T. A. (1981). Downward comparison principles in social psychology. *Psychological Bulletin, 90*, 245–271.

(1986). Stress and coping in early adolescence: Relationships to substance use in urban high schools. *Health Psychology, 5*, 503–529.

Wilson, E. O. (1975). *Sociobiology: The new synthesis*. Cambridge, MA: Harvard University Press.

Wine, J. D. (1971). Test anxiety and direction of attention. *Psychological Bulletin, 76*, 92–104.

(1980). Cognitive-attentional theory of test anxiety. In I. G. Sarason (Ed.), *Test anxiety: Theory, research, and application* (pp. 349–378). Hillsdale, NJ: Erlbaum.

Wong, P. T. P., & Weiner, B. (1981). When people ask "why" questions, and the heuristics of attributional search. *Journal of Personality and Social Psychology, 40*, 650–663.

Wood, J. V. (1989). Theory and research concerning social comparisons of personal attributes. *Psychological Bulletin, 106*, 231–248.

(1996). What is social comparison and how should we study it? *Personality and Social Psychology Bulletin, 22*, 520–537.

Wood, J. V., Saltzberg, J. A., & Goldsamt, L. A. (1990). Does affect induce self-focused attention? *Journal of Personality and Social Psychology, 58*, 899–908.

Wood, J. V., Taylor, S. E., & Lichtman, R. R. (1985). Social comparison in adjustment to breast cancer. *Journal of Personality and Social Psychology, 49*, 1169–1183.

Woodcock, A., & Davis, M. (1978). *Catastrophe theory*. New York: Dutton.

Worth, R. (1995). A model prison. *Atlantic Monthly, 276*, 38–44.

Wortman, C. B., & Brehm, J. W. (1975). Responses to uncontrollable outcomes: An integration of reactance theory and the learned helplessness model. In L. Berkowitz (Ed.), *Advances in experimental social psychology* (Vol. 8, pp. 277–336). New York: Academic Press.

Wright, J. C., & Mischel, W. (1988). Conditional hedges and the intuitive psychology of traits. *Journal of Personality and Social Psychology, 55*, 454–469.

Wright, R. A. (1996). Brehm's theory of motivation as a model of effort and cardiovascular response. In P. M. Gollwitzer & J. A. Bargh (Eds.), *The psychology of action: Linking cognition and motivation to behavior* (pp. 424–453). New York: Guilford.

Wright, R. A., & Brehm, J. W. (1989). Energization and goal attractiveness. In L. A. Pervin (Ed.), *Goal concepts in personality and social psychology* (pp. 169–210). Hillsdale, NJ: Erlbaum.

Wyer, R. S., Jr. (1973). Category ratings as "subjective expected values": Implications for attitude formation and change. *Psychological Review, 80*, 446–467.

Wyer, R. S., Jr., & Srull, T. K. (1989). *Memory and cognition in social context*. Hillsdale, NJ: Erlbaum.

Wylie, R. C. (1968). The present state of self theory. In E. F. Borgatta & W. W. Lambert (Eds.), *Handbook of personality theory and research* (pp. 728–787). Chicago: Rand McNally.

Wynne-Edwards, V. C. (1964). Population control in animals. *Scientific American, 211*, 68–74.

Young, M. A., Fogg, L. F., Scheftner, W., Fawcett, J., Akiskal, H., & Maser, J. (1996). Stable trait components of hopelessness: Baseline and sensitivity to depression. *Journal of Abnormal Psychology, 105*, 155–165.

Youngren, M. A., & Lewinsohn, P. M. (1980). The functional relation between depression and problematic interpersonal behavior. *Journal of Abnormal Psychology, 89*, 333–341.

Zajonc, R. B. (1965). Social facilitation. *Science, 149*, 269–274.

Zeeman, E. C. (1976). Catastrophe theory. *Scientific American, 234*, 65–83.

——— (1977). *Catastrophe theory: Selected papers 1972–1977*. Reading, MA: Benjamin.

Zeigarnik, B. (1927). Das behalten erledigter und unerledigter Handlungen. *Psychologische Forschung, 9*, 1–85.

Zevon, M. A., & Tellegen, A. (1982). The structure of mood change: An idiographic/nomothetic analysis. *Journal of Personality and Social Psychology, 43*, 111–122.

Zirkel, S., & Cantor, N. (1990). Personal construal of life tasks: Those who struggle for independence. *Journal of Personality and Social Psychology, 58*, 172–185.

Name Index

Subject Index